Inflation,
Tax Rules, and
Capital Formation

A National Bureau
of Economic Research
Monograph

Inflation, Tax Rules, and Capital Formation

Martin Feldstein

University of Chicago Press

Chicago and London

MARTIN FELDSTEIN is professor of economics at Harvard University (on leave) and chairman of the Council of Economic Advisers.

The University of Chicago Press, Chicago 60637
The University of Chicago Press, Ltd., London

Library of Congress Cataloging in Publication Data

Feldstein, Martin S.
   Inflation, tax rules, and capital formation.

   (A National Bureau of Economic Research monograph)
   Bibliography: p.
   Includes index.
   1. Inflation (Finance)—Addresses, essays,
lectures.   2. Taxation—Effect of inflation on—Ad-
dresses, essays, lectures.   3. Saving and investment—
Addresses, essays, lectures.   I. Title.   II. Series.
HG229.F35   1983   332.4'1   82-10854
ISBN 0-226-24085-1

Relation of the Directors to the
Work and Publications of the
National Bureau of Economic Research

1. The object of the National Bureau of Economic Research is to ascertain and to present to the public important economic facts and their interpretation in a scientific and impartial manner. The Board of Directors is charged with the responsibility of ensuring that the work of the National Bureau is carried on in strict conformity with this object.

2. The President of the National Bureau shall submit to the Board of Directors, or to its Executive Committee, for their formal adoption all specific proposals for research to be instituted.

3. No research report shall be published by the National Bureau until the President has sent each member of the Board a notice that a manuscript is recommended for publication and that in the President's opinion it is suitable for publication in accordance with the principles of the National Bureau. Such notification will include an abstract or summary of the manuscript's content and a response form for use by those Directors who desire a copy of the manuscript for review. Each manuscript shall contain a summary drawing attention to the nature and treatment of the problem studied, the character of the data and their utilization in the report, and the main conclusions reached.

4. For each manuscript so submitted, a special committee of the Directors (including Directors Emeriti) shall be appointed by majority agreement of the President and Vice Presidents (or by the Executive Committee in case of inability to decide on the part of the President and Vice Presidents), consisting of three Directors selected as nearly as may be one from each general division of the Board. The names of the special manuscript committee shall be stated to each Director when notice of the proposed publication is submitted to him. It shall be the duty of each member of the special manuscript committee to read the manuscript. If each member of the manuscript committee signifies his approval within thirty days of the transmittal of the manuscript, the report may be published. If at the end of that period any member of the manuscript committee withholds his approval, the President shall then notify each member of the Board, requesting approval or disapproval of publication, and thirty days additional shall be granted for this purpose. The manuscript shall then not be published unless at least a majority of the entire Board who shall have voted on the proposal within the time fixed for the receipt of votes shall have approved.

5. No manuscript may be published, though approved by each member of the special manuscript committee, until forty-five days have elapsed from the transmittal of the report in manuscript form. The interval is allowed for the receipt of any memorandum of dissent or reservation, together with a brief statement of his reasons, that any member may wish to express; and such memorandum of dissent or reservation shall be published with the manuscript if he so desires. Publication does not, however, imply that each member of the Board has read the manuscript, or that either members of the Board in general or the special committee have passed on its validity in every detail.

6. Publications of the National Bureau issued for informational purposes concerning the work of the Bureau and its staff, or issued to inform the public of activities of Bureau staff, and volumes issued as a result of various conferences involving the National Bureau shall contain a specific disclaimer noting that such publication has not passed through the normal review procedures required in this resolution. The Executive Committee of the Board is charged with review of all such publications from time to time to ensure that they do not take on the character of formal research reports of the National Bureau, requiring formal Board approval.

7. Unless otherwise determined by the Board or exempted by the terms of paragraph 6, a copy of this resolution shall be printed in each National Bureau publication.

(Resolution adopted October 25, 1926, as revised through September 30, 1974)

Contents

Preface

The research presented in this volume combines the traditional subjects of macroeconomics and public finance. From macroeconomics comes a concern with the rate of interest, the capital intensity of production, and the impact of monetary policy. From public finance comes an emphasis on the significance of the distortionary tax rules that have generally been ignored in macroeconomic analysis and a concern with the effects of tax rules and monetary policy on the distribution of income and on the value of assets. The results of this research show the importance of the interaction between tax rules and monetary policy and the importance of including explicit specifications of the tax system in the study of macroeconomic equilibrium.

The book brings together fourteen papers on the subject of inflation, tax rules, and capital formation that I wrote between 1975 and 1981. The volume begins with a brief overview of the research and of the principal conclusions. The first section of the volume then extends the traditional neoclassical models of monetary growth by including specific tax and debt-management policies. Since this is the most technical part of the volume, I have provided in chapter 2 a less formal discussion of these models and their implications. Subsequent sections of the book present both theoretical and empirical investigations of the interaction between the inflation in the United States in the 1960s and 1970s and the concurrent tax rules. The specific chapters analyze the impact of this interaction on effective tax rates, on the market rate of interest, on the prices of common stock and other portfolio assets, and on business investment in plant and equipment.

The research presented here is part of the NBER's Special Study of Capital Formation. The work was supported by the NBER and the National Science Foundation. I am grateful for this financial support and also for the comments and suggestions of my colleagues and students at the NBER and at Harvard University, especially the members of the NBER Taxation Program and the Harvard Public Finance Seminar.

Four of the chapters were originally written with coauthors: chapter 4 with Jerry Green and Eytan Sheshinski and an appendix by Alan Auerbach, chapter 7 with Joel Slemrod, and chapters 8 and 9 with Lawrence Summers. I am grateful to them for their collaboration in the original research and for their permission to include our joint papers in this volume. Charles Horioka and James Poterba provided valuable research assistance and Douglas Bernheim and George Sofianos rechecked all of the equations in the volume. Judy Frink prepared the manuscript and the bibliography for publication.

The papers in this volume reflect the evolution of my thinking over six years. Not surprisingly, I now understand things about this subject that I did not understand when some of these papers were written. Although there is a temptation therefore to write a completely new and more explicitly integrated volume, I do not believe that the improvement in the final product would justify the delays and the extra work involved. Since I believe that the analysis and conclusions of all of the papers are still basically correct, I have decided not to alter any of the articles.

Although I believe that the research presented here has significant implications for fiscal and monetary policies, in the National Bureau's tradition I have refrained in this volume from making any specific policy proposals. I hope that the papers in the present volume will contribute to a wider understanding of the fundamental aspects of these issues and, more generally, to an appreciation of the important effects of an economy's fiscal structure on its macroeconomic performance.

1   An Introductory Overview

The interaction of inflation and existing tax rules has powerful effects on the American economy. Inflation distorts the measurement of profits, of interest payments, and of capital gains. The resulting mismeasurement of capital income has caused a substantial increase in the effective tax rate on the real income from the capital employed in the nonfinancial corporate sector. At the same time, the deductibility of nominal interest expenses has encouraged the expansion of consumer debt and stimulated the demand for owner-occupied housing. The net result has been a substantial reduction in the accumulation of capital in nonfinancial corporations.

The rate of business fixed investment in the United States has fallen quite sharply since the mid-1960s. The share of gross national product devoted to net nonresidential fixed investment fell by more than one-third between the last half of the 1960s and the decade of the 1970s: the ratio of net fixed nonresidential investment to GNP averaged 0.042 from 1965 through 1969 but only 0.030 from 1970 through 1979. The corresponding rate of growth of the nonresidential capital stock declined by an even greater percentage: between 1965 and 1969, the annual rate of growth of the fixed nonresidential capital stock averaged 5.7 percent; in the 1970s, this average dropped to 3.8 percent. By the second half of the 1970s, the capital stock was growing no faster than the labor force, thereby eliminating the increase in capital per worker as a source of productivity growth.

This chapter is a slightly modified revised version of my paper "Inflation, Capital Taxation, and Monetary Policy," which was prepared for the October 1980 NBER Conference on Inflation and published in Hall (1982) © 1982 by the National Bureau of Economic Research. An earlier version of that paper was presented at the February 1980 Academic Consultants meeting with the Board of Governors of the Federal Reserve System.

The essays in this volume examine the interaction between tax rules and inflation and the impact of this interaction on net rates of return, on asset prices, and on real investment. Part 1 of this volume presents four theoretical studies of the way in which a steady and anticipated rate of inflation influences the long-run behavior of an economy. Each of those studies emphasizes a different aspect but all four feature an explicit analysis of the interaction of tax rules and inflation.

The present chapter begins with a summary and overview of the chapters in Parts 2–4. It then comments on the effects of the economy's fiscal structure for the impact of monetary policy. The next chapter then provides a brief nontechnical description of the four models of Part 1.

1.1   Inflation, Effective Tax Rates, and Net Rates of Return

Our tax laws were written for an economy with little or no inflation. With an inflation rate of 6 percent to 8 percent or more, the tax system functions very badly. The problem is particularly acute for the taxation of income from capital. Despite reductions in statutory rates over the past two decades, the effective tax rates on the income from savings have actually increased sharply in recent years because inflation creates fictitious income for the government to tax. Savers must pay tax not only on their real income from savings but also on their fictitious income as well.

Without legislative action or public debate, effective tax rates on capital income of different types have been raised dramatically in the last decade. This process of raising the effective tax rate on capital income is hard for the public at large or even for most members of Congress to understand. What appear to be relatively low rates of tax on interest income, on capital gains, and on corporate profits as measured under current accounting rules are actually very high tax rates, in some cases more than 100 percent, because our accounting definitions are not suited to an economy with inflation.

As anyone with a savings account knows, even a 10 percent interest rate was not enough in 1980 to compensate a saver for the loss in the purchasing power of his money that resulted from the 12 percent inflation. The present tax rules ignore this and tax the individual on the full nominal amount of his interest receipts. An individual with a 30 percent marginal tax rate would get to keep only a 7 percent return on an account that paid 10 percent. After adjusting this yield for the 12 percent inflation in consumer prices in 1980, such an individual was left with a real after tax return of *minus* 5 percent! The small saver was thus penalized rather than rewarded for attempting to save.

The effect of inflation on the taxation of capital gains is no less dramatic. In a study published in 1978 and presented in chapter 7, Joel Slemrod and I looked first at the experience of a hypothetical investor who bought a broad portfolio of securities like the Standard and Poors' 500 in 1957, held it for twenty years and sold it in 1977. An investor who did that would have been fortunate enough to have his investment slightly more than double during that time. Unfortunately, the consumer price level also more than doubled during that time. In terms of actual purchasing power, the investor had no gain at all on his investment. And yet, of course, the tax law would regard him as having doubled his money and would hold him accountable for a tax liability on this nominal gain.

After seeing this experience for a hypothetical investor, we were eager to know what has been happening to actual investors who have realized taxable capital gains and losses. Fortunately, the Internal Revenue Service has produced a very interesting set of data: a computer tape with a sample of more than 30,000 individual tax returns reporting realized capital gains or losses on corporate stock in 1973. While the sample is anonymous, it is the kind of scientific sample that can be used to make accurate estimates of national totals.

The results of this analysis were quite astounding. In 1973, individuals paid tax on $4.6 billion of capital gains on corporate stock. When the costs of those securities are adjusted for the increase in the price level since they were purchased, that $4.6 billion capital gain is seen correctly as a loss of nearly one billion dollars. Thus, people were paying tax on $4.6 billion of capital gains when in reality they actually sold stock that represented a loss of nearly a billion dollars. Moreover, although people paid tax on artificial gains at every income level, the problem was most severe for those investors with incomes of less than $100,000.

While the lower capital gains tax rates that were enacted in 1978 reduce the adverse effects of inflation, lowering the tax rate does not alter the fact that people will continue to pay taxes on nominal gains even when there are no real gains. They now pay a lower tax on those gains but they still pay a tax on what is really a loss.

Although interest recipients and those who realize nominal capital gains are taxed on fictitious inflation gains, by far the most substantial effect of inflation on tax burdens is the extra tax paid because of the overstatement of profits in the corporate sector. In the study presented in chapter 8, Lawrence Summers and I found that the mismeasurement of depreciation and inventories raised the 1977 tax burden on the income of nonfinancial corporations by $32 billion. This represents a 50 percent increase in the total tax paid on corporate source income by corporations, their shareholders, and their creditors.

Some lawyers and economists have previously argued that inflation does not increase the effective tax rate on real corporate income because firms deduct nominal interest payments (rather than real interest payments) in calculating taxable profits. Equivalently, corporations are not taxed on the fall in the real value of their debts that results from inflation.

Although this argument is valid if one looks only at the taxes paid by the corporation, it is wrong when one considers the taxes paid by creditors and shareholders. As our calculations show, the extra tax paid by the creditors on the inflated interest payments is as large as the tax savings by corporations and their owners. Debt can therefore be ignored in evaluating the net impact of inflation on the total tax burden on corporate capital.

More recently, James Poterba, Louis Dicks-Mireaux, and I have updated these calculations and extended the analysis to include the taxes paid to state and local governments on the capital used by nonfinancial corporations (Feldstein, Poterba, and Dicks-Mireaux, 1981). We found that the 1979 effective tax rate on the total real capital income of the nonfinancial corporate sector was 69 percent. Thus, taxes now take about three-fourths of the total real capital income on corporate capital. This represents a return to the tax level of the mid-1950s before accelerated depreciation and the investment tax credit began reducing the total tax burden. Even if attention is limited to federal taxes, our calculation shows that by 1979 the federal government taxes on corporations, their shareholders, and their creditors equaled 65 percent of the total real capital income of the nonfinancial corporations net of the state and local taxes paid by corporations.

The implication of a 69 percent total effective tax rate on corporate income is clear. Since the real rate of return on corporate capital before all taxes was 9.0 percent in 1979 (Feldstein, Poterba, and Dicks-Mireaux, 1981), the net rate of return was only about 30 percent of this, or 2.7 percent.

1.2 Inflation, Tax Rules, and Asset Prices

A potentially important way in which inflation can alter the rate of real investment is by changing the cost to the firm of equity capital, that is, the ratio of share value per dollar of pretax earnings. In a smoothly functioning economy with no distortionary taxes, inflation should have no effect on the cost of equity capital: both the earnings per share and the share price should increase over time at a faster rate because of inflation but their ratio should be unaffected. In fact, taxes interfere with this neutrality and alter the ratio of the share price to the pretax earnings.[1]

In thinking about the relation between inflation and share prices, it is crucial to distinguish between the effect of a *high* constant rate of inflation and the effect of an *increase* in the rate of inflation expected for the future. When the steady-state rate of inflation is higher, share prices

1. The relation between inflation, tax rules, and share prices is discussed in chaps. 10, 11, and 13.

increase at a faster rate. More specifically, when the inflation rate is steady, share prices rise in proportion to the price level to maintain a constant ratio of share prices to real earnings. In contrast, an *increase* in the expected future rate of inflation causes a concurrent fall in the ratio of share prices to current earnings. Although share prices then rise from this lower level at the higher rate of inflation, the ratio of share prices to real earnings is permanently lower. This permanent reduction in the price-earnings ratio occurs because, under prevailing tax rules, inflation raises the effective tax rate on corporate source income.

An important reason for the lower ratio of price to pretax earnings is that an increase in the permanent rate of inflation raises the effective tax rate on equity capital. The magnitude of this increase reflects the role of historic cost depreciation, the use of FIFO inventory accounting, and the extent of corporate debt. A numerical calculation with realistic values will indicate how these separate effects are combined. Consider an economy with no inflation in which each share of stock represents the ownership claim to a single unit of capital (i.e., one dollar's worth of capital valued at its reproduction cost) and to the net earnings that it produces. The marginal product of capital (net of depreciation), f', is subject to a corporate income tax at effective rate t_1. In the absence of inflation, this effective rate of tax is less than the statutory rate (t) because of the combined effect of accelerated depreciation and the investment tax credit. The corporation borrows b dollars per unit of capital and pays interest at rate r. Since these interest payments are deducted in calculating corporate income that is taxed at the statutory rate t, the net cost of these borrowed funds is $(1 - t)br$. The net return to equity investors per unit of capital in the absence of inflation is $(1 - t_1)f' - (1 - t)br$.

What happens to this net return when the inflation rate rises? For simplicity, consider an instantaneous and unanticipated increase to inflation at rate π that is expected to last forever. Under existing U.S. tax law, inflation raises taxable profits (for any fixed level of real profits) in two ways. First, the value of depreciation allowances is based on the original or "historic" cost of the asset rather than on its current value. When prices rise, this historic cost method of depreciation causes the real value of depreciation to fall and the real value of taxable profits to rise. Second, the cost of maintaining inventory levels is understated for firms that use the first-in/first-out (FIFO) method of inventory accounting. A linear approximation that each percentage point of inflation increases taxable profits per unit of capital by x implies that the existing treatment of depreciation and inventories reduces net profits by tx per unit of capital.

When there is a positive rate of inflation, the firms' net interest payments ($(1 - t)br$) overstates the true cost to the equity owners of the corporations' debt finance. Against this apparent interest cost it is necessary to offset the reduction in the real value of the corporations' net monetary liabilities. These net monetary liabilities per unit of capital are the difference between the interest-bearing debt (b) and the non-interest-bearing monetary assets (a).

Combining the basic net profits per unit of capital, the extra tax caused by the existing depreciation and inventory rules, and the real gain on net monetary liabilities yields the real net return per unit of capital,

$$(1) \qquad z = (1 - t_1)f' - (1 - t)br - tx\pi + (b - a)\pi$$

The effect of inflation on the real net equity earnings per unit of capital (z) depends on the response of the interest rate (r) to the inflation rate (π). In general, the change in equity earnings per unit change in the inflation rate ($dz/d\pi$) depends on the tax and finance parameters and on the effect of inflation on the interest rate ($dr/d\pi$) according to:

$$(2) \qquad \frac{dz}{d\pi} = -(1 - t)b \frac{dr}{d\pi} - tx + (b - a)$$

Econometric studies indicate that the nominal interest rate has risen approximately point-for-point with the rate of inflation. Assuming that $dr/d\pi = 1$ implies

$$(3) \qquad \frac{dz}{d\pi} = -(1 - t)b - tx + (b - a)$$

$$= t(b - x) - a$$

Thus, equity owners (1) gain tb (per unit of capital) from a rise in inflation because nominal interest expenses are deducted in calculating taxable income, (2) lose tx because of the understatement of cost due to the use of historic cost depreciation and FIFO inventory accounting, and (3) lose a because they hold non-interest–bearing monetary assets.

Recent values of these parameters imply that $dz/d\pi$ is negative and therefore that inflation would reduce the equity earnings per share. In 1977, nonfinancial corporations had a total capital stock of $1,684 billion and owed net interest-bearing liabilities of $509.7 billion,[2] implying that $b = 0.302$. The monetary assets of the NFCs had a value of $54.8 billion, implying that $a = 0.033$. Since the corporate tax rate in 1977 was $t = 0.48$, these figures imply that $dz/d\pi = 0.113 - tx$.

---

2. The capital stock, valued at replacement cost in 1977 dollars, is estimated by the Department of Commerce. The net liabilities are based on information in the Flow of Funds tables. The study by Feldstein and Summers presented in chap. 8 reports the net interest-bearing liabilities of NFCs as $595 billion. For the appropriate debt measure in this work, the value of the net trade credit ($72.7 billion) and government securities ($12.9 billion) must be subtracted from this $595 billion. The subtraction of net trade credit reflects the assumption that the profits of NFCs include an implicit interest return on the trade credit that they extend. The new information is from the *Federal Reserve Balance Sheets of the U.S. Economy*.

While it is difficult to calculate x as precisely as t, b, and z, it is clear that tx exceeds 0.113 and therefore that $dz/d\pi$ is negative. Recall that $x\pi$ is the overstatement of taxable profits per dollar of capital caused by inflation at rate π. The Feldstein and Summers study presented in chapter 8 estimates that in 1977 inflation caused an overstatement of taxable profits of $54.3 billion of which $39.7 billion was due to low depreciation and $14.6 was due to artificial inventory profits. Thus in 1977 $x\pi$ = 54.3/1684 = 0.032. The implied value of x depends on the rate of inflation that was responsible for these additional taxable profits. For the inventory component of the overstated profits, the relevant inflation rate is the one for the concurrent year; for the depreciation component, the relevant inflation rate is a weighted average of the inflation rates since the oldest remaining capital was acquired but with greater weight given to inflation in more recent years. The consumer price index rose 6.8 percent in 1977, an average of 7.2 percent in the preceding five years, and 4.5 percent and 1.9 percent in the two previous five-year periods.[3] An inflation rate of 7.0 percent is therefore a reasonable upper bond for the relevant rate and 5.0 percent is a reasonable lower bound. A value of π = 0.06 implies that x = 0.53 and therefore that tx = 0.256, even at the upper bound of π = 0.07, x = 0.46, and tx = 0.22. Both of these values are clearly above the critical value of 0.113 required for $dz/d\pi$ to the negative.

By itself, the fact that the inflation-tax interaction lowers the net of tax equity earnings tends to depress the price-earnings ratio. This is reinforced by the fact that the nominal increase in the value of the corporation's capital stock induces a capital gains tax liability for shareholders. But the net effect on the share price level depends on the effect of inflation on the investors' opportunity cost of investing in stocks. Because households pay tax on nominal interest income, inflation lowers the real net yield on bonds as an alternative to share ownership. At the same time, the favorable tax rules for investment in land, gold, owner-occupied housing, and so forth, imply that the real net opportunity cost of shareholding does not fall as much as the real net yield on bonds and may actually rise.[4] In considering these interactions of inflation and tax rules, it is important to distinguish households and nontaxable institutions and to recognize that share prices represent an equilibrium for these two groups.

In chapter 11, I evaluate the effect of inflation on the equilibrium share price, using a very simple model with two classes of investors. That analysis shows that if the opportunity cost that households perceive remains unchanged (at a real net-of-tax 4 percent), a rise in the inflation

3. The index of producer prices for finished goods rose 6.6 percent in 1977 and an average of 5.9 percent for the previous decade, essentially the same as the CPI.
4. This point is developed further in chaps. 6, 12, and 13 and in Hendershott (1979), Hendershott and Hu (1979), and Poterba (1980).

rate from zero to 6 percent would reduce the share value by 24 percent.[5] A one-fourth fall in the households' opportunity cost of share ownership (from 0.04 to 0.03) would limit the fall in the equilibrium share value to only 7 percent.

The real net cost of equity funds rose from about 7 percent in the mid-1960s to about 10 percent in the mid-1970s. On balance, I believe that the interaction of inflation and the tax rules is responsible for part, but only part, of this very substantial rise in the real cost of equity capital. Inflation may also depress share prices because of a perceived increase in risk (as Malkiel has stressed) or because investors confuse nominal and real returns (as Modigliani has emphasized). These additional explanations are not incompatible with the tax effect.

Although the tax rules cause inflation to depress share prices, they have the opposite effect on the prices of land, gold, and other "stores of value." Because the real opportunity cost of holding these assets is depressed by inflation while the return on these assets bears only a small extra tax because of inflation (i.e., the capital gains tax on realized nominal gains), an asset equilibrium requires a rise in their price. This notion is developed explicitly in chapters 12 and 13. The rise in the price of land, gold, and other stores of value not only redistributes wealth but also, by raising individual wealth, causes increased consumption and thus less saving.

1.3   Inflation, Tax Rules, and Investment

An important reason for the decline in nonresidential investment that I referred to in the beginning of this chapter has been the interaction of the high rate of inflation and the existing tax rules. As the discussion in the previous two sections has made clear, the nature of this interaction is complex and operates through several different channels. I have investigated this effect in the study presented in chapter 14 by estimating three quite different models of investment behavior. The strength of the empirical evidence rests on the fact that all three specifications support the same conclusion.

The simplest and most direct way relates investment to the real net return that the providers of capital can earn on business capital. As I noted in the first section of this chapter, the combined effects of original cost depreciation, the taxation of nominal capital gains, and other tax rules raise the effective tax rate paid on the capital income of the corporate sector and thus lowers the real net rate of return that the

---

5. This makes an allowance for the effect of the induced reduction of the capital stock on the subsequent pretax return. Summers (1980a) shows explicitly how that would reduce the fall in the equilibrium share value.

ultimate suppliers of capital can obtain on nonresidential fixed investment. This in turn reduces the incentive to save and distorts the flow of saving away from fixed nonresidential investment. Even without specifying the mechanism by which the financial markets and managerial decisions achieve this reallocation, the variations in investment during the past decades can be related to changes in the real net rate of return.

The real net rate of return varied around an average of 3.3 percent in the 1950s, rose by the mid-1960s to 6.5 percent while averaging 5.0 percent for the 1960s as a whole, and then dropped in the 1970s to an average of only 2.8 percent. A simple econometric model (relating net fixed business investment as a fraction of GNP to the real net rate of return and to capacity utilization) indicates that each percentage point rise in the real net return raised the ratio of investment to GNP by about one-half a percentage point. This estimated effect is quite robust with respect to changes in the specification, sample period, and method of estimation. It implies that the fall in the real net rate of return between the 1960s and the 1970s was large enough to account for a drop of more than one percentage point in the ratio of investment to GNP, a reduction that corresponds to more than one-third of the net investment ratio in the 1970s.

This general conclusion is supported by two quite different alternative models of investment. The first of these relates investment to the difference between the maximum potential rate of return that the firm can afford to pay on a "standard" project and the actual cost of funds. The second is an extension of the Hall-Jorgenson (1967) investment equation that incorporates all of the effects of inflation in the user cost of capital. Although none of the three models is a "true" picture of reality, the fact that they all point to the same conclusion is reassuring because it indicates that the finding is really "in the data" and is not merely an artifact of the model specification.

1.4   Fiscal Structure and Effects of Monetary Policy

The intellectual traditions of monetary analysis have caused the effects of the economy's fiscal structure to be ignored. Whatever the appropriateness of this division of labor between monetary specialists and tax specialists in earlier decades, it has clearly been inappropriate in more recent years. As I explain in chapters 3 through 6, the fiscal structure of our economy is a key determinant of the macroeconomic equilibrium and therefore of the effect of monetary policy. The failure to take fiscal effects into account has caused a misinterpretation of the expansionary and distortive character of monetary policy in the 1960s and 1970s.

During the dozen years after the 1951 accord between the Treasury and the Fed, the interest rate on Baa bonds varied only in the narrow range between 3.5 percent and 5 percent. In contrast, the next fifteen years saw the Baa rate rise from less than 5 percent in 1964 to more than 12 percent at the end of 1979. It is perhaps not surprising therefore that the monetary authorities, other government officials, and many private economists worried throughout this period that interest rates might be getting "too high." Critics of what was perceived as "tight money" argued that such high interest rates would reduce investment and therefore depress aggregate demand.

Against all this it could be argued, and was argued, that the *real* interest rate had obviously gone up much less. The correct measure of the real interest rate is of course the difference between the nominal interest rate and the rate of inflation that is *expected* over the life of the bond. A common rule of thumb approximates the expected future inflation by the average inflation rate experienced during the preceding three years. In 1964, when the Baa rate was 4.8 percent, this three-year rise in the GNP deflator averaged 1.6 percent; the implied real interest rate was thus 3.2 percent. By the end of 1979, when the Baa rate was 12.0 percent, the rise in the GNP deflator for the previous three years had increased to 7.8 percent, implying a real interest rate of 4.2 percent. Judged in his way, the cost of credit has also increased significantly over the fifteen-year period.

All of this ignores the role of taxes. Since interest expenses can be deducted by individuals and businesses in calculating taxable income, the net-of-tax interest cost is very much less than the interest rate itself. Indeed, since the *nominal* interest expense can be deducted, the *real net-of-tax* interest cost has actually varied inversely with the *nominal* rate of interest. *What appears to have been a rising interest rate over the past twenty-five years was actually a sharply falling real after-tax cost of funds.* The failure to recognize the role of taxes prevented the monetary authorities from seeing how expansionary monetary policy had become.

The implication of tax deductibility is seen most easily in the case of owner-occupied housing. A married couple with a $30,000 taxable income now has a marginal federal income tax rate of 37 percent. The 11.4 percent mortgage rate in effect in the last quarter of 1979 implied a net-of-tax cost of funds of 7.2 percent. Subtracting a 7.8 percent estimate of the rate of inflation (based on a three-year average increase in the GNP deflator) leaves a real net-of-tax cost of funds of *minus* 0.6 percent. By comparison, the 4.8 percent interest rate for 1964 translates into a 3.0 percent net-of-tax rate and a 1.4 percent real net-of-tax cost of funds. Thus, although the nominal interest rate had more than doubled and the real interest rate had also increased substantially, the relevant net-of-tax real cost of funds had actually fallen from 1.4 percent to a *negative* 0.6 percent.

As this example shows, taking the effects of taxation into account is particularly important because the tax rules are so nonneutral when there is inflation. If the tax rules were completely indexed, the effect of the tax system on the conduct of monetary policy would be much less significant. But with existing tax rules, the movements of the pretax real interest rate and of the after-tax real interest rates are completely different. I think that monetary policy in the last decade was more expansionary than it otherwise would have been because the monetary authorities and others believed that the cost of funds was rising or steady when in fact it was falling significantly.

The fall in the real after-tax interest rate has caused a rapid increase in the price of houses relative to the general price level and has sustained a high rate of new residential construction; this effect is analyzed in chapter 6. There were, of course, times when the ceilings on the interest rates that financial institutions could pay caused disintermediation and limited the funds available for housing. To that extent, the high level of nominal interest rates restricted the supply of funds at the same time that the corresponding low real after-tax interest cost increased the demand for funds. More recently, the raising of certain interest rate ceilings and the development of mortgage-backed bonds that can short-circuit the disintermediation process have made the supply restrictions much less important and have therefore made any interest level more expansionary than it otherwise would have been.

The low real after-tax rate of interest has also encouraged the growth of consumer credit and the purchase of consumer durables. It is not surprising that, with a negative real net rate of interest, house mortgage borrowing has soared to over $90 billion a year, more than double the rate in the early 1970s. More generally, even households that do not itemize their tax deductions are affected by the low real after-tax return that is available on savings. Because individuals pay tax on nominal interest income, the real after-tax rate of return on saving has become negative. It seems likely that this substantial fall in the real return on savings has contributed to the fall in the personal saving rate and the rise in consumer demand.

The evidence presented in chapter 8 shows that the analysis is more complex for corporate borrowers and investors because inflation changes the effective tax rate on investments as well as the real net-of-tax interest rate. More specifically, because historic cost depreciation and inventory accounting rules reduce substantially the real after-tax return on corporate investments, an easy-money policy raises the demand for corporate capital only if the real net cost of funds falls by more than the return that firms can afford to pay. This balance between the lower real net interest cost and the lower real net return on investment depends on the corporation's debt-equity ratio and on the relation between the real yields that must be paid on debt and on equity funds. It is difficult to say just what has happened on balance. In a preliminary study presented in chapter 9, Lawrence Summers and I concluded that the rise in the nominal interest rate caused by inflation was probably slightly less than the rise in the maximum nominal interest rate that firms could afford to pay.

However, that study made no allowance for the effect of inventory taxation or for the more complex effects of inflation on equity yields that I discuss in chapters 8, 10, and 11. My current view, based on the evidence developed in chapter 14, is that, on balance, expansionary monetary policy reduced the demand for business investment at the same time that it increased the demand for residential investment and for consumption goods.

It is useful to contrast the conclusion of this section with the conventional Keynesian analysis. According to the traditional view, monetary expansion lowers interest rates which reduces the cost of funds to investors and therefore encourages the accumulation of plant and equipment. In the context of the U.S. economy in recent years, this statement is wrong in three ways. First, a sustained monetary expansion raises nominal interest rates. Second, although the interest rate is higher, the real net-of-tax cost of funds is lower. And, third, the lower cost of funds produced in this way encourages investment in housing and consumer durables (as well as greater consumption in general) rather than more investment in plant and equipment. Indeed, because of the interaction of tax rules and inflation, a monetary expansion tends to discourage saving and reduce investment in plant and equipment. The low real net-of-tax rate of interest on mortgages and consumer credit is an indication of this misallocation of capital.

Perhaps the problems of misinterpretation and mismanagement might have been avoided completely if the monetary authorities and others in the financial community, as well as Congress and the economics profession, had ignored interest rates completely and focused their attention on the money supply and the credit aggregates. Presumably, under current Federal Reserve procedures, there will be more of a tendency to do just that. But since the temptation to look at rates as well is very powerful, it is important to interpret the rates correctly. What matters for the household borrower or saver is the real net-of-tax interest rate. A very low or negative real net-of-tax rate is a clear signal of an incentive to overspend on housing and on other forms of consumption. What matters for the business firm is the difference between the real net-of-tax cost of funds (including both debt and equity) and the maximum return that, with existing tax laws, it can afford to pay. The difficulty of measuring this difference should be a warning against relying on any observed rates to judge the ease or tightness of credit for business investment.

1.5   The Mix of Monetary and Fiscal Policies

There is widespread agreement on two central goals for macroeconomic policy: (1) achieving a level of aggregate demand that avoids both unemployment and inflation, and (2) increasing the share of national income that is devoted to business investment. Monetary and fiscal policy provide two instruments with which to achieve these two goals. The conventional Keynesian view of the economy has led to the prescription of easy money (to encourage investment) and a tight fiscal policy (to limit demand and prevent inflation). Our low rate of investment and high rate of inflation indicate that this approach has not worked. It is useful to review both the way such a policy is supposed to work and the reason why it fails.

Keynesian analysis, based on a theory developed during and for the depression, is designed for an economy with substantial slack and essentially fixed prices. This Keynesian perspective implies that real output can be expanded by increasing demand and that the policy mix determines how this increased output is divided between investment, consumption or government spending. An increase in the money supply favors investment while a fiscal expansion favors consumption or government spending. Whatever the validity of this analysis in an economy with vast excess capacity and fixed prices, it has not been appropriate for the U.S. economy in recent years.

There is a way in which a policy mix of easy money and fiscal tightness could in principal work in our relatively fully employed economy. The key requirement would be a persistent government surplus. Such a surplus would permit the government to reduce the supply of outstanding government debt. This in turn would induce households and institutions to substitute additional private bonds and stocks for the government debt that was removed from their portfolios. The result would be an increased rate of private capital accumulation. Under likely conditions, this substitution of private capital for government debt would require a lower rate of interest and a relative increase in the stock of money.[6]

Unfortunately, the traditional prescription of easy money and a tight fiscal position has failed in practice because of the political difficulty of achieving and maintaining a government surplus.[7] As a result, the pursuit of an easy money policy has produced inflation. Although the inflationary

6. See chap. 5 for a theoretical analysis in which this possibility is considered.
7. It might be argued that the inflationary erosion of the real government debt means that the government has in fact had real surpluses even though nominal deficits. But such an inflation adjustment also implies an equal reduction in private saving, indicating that private saving has in fact been negative. The conventional government deficit should also be augmented by the off-budget borrowing and the growth of government unfunded obligations in the social security and civil service and military service pension programs.

increase in the money supply did reduce the real after-tax cost of funds, this only diverted the flow of capital away from investment in plant and equipment and into owner-occupied housing and consumer durables. By reducing the real net return to savers, the easy money policy has probably also reduced the total amount of new savings.

The traditional policy mix reflects not only its optimistic view about the feasibility of government surpluses but also its overly narrow conception of the role of fiscal policy. In the current macroeconomic tradition, fiscal policy has been almost synonymous with variations in the net government surplus or deficit and has generally ignored the potentially powerful incentive effects of taxes that influence marginal prices.

An alternative policy mix for achieving the dual goals of balanced demand and increased business investment would combine a tight-money policy and fiscal incentives for investment and saving. A tight-money policy would prevent inflation and would raise the real net-of-tax rate of interest. Although the higher real rate of interest would tend to deter all forms of residential and nonresidential investment, specific incentives for investment in plant and equipment could more than offset the higher cost of funds. The combination of the higher real net interest rate and the targeted investment incentives would restrict housing construction and the purchase of consumer durables while increasing the flow of capital into new plant and equipment. Since housing and consumer durables now account for substantially more than half of the private capital stock, such a restructuring of the investment mix could have a substantial favorable effect on the stock of plant and equipment.

A rise in the overall saving rate would permit a greater increase in business investment. The higher real net rate of interest would in itself tend to induce such a higher rate of saving. This could be supplemented by explicit fiscal policies that reduced the tax rate on interest income and other income from saving.

In short, restructuring macroeconomic policy to recognize the importance of fiscal incentives and of the current interaction between tax rules and inflation provides a way of both reducing the rate of inflation and increasing the growth of the capital stock.

I   Inflation and Tax Rules in Macroeconomic Equilibrium

2 A Summary of the Theoretical Models

This chapter summarizes four rather abstract models of a very simple economy with a constant and known rate of inflation. These models, persented in chapters 3 through 6, examine what happens to asset yields and capital intensity when the rate of inflation changes from one "permanent" level to another. Within this framework, it is possible to examine the implications of different tax rules, especially different forms of indexing and of inflation nonneutrality. These theoretical models represent my own attempt to understand how inflation and the tax system interact to influence the rate of capital formation.

The first of these theoretical studies, reported in "Inflation, Income Tax Rules, and the Rate of Interest" (chap. 3) introduces a corporate tax and a personal tax on investment income into a simple neoclassical monetary growth model. The model is then used to study the effect of inflation on the rate of interest and on the capital intensity of the economy. Except for the capital income taxes, this model is very similar to the one developed by James Tobin (1965).

Tobin obtained his famous conclusion that inflation *increases* capital intensity by analyzing an economy in which all taxes were assumed to be of a lump sum variety. The capital-increasing effect of inflation is also a possible special case in my own more general analysis. But the richer description of the tax system shows that the tax rates and saving behavior together determine whether an increase in the rate of inflation will increase or decrease the steady-state capital intensity of the economy. In this more general model and with plausible parameter values, the most likely effect of an increase in the rate of inflation is a fall in the real net

The main part of this chapter appeared previously in my *Two Lectures on Macroeconomics*, in 1980 Woodward Lectures at the University of British Columbia, published by the University of British Columbia, 1982.

rate of interest received by savers and therefore a decrease in the capital intensity of production in the economy.

The model that leads to this conclusion involves two important simplifying assumptions. First, all corporate investment is financed by debt; equivalently, and perhaps more plausibly, only debt finance is used at the margin so that the corporate income tax produces revenue for the government because it taxes the intramarginal equity income.[1] The second assumption is that firms use a correct measure of economic depreciation in calculating taxable profits; in particular, inflation does not reduce the value of depreciation allowances. Both of these assumptions are replaced by more realistic descriptions of corporate finance and historic cost depreciation in subsequent papers that are described below. Although these more general analyses give results that more accurately reflect reality, analysis of the present model with debt-only finance and with economic depreciation is useful for highlighting some important features of the general mechanism by which inflation affects capital intensity and asset yields.

In this model, the effect of inflation on capital intensity depends on two countervailing forces. First, there is the liquidity or portfolio composition effect emphasized by Tobin (1965) and Mundell (1963). An increase in the rate of inflation raises the nominal interest rate, implying a higher cost of holding money balances. This induces a shift in portfolio composition from money to real capital. The portfolio composition effect in this two-asset model unequivocally implies that inflation raises capital intensity. This effect was the basis of Tobin's conclusion.

There is, however, a second effect of inflation that depends on the nature of the tax system and of saving behavior. Because the tax system is based on nominal interest payments and receipts rather than real interest payments and receipts, inflation is likely to alter the real net rate of interest received by savers. If saving is sensitive to the rate of return, inflation will alter the saving rate and therefore the long-run capital intensity of production. Although a positive relationship between the real net rate of return and the saving rate is not an unambiguous implication of economic theory,[2] it appears to be supported by empirical research and by the examination of plausible parameter values in theoretical models;[3] unless I say otherwise, I shall therefore be assuming in this chapter that a higher real net rate of return increases the saving rate or at least does not decrease it. I might add that only the first of the three theoretical models that I will describe assumes a variable saving rate; in the others, individuals save a fixed fraction of disposable income.

1. See Joseph Stiglitz (1973) for a model that incorporates this assumption of marginal debt finance.

2. This is time even for compensated changes in the rate of return; see Feldstein (1978c).

3. See Boskin (1978), Feldstein (1981a), Feldstein and Tsiang (1968), and Summers (1980).

The effect of inflation on the real net rate of interest depends on the entire tax structure. It is easy but wrong to fall into the trap of arguing as follows: "Since inflation raises the interest rate by the rate of inflation, and the inflation premium is subject to tax, the *net* interest rate rises by less than the rate of inflation and the *real net* interest rate therefore falls. For example, if an economy has a 4 percent interest rate with no inflation, an 8 percent inflation will raise the interest rate to 12 percent. With a 50 percent personal tax rate, the original 4 percent interest rate would leave a net yield of 2 percent; the 12 percent rate would leave a net yield of only 6 percent or 2 percent less than the rate of inflation. Thus the real net rate falls from a positive 2 percent to a negative 2 percent."

This argument is wrong in assuming that the interest rate necessarily rises by the rate of inflation. This famous theoretical proposition of Irving Fisher (1930) was based on an economy with no taxes. When borrowers can deduct their interest costs, they can afford to pay a higher inflation premium. More specifically, with economic depreciation and no other adverse effects of inflation on real profitability, the borrower can afford to raise the interest rate that it pays until the inflation rate equals the rise in the interest rate net of the borrower's tax deduction. Thus, if the borrower is in the 50 percent tax bracket, the interest rate will rise by two percentage points for every percentage point of inflation. In the numerical example that I considered in the previous paragraph, an 8 percent rate of inflation would raise the interest rate by 16 percentage points to 20 percent. The net interest rate to the lender in the 50 percent bracket is thus 10 percent and the net real rate becomes 2 percent, exactly what it was in the absence of inflation.

This example illustrates a general proposition that is shown more formally in the paper: The real net rate of return to savers will remain unchanged if and only if the tax rates paid by borrowers and lenders are equal. If the tax rate of borrowers exceeds that of lenders, the real net return to lenders will rise and saving will be encouraged. Conversely, if the tax rate of lenders is higher than that of borrowers, the real net return to lenders will fall and saving will be discouraged. The net effect of inflation on capital intensity in this case depends on the relative strength of the saving effect and the portfolio composition effect. Some calculations in the paper itself show that the relative size of the relevant money balances is so small that even a quite small sensitivity of saving to the net rate of interest will cause the saving effect to be more important than the portfolio composition effect.

The relation between the two tax rates and the real net rate of return can be derived explicitly by noting that, with all debt finance and economic depreciation, the real return on capital net of the corporate income tax [$(1 - \tau)f'$ where τ is the corporate tax rate and f' is the marginal product of capital] must equal the real net cost per dollar of borrowed funds $[(1 - \tau)i - \pi$ where i is the nominal interest rate and π is the rate of inflation]. Thus,

(1) $$(1 - \tau)f' = (1 - \tau)i - \pi$$

or

(2) $$i = f' + \pi/(1 - \tau)$$

The net rate of interest to the saver is $i_N = (1 - \theta)i$ or

(3) $$i_N = (1 - \theta)f' + \frac{1 - \theta}{1 - \tau}\pi$$

The real net rate of interest to the saver is $r_N = i_N - \pi$ or

(4) $$r_N = (1 - \theta)f' + \frac{\tau - \theta}{1 - \tau}\pi$$

Thus the real net rate of return to the saver rises or falls with inflation according to whether or not the borrowers' tax rate exceeds the lenders' tax rate.

These calculations highlight the importance of the deductability of nominal payments by borrowers and the taxation of nominal payments received by savers. While this emphasis is useful, it implies too strong a condition for inflation to depress capital intensity. A more general model shows that inflation can reduce capital intensity even when the borrowers' rate exceeds the lenders' rate if we also recognize the historical cost method of depreciation, the tax treatment of inventory accounting profits, and the taxation of capital gains. I will return to these more general conclusions later in this chapter.

But first, the implied impact of inflation on the interest rate in the first model deserves further comment. Equation (2) implies that $di/d\pi = 1/(1 - \tau)$ or approximately 2 and not the point-for-point relation between changes in inflation and in the interest rate that was predicted by Irving Fisher for a taxless economy and that has in fact been observed at least approximately in the United States in recent years. The difference between the pure inflation effect implied by the model and indicated by equation (2) and the actual one-for-one movements that have been experienced reflects four features of the U.S. economy that the present model ignores: (1) the additional tax burdens caused by inflation because of historic cost depreciation and inventory accounting rules; (2) the role of equity financing and the taxation of the return to equity; (3) the presence of government debt and debt management policies; and (4) the presence of other debt instruments that are not affected by inflation in the same way as the corporate bond market but that are close substitutes for corporate bonds in investors' portfolios (i.e., residential mortgages, state and local bonds, foreign bonds). A richer model that incorporates these features has implications that are consistent with the observed behavior of interest rates. The simpler model is nevertheless useful in focusing on the partial effect of nominal interest deductibility and taxation.

Despite its simple structure, or perhaps because of it, the current model also provides insights into the welfare effects of inflation. The economists' traditional objection to a positive constant rate of inflation is that it imposes an efficiency loss by distorting the demand for money balances.[4] This traditional conclusion refers to an economy with no distorting taxes. Phelps (1972) has stressed that the increase in the money supply that causes inflation is also a source of government revenue that in itself permits a reduction in the tax rate that distorts labor supply. Phelps concluded from this observation that the optimal inflation rate is positive and may even be substantial. The appropriate analysis is more complex when we recognize the nonneutrality of existing taxes on capital income.[5] Even in the absence of inflation, the net return to savers (r_N) is less than the marginal product of capital (by the rate of personal income tax: $r_N = (1 - \theta)f'$) and this distortion between the gross and net rates of return is itself a welfare loss. A positive rate of inflation affects the tax wedge between the marginal product of capital and the net return as well as the amount of revenue that the government collects at existing tax rates (and therefore its ability to reduce—or its need to increase—the distortionary tax on labor income). The effects of inflation on the "investment tax wedge" and on revenue are of opposite signs. If the lenders' tax rate exceeds the borrowers', inflation increases tax revenues but worsens the tax wedge between the marginal product of capital and the net return; conversely, if the borrowers' tax rate is higher, inflation reduces tax revenue but improves (i.e., reduces) the distorting wedge between the gross and net rates of return. Determining the optimal steady-state rate of inflation requires balancing at least three effects of inflation on economic welfare: (1) the welfare loss that results from reduced liquidity, (2) the change in welfare that results from the increase or decrease in the differential between the marginal product of capital and each individual's marginal rate of substitution, and (3) the change in other distorting taxes that results from the increase or decrease in the net tax revenue in response to inflation.

Although the analysis is necessarily more complex in richer models, the same conflict between the investment tax wedge and the revenue effect remains. With parameter values that provide a realistic description of the

4. See Bailey (1956), Friedman (1969), and Feldstein (1979).

5. Indeed, even within his own more limited framework, Phelps's conclusion is not correct. Recall that Friedman has shown that, ignoring the revenue effect of inflation, the optimal rate of inflation is not zero but is negative and equal to the marginal product of capital. The force of Phelps's argument is only that, when the revenue effect is considered, the optimal tax rate should be greater than this negative number and not that it should be positive.

U.S. economy, inflation does raise extra tax revenue (that could be used to reduce the distortionary tax on labor income) but accomplishes this only by increasing the distortionary wedge between the net return to savers and the pretax marginal product of capital. Since the existing mix of labor and capital income taxes places too heavy a relative tax on capital income even in the absence of inflation (i.e., the welfare loss of collecting the existing amount of total tax revenue could be reduced by switching more of the tax to labor),[6] the effect of inflation on the relative rates of tax on capital and labor is undesirable.

As I have emphasized several times, two important limitations in the realism of this first model are (1) the exclusive focus on debt finance and (2) the assumption that firms are allowed economic depreciation. Dropping these restrictions has important implications for the effects of inflation on the equilibrium of the economy. Jerry Green, Eytan Sheshinski and I extended this first model (in "Inflation and Taxes in a Growing Economy with Debt and Equity Finance," presented in chapter 4) to recognize that firms finance investment by both debt and equity (in a ratio that depends on tax rates and on the rate of inflation) and that the "historic cost" method of depreciation causes the effective tax rate on corporate income to rise with the rate of inflation. A complete analysis of such a model would follow the procedure of the first model and trace out the full general equilibrium effects that a change in the permanent rate of inflation would have on the asset yields, portfolio composition, the real rate of return, and the capital stock. We followed a simpler and more partial analysis. We took both the saving rate and the ratio of real money balances to real capital as fixed. This implies that the capital stock and the pretax marginal product of capital remain fixed when the inflation rate changes. In this framework we examined how a change in the rate of inflation alters the yields on debt and equity. It is easy to see how this could then be extended to allow for the general equilibrium effects of changes in the saving rate, portfolio composition, and capital intensity.

The analysis in this new paper showed that the historic cost method of depreciation has important effects on the yields of *both* debt and equity. Because depreciation for tax purposes is limited to the original or "historic" cost of the firm's capital stock, a higher rate of inflation reduces the real value of the depreciation allowance and thereby raises the real tax burden on corporate income. This extra real tax reduces the net return that firms can pay to the suppliers of debt and equity capital. This reduction in the real net return to capital is divided between debt and equity in a way that depends on the substitutability between debt and equity in the portfolios of individual investors. In general, inflation reduces both the real net return to equity and the real net rate of interest.

6. See Feldstein (1978*a*).

Understanding the role of historic cost depreciation helps to resolve the puzzling and counterfactual implication of the simpler model that the nominal interest rate rises by approximately twice the increase in the rate of inflation. Put simply, historic cost depreciation reduces the firm's ability to pay such high interest rates. With a constant marginal product of capital (f') and a constant debt to equity ratio, the relation between the interest rate and the rate of inflation can be written $di/d\pi = (1 - \delta)/(1 - \tau)$ where δ is the extra tax per 100 units of capital that is collected when the inflation rate rises by one percentage point. Thus, if a 10 percent inflation rate and historical cost depreciation together mean that the tax rate on capital rises by five percentage points, $\delta = 0.5$ and $di/d\pi = .5/(1 - \tau)$ or approximately one. More generally, the effect of inflation on the nominal interest rate depends on the relative magnitudes of the historical cost depreciation penalty (δ) and the benefits of deducting nominal interest rates (as measured by the corporate tax rate, τ). The analysis in our article is based on an approximation that δ is approximately 0.2, implying that the interest rate rises by significantly more than the inflation rate but that calculation still ignored the inventory accounting penalty, government debt management, and other financial assets.

The effect of inflation on the real net return to savers can be summarized by a simple expression if we limit attention to the special case in which investors wish to hold debt and equity in fixed proportions. With this assumption, it is not necessary to worry about changes in risk premia that would otherwise influence the interest rate and the yield on equities. In this case, the effect of inflation on the *real net* interest rate is given by

$$(5) \qquad \frac{dr_N}{d\pi} = \left[\frac{\tau - \theta}{1 - \tau} - \frac{\delta(1 - \theta)}{1 - \tau} \right]$$

The first term reflects the effects of basing taxes on nominal interest payments and expenses. The real net return to the saver rises or falls with inflation according to the relative tax rates on borrowers and lenders for the reasons that have been discussed above; this part of equation (5) is the same as the previous equation (4). The second term reflects the adverse effect of historical cost depreciation on the net return on debt. Note that $\theta \geq \tau$ is a sufficient (although not necessary) condition for inflation to reduce the real net return on debt.

The comparable effect on equity can also be calculated most easily if we assume that the debt equity ratio is constant. The Feldstein-Green-Sheshinski analysis then shows that:

$$(6) \qquad \frac{de_N}{d\pi} = -[c + \delta(1 - \theta)]$$

where e_N is the real net of tax return per unit of equity and c is the effective rate of capital gains tax. This is unambiguously negative. Note that the assumption that the debt-equity ratio is fixed implies that the gap between the real net yields on debt and on equity varies with inflation.

In general, inflation will also influence the firm's debt-equity.ratios. Although the nature of this dependence is complex, in the simple case in which the only nonneutrality in the tax system is in the treatment of interest (i.e., when there is economic depreciation and no taxation of nominal capital gains), inflation raises the debt-equity ratio in the economy if the borrowers' tax rate exceeds the lenders' tax rate ($\tau > \theta$) and reduces it if the borrowing rate is lower. It is easy to see why this is so since the higher tax rate for borrowers means that the government loses money to investors on every dollar of debt, therefore encouraging the substitution of debt for equity.

In this paper, Green, Sheshinski and I also examined the effects of alternative indexing rules. It is clear from equation (6) that indexing depreciation and capital gains ($\delta = c = 0$) would make the real net return to equity independent of the inflation rate as long as the debt-equity ratio remained unchanged. With economic depreciation ($\delta = 0$), the real net rate of interest is affected only by the difference between the tax rates on borrowers and lenders (equation 5). In the special case of equal tax rates, there is no need to adjust the tax treatment of interest payments and receipts in order to keep both the real net yield on both debt and equity unaffected by inflation. Indeed, even if the debt equity ratio is not fixed, the analysis in the paper shows that the net yields are unaffected by inflation if there is economic depreciation, no taxation of nominal capital gains, and equality of tax rates on borrowers and lenders. (Of course, the complete neutrality is true only if everyone has the same rate and not just if the average rate among borrowers equals the average rate among lenders. Even if the averages are equal, the individuals with the highest marginal tax rates will lose and those with the lowest marginal tax rates will gain.)

Illustrative but plausible parameter values suggested to Green, Sheshinski, and me that "With our current tax system, inflation decreases the net rate of return and therefore is likely to decrease the rate of saving. This in turn would decrease the ratio of capital to labor and thus increase the marginal product of capital. This in turn would partially offset the fall in the after-tax rate of return, but the qualitative results of our analysis would remain unchanged."

A theoretical model cannot be a complete picture of reality and still be simple enough to be analytically useful. Examining different models that emphasize different aspects of a problem can, however, provide useful insights about the complex reality that is of ultimate interest. In this spirit, the third paper ("Fiscal Policies, Inflation, and Capital Formation," chap. 5) explores another facet of the general subject of the interrelationship between inflation, fiscal policy, and capital formation: the role of government bonds and monetary (or debt-management) policy. More specifically, the monetary growth model with which I began in the first model is extended by recognizing that the government can finance its deficit by alternative combinations of money and bonds. The monetary policy that is selected (i.e., the combination of money and bonds) determines the extent to which a government deficit causes inflation, crowds out private investment, or both. The analysis emphasizes that the impact of any monetary policy depends crucially on the structure of the tax rules.

The importance of government bonds in this model of the economy is that they provide an alternative asset which, unlike money, *has* a nominal yield that can vary with the rate of inflation and into which individuals can channel their saving instead of acquiring claims to physical capital. This rechannelling of saving represents an important way in which inflation can reduce real capital accumulation even if the saving rate itself is not sensitive to the real rate of return. The availability of government bonds is thus a reason why, contrary to Tobin's earlier conclusion, a higher rate of inflation may not succeed in increasing investors' willingness to hold real capital and may have just the opposite effect.

The existence of both government bonds and money also provides a further way of explaining the observation that the real pretax interest rate has remained constant. The puzzling implication of the models that I have already described (i.e., that inflation would raise the real pretax interest rate) reflected the absence of any monetary or debt-management policy. The current analysis shows how the government can reduce the real yield on bonds by decreasing the ratio of government bonds to money. The government, in other words, can validate Irving Fisher's propositions by a relative increase in the money supply.

A surprising result of the formal analysis of this model is that the real per capita government deficit can increase permanently without inducing any changes in either inflation or capital intensity. This will happen, however, in a fully employed economy only if there is a corresponding reduction in the share of government spending in national income. In contrast, if the government's share of national income is constant, a permanent increase in the real per capita deficit must be accompanied by an increase in the rate of inflation, or by a decrease in equilibrium capital intensity, or both.

With the existing tax system and the type of monetary policy that has been pursued in the United States, an increase in the deficit is likely to cause both a higher rate of inflation and a reduced capital intensity of production. More specifically, this is the likely implication of a monetary policy that keeps the real interest rate on government debt constant by adjusting the mix of bonds and money when the size of the deficit changes. The basic reason for this is that an increase in inflation reduces the real net yield on private capital because of historic cost depreciation and other tax accounting rules. If the real net yield on government bonds is maintained while the real net yield on private capital falls, there will be incentive for individuals to switch from real investment to the holding of government debt. Capital intensity will fall except in the unlikely event that the adverse effect of inflation on the demand for money outweighs the positive effect of inflation on the demand for bonds. The greater responsiveness of bond demand than of money demand is quite likely in view of the relative magnitudes of both types of assets and the greater substitutability between debt and capital than between money and capital.

The formal analysis in this paper also shows that the reduced capital intensity in this case is accompanied by an increased rate of inflation. To prevent such an increase in the rate of inflation would require a greater rise in the interest rate, enough to cause the demand for government liabilities (i.e., the sum of bonds and money) to increase enough to absorb an increased deficit without a higher proportional rate of growth of either money or bonds. To state this same point in a slightly different way, the faster growth of government liabilities can be absorbed without increasing the *proportional* growth of either money or bonds (and therefore the inflation rate) if the *levels* of money and bonds that are demanded (i.e., the denominators of the proportional growth rates) are increased. The higher interest rate would make this possible by increasing the demand for bonds by more than it decreases the demand for money.

Although such a policy would prevent inflation, the government deficit would reduce real capital accumulation. The analysis makes it clear that a higher rate of real capital accumulation can only be achieved by either a reduction in the government deficit or an increase in private saving. If private saving is responsive to a higher real yield, the policy of high interest rates and the prevention of inflation can together increase private saving. Other specific fiscal incentives that reduce the wedge between the marginal product of capital and the real after-tax return might also be used to increase the rate of saving. In this context, a reduction in the subsidy for spending on consumer durables, housing, and other forms of what we might call "consumption capital" would also encourage the accumulation of more plant and equipment.

An explicit analysis of the effect of inflation on the equilibrium demand for housing capital is presented in chapter 6, "Inflation, Tax Rules, and the Accumulation of Residential and Nonresidential Capital." The essential framework is a monetary growth model with taxation of nominal corporate and household income. The model of chapters 3 and 4 is extended to include both a general goods sector and an owner-occupied housing sector. To facilitate this analysis, the earlier models are simplified by assuming that both savings and money demand are inelastic and that all investment is financed by debt.

Within this framework, the analysis shows that an increase in the rate of inflation raises the amount of housing stock per person and reduces the amount of plant and equipment. It is clear from the structure of the analysis that the same conclusion would hold in a model with all equity finance. If the saving rate is an increasing function of the real net-of-tax return, the total of both types of capital would be reduced but the change in the mix in favor of housing would remain. The basic reason for all of these effects is the adverse impact of historic cost accounting on the profitability of the corporate capital relative to the implicit return on housing capital.

This brings me back to the point with which I began this chapter. It is now time to turn to the four theoretical studies themselves and then to the empirical research presented in later chapters that they led me to— research on the impact of inflation on effective rates of tax as well as research on the effects of inflation on the real yields on corporate debt and equity as well as research on the effect that the interaction of inflation and our tax rules has had on private saving and on business fixed investment. I hope, however, that even this brief review of the four simplified models indicates the types of theoretical thinking that helped me to clarify my own analysis about the nature of the interaction between inflation, taxes, and capital formation.

3   Inflation, Income Taxes, and the Rate of Interest: A Theoretical Analysis

Income taxes are a central feature of economic life but not of the growth models that we use to study the long-run effects of monetary and fiscal policies. The taxes in current monetary growth models are lump sum transfers that alter disposable income but do not directly affect factor rewards or the cost of capital. In contrast, the actual personal and corporate income taxes do influence the cost of capital to firms and the net rate of return to savers. The existence of such taxes also in general changes the effect of inflation on the rate of interest and on the process of capital accumulation.[1]

The current paper presents a neoclassical monetary growth model in which the influence of such taxes can be studied. The model is then used in sections 3.2 and 3.3 to study the effect of inflation on the capital intensity of the economy. James Tobin's (1955, 1965) early result that inflation increases capital intensity appears as a possible special case. More generally, the tax rates and saving behavior determine whether an increase in the rate of inflation will increase or decrease steady-state capital intensity.

The analysis also shows that the net real rate of interest received by savers may be substantially altered by the rate of inflation. Section 3.3

Reprinted by permission from *American Economic Review* 66 (December 1976): 809–20.

I am grateful to the University of California at Berkeley for the opportunity to prepare this paper while I was Ford Research Professor. The National Science Foundation supported the project on the effects of fiscal programs on capital accumulation and income distribution, of which the current study is a part. I am grateful for discussions with Stanley Fischer, Steven Goldman, and David Hartman.

1. Income taxes have been studied in *nonmonetary* growth models by Peter Diamond (1970, 1975), Feldstein (1974*a, b*), and Kazuo Sato (1967). Of course, the effects of inflation cannot be examined in such models.

discusses the desirability of adjusting the taxation of interest income to eliminate these arbitrary effects of inflation. The fourth section discusses the implications of this for the welfare effects of inflation and the optimal rate of growth of the money supply.

3.1 A Growing Economy with Inflation and Income Taxes

This section presents a one-sector neoclassical model of economic growth with inflation and income taxes. The model differs from that of Tobin (1965) in two fundamental ways: (1) the savings rate depends on the net real rate of return earned by savers; (2) there are personal and corporate interest income taxes as well as a lump sum tax.[2] Because the analysis of the model in section 3.2 will focus on comparative steady-state dynamics, only these steady-state properties will be discussed here.

The steady-state economy will be characterized by an inflation rate $\pi = Dp/p$ and a nominal interest rate of i. The real rate of interest is, by definition, $r = i - \pi$. In order to consider the effects of adjusting the tax treatment for the rate of inflation, separate tax rates will be specified for the real and inflation components of the nominal rate of interest. The personal income tax will tax real interest payments at θ_1 and the inflation component at θ_2. The net nominal rate of return is thus $i_N = (1 - \theta_1)r + (1 - \theta_2)\pi$. In our current tax law $\theta_1 = \theta_2$ so that $i_N = (1 - \theta)(r + \pi) = (1 - \theta)i$. With complete inflation indexation, $\theta_2 = 0$ and $i_N = (1 - \theta_1)r + \pi$; the net real rate of interest received by households is thus $r_N = i_N - \pi = (1 - \theta_1)r$.

The economy is characterized by an exogenously growing population

$$(1) \qquad N = N_0 e^{nt}$$

The labor force is a constant fraction of the population. Production can be described by an aggregate production function with constant returns to scale. The relation between aggregate output per capita (y) and aggregate capital stock per capita (k) is

$$(2) \qquad y = f(k)$$

with $f' > 0$ and $f'' < 0$. For simplicity, both technical progress and depreciation are ignored.

3.1.1 The Demand for Capital

The investment and financing behavior of firms is influenced by the corporate income tax. An important feature of the corporation tax is that the interest paid on corporate debt may be deducted by firms in calculating taxable profits while dividends paid on corporate equity may not be

2. In the more general model of David Levhari and Don Patinkin, the savings rate does depend on the rate of return but there are no corporate or personal income taxes.

deducted. Although the method of finance need not affect the analysis in models without a corporate income tax, it is necessary in the current model to identify the method of finance. Because the focus of the current paper is on the effect of inflation on the rate of interest, I will assume that all corporate investment is financed by issuing debt.[3] The tax deduction of interest payments may also be adjusted for inflation: let τ_1 be the tax rate at which the real component of interest payments is deducted and let τ_2 be the tax rate at which the inflation component can be deducted. The net rate of interest paid by firms is then $(1 - \tau_1)r + (1 - \tau_2)\pi$.[4]

In the absence of the corporation tax, the firm maximizes its profit by investing until the marginal product of capital is equal to the real rate of interest, $i - \pi$. Stated somewhat differently, the firm's capital stock is optimal when the marginal product of capital $[f'(k)]$ plus the nominal appreciation in the value of the capital stock per unit of capital (π) is equal to the nominal rate of interest:

$$(3) \qquad f'(k) + \pi = i$$

The effect of the corporation tax on this optimality condition depends on the way that depreciation is treated by the law. Consider first the simple case in which capital lasts forever, i.e., in which there is no depreciation. The corporation tax then reduces the net-of-tax marginal product of capital to $(1 - \tau_1)f'(k)$. There is no tax on the unrealized appreciation of the capital stock. The firm maximizes profits by increasing the capital stock until the net nominal return on capital $(1 - \tau_1)f'(k) + \pi$ is equal to the net nominal rate of interest, $(1 - \tau_1) r + (1 - \tau_2)\pi$. The first-order optimum of equation (3) therefore becomes

$$(4) \qquad f'(k) = r - \left(\frac{\tau_2}{1 - \tau_1} \right) \pi$$

If the capital stock does depreciate, $f'(k)$ can be interpreted as the marginal product of capital net of the cost of replacing the capital that has been used up in production. If the corporation tax allows the deduction of

3. It would, of course, be desirable to have a more general model in which corporate debt and equity coexist. The exclusion of equity in the current analysis and the full deductibility of corporate interest payments imply that the present value of corporation taxes is zero. The present model might therefore be regarded as an approximation to a model in which equity profits are intramarginal and all marginal investments are financed by debt (see Joseph Stiglitz 1973). Dale Henderson and Thomas Sargent (1973) studied the effect of inflation in an economy in which firms finance all investment by issuing equity. Because they use a short-run analysis with no accumulation of capital, their conclusions cannot be compared with those of the current analysis. After this paper was accepted for publication, Jerry Green, Eytan Sheshinski, and I (1978; chap. 4 below) developed a more general extension of the current analysis in which firms use an optimal mix of equity and debt finance.

4. In steady-state growth with fully anticipated inflation there is no need to distinguish between short-term debt and long-term debt.

the replacement cost of this depreciation, the net-of-tax marginal product of capital is again $(1 - \tau_1)f'(k)$ and equation (4) continues to hold. I will use this condition to describe the demand for capital.[5]

3.1.2   Liquidity Preference

The real value of household assets is the sum of the real values of outside money (M/p) and corporate bonds (B/p):

$$(5) \qquad A = \frac{M}{p} + \frac{B}{p}$$

Since outside money bears no interest, the ratio of money to bonds that households will hold is a decreasing function of the after-tax nominal rate of return on bonds, $i_N = (1 - \theta_1)r + (1 - \theta_2)\pi$. The real value of bonds (B/p) is also the real value of the capital stock (K). The liquidity preference relation can therefore be written in per capita terms as

$$(6) \qquad \frac{m}{k} = L[(1 - \theta_1)r + (1 - \theta_2)\pi], L' < 0$$

where $m = M/pN$, the real money balances per capita. In steady state, m/k must remain constant. Equivalently, M/pK remains constant, i.e., the rate of growth of M is equal to the rate of growth of pK or $\pi + n$. Thus[6]

$$(7) \qquad \pi = \frac{DM}{M} - n$$

3.1.3   The Supply of Savings

In steady-state growth, the supply of savings (S) is proportional to the households' real disposable income (H). The savings propensity may of course depend on the real net return that savers receive:

$$(8) \qquad S = \sigma(r_N) \cdot H$$

Disposable income is equal to national income (Y) minus both the government's tax receipts (T) and the fall in the real value of the population's money balances $(\pi M/p)$.[7] The total taxes are the sum of the corporate tax, the personal interest income tax, and a residual tax that may be

---

5. The U.S. corporation tax does not allow replacement cost depreciation but partly offsets historic cost depreciation with accelerated depreciation schedules. An analysis of the effect of historic cost depreciation is presented in the paper by Feldstein, Green, and Sheshinski (1978; chap. 4 below).

6. Jerome Stein (1970) examined a more general Keynes-Wicksell model in which the adjustment of price to the excess demand for cash balances is not immediate. Stanley Fischer (1979a) explained that in the long run a steady rate of increase of the money supply will come to be anticipated, causing the Keynes-Wicksell behavior to converge to the familiar neoclassical behavior of equation (7). All of the results of the current paper will therefore continue to hold in a Keynes-Wicksell version of the current model.

7. The capital loss on corporate bonds is just offset by the difference between the real and nominal interest rates paid by firms. There are no corporate retained earnings.

regarded as a lump sum or payroll tax. The government uses these tax receipts plus the increase in the money supply (DM/p) to finance its purchases of public consumption (G). Disposable income is therefore

(9)
$$H = Y - T - \frac{\pi M}{p}$$

$$= Y - G + \frac{DM}{p} - \frac{\pi M}{p}$$

Since $\pi = DM/M - n$,

(10)
$$H = Y - G + nM/p$$

If public consumption is a constant fraction of real national income ($G = \gamma Y$), per capita disposable income is

(11)
$$h = y(1 - \gamma) + nm$$

Per capita saving is therefore

(12)
$$s = \sigma(r_N)\cdot[y(1 - \gamma) + mn]$$

3.1.4   Growth Equilibrium

All savings must be absorbed in either additional capital accumulation or additional real money balances:

(13)
$$S = DK + DM/p$$

The constant ratio of capital to labor in steady-state growth implies that $DK = nK$. Similarly, the constancy of $m = M/pN$ implies that the rate of growth of (M/p) is nM/p. The requirement of equilibrium growth is therefore, in per capita terms,

(14)
$$s = nk + nm$$

or

(15)
$$\sigma(r_N)\cdot[(1 - \gamma)y + nm] = nk + nm$$

This completes the specification of the model. It is useful to collect now the six equations that jointly determine y, h, k, m, r, and π:

(2)
$$y = f(k)$$

(11)
$$h = y(1 - \gamma) + mn$$

(13')
$$\sigma[(1 - \theta_1)r - \theta_2\pi]\cdot h = nk + nm$$

(4)
$$f'(k) = r - \left(\frac{\tau_2}{1 - \tau_1}\right)\pi$$

(6)
$$m = L[(1 - \theta_1)r + (1 - \theta_2)\pi]k$$

(7)
$$\pi = \frac{DM}{M} - n$$

The exogenous variables are the rate of population growth n, and the government policy variables θ_1, θ_2, τ_1, τ_2, and DM/M.

3.2   The Effects of Changes in the Rate of Inflation

The model of section 3.1 will now be used to study the effects of inflation on capital accumulation and interest rates. Although the rate of inflation is endogenous, the model can be decomposed to obtain π as the difference between the two exogenous variables, DM/M and n. The analysis can then proceed to use the remaining five equations with π regarded as predetermined.

By appropriate substitution for y, h, m, and r and equation (13′), the growth equilibrium provides the basic relation between the equilibrium capital intensity and the steady-state rate of inflation:

(16)
$$\sigma[(1 - \theta_1)(f' + \pi r_2/(1 - \tau_1)) - \theta_2\pi]$$
$$\cdot[(1 - \gamma)f + nkL] = nk(1 + L)$$

where the arguments of L in equation (6) are not explicitly specified. Total differentiation with respect to k and π yields equation (17).

(17)
$$\frac{dk}{d\pi} = \frac{(1 - \sigma)nk[(1 - \theta_1)\tau_2/(1 - \tau_1)}{\sigma[(1 - \gamma)f' + nL] - n(1 + L)}$$
$$\frac{+ (1 - \theta_2)]L' - h[(1 - \theta_1)\tau_2/(1 - \tau_1) - \theta_2]\sigma'}{- (1 - \sigma)nkL'(1 - \theta_1)f'' + h\sigma'(1 - \theta_1)f''}$$

The denominator can be shown to be unambiguously negative if the savings rate is a nondecreasing function of the real rate of return, $\sigma' \geq 0$.[8] With this condition, the denominator is clearly negative if $\sigma[(1 - \gamma)f' + nL] - n(1 + L) < 0$. To show that this inequality is true, multiply by k and substitute $m = kL$ to obtain the equivalent condition

$$\sigma[(1 - \gamma)kf' + nm] - (nk + nm) < 0$$

From equation (15),

$$nk + nm = \sigma[(1 - \gamma)f + nm]$$

The required condition is therefore

$$\sigma[(1 - \gamma)kf' + nm] < \sigma[(1 - \gamma)f + nm]$$

8. This is equivalent to $\sigma'(r_N) \geq 0$ in the asset demand equation (8). In a life cycle model, this occurs if an increase in the real net rate of interest causes a postponement in consumption. In the simple two-period model in which all income is earned in the first period, $\sigma'(r_N) \geq 0$ is equivalent to an elasticity of substitution of the two-period utility function that is greater than or equal to one. Although I will only discuss the implications of $\sigma' \geq 0$, the opposite may be true and its implications deserve examination.

or $kf' < f$ which clearly holds. The sign of $dk/d\pi$ is therefore the opposite of the sign of the numerator.

The first term of the numerator,

$$(1 - \sigma)nk[(1 - \theta_1)\tau_2/(1 - \tau_1) + (1 - \theta_2)]L'$$

is unambiguously negative because the demand for money is inversely related to the nominal rate of interest, $L' < 0$. If the savings rate is an increasing function of the real net rate of interest ($\sigma' > 0$), the sign of the second term and therefore of the entire numerator depends on the nature of taxation. In two important special cases, the second term is zero and therefore the numerator is negative:

1. *Full Tax Indexing*: There is full indexing of the taxation of interest income, i.e., the personal income tax is on the real rate of interest only ($\theta_2 = 0$), and the corporation tax allows a deduction only for real interest payments ($\tau_2 = 0$).
2. *Equal Tax Rates*: There is no indexing of the taxation of interest income but the rate of corporation tax is the same as the rate of personal income tax, i.e., $\theta_1 = \theta_2 = \tau_1 = \tau_2$.

In both these cases, $(1 - \theta_1)\tau_2/(1 - \tau_1) - \theta_2 = 0$ so that the second term is zero, the numerator is negative and $dk/d\pi > 0$. In these cases the sensitivity of the savings rate to the net rate of interest (σ') influences the magnitude but not the direction of the impact of inflation on equilibrium capital intensity. The direction of the impact reflects the reduction in desired liquidity that results from the higher nominal rate of interest that accompanies inflation. A smaller ratio of real money balances to capital implies that a larger fraction of savings is channeled into real capital accumulation. The resulting increase in capital intensity lowers the real net rate of interest; if savings respond positively to this rate of interest, there is a reduction in the rate of savings that partly offsets the portfolio composition effect but that cannot reverse its sign. This dampening effect of the savings response appears as the term $h\sigma'(1 - \theta_1)f''$ that increases the absolute size of the denominator.

Neither of the two cases considered above corresponds to the current situation in the United States. There is no indexing of the taxation of interest payments. The real and inflation components of the nominal interest rate are treated in the same way by both the personal and corporate income taxes: $\theta_2 = \theta_1$ and $\tau_2 = \tau_1$. Because of the progressivity of the personal income tax, a simple comparison of the corporate and personal income tax rates is not possible.[9] I will therefore consider the implications of both $\theta < \tau$ and $\theta > \tau$ where the common rate of income tax is denoted $\theta = \theta_1 = \theta_2$ and that of the corporate tax is denoted $\tau = \tau_1 =$

---

9. The actual problem of comparison is even more complex because individuals as well as corporations are borrowers.

τ_2. The analysis will assume that the savings rate is an increasing function of the net rate of interest; the reader can easily discover the implications of reversing this assumption.

When the corporation tax rate exceeds the personal tax rate, inflation induces an increase in the savings rate that reinforces the reduction in liquidity. To understand the nature of this reinforcing effect, recall from equation (4) that

$$(18) \qquad r = f'(k) + \left(\frac{\tau_2}{1 - \tau_1}\right) \pi$$

With $\tau_2 = \tau_1$, the nominal rate of interest is

$$(19) \qquad i = r + \pi = f'(k) + \frac{\pi}{1 - \tau}$$

Since the personal income tax is levied at rate θ on this nominal rate of interest, the real net rate received by savers is

$$(20) \qquad r_N = (1 - \theta)i - \pi$$

$$= (1 - \theta)f'(k) + \left(\frac{\tau - \theta}{1 - \tau}\right) \pi$$

At any given level of capital intensity, $f'(k)$ is a constant and the direct effect of an increase in π is to increase r_N whenever $\tau > \theta$. This increase in r_N induces a higher rate of saving and therefore greater capital accumulation. More formally, it is clear from equation (17) that increasing the value of τ causes an increase in $dk/d\pi$ whenever $\sigma' > 0$.

Equation (20) also shows that when the corporation tax rate is less than the personal tax rate, inflation induces a reduction in r_N and therefore in the savings rate. The net effect of inflation on capital intensity depends on the relative strength of the negative savings effect and the positive liquidity effect. There is no unambiguous a priori conclusion. Recall that inflation increases capital intensity if and only if the numerator of equation (17) is negative. With $\theta_1 = \theta_2 = \theta$ and $\tau_1 = \tau_2 = \tau$, this condition reduces to $dk/d\pi > 0$, if and only if,

$$(21) \qquad h(\theta - \tau)\sigma' + (1 - \sigma)nk(1 - \theta)L' < 0$$

A series of substitutions and manipulations shows that this condition is equivalent to

$$(22) \qquad \frac{\eta_L}{\eta_S} > \frac{a}{(1 - \sigma)m} \cdot \frac{\theta - \tau}{1 - \theta} \cdot \frac{i_N}{r_N}$$

where $\eta_L = -i_N L'/L$, the elasticity of the demand for real money balances relative to capital with respect to the nominal net rate of interest, and $\eta_S = r_N \sigma'/\sigma$, the elasticity of the savings rate with respect to the real net rate of interest.[10] Recall that $a = k + m$, total wealth per person, and that $r_N = i_N - \pi$. Note that (22) shows that $dk/d\pi > 0$ is more likely when the demand for liquidity is interest sensitive (η_L is large) and when savings behavior is not sensitive to the net yield (η_S is small). The required inequality is clearly satisfied in the cases that were previously considered: $\theta \leq \tau$ (or $\eta_S = 0$). But if $\theta > \tau$ and $\eta_S > 0$, the inequality in (22) may not be satisfied. When inequality (22) is false, an increase in the rate of inflation reduces equilibrium capital intensity. Consider therefore some plausible values for the right-hand side. At the end of 1974, total private wealth was approximately $4 trillion. A useful empirical measure of the stock of outside money is the monetary base, the sum of currency in circulation and member bank reserves at the Federal Reserve Banks. At the end of 1974, the monetary base was approximately $100 billion. With an average saving rate of $\sigma = 0.1$, the value of $a/(1 - \sigma)m$ is approximately 40.[11] If $\tau = 0.5$ and $\theta = 0.6$, (22) is equivalent to

$$(23) \qquad \frac{\eta_L}{\eta_S} > 10 \frac{i_N}{r_N}$$

Starting from a situation in which there is no inflation (i.e., $i_N = r_N$), the introduction of positive inflation will increase capital intensity only if $\eta_L > 10\eta_S$. With a substantial rate of inflation, the condition for $dk/d\pi > 0$ is even more difficult to satisfy. From equations (19) and (20), we obtain

$$(24) \qquad \frac{i_N}{r_N} = \frac{(1 - \theta)f'(k) + \left(\dfrac{1 - \theta}{1 - \tau}\right)\pi}{(1 - \theta)f'(k) + \left(\dfrac{\tau - \theta}{1 - \tau}\right)\pi}$$

If, for example, $\pi = f'(k) = 0.12$, equation (24) implies that $i_N/r_N = 0.144/0.024 = 6$. The inequality in (23) now implies that $dk/d\pi > 0$ only if $\eta_L > 60\eta_S$.[12]

---

10. If $r_N < 0$, η_S is not well defined. The inequality (22) can instead be written

$$\frac{L'/L}{\sigma'/\sigma} > \frac{a}{(1 - \sigma)m} \cdot \frac{\theta - \tau}{1 - \theta}$$

when $\sigma' > 0$ even if $r_N < 0$.

11. Restricting attention to outside money ignores the role of private banks in creating liquidity. A broader measure of the money supply, defined as currency plus demand deposits, was $285 billion at the end of 1974, implying $a/(1 - \sigma)m = 16$. However, most of the money supply measured in this way was "inside money" and not appropriate to the current model.

12. There is substantial controversy about the magnitudes of η_L and η_S. In earlier econometric studies, I found $di/d \ln M$ was approximately 10, implying that η_L is approximately 0.01 (see Feldstein and Chamberlain, 1973, and Feldstein and Eckstein, 1970). The estimates of η_S range from negative to positive, but none of the estimates measures r_N correctly as the real net-of-tax rate of return. Obviously, even a very moderate positive value of η_S would exceed the η_L reported above.

The above examples are only illustrative. They nevertheless indicate that, in an economy with a relatively high rate of tax on interest income, an increase in the rate of inflation may decrease capital intensity. More generally, the presence of taxes may reduce or magnify a positive effect of inflation on capital intensity.

3.3   Effects of Inflation on Interest Rates

The relation of the interest rate to the rate of inflation is substantially influenced by the presence of the corporation and personal income tax. This is true even if inflation has no effect on the capital intensity of production. As a result, the real net rate of return earned by savers also generally depends on the rate of inflation.

The basic marginal productivity relation derived above,

$$(25) \qquad r = f'(k) + \left(\frac{\tau_2}{1 - \tau_1}\right) \pi$$

implies that the nominal rate of interest is

$$(26) \qquad i = f'(k) + \left(\frac{1 + \tau_2 - \tau_1}{1 - \tau_1}\right) \pi$$

and the real rate of return is

$$(27) \qquad r_N = (1 - \theta_1)f'(k)$$
$$+ \left(\frac{(1 - \theta_1)\tau_2 - (1 - \tau_1)\theta_2}{1 - \tau_1}\right) \pi$$

Consider first the effect of inflation on the nominal rate of interest. Irving Fisher originally explained that the nominal interest rate would rise by the rate of inflation, thus leaving the real interest rate unchanged. The force of his argument rests on the equivalence of the real interest, the cost of capital to the firm, and the real return to savers. Although all three would be equal in the absence of taxation, the current analysis has shown that this is not true in an economy with corporate and personal income taxes. Tobin's analysis (1965) modified Fisher's conclusion: because inflation reduces the demand for money balances, it increases capital intensity, lowers the real rate of return, and thus causes the nominal rate of interest to rise by less than the rate of inflation. Again this analysis ignores the effect of the personal and corporate income tax.[13]

---

13. Martin Bailey (1956) provides a similar analysis of the effect of inflation on the rate of interest through the change in money balances. His analysis is static and also ignores taxation.

In contrast, equation (26) implies that

$$(28) \qquad \frac{di}{d\pi} = \frac{1 + \tau_2 - \tau_1}{1 - \tau_1} + \left(\frac{dk}{d\pi}\right) f''$$

Fisher's conclusion that $di/d\pi = 1$ corresponds to the special case of no taxes and an interest insensitive demand for real money balances.[14] In Tobin's analysis this is modified by the fall in the marginal product of capital, $df'/d\pi = (dk/d\pi)f'' < 0$, where $dk/d\pi$ reflects a portfolio composition effect but no savings effect. The magnitude of this portfolio composition effect is, however, very small. Even if the relevant money supply is defined to include inside money, the value of the money stock is less than 10 percent of the value of real assets. Thus, even if some rate of inflation would completely eliminate the demand for money, the equilibrium capital stock would rise by less than 10 percent. With a Cobb-Douglas technology, the marginal product of capital would fall by less than one-tenth of its previous value. It is difficult therefore to imagine that the absolute value of the portfolio effect, $(dk/d\pi)f''$, exceeds 0.01.

In the more general case in which taxes are recognized, the nominal rate of interest may rise by substantially more than the rate of inflation. With no tax indexing, $\tau_2 = \tau_1 = \tau$, and

$$(29) \qquad \frac{di}{d\pi} = \frac{1}{1 - \tau} + \left(\frac{dk}{d\pi}\right) f''$$

With no change in capital intensity, $di/d\pi = (1 - \tau)^{-1}$; a corporate tax rate of $\tau = 0.5$ implies that the nominal rate of interest rises by *twice* the rate of inflation. The analysis of section 3.2 shows that $dk/d\pi$ may be greater or less than zero. The nominal rate of interest may therefore rise by either more or less than *twice* the rate of inflation.[15]

With tax indexing, $\tau_2 = 0$, and

$$(30) \qquad \frac{di}{d\pi} = 1 + \left(\frac{dk}{d\pi}\right) f''$$

Here with no change in capital intensity the original Fisherian conclusion that $di/d\pi = 1$ obtains. Section 3.2 also showed that with full tax indexing ($\theta_2 = \tau_2 = 0$), the sign of $dk/d\pi$ is determined by the portfolio composi-

14. Equation (17) shows that $\tau_1 = \tau_2 = \theta_1 = \theta_2 = 0$ and $L' = 0$ imply $dk/d\pi = 0$.
15. Recent empirical studies suggest that during the past decade the long-term corporate bond rate has increased by approximately the increase in the rate of inflation (see Feldstein and Chamberlain, 1973, Feldstein and Eckstein, 1970, and Robert Gordon, 1971). This is smaller than the steady-state increase suggested by the analyses above, especially since it was unlikely that there had been any substantial induced change in capital intensity during so short a period. The difference reflects the failure of the above analysis to allow for equity financing, historic cost depreciation, and personal capital gains taxation. In addition, the estimated $di/d\pi$ in the studies noted above may differ from the value of $di/d\pi$ in a sustained inflation.

tion effect and thus $(dk/d\pi)f'' < 0$. With full tax indexing of interest payments, the nominal interest rate will rise by slightly less than the rate of inflation.

Consider now the effect of inflation on the real net rate of interest received by savers. Equation (27) implies

$$
(31) \qquad \frac{dr_N}{d\pi} = \left[\frac{(1 - \theta_1)\tau_2 - (1 - \tau_1)\theta_2}{1 - \tau_1} \right] \\ + (1 - \theta_1)\left(\frac{dk}{d\pi}\right) f''
$$

If there are no taxes and the demand for real balances is not sensitive to the rate of interest, equation (31) yields the Fisherian conclusion that the real return to savers is unaffected by inflation, $dr_N/d\pi = 0$. In two further special cases, the effect of inflation on the real net interest rate is limited to the relatively small portfolio composition effect: $(1 - \theta_1)(dk/d\pi)f'' < 0$. If there is full tax indexing ($\theta_2 = \tau_2 = 0$) or equal tax rates for corporations and households ($\theta_1 = \tau_1$ and $\theta_2 = \tau_2$), the first term of equation (31) is zero and the sign of $dk/d\pi$ depends only on the portfolio composition effect.[16]

More generally, however, inflation can have a substantial effect on the savers' real net rate of return. If there is no indexing, equation (31) reduces to

$$
(32) \qquad \frac{dr_N}{d\pi} = \left(\frac{\tau - \theta}{1 - \tau}\right) + (1 - \theta)\left(\frac{dk}{d\pi}\right) f''
$$

If the corporate tax rate exceeds the personal tax rate, the first term is positive and the second term is negative.[17] The real net rate of return may either rise or fall. If the personal tax rate is higher than the corporate tax rate, the first term is negative. Section 3.2 showed that in this case $dk/d\pi$ can be either positive or negative. If $dk/d\pi > 0$, an increase in the rate of inflation reduces the saver's real net return. If $dk/d\pi < 0$, the change in r_N depends on the balancing of the two effects.

The case in which $dk/d\pi = 0$ illustrates the potential magnitude of the effect of inflation on r_N when $\theta > \tau$. If the marginal product of capital is $f'(k) = 0.12$ and the personal tax rate is $\theta = 0.6$, the net rate of return in the absence of inflation is $r_N = (1 - \theta)f' = 0.048$. If the corporate tax rate is $\tau = 0.5$, a 12 percent rate of inflation reduces r_N by 0.024 to half of its previous value, $r_N = 0.024$.

---

16. Recall that equation (17) and the discussion in section 3.2 established that either of these conditions makes $dk/d\pi > 0$.

17. Section 3.2 showed that $\tau > \theta$ implies $dk/d\pi > 0$.

This substantial sensitivity of r_N to inflation is a result of our tax system. Equations (32) and (17) show that without taxes ($\theta = \tau = 0$), r_N is unaffected by inflation except for the small liquidity effect on capital intensity.[18] A tax system in which the effective tax rate on capital income changes with the rate of inflation is arbitrary and inequitable.[19] If the definition of taxable interest income is altered to tax only the real interest ($\theta_1 > 0$, $\theta_2 = 0$) and to allow companies to deduct only the real component of interest payments ($\tau_1 > 0$, $\tau_2 = 0$), the return to savers will remain constant except for the liquidity effect; this is seen for $\tau_2 = \theta_2 = 0$ in equations (31) and (17). Complete indexing in this way also keeps unchanged the ratio of the tax paid to the net return. The magnitude of the possible changes in effective tax rates and net yields under our current tax system indicates the importance of revising the definition of taxable income and expenses to neutralize the effects of inflation.

3.4   The Welfare Effects of Inflation

Studies of the welfare effects of anticipated inflation have focused on the distortion in the demand for money that results from inflation.[20] More recently, Edmund Phelps has pointed out that the revenue from inflation permits a reduction in other distorting taxes so that some inflation is part of an optimal set of taxes when lump sum taxation is not possible. These studies have been done with a basic model in which there are no interest income taxes. The current analysis suggests an additional important effect of inflation on economic welfare: inflation changes the distortion in saving that is due to the tax on interest income.

The corporation tax and the personal interest income tax introduce a differential between the marginal productivity of capital [$f'(k)$] and the real net rate of return received by savers (r_N). Equation (27) implies that with no indexing this relation is

$$(33) \qquad r_N = (1 - \theta)f'(k) + \left(\frac{\tau - \theta}{1 - \tau}\right)\pi$$

The differential between r_N and $f'(k)$ depends on the tax rates and the rate of inflation. If $\tau > \theta$, a positive rate of inflation can reduce the distorting effect of taxation. With $\pi = [\theta(1 - \tau)/(\tau - \theta)]f'(k)$, the net

18. With $L' = 0$, r_N is constant.

19. A number of recent discussions have emphasixed that real tax liabilities should be independent of inflation. This has prompted proposals to adjust the income tax by the consumer price index so that the progressivity of the rate schedule does not cause inflation to increase real tax burdens. There have also been proposals to change the taxation of capital gains by adjusting the "cost" basis for changes in the consumer price index.

20. The analysis of this issue began with Milton Friedman (1942) and Martin Bailey (1956). Subsequent contributions are discussed in Robert Clower (1971), Harry Johnson (1971), and Edmund Phelps (1973).

rate of return to savers is equal to the marginal product of capital. If, however, $\tau < \theta$, a positive rate of inflation increases the differential between $f'(k)$ and r_N.

Phelps stressed that the increase in money that causes inflation is also a source of government revenue that permits a reduction in distortionary tax rates.[21] With a corporation tax and a personal interest income tax, the effect of inflation on government revenue is more complex. With no indexing of interest income, a rise in nominal interest payments increases revenues from the personal income tax but decreases revenues from the corporation tax. Total tax payments will rise with an increase in nominal interest payments if $\theta > \tau$ and will fall if $\theta < \tau$.

Since nominal interest payments per capita are ik, the net tax revenue on these payments is $(\theta - \tau)ik$. The change in net revenue from this source when inflation increases is therefore

(34)
$$\frac{d[(\theta - \tau)ik]}{d\pi} =$$

$$\frac{\theta - \tau}{1 - \tau}\left\{ k + [\pi + (1 - \tau)\cdot(f' + kf'')]\left(\frac{dk}{d\pi}\right) \right\}$$

Since the sign of $f' + kf''$ depends on the form of the production function, the sign on the right-hand side of (34) cannot be unambiguously determined without further restrictions. In the most plausible case,[22] $[\pi + (1 - \tau)(f' + kf'')] > 0$ so that the change in net revenue is negative if $\tau > \theta$ and $dk/d\pi > 0$. Section 3.2 showed that $\tau > \theta$ does imply $dk/d\pi > 0$ and therefore that inflation reduces tax revenue. In the opposite case of $\theta > \tau$, an increase in inflation may increase revenue.[23]

The relation between the effect on revenue and the effect on the differential between $f'(k)$ and r_N should be noted. When $\tau > \theta$, a small positive rate of inflation reduces the differential between $f'(k)$ and r_N but also causes a reduction in tax revenue from this source. Although the distortion in the supply and demand for capital is reduced, the fall in net revenue requires an increase in tax rates that increases distortion else-

21. Phelps used a model in which the tax is levied on wage income and distorts the labor-leisure choice. The current model could easily be extended to include such a tax. Tax-induced changes in labor supply are equivalent to changes in the labor force participation rate and would not alter the effects of inflation on the capital intensity of production or the rate of interest. See Feldstein (1974b).

22. Note that kf''/f' is the elasticity of the marginal productivity of capital with respect to the capital intensity. With Cobb-Douglas technology, this is $\alpha - 1$ and $[\pi + (1 - \tau)(f' + kf'')]$ is unambiguously positive. Unless the elasticity of substitution is very great, the sign of $[\pi + (1 - \tau)(f' + kf'')]$ will be positive.

23. If $\theta > \tau$, net revenue will increase with inflation if $dk/d\pi > 0$. Section 3.2 showed that $\theta > \tau$ leaves the sign of $dk/d\pi$ uncertain. If the portfolio composition effect dominates the savings effect, $\theta > \tau$ does imply $dk/d\pi > 0$. In this case, an increase in inflation caused an increase in tax receipts.

where. Conversely, when $\tau < \theta$, a positive rate of inflation exacerbates the distortionary differential between $f'(k)$ and r_N but may yield an increase in tax revenue that permits a reduction in other distortionary taxes.

Of course, if the corporation tax and the personal income tax are fully adjusted so that they recognize only real interest payments, there is no effect of inflation on either the differential between $f'(k)$ and r_N or on the net tax revenue.[24] A more complete adjustment by the government would also provide interest-bearing money that would eliminate both the liquidity and revenue effects of inflation. But until such changes are made, determining the optimal steady-state rate of inflation requires balancing at least three effects of inflation on economic welfare: (1) the welfare loss that results from reduced liquidity; (2) the change in welfare that results from the increase or decrease in the differential between the marginal product of capital and individuals' marginal rate of substitution; and (3) the change in other distorting taxes that results from the increase or decrease in the net tax revenue in response to inflation. With this broader model of economic effects, it is no longer possible to conclude as Friedman (1969) did that the optimal rate of inflation is negative or as Phelps did that the optimal finance of government expenditures should include a heavy tax on liquidity through a high rate of inflation. A full evaluation of the optimal rate of inflation with our current tax rules is a subject for another study.

3.5   Conclusion

This paper has explored the impact of inflation in a growing economy. The presence of the corporate and personal income taxes substantially alters the effect of inflation on the capital intensity of production, the market rate of interest, and the real net return to savers. The existing theories of the optimal rate of anticipated inflation must be revised in light of these effects. The analysis also suggests that recent proposals to adjust the tax rules for inflation should be modified to include a specific adjustment for the inflation premium in the rate of interest.

There are several directions in which this research might usefully be extended. First, the model of financial behavior was highly simplified. It might be enriched to include corporate equity finance, household borrowing, and the use of inside money.[25] Second, the current paper focuses only on the steady-state effects of fully anticipated inflation. An analysis of the transition path would be valuable. Third, a model with two sectors

---

24. There will be a small effect on tax revenue because of the increase in capital intensity that results from the change in portfolio composition.
25. A model with equity finance is presented in Feldstein, Green and Sheshinski (1978; chap. 4 below).

would allow an analysis of the problems considered by Duncan Foley and Miguel Sidrauski (1971) as well as the issues raised by a tax that is limited to the corporate sector.

With a richer analytic structure, it would be both possible and necessary to introduce evidence with which to quantify the effects that have been discussed. The problem of inflation is likely to remain with us for a long time to come. It is important to improve our analytic understanding of its effects and to adjust our institutions accordingly.

4

Inflation and Taxes in a Growing Economy with Debt and Equity Finance

With Jerry Green and Eytan Sheshinski

The recent high rates of inflation have drawn professional and public attention to the undesirable ways in which inflation affects the functioning of our tax system.[1] The most widely perceived problem is that the progressive structure of the personal income tax causes effective tax rates to increase arbitrarily when inflation raises nominal incomes. Several economists (Friedman 1974; Bailey 1975; Fellner, Clarkson, and Moore, 1975) have suggested that the tax rates should be redefined as functions of real income by indexing to consumer prices all of the dollar amounts in the tax law, for example, personal exemptions and the limits of the rate brackets.

There is a second and more severe problem that has received less attention. Because we currently tax the nominal income from investment (nominal interest and nominal capital gains) and allow borrowers to deduct nominal interest costs, the real net-of-tax returns to debt and equity will be altered by a change in the rate of inflation. This occurs even if the tax is not progressive. This paper shows that, with the current U.S. tax laws, even moderate rates of inflation can cause very substantial changes in net real yields.

An unanticipated change in the rate of inflation would of course benefit debtors and harm creditors. In order to abstract from such temporary

Reprinted by permission from *Journal of Political Economy* 86 (April 1978): S53–S70.

We are grateful to the National Science Foundation for financial support under grants SOC75-14656, SOC71-03803, and SOC74-11446. We have benefited from comments on a previous draft by Alan Auerbach, who pointed out an error in our treatment of historic cost appreciation; the correct results derived by Auerbach are presented in the appendix, of which he is the author.

1. See Brinner (1973), Friedman (1974), Diamond (1975), Fellner, Clarkson, and Moore (1975), Aaron (1976), Feldstein (1976; see chap. 3 above), and Green and Sheshinski (1977).

effects and from the problems of the transition from one equilibrium to another, this paper focuses only on the comparative steady-state equilibria of a growing economy with different rates of inflation.

In earlier papers, Feldstein (1976; see chap. 3) and Green and Sheshinski (1977) examined the effects of inflation on the real net rate of interest in an economy in which all investment is financed by debt. In contrast, in this study firms finance investment by issuing both debt and equity. Because the interest rate and the equity yield that a firm must pay are increasing functions of the firm's debt-equity ratio, the firm can choose an optimal debt-equity ratio that minimizes its total cost of capital. The debt-equity ratio depends on the tax rates and on the rate of inflation.

The first section of this paper presents a model of the growing economy and of the firm's financial behavior. Section 4.2 derives the comparative steady-state dynamics and investigates the effects of inflation on the debt-equity ratio and the real net yields to debt and equity. Section 4.3 discusses the nature of complete adjustment of the tax law to neutralize the effect of inflation and the effect of partial adjustment. A brief concluding section then discusses the implications of inflation in a more general model than the one that is fully analyzed here.

4.1 The Model

We study the problems discussed above by uniting a simple variant of a full-employment monetary-growth model with a system describing the supply of capital to firms individually and collectively. The risks inherent in the ownership of financial assets will be determinants of the supply of capital to firms in the form of equity or debt obligations along with their respective rates of return.

The economy is thereby described at both the level of the aggregate and the individual firm. The assumption that all firms have the same constant returns-to-scale technology will serve to link these two levels via symmetry conditions in the equilibrium. We will be considering steady-state growth equilibria throughout this paper.

4.1.1 The Aggregative Structure

We consider a neoclassical one-commodity growth model. The labor force L is assumed to grow exogenously at rate n. Since firms are identical and have constant returns-to-scale technologies, aggregate output Y is also given by the same production function

(1) $$Y = F(K, L)$$

where K is the level of the aggregate capital stock. We will write this in its usual per capita form as

(2) $y = f(k)$

where $y = Y/L$ and $k = K/L$. Money does not enter the production function directly. It is, however, held as an asset by individuals. The equation

(3) $m = \mathscr{L}k$

describes the desired level of real money balances per capita, m, as a multiple of the real capital stock. This multiple, $\mathscr{L}$, may be a function of the relative rates of return to holding these assets. Either of these net returns may depend on the rate of inflation or the tax system. However, as Feldstein (1976; see chap. 3) has pointed out, the magnitude of the real effects of inflation induced through shifts in m/k is very small. We will therefore treat $\mathscr{L}$ as a constant for most of our analysis. Money balances are held by individuals directly, rather than by firms; this simple but somewhat unrealistic assumption is traditional in the monetary-growth literature.[2]

The government is assumed to have a desired level of expenditures equal to a fraction, γ, of national income. Its revenue sources are threefold: various corporate, interest-income, and capital gains taxes to be described below; the issuance of money; and a labor-income tax. When we compare steady states attainable through different rates of inflation, the labor-income tax will be assumed to vary so as to maintain the government's budget-balance condition. Even if labor is supplied elastically, this tax will affect the real variables of the system only insofar as it changes savings and ultimately the capital stock (Feldstein 1974b).

Since the real level of money balances is m, and the labor force is growing at rate n, which will therefore be the growth rate of output and capital in the steady state, the government can issue money at the rate of mn without causing any inflation in the price level. Inflation at rate π produces extra revenue of πm.

Disposable income per capita, d, is therefore given by the national income per capita, y, minus total taxes and the real capital losses induced by inflation, πm. Total taxes are just γy minus the part of government spending financed through the issuance of money $(\pi + n)m$. Thus,

(4) $d = (1 - \gamma)y + mn$

Savings are a proportion, σ, of disposable income. The number σ will depend, in general, on the real net rate of return to be earned on the assets that can be held by individuals, as well as their riskiness. In this way, the tax system and the rate of inflation will influence savings and hence the steady-state behavior of the model. This is the effect emphasized by Feldstein (1976; chap. 3).

---

2. Green and Sheshinski (1977) have studied a system in which firms hold money for production purposes. The comparative statics are similar to the traditional case.

In this paper we will be concentrating on the form in which saving is done and on the interplay between this, the tax structure, and corporate financial behavior. For simplicity, therefore, it is assumed that σ is a constant.

Savings, σd, is divided between capital and real money balances according to (3). The steady-state equation is therefore

$$(5) \qquad \sigma d = n(1 + \mathscr{L})k$$

expressing the equality between actual savings and that necessary to keep the real variables growing at the same rate as population. Because of the specification of the government budget equation that we have employed, d depends only on k, as can be seen directly in (4). Therefore, (5) determines the unique steady-state level of the aggregative variables independent of the government's monetary or tax policy. We will therefore take k, y, and m as predetermined in our analysis below.

4.1.2   The Disaggregated Structure: Corporate Financial Policy and the Supply of Capital

Both the supply and demand sides of the market for corporate financial obligations are intimately connected with the tax structure and with the rate of inflation. There are four basic features of the tax structure that we will be considering below: (1) a corporate income tax at rate τ, for which the base is corporate income net of interest payments on debt and net of depreciation based on historic costs; (2) a personal capital income tax at rate θ, which is the same for interest on debt and for equity income (this equity income consists of both dividends and retained earnings, including the inflation-induced real gain that holders of equity receive because of the fall in the real value of debt claims on the firm's assets);[3] (3) the cost of depreciation, which is deductible from corporate income at the historic nominal value of the capital rather than at replacement cost (this induces an extra tax proportional to the rate of inflation, whose effective rate we denote by δ); (4) nominal capital gains caused by inflation and taxed at rate c.

Let us first consider the decision to be made by firms. Since we have assumed that all firms have identical production functions, we study the behavior of a representative producer whose financial goal is to minimize the cost of financing a unit of capital. His only decision is the mixture of debt and equity to use. Let b = proportion of capital financed by debt; e = dividends paid by firms plus retained earnings, per unit of equity; i = gross interest cost to firm, per unit of debt obligation. The real cost of

---

3. In an earlier version of this paper, we assumed that the personal tax rate on interest income was higher than the rate on equity income because of the relatively favorable treatment of retained earnings. Subsequent work has shown us that the problem is more complex because the ratio of dividends to retained earnings varies with the rate of inflation. We therefore ignore the distinction between dividends and retained earnings until we can provide a more complete analysis.

capital to the firm is computed as follows: Since the interest costs are deductible from profits for computing taxable corporate income, the net interest cost of debt is only $(1 - \tau)i$. Moreover, the real value of the debt is falling at the rate of inflation, since the principal is denominated in nominal terms. Therefore, the real net cost of debt finance is $(1 - \tau)i - \pi$. Equity finance, however, simply costs e, as the value of the equity-holders claim on real capital rises with the rate of inflation. Therefore, a unit of capital financed by b units of debt and $(1 - b)$ units of equity has a real net cost of

(6) $$N = b(1 - \tau)i + (1 - b)e - b\pi$$

We assume that the firm perceives the effect of its choice of b on the net rates of return it must provide to its two classes of investors and hence on the cost it must incur for this financing. In a model in which the securities of all corporations were perfect substitutes, e and i would have an infinite elasticity with respect to b. Here we will be implicitly supposing that there are few enough risk classes of firms so that e and i have nonzero derivatives with respect to b. The supply-of-funds schedule faced by an individual firm depends also on the riskiness and returns from other assets. In this model, due to symmetry conditions, we can use the market's debt-equity ratio and promised yields on the two classes of assets.

We indicate variables relevant to the rest of the market, treated as parameters by the individual firm, by the symbol ˆ. Thus we denote

> $\hat{e}_N$ = real net rate of return promised on equity holdings by the "market,"
>
> $\hat{i}_N$ = real net rate of return promised on debt holdings by the "market,"
>
> $\hat{b}$ = proportion of capital in the "market" financed by debt,
>
> e_N = real net rate of return on holdings of equity in the representative firm,
>
> i_N = real net rate of return on holdings of debt issued by the representative firm.

The supply of investment funds to the firm can then be written through the inverse supply function as:

(7) $$e_N = \phi(b, \hat{b}, \hat{e}_N, \hat{i}_N)$$

(8) $$i_N = \Psi(b, \hat{b}, \hat{e}_N, \hat{i}_N)$$

To determine the net return to the holders of equity after inflation and taxation, it is necessary to describe the financial and accounting rules used by the tax authorities. The real earnings of equity per dollar of equity capital, after corporate taxes and payments of the other factors have been deducted from sales revenue, is e. In the absence of inflation, the net return to the equity owners per unit of equity capital is $(1 - \theta)e$, where θ is the personal tax rate on capital income. Inflation raises the nominal value of the firm's capital stock at rate π. Since the value of the debt is fixed in nominal terms, all of this increase in the nominal value of the firm's capital accrues to holders of equity. These nominal capital gains are taxed at the capital gains tax rate, c. Thus the net yield per unit time on a unit of equity is[4]

$$(9) \qquad\qquad e_N = (1 - \theta)e - c\pi$$

This implies directly that

$$(10) \qquad\qquad e = \frac{e_N}{1 - \theta} + \frac{c\pi}{1 - \theta}$$

The case of the holders of debt is somewhat simpler. They are taxed at a rate θ on their nominal return and experience inflation-produced capital losses at rate π which are uncompensated by the tax system. Therefore,

$$(11) \qquad\qquad i_N = (1 - \theta)i - \pi$$

and

$$(12) \qquad\qquad i = \frac{i_N + \pi}{1 - \theta}$$

In minimizing (6) with respect to b, the firm uses (10) and (12) together with the specification of the supply functions given in (7) and (8). This minimization is carried out in the next section, which is concerned with the long-run comparative statics of the model.

A second equilibrium condition for the system is that the firm's promised payments can be exactly met by its net profits. One can either view this as a type of zero-profit condition arising because the firms are numerous, or a cash-flow balance condition for feasibility and equilibrium within the firm.

---

4. The situation would be more complex if dividends and retained earnings were taxed differently. Consider an increase in the rate of inflation. This means that the debt-equity ratio would tend to fall continuously since the nominal value of equity is rising. To offset this tendency and maintain a stable value of b (which may, of course, differ from the b chosen before the change in π), the firm must issue new debt and pay out the proceeds as dividends: Note that it cannot retain these proceeds because doing so would cause the firm to depart from its equilibrium growth rate. This process of converting these real gains (that result from the inflation-induced fall in the value of existing debt) from retained earnings to dividends has no tax consequence if dividends and retained earnings are taxed equally. The process is therefore ignored in equation (9). In a more realistic model, in which dividends are taxed more heavily than retained earnings, inflation would raise the effective tax rate by causing more of the real return to have the apparent form of dividends rather than retained earnings.

Since the labor market is competitive, the real gross rate of profit is equal to the marginal product of capital, f'. This is taxed at a rate τ. Nominal income of the firm includes this plus the inflation-produced gain on the capital stock which is π. Moreover, since the real value of the debt has fallen at the rate π, the firm can borrow $b\pi$ continually without changing its debt-equity ratio. Therefore, the sources of funds amount to

$$(13) \qquad (1 - \tau)f' + \pi + b\pi$$

The uses of funds are composed of the direct capital costs (which are being minimized as discussed above) of $b(1 - \tau)i + (1 - b)e$, the increased nominal value of the equity π, and a tax allowance for depreciation.

Ordinarily we can regard depreciation of the capital stock as being included in the definition of the production function. But in a world with both taxes and inflation, depreciation allowances at historic cost underestimate the necessary capital requirements. We suppose, therefore, that the additional funds used up by the difference between real depreciation and the historic cost allowed by the tax system are $\delta\pi$. The parameter δ reflects the timing and the rate of depreciation. (An example of the calculation of δ will be presented in the appendix.) The total uses of funds are, therefore,

$$(14) \qquad b(1 - \tau)i + (1 - b)e + \pi + \delta\pi$$

Equating (13) and (14) we have the condition

$$(15) \qquad (1 - \tau)f' = b(1 - \tau)i + (1 - b)e + (\delta - b)\pi$$

describing the cash flow of the representative firm in equilibrium.

In equilibrium, firms must be choosing identical financing mixes and rates of return on the two assets. Thus,

$$(16) \qquad b = \hat{b}$$
$$e_N = \hat{e}_N$$
$$i_N = \hat{i}_N$$

are equilibrium conditions.

Finally, recall that the supply of savings to the entire sector is fixed, being a constant fraction of disposable income. The mixture of debt and equity assets acceptable to the market depends on the net rates of return that the market provides. Specifically, we assume that the differences in the net real rates of return are the determining variables,

$$(17) \qquad \hat{b} = \eta(\hat{i}_N - \hat{e}_N)$$

and that $\eta' > 0$, reflecting the fact that higher returns on bonds make them relatively more attractive in the aggregate portfolio.

In summary, therefore, the level of capital per head is fixed by (5) and will be treated as constant throughout our analysis. The remaining six variables, b, $\hat{b}$, e_N, $\hat{e}_N$, i_N, $\hat{i}_N$, are determined through the system of equations given by the conditions for a minimum of (6) and by (15)–(17). The remaining variables e and i can be recomputed from (10) and (12), respectively.

4.2   Effects of Changes in Inflation

We are now ready to study how a permanent change in the rate of inflation changes the steady-state equilibrium of the economy. In general, an increase in the rate of inflation will change the capital intensity of the economy and, for any capital intensity, will change the debt-equity ratio and the real net yields on debt and equity. In order to focus on the effects that do not depend on the change in capital intensity, we are examining the special case in which inflation does not alter the capital labor ratio; we return in section 4.4 to consider the effect of inflation on capital intensity.

We are therefore considering an economy in which the ratio of saving to disposable income (σ) and the ratio of money to capital ($\mathcal{L}$) are constant. Equation (5) then implies a unique capital-labor ratio that is independent of the rate of inflation. Although the assumption of inelastic saving and liquidity preference thus makes the economy decomposable, this is not quite the classical dichotomy between real and nominal quantities. The first part of the model can be solved for an equilibrium capital intensity and the corresponding real national income and marginal products of labor and capital. Conditional on this marginal product of capital, the second part of the model finds the equilibrium debt equity and the real after-tax yields on debt and equity. It is this part that we now examine.

Equation (15) showed that the firm's after-tax income $[(1 - \tau)f' - \delta\pi + b\pi]$ is divided between net interest payments $[b(1 - \tau)i]$ and a return to equity $[(1 - b)e]$:

(18) $$(1 - \tau)f' - \delta\pi + b\pi = b(1 - \tau)i + (1 - b)e.$$

Using (10) and (12), we can rewrite the cash-flow equation (18) as

(19) $$(1 - \tau)f' = \frac{b(1 - \tau)i_N}{1 - \theta} + \frac{(1 - b)e_N}{1 - \theta}$$
$$+ \pi \left[\frac{b(\theta - \tau)}{1 - \theta} + c\frac{(1 - b)}{1 - \theta} + \delta \right]$$

Multiplying (19) by $(1 - \theta)$ we have

$$(20) \qquad (1 - \theta)(1 - \tau)f' = b(1 - \tau)i_N + (1 - b)e_N$$
$$+ \pi[b(\theta - \tau) + c(1 - b)$$
$$+ \delta(1 - \theta)]$$

This is the first of the three basic equations to be solved for b, e_N, and i_N.

The net cost of capital to the firms (N) was shown in equation (6) to be $b(1 - \tau)i + (1 - b)e - b\pi$. Substituting again for i and e yields

$$(21) \qquad (1 - \theta)N = b(1 - \tau)i_N + (1 - b)e_N$$
$$+ \pi[(\theta - \tau)b + (1 - b)c]$$

The firm selects b to minimize this cost, implying

$$(22) \qquad (1 - \tau)i_N - e_N + \pi(\theta - \tau - c)$$
$$+ b(1 - \tau)\Psi_1 + (1 - b)\phi_1 = 0$$

where $\Psi_1 = \partial i_N / \partial b$ and $\phi_1 = \partial e_N / \partial b$ along the firm's financial supply equations (7) and (8).

The final equation is the market's demand for debt relative to all capital. Equation (17) and the equilibrium condition $b = \hat{b}$, $i_N = \hat{i}_N$, and $e_N = \hat{e}_N$ imply

$$(23) \qquad b = \eta(i_N - e_N)$$

Totally differentiating equations (20), (22), and (23) with respect to b, e_N, i_N, and the predetermined π yields (assuming $\Psi_{ij} = \phi_{ij} = 0$):

$$(24) \qquad \begin{bmatrix} Q & (1 - b) & b(1 - \tau) \\ Z & -1 & (1 - \tau) \\ 1 & \eta' & -\eta' \end{bmatrix} \begin{pmatrix} db \\ de_N \\ di_N \end{pmatrix}$$
$$= - \begin{bmatrix} b(\theta - \tau) + (1 - b)c + \delta(1 - \theta) \\ \theta - \tau - c \\ 0 \end{bmatrix} d\pi$$

where $Q = (1 - \tau)i_N - e_N + \pi(\theta - \tau - c)$ and $Z = \partial^2(1 - \theta)N/\partial b^2$. Since both i_N and e_N are increasing functions of $b(\Psi_1 > 0$ and $\Phi_1 > 0)$, equation (22) implies $Q < 0$. The second-order condition for choosing b to minimize the cost of capital implies $Z > 0$.

4.2.1   The Debt-Equity Ratio

Solving (24) for $db/d\pi$ we have:

$$(25) \qquad \frac{db}{d\pi} = \frac{\eta'[(\tau - \theta) + c(1 - \tau) - \tau\delta(1 - \theta)]}{\Delta}$$

where Δ is the determinant of the matrix on the left-hand side of (24). We have that $\Delta = (1 - \tau) + \eta'[\tau Q + Z(1 - b\tau)]$. Clearly, $\Delta > 0$ when $\eta' = 0$; although the sign of Δ is ambiguous when $\eta' > 0$ (because Q and Z are of opposite sign), we will continue to assume throughout this paper that $\Delta > 0$ even when we consider $\eta' > 0$.

When c and δ are both zero, so that economic depreciation is allowed and the taxation of capital gains has been adjusted for inflation, we see that $db/d\pi$ has the sign of $\tau - \theta$.

It is important to note that the parameter values $c = \delta = 0$ do not correspond to a full indexing of the tax system, in the sense of making it inflation proof. There are two reasons for this, which we will explore in detail in section 4.3. First, it is still nominal interest cost and not the real costs that is deductible from profits of firms for tax purposes. Second, nominal interest income, rather than real interest, is taxed at the individual level. Thus, although the purely inflationary gains of equity holders are not taxed when $c = 0$, bond holders are not treated symmetrically. (Under a full indexing of the tax system, we would have $i_N = [1 - \theta][i - \pi]$, and not $[1 - \theta]i - \pi$.)

These two distortions account for the nonneutrality of inflation with respect to the debt-equity ratio as derived above.

The sign of the numerator of (25) cannot be determined on purely theoretical grounds. However, for values of the tax parameters corresponding roughly to the current U.S. tax laws ($\tau = .45$ and $\theta = .30$), we can see that $db/d\pi$ would be positive even if $c = 0$ and $\delta = .3$, which are, as we will see, lower and upper bounds on the values of these parameters, respectively.

4.2.2 The Real Net Rate of Interest

The effect of inflation on the real rate of interest has been the subject of theoretical and empirical research at least since Irving Fisher (1930). Equation (26) shows that the real net rate of interest is unlikely to remain unchanged with our tax system:

$$(26) \qquad \frac{di_N}{d\pi} = \frac{\begin{array}{c}(\tau - \theta) - \delta(1 - \theta) + \eta'\{Q(\theta - \tau - c) \\ - Z[b(\theta - \tau) + (1 - b)c + \delta(1 - \theta)]\}\end{array}}{\Delta}$$

Consider first the case in which $c = \delta = 0$. The real net yield now increases if $\tau > \theta$ and decreases if $\tau < \theta$. With $\tau > \theta$, i_N rises for two reasons. With a fixed debt-equity ratio, the firm can increase the nominal rate of interest by $\pi/(1 - \tau)$ and keep the same real net rate of interest. This raises the net nominal yield to households by $(1 - \theta)\pi/(1 - \tau)$ and the real net yield by $(1 - \theta)\pi/(1 - \tau) - \pi = \pi(\tau - \theta)/(1 - \tau)$. In addition, with $\tau - \theta > 0$, inflation induces firms to substitute debt for equity, thus raising the interest rate further by a risk premium. Positive taxation of nominal capital gains and historic cost depreciation reduce the overall net profits of the firm available for interest payments.

In a previous study, Feldstein (1976; see chap. 3) found that in an all debt-financed economy with economic depreciation ($\delta = 0$ and $c = 0$), the real net rate of interest would remain unchanged only if $\tau = \theta$. Equation (27) shows that this continues to be true when the firms choose an optimal mix of debt and equity finance.

The magnitude of the change in i_N can be crudely approximated by assuming $\eta' = 0$, that is, ignoring the shift in the debt-equity ratio. Equation (26) then implies

$$(27) \qquad \frac{di_N}{d\pi} = \frac{\tau - \theta - \delta(1 - \theta)}{1 - \tau}$$

It is of interest to note first that this expression is independent of c, the inflation-induced taxation of equity earnings. As noted above, $di_N/d\pi$ is positive when $\tau > \theta$ if $\delta = 0$. However, for tax rates close to those currently in force in the United States, even modest values of δ may completely offset this positive effect. If $\delta = .2$, the real net yield on debt would be approximately insulated from inflation, but only as the consequence of two equal and opposite forces.

Intuitively, historic cost depreciation causes an implicit taxation of the firm's cash flow which increases with the rate of inflation. Part of this is borne by equity and part by debt. But, at the same time, the deductibility of nominal interest costs is making debt a cheaper source of finance for firms, on the margin. Firms attempt to issue more debt in order to take advantage of this effect, but in the aggregate the market is not willing to absorb any more debt, since $\eta' = 0$. Therefore, the gross interest costs, i, get bid up because the shift in the supply curve for bonds decreases their price. Although some of this increase is taxed at the personal level and some further losses are caused by the increased inflation itself, the net return to holders of debt would be increased for a given level of gross profits. Because corporate and personal tax rates are close in magnitude, the historic cost-depreciation effect is important and may actually change the direction that would be predicted by analyzing the capital markets in isolation.

Note, moreover, that the effect of inflation on i_N will vary among individual investors in a way that depends on their own personal tax rates. Bond holders with low values of θ will benefit from inflation, while those with high tax rates will receive a lower net interest rate as inflation rises. Equation (27) implies that an individual with a 50 percent marginal rate ($\theta = .5$) will find that even a moderate rate of inflation eliminates his real interest income. To see this, note that in the late 1950s and early 1960s when there was no inflation, the interest rate was $i = .04$, and therefore for a 50 percent marginal rate individual, $i_N = (1 - \theta) i = .02$. The appendix shows that $\delta = .20$ is a reasonable value for U.S. conditions. With $\tau = .45$, equation (27) implies $di_N/d\pi = -.27$. Thus, an inflation rate of $\pi = .08$ would eliminate all of the real net interest because of the way in which the tax law operates.

Since $i = (i_N + \pi)/(1 - \theta)$,

$$(28) \qquad \frac{di}{d\pi} = \frac{1}{1 - \theta}\left[\frac{di_N}{d\pi} + 1\right] = \frac{1 - \delta}{1 - \tau}$$

With the value of $\delta = .20$ derived in the appendix, equation (28) implies $di/d\pi = 1.45$.[5]

4.2.3   The Net Real Return on Equity

The response of the real after-tax return of equity owners is, from equation (24),

$$(29) \qquad \frac{de_N}{d\pi} = \frac{-(1 - \tau)[c + \delta(1 - \theta)] + \eta'\{Q(\theta - \tau - c) - Z[b(\theta - \tau) + (1 - b)c + \delta(1 - \theta)]\}}{\Delta}$$

It is again useful to begin with the case $\delta = c = 0$:

$$(30) \qquad \frac{de_N}{d\pi} = (\tau - \theta)\eta'(bZ - Q)/\Delta = (bZ - Q)\frac{db}{d\pi}$$

Since $Z > 0$ and $Q < 0$,[6] the sign of $de_N/d\pi$ is the same as the sign of $db/d\pi$. In this case, the yield on equity increases because the debt-equity ratio rises, increasing the riskiness of equity. If inflation decreases the real value of depreciation ($\delta > 0$) or if nominal capital gains are taxed ($c > 0$), the return to equity owners is thereby reduced.

A rough approximation of the magnitude of the change in the yield on equities can be obtained by ignoring the change in the debt-equity ratio, that is, by setting $\eta' = 0$:[7]

5. The empirical evidence indicates that a sustained change in the inflation rate leads after a few years to an approximately equal change in the nominal interest rate; see Yohe and Karnovsky (1969), Feldstein and Eckstein (1970), and Feldstein and Chamberlain (1973). Feldstein's 1976 model (see chap. 3 above), which ignored both depreciation and equity finance, implied that the nominal interest rate should rise by twice the change in the rate of inflation; this contradiction with the evidence is substantially resolved by the current and more satisfactory model. The calculation of δ in the appendix ignores the accelerated depreciation features in the actual tax laws. The empirical analyses also failed to incorporate taxation explicitly and may provide biased estimates of the effects of inflation on interest rates.

6. See the discussion following equation (24).

7. With $\eta' \neq 0$, part of the increase in e_N reflects an increase in risk. That ambiguity is avoided by assuming $\eta' = 0$.

$$(31) \qquad \frac{de_N}{d\pi} = -[c + \delta(1 - \theta)]$$

The statutory rate of tax on capital gains is approximately one-half of the individual rate on ordinary income. In addition, the effective rate is reduced by the rule delaying the tax liability until the gain is realized. It may be reasonable to estimate $c = .2\theta$.[8] With the estimate that $\delta = .2$, equation (31) implies $de_N/d\pi = -.2$ for all values of θ. A 10 percent rate of inflation reduces the real net return to equity by 2 percentage points.

What is the corresponding value of e_N when π is zero? Equation (18) implies

$$(32) \qquad e = (1 - \tau)(f' - bi)/(1 - b)$$

and, since $e_N = (1 - \theta)e$ when $\pi = 0$,

$$(33) \qquad e_N = (1 - \theta)(1 - \tau)(f' - bi)/(1 - b)$$

Using the values of $i = .04$ and $b = .3$ to represent conditions when the inflation rate was zero and $f' = .12$ as the pretax marginal product of capital (Feldstein and Summers 1977), equation (33) implies $e_N = .085$ $(1 - \theta)$. An investor with a marginal tax rate of $\theta = .3$ receives $e_N = .059$; a 10 percent rate of inflation cuts the real net return to equity by about one-third. With $\theta = .5$, $e_N = .042$ when there is no inflation and a 10 percent rate of inflation cuts the real net return to equity in half.

4.3   Adjusting Taxes for Inflation

It is a very undesirable feature of our tax system that the equilibrium real net rates of return on debt and equity vary with the rate of inflation. This section considers how the definitions of taxable income and expenses can be varied to eliminate the effect of inflation on equilibrium real' yields.

The most obvious adjustments to the tax law are to end the taxation of nominal capital gains $(c = 0)$[9] and to allow replacement cost depreciation of capital assets $(\delta = 0)$.[10] Two further changes should be made, both in the tax treatment of interest. First, individuals should be taxed on their real interest receipts, $b(i - \pi)$. Second, firms should be permitted to deduct only their real interest expense in calculating their taxable profits; that is, taxable profits per unit of capital are $f' - b(i - \pi)$, so that the

8. See Bailey (1969) for estimates of the effect of the deferral of taxation on the effective rate of capital gains tax.
9. Specific proposals to adjust the capital gains tax in this way have been made by Brinner (1973) and Diamond (1975).
10. See Fellner, Clarkson, and Moore (1975) for a discussion of this subject.

company tax is $\tau[f' - b(i - \pi)]$. Note that this is equivalent to allowing a deduction of the nominal interest payment and taxing the real gain that results from the decline in the real value of the debt: $\tau(f' - bi) + \tau b\pi$.

With these changes, the firm's nominal after-tax income $[(1 - \tau)f' + b\pi]$ is divided between net interest payments $[bi - \tau b(i - \pi)]$ and a return to equity $[(1 - b)e]$:[11]

$$(34) \qquad (1 - \tau)f' + b\pi = bi - \tau b(i - \pi) + (1 - b)e$$

With this change, $i_N = (1 - \theta)(i - \pi)$, or $i = \pi + i_N/(1 - \theta)$. Similarly, equation (9) becomes $e_N = (1 - \theta)e$, or $e = e_N/(1 - \theta)$. Substituting into (34) and rearranging yields

$$(35) \qquad (1 - \tau)f' = \frac{(1 - \tau)bi_N}{1 - \theta} + \frac{(1 - b)e_N}{1 - \theta}$$

This equilibrium condition (which is analogous to [19] without indexing) is now completely independent of the rate of inflation.

Since the net cost of capital to the firm is the right-hand side of (35), the condition for choosing b to minimize the cost of capital is also independent of π:

$$(36) \qquad (1 - \tau)i_N - e_N + b(1 - \tau)\psi_1 + (1 - b)\phi_1 = 0$$

The third equation, the market demand for bonds, is always defined in terms of real net yields:

$$(37) \qquad b = \eta(i_N - e_N)$$

Thus the three equations that determine the equilibrium values of b, i_N, and e_N are independent of the rate of inflation. The tax changes described above are sufficient to eliminate completely the arbitrary effects of inflation.

At the current time, most discussions of adjusting the tax law for inflation have stopped short of the complete indexing that has just been described. The most common proposals call for replacement cost depreciation and taxing only real capital gains. This partial indexing corresponds to the special case of $\delta = c = 0$ that was examined in section 4.2. The effect of the different approaches to indexing in comparison to the current tax rules can be seen in table 4.1 for individuals at three different marginal tax rates. Note that replacement cost depreciation only ($\delta = 0$, indexing rule 1) still causes e_N to fall with inflation, while $\delta = 0$, and $c = 0$ (rule 2) makes e_N independent of inflation. Any of the partial rules makes i_N sensitive to inflation with the direction of the change depending on the level of δ.

---

11. Note that this is analogous to equation (18) without indexing.

Table 4.1   **Equilibrium Real Net Rates of Return under Various Tax Rules**

Personal Tax Rate (θ) and Net Real Return	No. Inflation	Current Rule	Partial Indexing Rules[a]			Complete Indexing
			1	2	3	
θ = .50:						
e_N	.042	.022	.032	.042	.042	.042
i_N	.020	−.007	.011	.011	.061	.020
θ = .30:						
e_N	.059	.039	.053	.059	.059	.059
i_N	.028	.030	.055	.055	.085	.028
θ = .0:						
e_N	.085	.065	.085	.085	.085	.085
i_N	.040	.084	.122	.122	.122	.040

NOTE: The calculations are based on the following assumptions: $f' = .12, \eta' = 0, b = .3, \tau = .45, c = .20$, and $i = .04$ at $\pi = 0$. See text for details of equilibrium relationships.
a. Partial indexing rules: (1) replacement cost depreciation ($\delta = 0$); (2) replacement cost depreciation ($\delta = 0$), no taxation of nominal capital gains ($c = 0$); (3) replacement costs depreciation ($\delta = 0$), no taxation of nominal capital gains ($c = 0$), personal taxation of real interest only $[(i_N = (1 - \theta)(i - \pi)]$.

4.4   Conclusion

Our tax system was designed for an economy with little or no inflation. In this paper we have shown that the rates of inflation that can be expected in the future will cause capricious and undesirable changes in the effective rates of tax on capital income. This would be true even with a proportional tax, but a progressive structure can exacerbate distortions.

The inflation-induced change in the effective rate of tax implies a corresponding change in the real net rate of return on capital that savers receive. This is not only a temporary disequilibrium effect but one which persists in steady-state equilibrium.

We have purposely simplified the analysis by abstracting from the effect of inflation on portfolio composition and the potentially more important effect on the rate of saving.[12] With our current tax system, inflation decreases the net rate of return and therefore is likely to decrease the rate of saving. This in turn would decrease the ratio of capital to labor and thus increase the marginal product of capital. This in turn would partially offset the fall in the after-tax rate of return, but the qualitative results of our analysis would remain unchanged. In contrast, the partial indexing described in section 4.3 allows for real economic

12. See Boskin (1978) for estimates of the effect of the real net rate of return on savings. Feldstein (1976; see chap. 3 above) discusses the small size of the liquidity portfolio composition effect.

depreciation for firms but does not tax the real return to savings. The likely result would be an increase in saving which would reduce the marginal product of capital, again partially reducing the effect described above but not changing the qualitative conclusions. Only complete index-ing—recognizing only the real component of interest payments as well as altering the treatment of depreciation and capital gains—would make real yields and therefore saving independent of the rate of inflation.

4.5   Appendix: The Effect of Inflation on the Tax Value of Depreciation

by *Alan Auerbach*

In this appendix we calculate the implicit rate of tax induced by historic cost depreciation in a period of inflation, that is, the value of the para-meter δ used in the text. We shall investigate the special case in which capital decays ("evaporates") exponentially.

Consider an investment of $1 of capital at time $t = 0$. With exponential depreciation at rate d, the net marginal product of capital f' can be written as $f' = g' - d$, where g' is thus the gross marginal product of capital. In any future period, the firm pays a tax at rate τ on $g' - bi - D(s)$, where $D(s)$ is the real tax depreciation allowed on a "machine" of age s. The firm's first-order condition, analogous to equation (15) is

$$(38) \qquad (1 - \tau)g' = (N + d)(1 - \tau Z)$$

where Z is the present value of the tax depreciation as of the time that the investment is made:

$$(39) \qquad Z = \int_0^\infty e^{-Ns} D(s)\, ds$$

Note that when $D(s)$ corresponds to economic depreciation, that is, $D(s) = de^{-ds}$, $Z = d/(N + d)$, and (38) becomes

$$(40) \qquad (1 - \tau)g' = (N + d)\left(1 - \frac{rd}{N + d}\right)$$

or

$$(41) \qquad (1 - \tau)(g' - d) = N$$

This is identical with the condition of (15) when $\delta = 0$, that is, when economic depreciation is allowed.

The method of historic cost depreciation that is in current use[13] implies that $D(s) = de^{-ds}e^{-\pi s}$, that is, the real value of the depreciation falls

---

13. We ignore the special features of the investment credit and accelerated depreciation.

below economic depreciation by a factor that grows with time at the rate π. Thus, for historic cost depreciation we have $Z_H = d/(N + d + \pi)$, and (38) becomes

$$(42) \qquad (1 - \tau)g' = (N + d)\left(1 - \frac{\tau d}{N + d + \pi}\right)$$

This can be rewritten as

$$(43) \qquad (1 - \tau)f' + (1 - \tau)d = N + d \; \frac{(N + d)(1 - \tau) + \pi}{N + d + \pi}$$

or

$$(44) \qquad (1 - \tau)f' = N + \left(\frac{\tau d}{N + \pi + d}\right)\pi$$

Comparing (44) with (15) and using (6) shows that

$$(45) \qquad \delta = \frac{\tau d}{N + \pi + d}$$

For a machine that depreciates one-tenth per year, $d = .10$. At $\pi = 0$, $N = (1 - \tau)f'$ or approximately $N = .55\,(.12) = .066$. Thus at $\pi = 0$, $\delta = .27$. At $\pi = .10$, equation (44) implies $N = .048$ and therefore $\delta = .18$. Lower values of d imply smaller values of δ at each depreciation rate. For example, at $\pi = 0$, a decay rate of $d = .067$ implies $\delta = .23$. In the text we used $\delta = .20$, a relatively conservative value for the inflation rates that have been observed in the United States.

5   Fiscal Policies, Inflation, and Capital Formation

The large unprecedented government deficits in recent years have stimulated speculation about their adverse effects on inflation and private capital formation. While it is clear that deficits may have no adverse effect in an economy with sufficient unemployed resources, the effects of a deficit when there is full employment are less clear. Is a persistent increase in the government deficit necessarily inflationary? Does it necessarily reduce private capital formation? Is it possible to avoid both adverse effects? A primary purpose of this paper is to answer these questions in the context of a fully employed and growing economy.

A closely linked issue is the relation between private saving and capital formation when money and other government liabilities are alternatives to real capital in individual portfolios. John Maynard Keynes, Roy Harrod, and James Tobin have all emphasized the possibility of excess saving when individuals will not hold capital unless its yield exceeds some minimum required return. When the return on capital is too low, an increase in saving only reduces aggregate demand. If prices are flexible downward, this causes deflation until the increased value of real balances causes a sufficient reduction in saving; if prices cannot fall, the excess saving results in unemployment.

Three ways of averting such "excess saving" have been emphasized in both theory and practice. The thrust of the Keynesian prescription was to increase the government deficit to provide demand for the resources that

Reprinted by permission from *American Economic Review* 70 (September 1980): 636–50.

This paper is part of the NBER Program of Research on Capital Formation; a previous version was circulated as NBER working paper no. 275 (August 1978). I am grateful for financial support from the National Science Foundation and the NBER. The paper presents my views and not those of the NBER.

would not otherwise be used for either consumption or investment. In this way, aggregate demand would be maintained by substituting public consumption for private consumption. A second alternative prescription was to reduce the private saving rate. Early Keynesians like Seymour Harris saw the new Social Security program as an effective way to reduce aggregate saving. The third type of policy, developed by Tobin, relies on increasing the rate of inflation and making money less attractive relative to real capital. In Tobin's analysis, the resulting increase in capital intensity offsets the higher saving rate and therefore maintains aggregate demand.

This paper will examine ways of increasing capital intensity without raising the rate of inflation. The analysis will also show why, contrary to Tobin's conclusion, a higher rate of inflation may not succeed in increasing investors' willingness to hold real capital.

An important feature of the analysis in this paper is a monetary growth model that distinguishes between money and interest-bearing government bonds. With this distinction, we can compare government deficits financed by borrowing with deficits financed by creating money. It is possible also to examine the effect of changes in the interest rate on government debt while maintaining the fact that money is not interest bearing. The two types of government liabilities also permit analyzing the distinction between the traditional liquidity preference and a demand for government bonds that I shall call "safety preference." In practice, this safety preference may be much more important than the traditional liquidity preference.

The first section of the paper develops the three-asset monetary growth model that will be used in the remaining analysis. Section 5.2 then considers the effects of changes in the government deficit. The effects of increased saving on aggregate demand and capital intensity are developed in section 5.3.

5.1   A Three-Asset Model of Monetary Growth

The model developed here differs from the traditional monetary growth model (see, e.g., Tobin, 1955, and David Levhari and Don Patinkin, 1968) in two important ways. First, instead of the usual assumption that all taxes are lump sum levies, the current analysis recognizes taxes on capital income that lower the net rate of return! Second, the government deficit is financed not only by increasing the money supply

---

1. My 1976 paper (chap. 3 above) and my 1978 paper with Jerry Green and Eytan Sheshinski (chap. 4 above) show the importance of recognizing capital income taxes in analyzing the effects of inflation in a monetary growth model. Corporate and personal taxes were distinguished there but will not be in this paper.

but also by issuing interest-bearing government debt.[2] Throughout the analysis we maintain the simplifying assumption that the savings rate out of real disposable income is fixed; the tax on capital income affects the allocation of saving but not the saving rate itself. Because the analysis in the sections that follow will focus on comparative steady-state dynamics, only these steady-state properties will be discussed here.[3] Note that this assumption of steady-state dynamics implies that all growth rates are constant and therefore that all quantities are correctly anticipated.

The economy is characterized by an exogenously growing population

$$(1) \qquad N = N_0 e^{nt}$$

The labor force is a constant fraction of the population and technical progress is subsumed into population growth. Production can be described by an aggregate production function with constant returns to scale. The relation between per capita output (y) and the per capita capital stock (k) is

$$(2) \qquad y = f(k)$$

with $f' > 0$ and $f'' < 0$. For simplicity, output is measured net of depreciation and real depreciation is not explicitly included in the analysis.

5.1.1   The Government Budget Constraint

Government spending (G) plus the payment of interest on the government debt must be financed by either tax receipts, money creation, or borrowing. Total real tax receipts (T) are the sum of a lump sum tax (T_0) and the revenue that results from taxing the income from real capital at rate τ.[4] The money created by the government (M) is the only money in the economy and does not bear interest. The time rate of change of the stock of nominal money is DM; the real value of the extra money created in this way is DM/p. Government bonds bear interest at rate i; the

---

2. Green and Sheshinski (1977) examine an economy with both bonds and money but assume that such bonds are perfect substitutes for private capital in investors' portfolios. Their analysis generally focuses on quite different issues. Tobin and Willem Buiter (1978) recently developed a three-asset model in which government bonds and money are imperfect substitutes for each other as well as for real capital. I received a copy of their unpublished paper only after this paper was submitted for publication. Because the tax structure that they assume is very different from the taxes described herein, their conclusions are frequently different from my own. Benjamin Friedman (1978) also recently developed a three-asset model but used it to analyze quite different questions (the short-run effects of monetary and fiscal policies in an economy with unemployment and fixed prices) from those that are the focus of my own research.

3. Section 5.3 will, however, consider the possibility of disequilibrium behavior associated with excess saving.

4. The tax rate τ is best thought of as a corporation tax rate. The personal tax on real capital income and on the interest on government debt is not specially recognized.

nominal market value of these bonds is B and the real value of new borrowing is DB/p.[5]

The government's budget constraint may be written

(3) $$G + \frac{iB}{p} = T + \frac{DM}{p} + \frac{DB}{p}$$

Alternatively, it will be convenient to denote the real government deficit by Δ and write

(4) $$\Delta = \frac{DM}{p} + \frac{DB}{p}$$

In the steady state, the ratio of real money per unit of real capital (M/pK) must remain constant. This implies that the rate of growth of M is equal to the rate of growth of pK, or with $Dp/p = \pi$,[6]

(5) $$\frac{DM}{M} = \pi + n$$

Similarly, the steady-state rate of growth of nominal government bonds equals the inflation rate plus the real growth rate of the economy:

(6) $$\frac{DB}{B} = \pi + n$$

Substituting these expressions into (4) and dividing by the population gives the steady-state per capita deficit:

(7) $$\frac{\Delta}{N} = (\pi + n)\frac{M}{pN} + (\pi + n)\frac{B}{pN}$$

With lowercase letters representing real per capita values, (7) can be rewritten

(8) $$\delta = (\pi + n)(m + b)$$

The real per capita deficit equals the product of the economy's nominal growth rate and the real per capita government liabilities.

5.1.2   Portfolio Behavior[7]

The real value of household assets is the sum of the real values of government liabilities and the capital stock:[8]

---

5. These bonds may be thought of as Treasury bills although their maturity is irrelevant for steady-state analysis as long as that maturity is finite. I ignore changes in the market value that would temporarily result from changes in the interest rate if the maturity were not very short.

6. This uses the fact that in the steady state $k = K/N$ is constant, implying $DK/K = n$.

7. The description of portfolio behavior and saving in this model assumes that households as a whole regard government bonds as net wealth, implicitly ignoring the corresponding tax liabilities that they and future generations must bear in order to pay the interest and

(9) $$a = b + m + k$$

I shall simplify the description of the households' portfolio behavior by assuming that the equilibrium ratio of real bonds to capital depends on the difference between the net real yield on capital (r) and the real yield on government bonds $(i - \pi)$:[9]

(10) $$\frac{b}{k} = \beta[r + \pi - i] \qquad \beta' < 0$$

Because the depreciation method used in the United States and in most other countries is based on the original costs of plant and equipment, the tax liability per unit of capital increases with the rate of inflation.[10] I shall therefore write the net rate of return as

(11) $$r = f' - \tau(f' + \lambda\pi)$$

where the parameter λ indicates the extent to which a higher inflation rate increases the tax liability.[11] Substituting into (10) yields the equilibrium bond portfolio condition:

(12) $$\frac{b}{k} = \beta[(1 - \tau)f' + (1 - \tau\lambda)\pi - i] \qquad \beta' < 0$$

With safe short-term interest-bearing government debt available, individuals should hold money only for transaction purposes. As William Baumol (1952) and others have shown, this demand for money varies positively with the level of income and inversely with the rate of interest:[12]

(13) $$\frac{m}{y} = L(i), L' < 0$$

---

principal on these bonds. The alternative view, based on the so-called Ricardian equivalence theorem, depends on extremely strong and improbable assumptions. To the extent that households do partially reduce their perceived value of government bonds because of future tax liabilities, the variable B (or b) in household portfolios might be scaled down to some fraction of B. This need not change any of the qualitative conclusions of the current analysis.

8. The private bonds and equities that represent the ownership claims to the capital stock are not explicitly recognized. The tax rate τ can be regarded as the effective tax rate corresponding to the steady-state mix of debt and equity finance. See my paper with Green and Sheshinski (1979).

9. Recall that we are ignoring the *personal* tax on investment income.

10. See my paper with Green and Sheshinski (1978; chap. 4), especially the appendix by Alan Auerbach, and my paper with Lawrence Summers (1977).

11. Accelerated depreciation affects τ and λ but λ exceeds zero even if, at the equilibrium value of π, tax depreciation exceeds economic depreciation.

12. This simplifies by assuming that individuals regard the interest-bearing government debt rather than real capital as an alternative to transaction balances. Transaction balances are also assumed to depend on income rather than wealth when in reality both are important.

An important feature of an economy with money or other government liabilities is the possibility that individuals will be unwilling to hold capital unless its yield is above some minimum level. In the traditional two-asset Keynesian model, this is represented as a liquidity trap, that is, as an infinitely elastic demand for money at some low rate of interest. A more realistic description is possible with the current three-asset model. When the real net yield on capital becomes very low relative to the real yield on government bonds, investors will want to hold government bonds instead of capital; in the notation of equation (12), the absolute value of β' becomes infinite when the real differential becomes very small.[13] The reason that investors prefer government bonds in this situation is that the pretax profitability of private capital is uncertain. The bond-demand behavior will therefore be referred to as a "safety preference" relation to distinguish it from the liquidity preference relation that governs the demand for money.[14]

5.1.3   The Supply and Demand for Savings

The supply of savings (S) is proportional to the households' real disposable income (H):

(14) $$S = \sigma \cdot H$$

The saving propensity will be assumed to be constant. Disposable income is equal to national income (Y) minus both the government's tax receipts (T) and the fall in the real value of the population's money and government bonds $(\pi M/p$ and $\pi B/p)$.[15] Saving is therefore

(15) $$S = \sigma \left(Y - T - \frac{\pi M}{p} - \frac{\pi B}{p} + \frac{iB}{p} \right)$$

or, using equation (3),

(16) $$S = \sigma \left(Y - G + \frac{DM}{p} + \frac{DB}{p} - \frac{\pi M}{p} - \frac{\pi B}{p} \right)$$

In the steady state, government spending must bear a stable relation to national income. The analysis that follows assumes that a fraction γ of national income is devoted to government spending exclusive of interest on the government debt. This implies that any increase in interest on the government debt causes a corresponding increase in the government deficit or in lump sum taxes.

13. This unwillingness to own real capital may also increase the demand for money, but that effect is likely to be small relative to the increased demand for bonds.

14. The private securities are generally as marketable as government bonds, and, to the extent that they have the same maturity structure, their price will be as sensitive to interest rate fluctuations. Their liquidity is therefore similar even thought the safety and predictability of the yields differ substantially.

15. Recall that this analysis assumes that households as a whole regard government bonds as net wealth.

All saving must be absorbed in either real capital accumulation or additional real money and bonds:

(18) $S = DK + D(M/p) + D(B/p)$

The constant ratio of capital to labor in steady-state growth implies $DK = nK$. Similarly, the constancy of $m = M/pN$ and $b = B/pN$ implies that $D(M/p) = nM/p$ and $D(B/p) = nB/p$. Thus

(19) $$S = nK + \frac{nM}{p} + \frac{nB}{p}$$

Combining equations (17) and (19), writing γY for G, and dividing by N yields the per capita growth equilibrium condition:

(20) $\sigma[y(1 - \gamma) + nm + nb] = nk + nm + nb$

This completes the presentation of the model that will be analyzed in the remainder of this paper. Although the model contains important features that were lacking in earlier monetary growth models, it is still very simple. It would be desirable to investigate a richer class of models that includes personal taxes on portfolio income, that distinguishes households from institutional investors, that recognizes substitutes for business capital other than bonds and money, and that separates corporate bonds from equity. The reader should bear in mind the strong simplifying assumptions that have been made, and the fact that the subsequent analysis will compare steady-state growth patterns with no attention to the transitions. Any such short-run or transitional analysis raises difficult problems of specifying how expectations are formed when the economy is not on a steady-state growth path.

5.2   Deficits, Inflation, and Capital Intensity

The model developed in section 5.1 can now be used to analyze how changes in the government deficit affect the rate of inflation and the capital intensity of the economy. Can the government increase the real steady-state deficit in this fully employed economy without causing either inflation, reduced capital intensity, or both? What policies can be pursued to mitigate the adverse effects of the deficit? What happens when the policy options of the government are restricted?

To answer these questions, it is useful to collect the four equations that describe the steady-state behavior of the economy:

(21) $\delta = (\pi + n)(m + b)$ (previously 8)

(22) $m = L(i) \cdot f(k)$ (previously 13)

(23) $b = \beta[(1 - \tau)f'(k) + (1 - \tau\lambda)\pi - i] \cdot k$ (previously 12)

(24) $\sigma[(1 - \gamma)f(k) + nm + nb]$

                     $= n[k + m + b]$ (previously 20)

where $f(k)$ has been substituted for y in (22) and (24). The policy
instruments controlled by the government are the size of the deficit (δ),
the share of government spending in national income (γ), the interest
rate on government bonds[16] (i), and the tax rates on capital income (τ and
λ). For given values of these policy instruments and the exogenous
growth rate (n), the four equations determine the values of k, π, m, and
b.

It is clear from these four equations that the government can increase
its deficit without inducing any changes in inflation or capital intensity if it
can vary all of the other policy instruments (γ, i, τ, and λ). In practice,
however, the government does not alter the share of government spend-
ing in national income (γ) in order to neutralize the effect of a deficit.[17] It
is tempting to conclude that, even if γ is held constant, the government
can still increase the deficit without changing π or k because it still has
three unconstrained instruments. It is easily shown, however, that this is
not true; an increased deficit must then be accompanied by a change in
either inflation, capital intensity, or both. To see this note that (with γ
constant) equation (4) implies that if $dk = 0$ it is also true that $d(m + b)$
$= 0$. Equation (21) shows that $d(m + b) = 0$ and $d\pi = 0$ together imply
$d\delta = 0$. The deficit must be unchanged if both inflation and capital
intensity are unchanged.

The government can, however, affect the combination of changes in
inflation and capital intensity that occur by its debt-management policy
and its tax policy. Because changes in tax policy (in τ and λ) are not a
typical government response, most of this section will assume that τ and λ
as well as γ are unchanged. My analysis focuses on debt-management
policy, that is, on the way that the government adjusts the relative supply
of money and bonds or, equivalently, the rate of interest on government
debt.

5.2.1 A Deficit Causing Both Increased
Inflation and Reduced Capital Intensity

With the type of debt policy that has been pursued in the United States,
an increase in the steady-state deficit is likely to cause both a higher rate

---

16. Recall that this would not in general equal the rate of return on private capital. This
interest rate could equivalently be regarded as endogenous if the government is assumed to
choose the supply of nominal bonds, or the supply of money, or the ratio of these two.

17. This would in particular require reducing the share of government spending in
national income. To see this, note that equation (21) implies $d\delta = (\pi + n)d(m + b)$ if
$d\pi = 0$. Equation (24) implies $- \sigma fd\gamma + (1 - \sigma)nd(m + b)$ since $dk = 0$. Combining these
two shows $d\gamma/d\delta < 0$.

of inflation and a reduced capital intensity of production. More specifically, most empirical research indicates that the government has issued a mix of money and debt in such a way that the *real* interest rate on government debt remains approximately unchanged.[18] This section analyzes the consequences of this policy; alternative debt policies are examined in the subsequent section. To analyze the effect of an increased deficit with a constant *real* interest rate on government debt, equations (21)–(24) are totally differentiated subject to the condition $di = d\pi$.

The key to the adverse effect of inflation on capital intensity is seen in the total differential of (23), subject to $di = d\pi$:

$$(25) \qquad db = (\beta + k\beta'(1 - \tau)f'')dk - k\beta'\tau\lambda d\pi$$

The partial effect of an increase in inflation is to increase the demand for bonds rather than capital because the real yield on bonds is maintained while the real yield on capital falls by $\tau\lambda d\pi$. If this positive effect of inflation on the demand for bonds is large enough to outweigh the negative effect of inflation on the demand for money that is implied by equation (22) with $di = d\pi$:

$$(26) \qquad dm = Lf' dk + fL' d\pi$$

the effect of an increased deficit can be shown unambiguously to reduce k. To see this, note first that (24) implies

$$(27) \qquad d(m + b) = \frac{\sigma(1 - \gamma)f' - n}{(1 - \sigma)n} dk$$

Adding (25) and (26) and then using (27) to eliminate $d(m + b)$ yields

$$(28) \qquad \frac{\sigma(1 - \gamma)f' - n}{(1 - \sigma)n} dk = (Lf' + \beta)$$
$$+ k\beta'(1 - \tau)f'')dk + (fL' - k\beta'\tau\lambda)d\pi$$

Similarly, differentiating equation (21) and using (27) yields

$$(29) \qquad d\delta = (\pi + n)\frac{\sigma(1 - \gamma)f' - n}{(1 - \sigma)n} dk + (m + b)d\pi$$

Using (28) to eliminate $d\pi$ from (29) yields

---

18. Evidence that the nominal interest rate rises by approximately the rate of inflation was presented by Irving Fisher and has been verified by William Yohe and Denis Karnovsky (1969), my paper with Otto Eckstein (1970), my paper with Summers (1977), and others. The assumption in Tobin that $di = 0$ is clearly inconsistent with experience when i is interpreted as the yield on government debt rather than the yield on money.

$$(30) \quad \frac{dk}{d\delta}\bigg|_{di=d\pi} = [(1-\sigma)n(fL' - k\beta'\tau\lambda)]/$$

$$[(\pi + n)(\sigma(1-\gamma)f' - n)(fL' - k\beta'\tau\lambda)$$
$$+ (m + b)(\sigma(1-\gamma)f' - n - n(1-\sigma)$$
$$\times (Lf' + \beta + k\beta'(1-\tau)f''))]$$

With the increased demand for bonds induced by higher inflation greater than the reduced demand for money, $fL' - k\beta'\tau\lambda > 0$, and the numerator is positive. Note that stability of the simpler nonmonetary economy requires $\sigma(1-\gamma)f' - n < 0$; with this assumption, the denominator is negative. Under these quite plausible conditions, a higher deficit reduces capital formation. Since (28) implies that dk and $d\pi$ are of opposite signs, the higher deficit also increases inflation.

5.2.2 A Deficit without Inflation

The bleak outcome of increased inflation and reduced capital intensity is not a necessary implication of a greater deficit. A different debt policy would permit a deficit with no inflation. By totally differentiating equations (21)–(24) with the constraint that $d\pi = 0$, it is possible to find the change in the interest rate and corresponding debt policy that permits such a noninflationary increase in the deficit:

$$(31) \quad d\delta = (\pi + n)d(m + b)$$

$$(32) \quad d(m + b) = (fL' - k\beta')di$$
$$+ (Lf' + \beta + k\beta'(1-\tau)f'')dk$$

$$(33) \quad (\sigma(1-\gamma)f' - n)dk = (1-\sigma)nd(m + b)$$

The separate behavior of m and b is irrelevant for determining the change in i that is required to keep the inflation rate unchanged. Equation (33) can be substituted into (32) to eliminate dk and (31) can then be used to eliminate $d(m + b)$. The resulting equation shows that

$$(34) \quad \frac{di}{d\delta}\bigg|_{d\pi=0} = [\sigma(1-\gamma)f' - n$$

$$- (Lf' + \beta + k\beta'(1-\tau)f'')(1-\sigma)n]$$
$$+ [(\pi + n)(\sigma(1-\gamma)f' - n)(fL' - k\beta')]$$

The numerator is unambiguously negative since, first, $\sigma(1-\gamma)f' - n < 0$ was assumed from stability considerations, and second, $f' > 0$, $\beta' < 0$ and $f'' < 0$ make $-(Lf' + \beta + k\beta'(1-\tau)f'')(1-\sigma)n < 0$. The first term of the denominator is positive while, as already noted, the second term is negative. The final term in the denominator is the difference between the effect on the demand for money of an increase in the interest rate on government debt and its effect on the demand for the bonds themselves. Since a higher value of i can be expected to increase the demand for bonds by more than it reduces the demand for money, this term will be taken to be positive. The denominator as a whole is therefore negative. Thus, $di/d\delta > 0$.

In short, the interest rate must increase when the deficit increases if the inflation rate is to remain constant. It is easy to understand why this interest rate increase is necessary. Equation (31) indicates that a stable inflation rate requires that $m + b$ must increase with the deficit. This is so because a higher value of $m + b$ permits the larger annual increase in the money supply, and/or government borrowing that must accompany an increased deficit to be absorbed without a higher proportional rate of growth of either money or bonds. To state this same point in a slightly different way, the faster growth of government liabilities can be absorbed without increasing the *proportional* growth rate of either money or bonds if the *level* of money and bonds that is demanded (i.e., the denominators of the proportional growth rates) is increased. The higher interest rate makes this possible by increasing the demand for bonds by more than it decreases the demand for money.

Note that in practice the required change would come about by financing the increased deficit with a higher ratio of bonds to money than had prevailed in the initial equilibrium. Achieving this reduction in liquidity would require paying a higher rate of interest on those bonds.

It is clear that this policy of a higher interest rate and an increased supply of real government debt must reduce the capital intensity of production. This can be seen directly by combining equations (31) and (33):

$$(35) \qquad \frac{dk}{d\delta}\bigg|_{d\pi=0} = \frac{(1-\sigma)n}{(\pi+n)(\sigma(1-\gamma)f'-n)} < 0$$

The cost of avoiding the higher inflation rate that would otherwise accompany an increased deficit is a lower level of capital intensity and a smaller real income.

5.2.3   A Deficit without Reduced Capital Intensity

The crowding out of real capital accumulation by the government deficit can be avoided by allowing inflation to occur. It is worth examining how much inflation and what change in the interest rate are needed to keep capital intensity unchanged.

Differentiating (24) with $dk = 0$ shows immediately that $m + b$ must also remain unchanged. Equation (21) then implies that $d\delta = (m + b)d\pi$, i.e., that an increase in the deficit must increase inflation. With $d(m + b) = 0$, equations (22) and (23) together imply

(36) $0 = (fL' - k\beta')di + (1 - \tau\lambda)k\beta'd\pi$

Substituting $(m + b)^{-1}d\delta$ for $d\pi$ yields the change in i required to keep k fixed:

(37) $$\left.\frac{di}{d\delta}\right|_{dk=0} = \frac{-(1 - \tau\lambda)k\beta'}{(m + b)(fL' - k\beta')}$$

As explained above, the denominator is positive in the likely case that a rise in the interest rate increases the demand for bonds by more than it decreases the demand for money. The value of λ would be zero if the tax law did not cause inflation to reduce the real net return on capital. In that case, the numerator is positive and $di/d\delta > 0$. More generally, even when historic cost depreciation rules do raise the effective tax rate on real profits ($\lambda > 0$), the numerator will still be positive as long as inflation raises the *nominal* after-tax return on capital.[19]

The mechanism by which a higher interest rate permits a constant value of k is clear from the derivation. A constant value of k implies a constant value of $m + b$ and therefore an increased value of π. With a constant value of k, a higher rate of inflation would actually decrease b (and therefore $m + b$) unless i is raised to prevent this.

Comparing equation (37) and (34) shows that the increase in i that keeps k unchanged is less than the increase in i that keeps π unchanged:

(38) $\left.\dfrac{di}{d\delta}\right|_{d\pi=0} - \left.\dfrac{di}{d\delta}\right|_{dk=0}$

$= [\{\sigma(1 - \gamma)f' - n - (Lf' + \beta + k\beta'(1 - \tau)f'')(1 - \sigma)n\}$

$(m + b) + (\pi + n)(\sigma(1 - \gamma)f' - n)(1 - \tau\lambda)k\beta']/$

$[(m + b)(fL' - k\beta')(\pi + n)(\sigma(1 - \gamma)f' - n)] > 0$

The reason for this is clear. Holding k and therefore $m + b$ constant implies $d\pi > 0$. Making $d\pi = 0$ requires an increase in $m + b$ and therefore a higher rate of interest.

5.2.4   A Deficit Financed by Interest-Bearing Debt

A particularly interesting debt policy requires that any increase in the deficit be financed only by additional borrowing. The real growth of the money supply remains constant. This section looks briefly at the effect of such a policy. This specification of debt policy implies that the real rate of new money creation remains unchanged: DM/pN is constant. Since $DM/pN = m(DM/M) = m(\pi + n)$, this debt policy implies $m(\pi + n) = c$, a constant. The implication of this for capital intensity and inflation depends on the interest elasticity of the demand for money. On the simplify-

---

19. The nominal after-tax return on capital is $(1 - \tau)f + (1 - \tau\lambda)\pi$.

ing assumption that the money demand is completely inelastic ($L' = 0$), it is easily shown that the deficit unambiguously decreases capital intensity and increases inflation. With $m(\pi + n) = c$,

$$(39) \qquad d\delta = (\pi + n)db + bd\pi$$

$$(40) \qquad dm = \frac{-m}{\pi + n}\, d\pi$$

Combining $m = Lf$ and $m(\pi + n) = c$ yields

$$(41) \qquad (\pi + n)f'dk = -fd\pi$$

Thus inflation and capital intensity move in opposite directions. The growth equilibrium condition of equation (24) implies

$$(42) \qquad \frac{\sigma(1 - \gamma)f' - n}{(1 - \sigma)n}\, dk = db + dm$$

Using (40) and (41) to eliminate dm yields

$$(43) \qquad db = \left(\frac{\sigma(1 - \gamma)f' - n}{(1 - \sigma)n} - \frac{mf'}{f}\right) dk$$

Equation (39) can thus be rewritten using (41) and (43) as

$$(44) \qquad d\delta = (\pi + n)\left\{\frac{\sigma(1 - \gamma)f' - n}{(1 - \sigma)n} - \frac{mf'}{f} - \frac{bf'}{f}\right\} dk$$

This shows that $dk/d\delta < 0$ and (41) then implies that $d\pi/d\delta > 0$. Thus even with a debt policy that keeps the growth of real money balances unchanged, the deficit increases inflation and reduces capital intensity.

5.3   Fiscal Incentives, Saving, and Aggregate Demand

The three-asset growth model can be used to analyze the effects of an exogenous increase in the saving rate.[20] The most important issue to be examined is the possibility of excess saving. Under quite reasonable conditions, an increase in the saving rate will be absorbed into higher capital intensity without any problem for aggregate demand if there is accommodating monetary policy. The possibility of excess saving arises when investors are unwilling to hold real capital in their portfolio at a lower rate of return; I shall refer to this as a "safety trap" by analogy to the traditional Keynesian liquidity trap. The problem is exacerbated if the yield on government bonds also cannot be lowered, that is, if the economy is also in a liquidity trap.

20. Such an increase in the saving rate (σ) may reflect a change in taste or a change in institutions such as Social Security that are not explicitly included in the model.

The problem of excess saving can manifest itself in two ways. Under some conditions, the extra saving could be absorbed in additional capital if the steady-state rate of inflation is reduced. If there is no inflation in the initial equilibrium, the increased saving rate would involve a continuous price deflation. While there may be no theoretical problem with this, as a practical matter, the downward rigidity of money wages could prevent this from occurring. The additional saving would not be absorbed but would result in unemployment. The problem is even worse when the safety trap and liquidity trap conditions both prevail. Under these conditions, the extra savings cannot be absorbed in increased capital even if the inflation rate could be permanently reduced.

The problem of excess saving arises only if the government restricts its accommodating action to monetary policy. This section shows how tax incentives, or under some conditions are increased deficit, can be used to assure than an increase in the saving rate results in a greater rate of capital formation.

5.3.1   Increased Saving with Accommodating Monetary Policy

Before studying the problem of excess saving, it is useful to examine the nature of the well-behaved equilibrium in which additional saving can be absorbed with the help of only accommodating monetary policy. Let us impose the requirement that the real deficit (δ), the share of the government in national income (γ), and the tax rates on capital income $(\tau$ and $\lambda)$ remain constant. The rate of inflation will also be required to remain unchanged, thus precluding the problem of unattainable price deflation.

The key change from the analysis of section 5.2 is that the differential of the growth equilibrium condition (equation 24 now involves a change in the saving rate:

(45)
$$[(1 - \gamma)f + n(m + b)]d\sigma$$
$$+ [\sigma(1 - \gamma)f' - n]dk - (1 - \sigma)nd(m + b) = 0$$

with a constant deficit $(d\delta = 0)$ and constant inflation rate $(d\pi = 0)$, the government budget constraint

(46)
$$d\delta = (\pi + n)d(m + b) + (m + b)d\pi$$

implies $d(m + b) = 0$. Together with (45) this shows immediately that the higher saving rate increases capital intensity

(47)
$$\frac{dk}{d\sigma} = -\frac{(1 - \gamma)f + n(m + b)}{\sigma(1 - \gamma)f' - n} > 0$$

The required change in the interest rate can then be derived from the money-demand relation (equation 22) and the bond-demand relation (equation 23). Together these imply

(48)
$$d(m + b) = [Lf' + \beta + k\beta'(1 - \tau)f'']dk$$
$$+ (fL' - k\beta')di + k\beta'(1 - \tau\lambda)d\pi$$

With $d(m + b) = d\pi = 0$,

(49)
$$\frac{di}{dk} = -\frac{Lf' + \beta + k\beta'(1 - \tau)f''}{fL' - k\beta'}$$

If the effect of a change in the interest rate on the demand for bonds exceeds its effect on the demand for money, the denominator is positive and $(di/dk) < 0$. To achieve this reduction in the equilibrium interest rate on government debt, the money supply must be increased relative to real income and the supply of bonds must be reduced relative to the capital stock. The precise changes are indicated by equations (22) and (23) and satisfy $d(m + b) = 0$.

In short, if investors are willing to accept a lower return on capital accompanied by a less than equal reduction in the yield on government debt, an increase in the saving rate can raise capital intensity without any change in inflation or other government policies.[21]

5.3.2   Safety Preference and Excess Saving

The basic insight of the Keynesian analysis is that, in a monetary economy, additional saving will not automatically be invested. When the yield on real capital becomes too low, individuals will prefer to hold government bonds rather than to assume the greater risk associated with the ownership of real capital. More precisely, the demand for government bonds becomes infinitely elastic at some low differential between the yield on real capital $((1 - \tau)f' + (1 - \tau\lambda)\pi)$ and the yield on government bonds (i). In the notation of the bond-demand equation,

(50)
$$b = k\beta((1 - \tau)f' + (1 - \tau\lambda)\pi - i)$$

assume that $\beta' = -\infty$ at some low value of $(1 - \tau)f' + (1 - \tau\lambda)\pi - i$. We can refer to this situation as "being in a safety trap."

When the economy has reached this condition, a further fall in $(1 - \tau)f' + (1 - \tau\lambda)\pi - i$ is not possible. This additional constraint on the adjustment of the economy can be the source of an excess saving problem. When certain further conditions exist, the increase in capital intensity could only occur if the rate of inflation could be reduced. If the initial equilibrium had no inflation (or a very low rate), the required reduction

---

21. If the interest rate on government debt cannot be reduced, an increase in the rate of inflation could achieve the same thing (as long as $1 - \tau\lambda > 0$). This is essentially Tobin's solution since he assumes $di = 0$. The implication of section 5.3.1 and the remainder of section 5.3 is that Tobin's inflationary policy is unnecessary and may be counterproductive.

in inflation might not be achievable and the extra savings would result in an unemployment disequilibrium.[22]

To see the conditions under which this problem would arise, note that the safety trap condition implies

$$(51) \qquad (1 - \tau)f'' \, dk + (1 - \tau\lambda)d\pi - di = 0$$

This in turn implies that $db = \beta dk$ and therefore that

$$(52) \qquad d(m + b) = fL' \, di + (Lf' + \beta)dk$$

With no change in the government deficit, the government budget constraint entails

$$(53) \qquad (\pi + n)d(m + b) + (m + b)d\pi = 0$$

Using this equation to eliminate $d(m + b)$ from (52) and using (51) to rewrite di in terms of $d\pi$ and dk yields

$$(54) \qquad \frac{d\pi}{dk} = - \frac{fL'(1 - \tau)f'' + Lf' + \beta}{\dfrac{m + b}{\pi + n} + fL'(1 - \tau\lambda)}$$

The numerator is unambiguously positive. If the denominator is also positive, an increase in capital intensity must be accompanied by a lower rate of inflation. There are two different plausible conditions under which the denominator will be positive. If the demand for money is interest inelastic ($L' = 0$), or, more generally, if the effect of interest on money demand is small ($(\pi + n)fL'(1 - \tau\lambda) < m + b$), the denominator will be positive. Alternatively, regardless of the size of L', if inflation raises the effective tax rate on capital income by enough to make the nominal after-tax yield on capital vary inversely with inflation ($1 - \tau\lambda < 0$), both terms in the denominator will be positive. In either case, increased capital intensity could not accompany a higher saving rate unless the rate of inflation could be reduced.

It is easy to see why the safety trap condition implies that a greater capital intensity entails a lower rate of inflation. Consider the case of inelastic money demand. The safety trap implies that the demand for bonds increases in proportion to the capital stock: $db = \beta dk$. With inelastic money demand, the money supply also increases with the capital stock: $dm = Lf'dk$. But with no change in the government deficit, the steady-state value of $m + b$ can increase only if the inflation rate is lower. In the alternate case in which inflation increases the effective tax rate, the analysis is only slightly more complex. If there were no change in infla-

---

22. The dynamics of such an employment disequilibrium will not be considered. The relative strength of the Pigou effect and Wicksell effect would influence the ultimate path. For the current purpose, it is sufficient that price deflation and unemployment would be required for at least some period of time.

tion, the interest rate would have to fall to maintain the minimum yield differential with greater capital intensity. But this would increase the demand for money, raising $m + b$. This is incompatible with a constant inflation rate. If the inflation rate increased, this would further reduce the yeld on capital relative to government bonds.

The problem of excess saving under these conditions can be avoided if the government uses fiscal policy as well as monetary policy to accommodate the additional saving. Consider first the possibility of responding to a higher saving rate by reducing the rate of tax on capital income, τ. With a lower tax rate, the net of tax yield on the real capital stock can be maintained while the greater capital intensity depresses the pretax yield. To confirm explicitly that this fiscal incentive is sufficient to permit greater capital intensity, with no change in the rate of inflation, consider the four equations that describe the safety trap equilibrium with $d\tau \neq 0$. The government budget constraint with $d\pi = 0$ and $d\delta = 0$ implies $d(m + b) = 0$. Substituting this into the growth equilibrium (equation 45) shows $dk/d\sigma > 0$ exactly as in equation (47). The two remaining conditions that must be satisfied are the safety trap condition with $d\pi = 0$:

$$(55) \qquad (1 - \tau)f''dk - di - (f' + \lambda\pi)d\tau = 0$$

and the condition that the change in the demands for debt and money leave $m + b$ unchanged:

$$(56) \qquad 0 = fL'\,di + (\beta + Lf')dk$$

Equation (56) shows that the interest rate must rise, reducing the demand for money per unit of capital. With the unique increase in di determined by (56) and the unique increase in k determined by (47), equation (55) shows the required decrease in the tax rate τ.

A higher saving rate can be transformed into greater capital intensity with no change in inflation even without changing the tax rate on capital income by an accommodating increase in the government deficit accompanied by a lower rate of interest. The lower rate of interest balances the fall in the return on real capital, permitting the real capital to be absorbed. The greater deficit with the unchanged rate of inflation permits an increase in both money and bonds that is required by the fall in i and increase in k.

To see all of this explicitly, note that with $d\tau = d\pi = 0$, the safety trap condition becomes

$$(57) \qquad (1 - \tau)f''dk - di = 0$$

The increased demand for money and bonds is

$$(58) \qquad d(m + b) = fL'\,di + (Lf' + \beta)dk$$

which, from (57), is

(59) $d(m + b) = (fL'(1 - \tau)f'' + Lf' + \beta)dk$

Substituting this value of $d(m + b)$ into the growth equilibrium (equation 45) yields

(60) $$\frac{dk}{d\sigma} = -\frac{(1 - \gamma)f + n(m + b)}{\sigma(1 - \gamma)f' - n - n(1 - \sigma)(fL'(1 - \tau)f'' + Lf' + \beta)}$$

This is unambiguously positive. The last term in the denominator, which reflects the increased deficit (i.e., $d(m + b)$), reduces the size of $dk/d\sigma$ but does not alter the fact that it is positive. With dk determined by (60), equation (59) implies a unique value of $d(m + b) > 0$. The government budget constraint with $d\pi = 0$ then gives the required change in the deficit, $d\delta = (\pi + n) d(m + b) > 0$.

Although both the reduced tax on capital income and the increased deficit are capable of turning additional saving into greater capital intensity without a change in the price level (and therefore without the possibility of a deflationary unemployment disequilibrium), the reduced tax on capital income has at least three advantages over the increased government deficit. First, and probably most important, the equilibrium capital intensity is greater if the increased saving is accommodated by a lower tax rate. Second, the lower tax rate on capital income reduces the excess burden caused by a distorting tax.[23] Finally, the tax reduction can be effective under special conditions when the increased deficit would fail. More specifically, the lower interest rate that must accompany the increased deficit would not be possible if the economy is also in a liquidity trap, that is, if investors are unwilling to hold any asset other than money at a lower rate of interest.[24] Even in this case, the tax reduction (and increased rate of interest) can be used to accommodate a higher rate of saving.

5.4   Some Conclusions

This paper has studied the long-run impact of fiscal policies on inflation and capital formation. The analysis uses an expanded monetary growth model in which the government finances its deficit by issuing both money and interest-bearing debt.

23. The welfare gain from reducing the tax rate on capital income depends on the way in which the lost tax revenue is recovered. My 1978a paper shows that even when the uncompensated elasticity of saving with respect to its return is zero, the excess burden of the tax system would be reduced by lowering the tax on capital income and raising it on labor income. In the current context there is the further complication that the increased deficit and lower interest rate would permit lower total taxes.

24. In the notation of the model, $L' = -\infty$ at some low level of i. This implies the extra constraint $di > 0$ which is consistent with equation (56) in the context of a tax rate reduction but not with equation (57) when $d\tau = 0$ and $d\delta > 0$. An increased deficit could avoid unemployment by the Keynesian remedy of absorbing all of the additional saving, i.e., with $dk = 0$.

One major focus of the paper is the effect of a permanent increase in the government's real deficit in a fully employed economy. An important conclusion is that such an increased deficit must raise the rate of inflation or lower the capital intensity of production or both. The analysis shows that the combination of *both* increased inflation and reduced capital intensity in a likely outcome with current *U.S.* tax rules and the prevailing monetary policy of allowing the interest rate to rise with inflation in a way that keeps the real interest rate unchanged. Section 5.2 determines the debt management policy (and the corresponding change in the interest rate) that would be required to maintain either a constant inflation rate or a constant capital-labor ratio.

The second purpose of the paper is to analyze the effect of an exogenous increase in the saving rate and the possibility of "excessive saving." The problem of excessive saving arises when the yield on capital becomes so low that individuals prefer to hold government bonds rather than the more risky claims to real capital. Under some conditions, an increased rate of saving could only be absorbed in increased capital intensity if the rate of inflation could be permanently reduced. This requirement might entail a negative inflation rate which, as a practical matter, would be precluded by the downward rigidity of money wages. In this case, the addtional saving would not be absorbed but would result in unemployment.

Section 5.3 shows first that there is no problem of excessive saving (1) if investors are willing to hold real capital even though the differential between its yield and that on government bonds is narrowed, and (2) if the government reduces the interest rate on government bonds by expanding the money supply more rapidly than the stock of bonds. When these conditions are met, an increase in saving can be absorbed in greater capital intensity without any change in either inflation or the government deficit.

A problem can arise if the economy is in a safety trap, that is, if investors would be unwilling to hold real capital if the difference between its yield and that on government debt were reduced. In that case, an increased saving rate can imply price deflation and therefore possible unemployment. This problem can be avoided however by reducing the tax on capital income (or, in some cases, by an increased deficit that absorbs some but not all of the higher savings rate). In short, by using fiscal incentives as well as monetary accommodation, an increased saving rate can be converted to greater capital intensity.

The analysis as a whole, although clearly a theoretical study of a simplified economy, suggests some insights that may help in understanding the unsatisfactory macroeconomic experience of the past decade and in designing more appropriate economic policies for the future. The recent years have been characterized by substantial inflation, a low rate of investment, and large government deficits. Section 5.2 shows how an increased government deficit can give rise to both greater inflation and reduced capital intensity. The combination of inflation and historic cost depreciation raised the effective tax rate on the income from real capital while the monetary and debt management policies have kept the real interest rate on government debt unchanged. The reduced-equilibrium capital-labor ratio that this implies manifests itself as a lower rate of investment. The problem is then exacerbated when the government responds to decreased investment by further enlarging its deficit. The analysis suggests that a more appropriate solution would be to reduce the deficit while stimulating investment through a lower tax rate and a depreciation method based on current rather than historic costs.

I have argued elsewhere that the United States should increase its saving rate to take advantage of the high social rate of return on additional investment.[25] Such an increase in the private saving rate could be achieved by reducing the growth of Social Security benefits or by tax reforms that make the personal income tax more like a consumption tax. These proposals implicitly assumed that such extra saving would result in greater capital intensity rather than in a fall in aggregate demand. Section 5.3 implies that this assumption is warranted. With appropriate fiscal incentives and accommodating monetary policies, an increase in saving can be absorbed in greater capital intensity without any change in the rate of inflation.

25. See my 1976 (chap. 3) and 1977b papers.

6   Inflation, Tax Rules, and the Accumulation of Residential and Nonresidential Capital

For nearly two decades, the United States has pursued a series of short-run policies that have increased the rate of inflation and sustained it at a high level. The rate of increase of the general price level (as measured by the GNP deflator) rose from less than 2 percent a year in the early 1960s to more than 8 percent a year in the late 1970s. The expansionary monetary and fiscal policies began in the early 1960s as an attempt to lower the unemployment rate and expand the level of output. Easy money, lower tax rates on capital income, and specific incentives for business investment were combined with the aim of stimulating investment and thereby, through the traditional multiplier process, reducing unemployment. Although the rate of inflation began to rise, many economists argued that "moving up the Phillips curve" to higher inflation and lower unemployment represented a desirable trade off. Then came the decision by President Johnson to expand both the Vietnam war and his Great Society programs. He insisted on doing so without a tax increase but with an easy money policy aimed at keeping interest rates from rising. This moved the inflation rate up sharply, to more than 5 percent as the 1970s began.

In the 1970s, inflationary monetary and fiscal policies continued to be pursued despite a lack of agreement on the rationale for those policies even among the prevailing economists of that decade. In effect, these economists and the politicians agreed on the treatment of the economy even though they disagreed about the proper diagnosis of its economic condition. First, there were those who continued to believe in a long-run

Reprinted by permission from *Scandinavian Journal of Economics* 84 (June 1980): 636–50.

This paper is part of the NBER study of capital formation. I am grateful to my colleagues at the NBER for numerous discussions of this subject and for comments on an earlier draft.

Phillips curve trade-off between inflation and unemployment. They advocated expansionary policy in the hope of reducing unemployment permanently even if that meant accepting a higher inflation rate. Second, there were those who recognized that no long-run trade-off exists but who misjudged how high the noninflationary unemployment rate had become because of changes in the demographic structure of the labor force and in the transfer programs that encouraged higher unemployment. They advocated expansionary monetary and fiscal policies because they believed that the economy was still operating with "too much unemployment." Finally, there were those who correctly perceived that the economy was at or below the noninflationary unemployment rate but who resisted a tightening of monetary and fiscal policy because they were unwilling to pay the price in higher unemployment for slowing the rise in inflation or reducing its level.

In this way the economy drifted to higher and higher rates of inflation.[1] Although some of the year-to-year changes in inflation were unexpected, the general level and even some of the upward drift clearly came to be anticipated. For more than a decade now, a major debate among American macroeconomists has been about whether such anticipated inflation has any effects on the real economy. At least since Milton Friedman's (1968) presidential address, economists have recognized that expected inflation is perfectly neutral in a simplified economy with flexible prices, inelastic money demand, and no taxes. Subsequent research by Barro (1977) Lucas (1972), Sargent and Wallace (1975), and others has refined this idea and emphasized the corresponding neutrality of expected changes in the stock of money.[2]

The important question, however, is whether the neutrality of anticipated changes in money and in the price level are relevant to the actual economy in which we live. James Tobin (1965) emphasized that even fully anticipated inflation is not neutral because the demand for money balances varies inversely with the nominal interest rate and therefore with the expected rate of inflation. An increase in inflation caused by a more rapid growth of money would therefore raise the capital intensity of the economy by inducing households to substitute real capital for money in their portfolios. Stanley Fischer (1979b) has recently examined the lead and lag patterns by which expected changes in the money stock can alter the capital stock and real output through the Tobin money-capital substitution effect. Although this portfolio substitution process is analytically correct, it is generally agreed that the magnitude of the Tobin effect is extremely small.[3]

---

1. The OPEC price shocks played a significant part in this process but do not alter the basic story that I have told above. For more extensive accounts, see Blinder (1979), Eckstein (1978), Feldstein (1981c), and Gordon (1981).

2. See also the papers and discussion in Fischer (1979a).

3. See sec. 6.1, especially sec. 6.1.5, for a discussion of why the Tobin effect is empirically too small to matter.

By contrast, the interaction of inflation and the tax rules can have very substantial effects on the incentive to save and on the relative returns to different types of investments. In Feldstein (1976; chap. 3) I examined the way in which the tax-inflation interaction could lower total capital formation by reducing the incentive to save. Then in Feldstein (1980; chap. 5) I showed how the tax-inflation interaction would encourage individual investors to substitute interest-bearing government debt for real capital in their portfolios and thereby reduce the real capital intensity of the economy. The present paper extends this analysis to examine how inflation diverts capital from plant and equipment to owner-occupied housing.[4]

The tax burden on business capital rises when there is inflation. Under existing U.S. tax rules,[5] inflation affects the taxation of business capital in three important ways. First, because of the "historic cost" approach to calculating the cost of production, a higher rate of inflation reduces the real value of depreciation allowances and understates the cost of replacing the goods withdrawn from inventory. Second, the owners of the equity of business firms pay capital gains tax on the rise in the nominal value of the capital stock. And, third, the firm gets to deduct nominal interest payments (thereby understating its taxable profits) but the creditors must pay tax on nominal interest receipts (thereby overstating their taxable income). Since the effective tax rate on the reduced corporate income is very close to the effective tax rate on the increased creditor income (Feldstein and Summers, 1979), this third effect is very small. On balance, inflation therefore raises the tax burden on the income from business investment.

Under present U.S. tax law, an individual who owns his own house may deduct the nominal interest payment in calculating taxable income and does not pay tax on the implicit rental income provided (in kind) by his house. In addition, the capital gains on owner-occupied housing are virtually untaxed.

Since the stock of housing capital is about 74 percent of the stock of nonresidential capital,[6] an incentive to shift capital from plant and equipment to housing can have a significant effect on the amount of plant and equipment in the economy. The ratio of net investment in residential capital to net investment in plant and equipment rose from 52 percent in the last half of the 1960s to 76 percent in the last half of the 1970s. In

4. I have previously discussed the way that inflation and tax rules combine to achieve this distortion in Feldstein (1980a, b) but have not previously presented a formal model. For other analyses of the way that the tax-inflation interaction affects the demand for residential capital, see Hendershott (1979, 1980), Hendershott and Hu (1979), Hendershott and Shilling (1980), Poterba (1980), and Summers (1981).

5. I.e., the tax rules as of July 1981.

6. This excludes land and includes inventories as well as fixed capital. Owner-occupied housing accounts for 42 percent of fixed capital alone. The data on capital stocks and inventories are from the Federal Reserve Board's *Balance Sheets of the U.S. Economy*.

Feldstein (1980*e*; chap. 14 below), I presented econometric evidence that the interaction of tax rules and inflation reduced the incentive to invest in plant and equipment and that this can explain most of the variation in the share of GNP devoted to such investment during the past three decades.

The present paper analyzes the effect of the interaction between tax rules and inflation on the size and allocation of the capital stock with particular emphasis on the role of owner-occupied housing. The analysis is developed in the framework of an economy that is in equilibrium and in which a constant fraction of disposable income is saved. In this model, I show that, with current U.S. tax laws, an increase in the rate of inflation reduces the equilibrium amount of business capital employed in the economy and raises the amount of housing capital. The analysis also shows that a higher rate of inflation lowers the real net-of-tax rate of return to the provider of business capital. In a richer model than the current one, that is, in a model in which the rate of personal saving was an increasing function of the net rate of return, a higher inflation rate would therefore lower the rate of saving.

The present analysis also shows that permitting firms to depreciate investments more rapidly for tax purposes increases the accumulations of business capital but that, unless firms are permitted to expense all investment immediately, an increase in inflation continues to depress the accumulation of business capital.

The model considered in this paper is a very simple one. I ignore several issues that I have considered in earlier papers: changes in the saving rate, changes in the demand for money, government debt, and the mixture of debt and equity in corporate finance.[7] A model cannot be a complete picture of reality but should help to elucidate some particular aspect of reality.

One final point should be emphasized before turning to the formal analysis. Because the relation between inflation and capital formation depends on the fiscal structure of the economy, the specific distorting effect of inflation is not a universal constant but differs among countries and even within the same country from time to time.

6.1   A Growing Economy with Inflation and Housing

The simplest framework within which to examine the effect of inflation on the composition of the capital stock is an economy with two sectors. The corporate business sector produces a general good that can be used for both consumption and investment. The unincorporated household sector produces the services of the owner-occupied housing stock. The population grows exogenously in this economy at a constant rate (n) and the labor force is a fixed fraction of the population. Labor is employed

---

7. See Feldstein (1976, chap. 3 above; 1980) and Feldstein, Green, and Sheshinski (1978).

only in the production of the general good; housing services are proportional to the stock of housing and are produced without labor.[8]

6.1.1 The Business Sector

If the general good is produced with constant returns to scale, the technology can be described by a production function that relates output per employee (y) to the capital stock per employee used in this sector (k):

$$(1) \qquad y = f(k)$$

For simplicity, output is measured net of depreciation and all technical progress is ignored.

The pretax rate of return on corporate capital is f'. In the absence of inflation, corporations pay tax at rate τ on this return to capital. The net-of-tax returns on the marginal investment, $(1 - \tau)f'$, must in equilibrium be equal to the firms' net cost of funds. The analysis is greatly simplified by assuming that all marginal investments are financed by debt.[9] On these funds, firms pay interest rate i. Since interest expenses are deducted in calculating a firm's taxable income, the net cost of borrowed funds is $(1 - \tau)i$ and the firm's equilibrium condition is $(1 - \tau)f' = (1 - \tau)i$ or just $f' = i$.

If there is inflation and the price level rises at a constant rate, π, the nominal pretax rate of return on capital is $f' + \pi$. If inflation did not alter the measurement of real taxable profits, the tax liability per unit of capital (ignoring for a moment the tax treatment of debt) would be $\tau f'$ and the resulting nominal after-tax rate of return would be $(1 - \tau)f' + \pi$. In fact, with the tax accounting rules that have prevailed in the United States, inflation causes taxable profits to increase relative to real profits. Both historic cost depreciation and the use of FIFO inventory accounting cause an understatement of the true cost of production and therefore an overstatement of taxable profits.[10] As an approximation, the increase in tax-

8. The model also ignores the land used in housing. In the current framework, inflation would raise the relative price of land.

9. The rationale for all "debt at the margin" finance is developed in Stiglitz (1973) and a model of growth equilibrium with such finance is presented in Feldstein (1976). More realistically, the costs of debt and equity funds depend on a firm's debt-equity ratio; see Gordon and Malkiel (1981) and Feldstein, Green, and Sheshinski (1978, chap. 4 above; 1979). It is worth noting that the analysis of this paper could be done equally easily for an economy without any debt finance. In such an economy, firms would use only equity finance and homeowners would have no mortgages. The same basic results about the allocation of capital would be obtained, indicating that the fundamental issue is the inflation-induced rise in the relative taxation of business income and not the deductibility of nominal interest payments on mortgages.

10. If depreciation schedules permit tax depreciation that is faster than economic depreciation, taxable profits in the absence of inflation will be less than true profits. The increase in real taxable profits caused by inflation may leave taxable profits greater or less than true profits. What matters is the *change* in the size of this difference, i.e., profits relative to real profits, and not the sign of the difference.

able income per unit of capital can be written as a constant multiple of the inflation rate, $\lambda\pi$, per unit of capital.[11] The additional tax is thus $\tau\lambda\pi$. The nominal rate of return to the corporation net of tax is therefore $(1 - \tau)f' + \pi - \tau\lambda\pi$.

Since the nominal interest rate is deducted in calculating taxable income, the net-of-tax cost of borrowed funds is $(1 - \tau)i$. The equilibrium condition that requires equating the nominal net returns on the marginal unit of capital to the net cost of funds therefore implies

$$(2) \qquad (1 - \tau)f' + (1 - \tau\lambda)\pi = (1 - \tau)i$$

Before proceeding to discuss the housing sector, it is interesting to note that equation (2) implies

$$(3) \qquad i = f' + \frac{1 - \tau\lambda}{1 - \tau}\pi$$

In contrast to the traditional conclusion of Irving Fisher that the nominal interest rate rises point for point with the rate of inflation, equation (3) shows that, *for a fixed real marginal product of capital*, the rise in the interest rate reflects the tax deductibility of nominal interest and the mismeasurement of depreciation and inventory profits. With economic depreciation and no artificial inventory profits, $\lambda = 0$ and $di/d\pi = 1/(1 - \tau)$. With existing depreciation and inventory rules, $0 < \lambda < 1$ and $1 < di/d\pi < 1/(1 - \tau)$.[12]

If the individuals who provide capital to the business sector pay tax at rate θ on nominal interest income, the real net-of-tax interest that they earn is $(1 - \theta)i - \pi$. From equation (3) it follows that

$$(4) \qquad (1 - \theta) - \pi = (1 - \theta)f' + \frac{[\tau - \theta - (1 - \theta)\tau\lambda]}{1 - \tau}\pi$$

The impact of inflation on the real net return to lenders depends on two things. First, $\tau - \theta$ reflects the difference between the advantage of deducting nominal interest payments at the corporate level and the disadvantage of paying tax on nominal interest income at the personal level. Second, $(1 - \theta)\tau\lambda$ reflects the additional tax paid at the corporate level because of the mismeasurement of depreciation and inventory costs. For any marginal personal income tax rate greater than 30 percent, i.e. for $\theta > .30$, the coefficient of π is negative.[13]

11. See Auerbach (1978, appendix to chap. 4 above) for an explicit derivation of the relation between the true rate of depreciation and the increase in taxable income caused by historic cost depreciation. Feldstein (1980d, see chap. 11 below) discusses the additional contribution of FIFO inventory accounting. For the United States, a value of $\lambda = 0.50$ is a reasonable approximation with the tax laws in effect in the late 1970s.

12. The expression is more complex when firms use equity as well as debt in marginal finance. It is important to emphasize that these expressions for $di/d\pi$ are partial equilibrium relations that assume f' fixed.

13. The corporate tax rate τ is 0.46 and, as noted above, λ has been estimated to be 0.50 (Feldstein, 1980d; see chap. 11 below).

6.1.2 The Housing Sector

The owner-occupied housing sector uses capital but no labor to produce housing services. Since in the long-run capital can move freely between the two sectors, the equilibrium price of a unit of housing capital is the same as the price of a unit of business capital which in turn is the price of a unit of the general good.[14] The price of housing services therefore depends on the cost of owning one unit of housing capital and of maintaining that capital.

More specifically, for each dollar of housing capital the individual pays or foregoes net interest of $(1 - \theta)i$.[15] Local property tax, maintenance, depreciation, and a standard risk premium add an additional net cost of z per unit of housing capital.[16] Since the value of net housing capital rises at the rate of inflation, the real net cost of owning and maintaining a unit of housing capital is:

$$(5) \qquad r = (1 - \theta)i + z - \pi$$

Note that r is thus the implicit rental cost of a unit of owner-occupied housing capital.

The demand for housing capital by individual homeowners reflects both the demand for housing services and the demand for housing capital as a portfolio asset. Since I have assumed that the amount of housing service is proportional to the housing stock it is not necessary to distinguish the demand for services from the demand for a portfolio asset. Instead, the demand for housing capital can be considered directly with its determinants reflecting both the portfolio and service characteristics. The simplest such specification is equation (6) where h is the housing capital stock per employee and $\phi' < 0$. This equation implies that the relative demand for housing services and for other goods varies inversely with the implicit rental price of housing.[17]

---

14. By contrast, in the short run the stocks of housing capital and business capital are given and equilibrium must be achieved by changes in the prices of these capital stocks. See Poterba (1980) and Summers (1981).

15. This assumes that individuals borrow and lend at the same interest rate. It also reflects the U.S. tax rule that permits individuals to deduct mortgage interest payments in the calculation of taxable income.

16. I say "net" cost because local property taxes are a deductible expense in calculating individual taxable income. By "standard risk premium" I mean the premium for a "standard" or "basic" amount of housing capital; the risk premium may be a function of the amount of housing capital in a way specified below.

17. Since the other goods represent the numeraire, r is also the rental price of housing relative to the price of other goods. A more general specification would make the demand for housing a function of real income and of wealth. Within the current paper, however, the equilibrium values of real income and wealth remain constant except for changes in the efficiency of resource allocation. If the initial condition of the economy is regarded as one of optimal resource allocation, the changes in resource allocation that result from a small increase in the rate of inflation do not change real income to a first-order approximation. A large change in inflation would, however, reduce real income. Similarly, a small increase in inflation would reduce real income if, in the initial condition, nonneutral tax rules cause

(6) $h = \phi(r)$

Even in the restricted form of equation (6), the demand for housing capital as an asset influences the form of the demand function, ϕ. In particular, since each individual must own the housing capital that produces his housing services, an increase in the consumption of housing services beyond some level involves increasing portfolio risk.[18] This implies that, for high values of h, the demand for housing capital is less responsive to the implicit rental price than would be true if individuals did not have to own their housing capital.[19] Even when the implicit rental price would otherwise be zero or negative, risk considerations limit the demand for housing capital.[20]

6.1.3   The Demand for Money

Money plays two quite distinct roles in a model of equilibrium growth. First, the exogenously given rate of growth of the nominal money stock determines the rate of inflation. This follows directly from the fact that the stock of real money balances per employee must remain constant in equilibrium growth since real income per employee, real assets per employee, and the rate of interest are all constant.[21] If real money balances per employee are to remain constant, the rate of growth of the nominal money stock ($\dot{M}/M$) must equal the rate of growth of prices plus the rate of growth of the labor force:

(7) $$\frac{\dot{M}}{M} = \pi + n$$

The second role of money is as an asset that absorbs savings and thereby reduces the equilibrium size of the real capital stock, $k + h$. As mentioned above, Tobin (1965) has emphasized that an increase in

---

there to be too much housing capital. A reduction in real income would cause individuals to consume less housing and this would partially offset the inflation-induced transfer of capital from the business sector to housing. Shifting one unit of capital from the business sector to housing reduces real income by the difference between the real marginal products of capital in the two sections and this income effect reduces the demand for housing capital by the marginal propensity to own housing capital as a function of real income. The real marginal product difference is less than f' which is approximatley 0.12 in the United States. The marginal housing-to-income ratio is less than three. Thus this real income effect offsets at most about one-third of any shift of capital from the business to housing sectors.

18. This is particularly true when the acquisition of housing capital is financed by borrowing.

19. The model assumes that all housing is owner-occupied when in reality about 75 percent of the housing capital stock is owner-occupied. The tax advantages and other aspects of home ownership probably outweigh risk considerations at most income levels. The tax advantage of homeownership is increased by inflation since rental property is adversely affected by historic cost depreciation rules.

20. This was probably the case in the 1970s.

21. If there is technical progress, the statement is true with "employee" interpreted as "effective employee."

inflation, by increasing the real cost of holding money balances, encourages households to economize on real money balances and therefore to devote a larger share of their wealth to real capital formation. The importance of this substitution effect depends on the size of the stock of "outside money" (i.e., money that does not represent a liability of any private entity) relative to total wealth and on the elasticity of money demand with respect to the nominal rate of interest. The monetary base, a reasonable measure of the stock of outside money,[22] was only $160 billion in 1980 or less than 3 percent of the total stock of private wealth. Since all estimates of the interest elasticity of money demand are substantially less than one, it is clear that even major changes in the nominal rate of interest would have very little effect on the fraction of savings devoted to real capital formation. I shall therefore ignore the interest elasticity of demand completely and write the demand for real money balances per employee (m) as a constant fraction (μ) of the corresponding real capital assets:

$$(8) \qquad m = \mu(k + h)$$

6.1.4 Public and Private Consumption

The government consumes a fraction (γ) of real national income and households consume a fraction $(1 - \sigma)$ of real disposable income. National income consists of the output of the business sector plus the output of the owner-occupied housing sector.[23] To combine these two products, I assume a constant relative price of housing services, that is, an implicit rental of ρ per unit of housing capital; national income per employee is thus $y + \rho h$.[24] Real government spending per employee is

$$(9) \qquad g = \gamma\,(y + \rho h)$$

Disposable income may be defined as national income minus both taxes paid (t) and the loss in real money balances caused by inflation (πm).[25] Thus consumption per employee is

---

22. It would be wrong to include in the measure of outside money any interest-bearing government debt since the market interest rate would adjust with inflation. Tobin's procedure of combining money and government debt is therefore misleading; see Feldstein (1980c; chap. 5 above) for a model that distinguishes money, government debt, and private real capital.

23. This ignores the value of the services of the stock of money, an omission that has no qualitative effect on the results of this analysis.

24. The value of ρ is the initial rental price of housing services. A small change in the rental price changes real income to the extent that (a) it reallocates capital between h and k and (b) the marginal product of business capital differs from ρ. That is, the change in real income is $f'dk + \rho dh$. It would be incorrect to include a term of the form hdr in evaluating the change in real income since dr represents either a change in the implicit price that individuals pay themselves on housing or a change in the tax consequences of homeownership that would merely be offset by a change in other taxes.

25. Taxes include the taxes on capital income from corporations and industries and an additional nondistorting tax. Changes in tax revenue that result from changes in inflation are

(10) $$c = (1 - \sigma)(y + \rho h - t - \pi m)$$

Since the government deficit equals the increase in the stock of money balances, that is $g - t = (\pi + n)m$, equation (10) can be rewritten:

(11) $$c = (1 - \sigma)(y + \rho h - g + nm)$$

This formulation, which is essentially due to Tobin (1965), assumes that households regard their increase in real balances as a component of disposable income even though the real resources available to households (i.e., the maximum feasible consumption) are only $y + \rho h - g$.[26] The amount that households save, including the amount that is saved in the form of increased real money balances, is therefore

(12) $$s = \sigma(y + \rho h - g + nm)$$

or, using (9) to substitute for g,

(13) $$s = \sigma[(1 - \gamma)(y + \rho h) + nm]$$

6.1.5 Growth Equilibrium

Real savings per employee are divided into the increase of real business capital per employee ($\dot{K}/N$), the increase of real housing capital per employee ($\dot{H}/N$), and the increase of real money balances per employee ($(\dot{M}/p)/N$). Denoting total real wealth by A and total real wealth per employee by a, we have

(14) $$s = \frac{\dot{A}}{N} = \frac{\dot{K}}{N} + \frac{\dot{H}}{N} + \frac{(\dot{M}/p)}{N}$$
$$= \frac{\dot{K}}{K}k + \frac{\dot{H}}{H}h + \frac{(\dot{M}/p)}{M/p}m$$

In steady-state equilibrium, all three stocks grow at the same rate as the population, implying that

(15) $$s = na = n(k + h + m)$$

Combining (13) and (15) gives the basic equation of growth equilibrium:

(16) $$\sigma[(1 - \gamma)(y + \rho h) + nm] = n[k + h + m]$$

Using (8) to substitute for m, (6) to substitute for h, and (1) to substitute for y, equation (16) can be rewritten

(17) $$\sigma[(1 - \gamma)(f + \rho\phi) + n\mu(k + \phi)] = n[k + \phi + \mu(k + \phi)]$$

---

offset by changes in the nondistorting tax to keep total tax revenue unchanged. If the offsetting change in other sources of tax revenue were in a distortionary tax, the effect of inflation on real income would be more complex than the current analysis indicates. See Feldstein (1976, chap. 3 above) for a discussion of this issue.

26. Ignoring nm in (11) or πm in (10) would not change any of the qualitative results.

Recall that ϕ is a function of r and that equation (5) shows this implicit rental price to be $r = (1 - \theta)i + z - \pi$. Equation (4) shows that the households' real net interest rate is given by $(1 - \theta)i - \pi = (1 - \theta)f' + x\pi$ where $x = [\tau - \theta - (1 - \theta)\tau\lambda]/(1 - \tau)$. Thus

(18) $\phi = \phi[(1 - \theta)f' + x\pi + z]$

If (18) is used to substitute for ϕ in (17), it provides an equation that determines the stock of business capital as a function of the inflation rate and the tax rules.

6.1.6   Disequilibrium Adjustments

The next section uses equations (17) and (18) to examine the equilibrium effects of changes in the rate of inflation and the tax rules. The complex expressions that result are readily interpreted in terms of the disequilibrium adjustments of the capital stock. This permits determining the directions of equilibrium change without having to specify numerical values for individual parameters.

Two very plausible disequilibrium adjustment assumptions will be made. The first is labelled the "net adjustment assumption": an increase in either type of capital stock per employee above its equilibrium value causes total wealth per employee to decline:

(19) $\dfrac{d\dot{a}}{dk} < 0$

and

(20) $\dfrac{d\dot{a}}{dh} < 0$

Equation (19) is satisfied if, when k exceeds its equilibrium value, k falls and the other types of wealth (housing plus real money balances) do not increase by an even greater amount. A similar interpretation holds for equation (20).

The second assumption is labelled the "partial adjustment assumption": when the stock of business capital per employee exceeds its equilibrium value, the total wealth per employee will decline even if housing wealth per employee is held constant:

(21) $\left.\dfrac{\partial\dot{a}}{\partial k}\right|_h < 0$

Since the fall in k is likely to raise the housing stock, holding housing constant should make it easier to satisfy the condition that a positive perturbation of k causes total wealth to decline. In this sense, equation (21) is a weaker assumption than (19) and (20).

6.2   Effects of Changes in Inflation

We are now in a position to examine the effect of inflation on the capital intensity of the business sector, on the consumption of housing services, and on the real net return to savers. Before beginning the formal derivations, it is useful to consider the general logic of the process.

A higher rate of inflation reduces the after-tax profitability of investment because the tax accounting procedures for dealing with depreciation and inventories raise the effective tax rate. This lower after-tax profitability means that firms can pay only a lower real net rate of return to the creditors who supply their capital.

The net return to the suppliers of business capital is also affected by the fact that firms deduct *nominal* interest payments and that lenders pay tax on *nominal* interest receipts. This matters, however, only to the extent that the tax rates of borrowers and lenders are different.

On balance, inflation lowers the real net rate of return and therefore reduces the implicit rental cost of housing. This in turn raises the consumption of housing services relative to the output of other goods. The present section will now show explicitly that this reduces the equilibrium amount of business capital per employee and therefore the productivity of the labor force. The decrease in productivity and the reallocation of production to housing also lowers the real income per capita.[27]

Substituting equation (18) into (17) and totally differentiating with respect to k and π yields:

$$(22) \qquad Q_1 dk + Q_2 \phi' x d\pi = 0$$

and thus

$$(23) \qquad \frac{dk}{d\pi} = - \frac{Q_2 \phi' x}{Q_1}$$

where the expressions for Q_1 and Q_2, derived in the appendix, are shown to satisfy $Q_1 = d\dot{a}/dk$ and $Q_2 = d\dot{a}/dh$. From equations (19) and (20) we have $Q_1 < 0$ and $Q_2 < 0$. Consequently, since $\phi' < 0$, the sign of $dk/d\pi$ is the same as the sign of $x = [\tau - \theta - (1 - \theta)\tau\lambda]/1 - \tau$. As I noted above, with realistic values of λ and τ, $x < 0$ for any $\theta > 0.30$ and therefore $dk/d\pi < 0$.

Since a higher rate of inflation unambiguously reduces the real equilibrium capital intensity of the business sector, it increases the pretax real rate of return (f'). The net-of-tax real rate of return and the rental cost of housing nevertheless declines. To see this, note that since $(1 - \theta)i - \pi = (1 - \theta)f' + \pi x$,

---

27. Although the analysis takes the saving rate (σ) as fixed, the reduction in the real net rate of return implies that the saving rate in a more general model would probably also be reduced, thereby further decreasing the capital intensity of production.

(24)
$$\frac{d[(1-\theta)i-\pi]}{d\pi} = \frac{d[(1-\theta)f'+\pi x]}{d\pi}$$

$$= (1-\theta)f''\frac{dk}{d\pi} + x$$

Since f'', $dk/d\pi$, and x are all negative, it seems at first as if the effect of inflation on the real net return is ambiguous. However, substituting (23) for $dk/d\pi$ yields

(25)
$$\frac{d[(1-\theta)i-\pi]}{d\pi} = [Q_1 - (1-\theta)f''\phi' Q_2]x/Q_1$$

Using the expressions for Q_1 and Q_2 in the appendix gives

(26)
$$\frac{d[(1-\theta)i-\pi]}{d\pi} = [\sigma(1-\gamma)f' + \sigma n \mu - n(1+\mu)]x/Q_1$$

Since both x and Q_1 are negative, the sign of $d[(1-\theta)i-\pi]/d\pi$ is the same as the sign of

(27)
$$Q_3 = \sigma(1-\gamma)f' + \sigma n \mu - n(1+\mu).$$

The appendix shows that $Q_3 = \partial \dot{a}/\partial k \mid h$. The partial adjustment assumption implies $Q_3 < 0$ and therefore, from equation (26) $d[(1-\theta)i-\pi]/d\pi < 0$.[28]

Since the demand for housing is a function of the real interest rate, an increase in inflation unambiguously increases the equilibrium stock of housing capital:[29]

(28)
$$\frac{dh}{d\pi} = \phi'\frac{dr}{d\pi}$$

$$= \phi'\frac{d[(1-\theta)i - \pi + z]}{d\pi}$$

$$= \frac{\phi' Q_3 x}{Q_1} > 0$$

Since all four terms are negative, $dh/d\pi > 0$.

---

28. An alternative suggested by Pentti Kouri is a model in which saving is optimized in a Ramsey model by invididuals who live forever. In this case, the real net rate of return, $(1-\theta)i - \pi$, is fixed. This in turn means that r and therefore h are not influenced by inflation. It follows, however, from equation (4) that f' must rise to keep the right-hand side constant; since $f'' < 0$, $dk/d\pi < 0$. In words, to earn the same real net return when inflation raises the effective tax rate, the pretax return would have to increase and therefore the business capital stock would have to decrease.

29. Note again that, to the extent that housing is also a function of real income and real income declines, this will partially offset the value of $dh/d\pi$ derived in equation (28).

The final effect of inflation that I wish to examine is on total real income, $y + \rho h$. If the initial allocation of capital between business and housing were optimal, a small increase in inflation would leave real income unchanged; since any small change from an optimum involves no loss to a first order approximation. But if taxes and inflation make the initial condition suboptimal, the reallocation of capital caused by an increase in inflation will have a first-order effect on real income. More specifically, the very favorable tax treatment of owner-occupied housing implies that even in the absence of inflation the real return to marginal housing capital (ρ) is less than the return to business capital (f'). A positive inflation rate widens the gap. This implies that a reallocation of capital from the business sector causes a loss of real income. More formally the change in real income induced by an inflation-induced change in the allocation of capital is

$$(29) \qquad \frac{d(y + \rho h)}{d\pi} = f'\frac{dk}{d\pi} + \rho\frac{dh}{d\pi}$$

Substituting from (23) and (28) implies

$$(30) \qquad \frac{d(y + \rho h)}{d\pi} = (\rho Q_3 - f'Q_2)\frac{\phi'x}{Q_1}$$

Substituting for Q_2 and Q_3 from the appendix yields,

$$\frac{d(y + \rho h)}{d\pi} = [\rho(\sigma(1 - \gamma)f' + \sigma n\mu - n(1 + \mu))$$

$$- f'(\sigma(1 - \gamma)\rho + \sigma n\mu$$

$$(31) \qquad - n(1 + \mu))]\phi'x/Q_1$$

$$= (f' - \rho)n[1 + (1 - \sigma)\mu]\phi'x/Q_1$$

Thus with $f' > \rho$, real income falls since $\phi' < 0$, $x < 0$ and $Q_1 < 0$.

6.3 Indexing the Tax Rules

Inflation causes a misallocation of capital between the business and housing sectors because the tax laws mismeasure capital income and expenses. A complete indexing of the tax laws would eliminate this source of the distortion caused by inflation. Complete indexing has three aspects: (1) eliminating the mismeasurement of depreciation and inventory profits that causes business operating profits to be overstated; (2) limiting the deductions for business interest to real interest payments only; and (3) limiting the taxation of household interest income and expenses to the real interest rate. This section shows the neutrality of

inflation when all three of the features are present and examines nonneutrality when there is only partial indexing.[30]

Consider a general tax-indexing rule under which firms pay tax at rate
τ_1 on operating profits net of real interest expenses but deduct the
inflation component against their tax liability at rate τ_2; under existing law
$\tau_1 = \tau_2$ while with complete indexing $\tau_2 = 0$. With these rules, the firms'
equilibrium condition (analogous to equation 2) is

$$(32) \qquad (1 - \tau_1)f' + (1 - \tau_1\lambda)\pi = i - \tau_1(i - \pi) - \tau_2\pi$$

If households are taxed on real interest receipts at rate θ_1 and on the
inflation component of interest payments at rate θ_2, the real net rate of
interest is $i - \theta_1(i - \pi) - \theta_2\pi - \pi = (1 - \theta_1)i + (\theta_1 - \theta_2)\pi - \pi$. Since
the implicit rental cost of housing is the real net rate of interest plus the
"other costs per unit of housing capital" (z), the rental cost of housing is

$$(33) \qquad r = (1 - \theta_1)i + (\theta_1 - \theta_2)\pi - \pi + z$$

and, using (32) to eliminate i,

$$(34) \qquad r = (1 - \theta_1)f' + \frac{1 - \theta_1}{1 - \tau_1}(1 - \tau_1\lambda)\pi - \frac{1 - \theta_1}{1 - \tau_1}(\tau_1 - \tau_2)\pi$$
$$+ (\theta_1 - \theta_2)\pi - \pi + z$$

When there is no indexing ($\tau_1 = \tau_2$ and $\theta_1 = \theta_2$), equation (34) reduces to
the same implicit rental cost that has already been analyzed. With com-
plete indexing ($\theta_2 = \tau_2 = \lambda = 0$), equation (34) reduces to

$$(35) \qquad r = (1 - \theta_1)f' + z$$

Here the implicit rental price is independent of inflation.[31]

It is sometimes proposed that the elimination of historic cost depreciation be coupled with limiting the business interest deduction to the real
cost of funds. In terms of equation (34), this implies $\lambda = \tau_2 = 0$ but $\theta_1 = \theta_2$. The resulting implicit rental cost of housing is then:

$$(36) \qquad r = (1 - \theta)f' + z + \left[\frac{1 - \theta}{1 - \tau_1} - \frac{1 - \theta}{1 - \tau_1}\tau_1 - 1\right]\pi$$
$$r = (1 - \theta)f' + z - (1 - \tau_1)\theta\pi$$

---

30. These three forms of indexing are discussed in Feldstein, Green, and Sheshinski
(1978, chap. 4 above), but there is no housing sector in that model and all of the distortions
are in financial returns.

31. The allocation of capital still favors housing because the net services of housing are
not taxed while interest income is taxable and the mortgage interest payments are deductible ($\theta_1 > 0$), but this is a separate matter.

An increase in inflation reduces the implicit rental cost because the firm is denied a deduction for the inflation premium in the interest rate but the household pays tax on that premium. An increase in the rate of inflation thus reduces the real net return to households on business capital and thereby lowers the cost of funds that enters the housing rental cost. Thus a partial indexing approach that focuses only on the firm may exacerbate the bias in favor of housing that is caused by inflation and clearly does not leave an inflation-neutral allocation of capital. More specifically, comparing (36) with (18) shows that the partial indexing rule causes a lower value of r than the existing unindexed tax law if $(1 - \tau_1)\theta > -x$; with $\tau = 0.46$ and $\lambda = 0.5$, this is satisfied for all values of $\theta < 0.48$.[32]

Most countries have dealt with inflation by accelerating the rate of depreciation used for calculating taxable profits but without changing the tax treatment of interest income and expenses. Accelerating depreciation has two distinct effects. First, at any rate of inflation (including zero), this lowers the effective tax rate on operating profits. In the notation of equation (32), it is equivalent to increasing f'; note that it is not equivalent to lowering τ_1 since that would also affect the tax treatment of interest. Second, more rapid depreciation reduces the sensitivity of the tax to the rate of inflation, i.e., it lowers λ. To see the effects of these changes on the implicit rental cost of housing, set $\tau_2 = \tau_1$ and $\theta_2 = \theta_1$ in equation (34) and evaluate the total differential of r with respect to f' and λ:

$$(37) \qquad dr = (1 - \theta)df' - \frac{(1 - \theta)}{(1 - \tau)} \tau\pi d\lambda$$

The decrease in λ raises the implicit rental cost of housing since it reduces the excess tax on business capital caused by historic cost accounting methods. Similarly the rise in f' raises the return on business investment and thus directly increases the implicit rental cost of owner-occupied housing. Although full indexing avoids all of the tax-induced distortions associated with inflation, any specific acceleration of depreciation can achieve the same effect only for one particular rate of inflation.

6.4   Conclusion

It is ironic that an easy money policy aimed at stimulating investment in plant and equipment is likely to have just the opposite effect: reducing the long-run capital intensity of production. Whatever the short-run virtue of expansionary policies, the long-run consequence of inflation under existing U.S. tax laws is to reduce investors' demand for business capital and to increase it for owner-occupied housing.

32. Note that correcting the depreciation and inventory rules (i.e., making $\lambda = 0$) is sufficient to achieve inflation neutrality if $\tau = \theta$.

The simple model developed in this paper shows more generally how the expectation of further inflation of the sort that resulted from the inflationary experience of the 1960s and 1970s can have very substantial effects on the real economy. The notion that a fully anticipated monetary expansion or inflation has no effect on the real economy is not plausible in a modern economy with a complex set of tax rules. The specific effect of inflation will, moreover, vary from country to country and from time to time as a function of the particular features of the country's fiscal structure.

It would be useful to extend the current analysis in a variety of ways. Of particular interest would be replacing the debt-only assumption of corporate finance with a mixture of debt and equity. This would bring out the more limited significance of the corporate deductibility of nominal interest payments and would show the relevance of the taxation of nominal capital gains. A further (or alternative) extension to include interest-bearing government debt as well as money would permit the government to vary the real interest rate through its debt management policy and would show the effect of inflation on residential investment when low-risk government debt is an alternative asset. Finally, since the analysis here is limited to U.S. tax rules, it would be quite interesting to see it altered to describe the tax rules of other countries and used to analyze the effect of inflation in these settings.

The present model, either in its current form or with the extensions described above, could be the basis for a more explicit dynamic analysis of the transition path when the expected rate of inflation changes. This in turn would provide a sounder foundation for the empirical analysis of the effect of inflation on the accumulation of residential and nonresidential capital.

6.5 Appendix

This appendix discusses the relation of Q_1, Q_2, and Q_3 of section 6.2 to the disequilibrium adjustment process.

Combining equations (13) and (14) yields

$$(38) \qquad \sigma[(1 - \gamma)(y + \rho h) + nm] = \frac{\dot{A}}{N}$$

It follows directly from differentiating a with respect to time that

$$(39) \qquad \frac{\dot{A}}{N} = \dot{a} + na$$

Thus (38) can be rewritten

$$(40) \qquad \sigma[(1 - \gamma)(y + \rho h) + nm] = na + \dot{a}$$

Along a balanced growth path, $\dot{a} = \dot{k} = \dot{h} = \dot{m} = 0$. This condition was imposed for the analysis in the text. But when k, h or m are not at their equilibrium values, these ratios will change to bring about equilibrium.

By substituting $h = \phi$ and $m = \mu(k + h)$, equation (40) can be rewritten:

$$(41) \qquad \sigma[(1 - \gamma)(f + \rho\phi) + n\mu(k + \phi)] - n(1 + \mu)(k + \phi) = \dot{a}$$

Taking the derivative of both sides with respect to k yields:

$$(42) \qquad Q_1 = \sigma(1 - \gamma)f' + \sigma n\mu - n(1 + \mu)$$
$$+ (\sigma[(1 - \gamma)\rho + n\mu] - n(1 + \mu))\phi'(1 - \theta)f''$$
$$= d\dot{a}/dk.$$

Similarly the derivative of (41) with respect to h yields

$$(43) \qquad Q_2 = \sigma[(1 - \gamma)\rho + n\mu] - n(1 + \mu) = d\dot{a}/dh$$

The net adjustment assumptions (19 and 20) imply directly that $Q_1 < 0$ and $Q_2 < 0$.

To derive the interpretation of Q_3 of equation (27), take the partial derivative of both sides of equation (41) with respect to k holding h (i.e., ϕ) constant:

$$(44) \qquad Q_3 = \sigma[(1 - \gamma)f' + n\mu - n(1 + \mu)] = \left.\frac{\partial\dot{a}}{\partial k}\right|_h$$

II   Inflation and Effective Tax Rates

7   Inflation and the Excess Taxation of Capital Gains on Corporate Stock

With Joel Slemrod

Inflation distorts all aspects of the taxation of personal income but is particularly harsh on the taxation of capital gains. When corporate stock or any other asset is sold, current law requires that a capital gains tax be paid on the entire difference between the selling price and the original cost even though much of that nominal gain only offsets a general rise in the prices of consumer goods and services. Taxing *nominal* gains in this way very substantially increases the effective tax rate on *real* price-adjusted capital gains. Indeed, many individuals pay a substantial capital gains tax even though, when adjustment is made for the change in the price level, they actually receive less from their sale than they had originally paid.

The present study shows that in 1973 individuals paid nearly $500 million of extra tax on corporate stock capital gains because of the distorting effect of inflation. The detailed evidence presented below shows that this distortion is greatest for middle income sellers of corporate stocks.

More specifically, in 1973 individuals paid capital gains tax on more than $4.5 billion of nominal capital gains on corporate stock. If the costs of these shares are adjusted for the increases in the consumer price level since they were purchased, the $4.5 billion nominal gain becomes a real capital loss of nearly $1 billion. As a result of this incorrect measurement of capital gains, individuals with similar real capital gains were subject to very different total tax liabilities.

Reprinted by permission from *National Tax Journal* 31 (June 1979): 107–18.

This study is part of the NBER program of research on business taxation and finance. We are grateful to Daniel Frisch, Sy Rottenberg, and Shlomo Yitzhaki for helpful discussions, to the U.S. Treasury for providing the data, and to the National Science Foundation for financial support.

These findings are based on a new body of official tax return data on individual sales of corporate stock. The first section of the paper describes the data and the method of analysis. The basic results are presented in section 7.2 Section 7.3 analyzes the extent to which equal real gains are taxed unequally under current rules. Several alternatives to the current law are then examined in detail. A final section examines how a permanent inflation rate of 6 percent would quadruple the effective rate of tax on capital gains.[1]

7.1   The Data and Estimation Method

Each year the Treasury Department and the Internal Revenue Service select a large scientific sample of tax returns with which to study various aspects of income sources and tax liabilities. In order to provide adequate information on high income taxpayers, the sample contains a much larger fraction of high income returns than of low and middle income returns. Since the sampling rates are known, the sample can be used to construct accurate estimates for the entire population.

In 1973, the information collected for the annual sample of tax returns was extended in a special study to include detailed data on capital asset transactions. The complete record on each sale of a capital asset (as recorded in Schedule D of Form 1040) was combined with the other information from that taxpayer's return. In the current study, we consider only the sales of corporate stock. Our sample consists of information for 30,063 individuals and 234,974 individual corporate stock sales in 1973.[2]

We supplemented the record for each transaction by calculating a price-indexed capital gain. More specifically, we multiplied the acquisition price of the stock by the ratio calculated by dividing the consumer price index (CPI) for 1973 by the CPI for the year of purchase. This has the effect of restating the cost of the stock in 1973 dollars. Substracting this price-indexed cost from the amount for which the stock was sold in 1973 yields a correct real capital gain in 1973 dollars. Since the CPI was higher in 1973 than in any previous year, the real capital gain is less than

1. For previous discussions of the taxation of capital gains in an inflationary economy see Brinner (1973, 1976) and Diamond (1975). The theory of the effect of income taxation in an inflationary economy, including the tax treatment of interest and capital gains, is developed in Feldstein, Green, and Sheshinski (1978; see chap. 4 above).

2. In a relatively small number of transactions, there is a discrepancy between the reported gain or loss and the difference between the reported purchase and sale prices. These nonmatching transactions were dropped from our sample, reducing the total capital gain on corporate stock from $5.01 billion to $4.63 billion. Our sample also excludes transactions in which the taxpayer did not specify the asset type and transactions recorded on partnership and fiduciary returns. Our estimate of the excess tax paid because of inflation is therefore an underestimate of the true value.

the nominal gain for all regular sales and greater than the nominal gain for all short sales.

Of the $4.63 billion in nominal capital gains, transactions representing $1.79 billion do not have a correctly coded year of purchase, presumably because the taxpayer failed to provide this information on his tax return. In order to calculate the price-adjusted cost of these stocks, we estimated the year of purchase by using the adjusted gross income (AGI) of the taxpayer and the ratio of the selling price to the original cost of the transaction. More specifically, all of the transactions for which we have correctly coded years of purchase were classified into one of eight AGI groups and one of 25 classes of the ratio of selling price to original cost. For each of these 200 categories, the average holding period was calculated. This average holding period was then applied to each of the transactions that had no purchase data on the basis of the taxpayer's AGI and the transaction's ratio of sale price to purchase price. When the holding period predicted in this way involved a fraction of a year, the price index was interpolated between the two bordering years' indices.[3]

To assess the excess tax that resulted from the mismeasuring of the capital gains, we must calculate the tax liability that individuals incurred in 1973 on their nominal capital gain and the liability that they would have incurred if the real capital gain had been included instead. To do this we use a special computer program that incorporates the relevant features of the income tax law as of 1973 and that calculates each individual's total tax liability for different measures of the capital gain.[4] Comparing the total tax liability based on the *nominal* capital gain (or loss) as recorded for 1973 with the liability if there were *no* gain (or loss) on corporate stocks provides the value for each individual of the actual capital gains tax on nominal gains. Similarly, comparing the total tax liability with the *real* capital gain for 1973 as described above with the liability if there were no gain provides the value for each individual of the capital gains tax on real gains. These tax calculations distinguish short-term and long-term capital gains in the usual way.

All calculations are done using the provision of the law of 1973 that limited the loss to be charged against current income to $1,000. Because using a real capital gains measure makes capital losses much more com-

---

3. Although there is no reason to believe that our procedure introduces any bias in the calculation of the excess tax, there is no way to test this directly. As a partial test of our method, the real gains of the transactions with known purchase dates were calculated using the predicted holding period rather than the actual. The resulting distribution of real gains is very similar to the actual real gains. To the extent that the transactions with purchase year missing are similar to those with a correctly coded date, our procedure will accurately approximate the real gain.

4. The program includes such features as the alternative tax, the preference tax, and the limit on tax losses as well as full information on each individual's income, deductions, etc. This TAXSIM program is described and used in Feldstein and Frisch (1977).

mon than they now appear to be, we also show the effect of removing the loss limitation. Several other changes in the tax law were also studied and will be described below.[5]

7.2 The Excess Tax on Capital Gains

The current practice of taxing nominal capital gains resulted in a tax liability of $1,138 million on the sales of corporate stock in 1973.[6] If capital gains were measured instead in real terms, the tax liability would only have been $661 million.[7] The excess tax was thus $477 million, an increase of more than 70 percent. If the current limit on deducting capital losses were also eliminated, the tax on real capital gains would only have been $117 million.

Table 7.1 shows the detailed calculations by income class that underlie these total figures. The first row presents the net capital gain as defined by the current law. For each of the eight adjusted gross income (AGI) classes, the net capital gain figure is the weighted sum of all of the individual net capital gains of taxpayers in the AGI class; the weights reflect the sampling probabilities, making our total figure a valid estimate of the total net capital gain for all taxpayers in that class.[8] Note that the current law's nominal measure of the capital gains implies that there is a positive net gain in each income class. The sum of these gains is $4.63 billion.

Row 2 presents the corresponding *real* net capital gains. This adjustment for the rise in the price level changes the $4.63 billion nominal gain into a $910 million real loss. Although adjusting for the price change reduces the gain at every income level, the effect of the price level correction is far from uniform. For taxpayers with AGI's below $100,000, the price adjustment indicates that real capital gains were negative. This group had $1.27 billion of nominal capital gains but, after adjusting for the rise in consumer prices, had a real capital loss of $3.31 billion. In

---

5. Because of the new Treasury data, our method represents a substantial improvement over the estimation procedure used by Brinner (1976). He worked with published data on capital gains in 1962 and did not have adequate measures of individual marginal tax rates on capital gains. Moreover, 1962 came after a period of relative price stability; the CPI rose at an average annual rate of less than 1.3 percent during the previous decade. Brinner was, of course, careful to warn his readers of these limitations.

6. Recall that our sample excludes sales in partnership and trusts and omits a small fraction of sales in which the reported gain or loss did not correspond exactly to the difference between selling price and original basis.

7. This calculation and all other calculations used here are based on the actual stock sales in 1973. Changing the law to tax only real capital gains would, of course, increase the amount of stock that is sold. On the sensitivity of common stock sales to the taxation of capital gains, see Feldstein and Yitzhaki (1978) and Feldstein, Slemrod, and Yitzhaki (1980).

8. See footnote 6 above.

Table 7.1 Capital Gains and Associated Tax Liabilities

				Adjusted Gross Income Class				
	Less than Zero	Zero to $10,000	$10,000 to $20,000	$20,000 to $50,000	$50,000 to $100,000	$100,000 to $200,000	$200,000 to $500,000	More than $500,000	All
					(millions of dollars)				
1. Nominal capital gains	86	77	21	369	719	942	1135	1280	4629
2. Real capital gains	−15	−726	−895	−1420	−255	437	839	1125	−910
3. Tax on nominal capital gains	1	−5	23	80	159	215	291	374	1138
4. Tax on real capital gains	0	−25	−34	−52	58	141	235	337	661
5. Tax on nominal capital gains, no loss limit	0	−7	−6	−31	91	191	288	372	897
6. Tax on real capital gains, no loss limit	−1	−38	−94	−259	−97	72	209	325	117
7. Total tax liability, those with corporate stock capital gain	10	224	1556	5492	3986	2467	1582	1133	16450
8. Total tax liability, all individuals	16	15490	40895	32275	10367	4922	2480	1638	108084

Note: All figures relate to capital gains on corporate stock sold in 1973.

contrast, taxpayers with AGI's above $100,000 had nominal gains of $3.36 billion and real gains of $2.40 billion.

The tax liabilities corresponding to these two measures of capital gains are compared in rows 3 and 4. In calculating these tax liabilities, individual losses are subject to the limit of $1,000. In each AGI class up to $50,000, recognizing real gains makes the tax liability negative. At higher income levels, tax liabilities are reduced but remain positive on average; the extent of the current excess tax—both absolutely and relatively—decreases with income. Thus taxpayers with AGI's between $50,000 and $100,000 paid an excess tax of $101 million or nearly three times the appropriate tax on their real capital gains. By contrast, taxpayers with AGI's over $500,000 paid an excess tax of $37 million or only 11 percent more than the tax on their real capital gains. This pattern of capital gains and of tax liabilities shows why the total tax on real capital gains remains positive even though total real capital gains are negative.

The substantial real capital losses for taxpayers with AGI's below $100,000 that are shown in row 2 suggest that the limit on the deductibility of capital losses has a substantial effect on tax liabilities when capital gains are measured in real terms. Lines 5 and 6 show the tax liabilities corresponding to nominal and real capital gains if the loss limitation is disregarded.[9] For nominal capital gains there is only a modest difference since the general rise in prices substantially reduces losses. The total tax liability is reduced from $1.14 billion to $0.90 billion, with almost all of the difference in the liabilities of taxpayers with AGI's between $20,000 and $100,000. By contrast, with real capital gains the current loss limit raises tax liabilities by $544 million or more than 80% of the $661 million tax liability.

The importance of the current excess taxation of capital gains can be seen by comparing the excess tax with the total tax liabilities shown in rows 7 and 8. Row 7 shows the total tax liabilities for taxpayers who had any capital gain or loss on corporate stock. The excess tax liability can thus be compared with the total liability for the same groups of individuals. With the current loss limitation retained, this excess tax is roughly constant as a percentage of total tax for all groups with AGI's over $20,000. For example, individuals with AGI's between $20,000 and $50,000 paid $132 million in excess tax or 2.4 percent of their total tax liability of $5.49 billion. For individuals with AGI's between $100,000 and $200,000, the extra tax is $74 million or 3.0 percent of their total tax of $2.47 billion. A maximum of 3.3 percent occurs for those with AGI's over $500,000.

---

9. Recall that we are looking only at the stocks actually sold in 1973. Allowing unlimited deduction for losses would induce more sales of stocks with accrued losses. Our estimates should be interpreted as the extent of overtaxation of the stocks actually sold rather than as estimates of the effect of changing the law to remove the limit.

7.3 Taxing Equal Gains Unequally

The mismeasurement of capital gains does more than raise the effective tax rate on real capital gains. It also introduces an arbitrary randomness in the taxing of capital gains. Two individuals with the same real capital gain can pay tax on very different nominal gains. This section presents striking evidence that equal real capital gains are taxed unequally to a very substantial extent.

Table 7.2 compares the tax liability that would be due on real capital gains with the tax liability that was actually assessed on nominal gains.[10] There is very substantial variation among individuals in the ratio of the tax liability on real gains to the liability on nominal gains. Consider, for example, the taxpayers with adjusted gross incomes between $20,000 and $50,000. Only 26.5 percent of the actual tax liability on nominal gains was incurred by taxpayers whose liabilities on real gains were between 90 percent and 100 percent of these nominal liabilities. An additional 18.4 percent of the actual tax liability was incurred by taxpayers whose liabilities on real gains would have been between 80 and 90 percent of their actual liabilities. The remaining 55 percent of actual tax liabilities were incurred by individuals whose liabilities on real gains would have been less than 80 percent of their actual statutory liabilities.

The disparities are even greater for taxpayers with lower AGI. Among those with AGI's between $10,000 and $20,000, 27 percent of actual liabilities were incurred by taxpayers whose liabilities on real capital gains were less than 40 percent of their actual statutory liabilities while an equally large amount (28.4 percent) of liabilities were incurred by taxpayers whose liabilities on real gains would have been nearly as large as their liabilities on nominal gains.

Table 7.3 shows this pattern of unequal taxation of real capital gains in a different way. This table shows the numbers of taxpayers at each level of liability on real capital gains who pay quite different amounts on nominal gain.[11] Thus, more than 220,000 of the taxpayers with real capital losses paid tax on nominal capital gains. Within this group, more than 3,000 paid capital gain taxes of over $2,000 and nearly 1,000 paid taxes of over $5,000. Similarly, among taxpayers who had real gains but with corresponding tax liabilities of less than $1,000, more than 40,000 paid tax liabilities of more than $1,000 and nearly 1,000 paid tax liabilities of more than $5,000.

The same sense of substantial and arbitrary randomness is evident if we look at the rows of the table. For example, if we look at the 3,355

---

10. We have considered here only those returns with a positive nominal gain so as to avoid ambiguity in interpreting the sign of the ratios.

11. Our calculation ignores the small number of taxpayers whose short sales meant that their nominal gain would actually be less than their real gain.

Table 7.2 Distribution of Actual Tax Liabilities by Tax Liability on Real Gains as a Percentage of Tax Liability on Nominal Gains

Tax Liability on Real Gains as Percentage of Tax Liability on Nominal Gains	Adjusted Gross Income (thousands of dollars)							
	0-10	10-20	20-50	50-100	100-200	200-500	500+	All Taxpayers
Less than 0	13.5	11.0	6.1	5.6	2.5	1.1	0.3	3.4
0	21.7	8.8	3.8	4.1	1.6	1.1	0.4	2.6
10%	0.8	1.7	0.8	1.3	1.0	0.4	0.1	0.7
20%	1.6	0.8	1.7	2.1	1.8	0.8	0.8	1.3
30%	3.8	4.5	5.0	4.1	1.7	1.2	0.3	2.4
40%	9.0	9.3	2.0	3.6	2.3	1.7	1.1	2.5
50%	9.7	5.3	4.4	3.4	3.5	2.5	0.6	2.9
60%	8.5	5.1	17.1	6.2	7.0	4.1	2.0	6.7
70%	2.3	9.2	14.1	12.9	11.7	8.5	3.9	9.6
80%	16.0	16.0	18.4	20.3	18.6	16.2	11.2	16.4
90%	24.5	28.4	26.5	36.3	48.2	62.3	79.3	51.5

NOTE: Each entry is the percentage of the tax liability on the nominal capital gains as actually incurred by taxpayers in that AGI class. Computations consider only those returns which showed a positive nominal gain on corporate stock capital gains.

Table 7.3   Numbers of Taxpayers Classified by Tax Liabilities on Real Gains and Nominal Gains

Tax Liability on Nominal Capital Gains (thousands of Dollars)	Tax Liability on Real Capital Gains (thousands of dollars)									
	Negative	0–1	1–2	2–5	5–10	10–20	20–30	30–50	50–100	>100
Negative	1,281,463									
0–1	213,632	1,083,048								
1–2	7,416	33,820	36,055							
2–5	2,212	7,033	19,269	29,083						
5–10	708	477	753	8,038	11,453					
10–20	196	174	49	616	2,617	6,402				
20–30	54	34	127	40	208	1,049	1,843			
30–50	23	13	10	19	30	135	722	2,111		
50–100	12	9	4	5	6	13	42	359	1,804	
>100	1	5	0	1	0	2	3	19	234	1,810

NOTE: "Tax liability on nominal capital gains" is the actual 1973 liability. The "tax liability on real gains" is the corresponding liability if real gains were calculated by adjusting the basis for the change in the CPI.

taxpayers who incurred tax liabilities of $20,000 to $30,000, we find that 463 would have had liabilities of less than $10,000 on their real gains.

In short, the effect of taxing nominal gains rather than real gains is of very little significance for some taxpayers but involves a very substantial distortion for others.

7.4   Alternative Tax Rules

This section examines the implication of price indexing the basis of capital gains in combination with two other proposals that have been frequently advocated: (1) taxing all corporate stock capital gains like short-term capital gains, i.e., eliminating the alternative tax method and the current exclusion of one-half of long-term gain, and (2) limiting income tax rates to 50 percent on so-called "unearned income" as well as "earned income."[12] Again we limit our attention to the tax consequences for the stocks actually sold in 1973 and thus disregard the way in which portfolio selling would be altered by these tax changes.

The current treatment of capital gains could be modified in either of two different ways. First, the current method of excluding one-half of long-term capital gains and of allowing the alternative tax could be ended while still limiting the deductible losses to $1,000. Alternatively, the limit on loss deductibility could be suspended at the same time. Table 7.4 shows the effects of applying each of these rules to the corporate stock sales in 1973.

For convenience, the first four rows show the tax liabilities based on the current exclusion and alternative tax rules. The next four rows show the corresponding tax liabilities when the exclusion and alternative tax rules are eliminated. Simply eliminating these features while retaining the use of nominal gains and the loss limitation would have raised the tax liability from $1.14 billion (row 1) to $3.06 billion (row 5). Taxing only real gains but eliminating the exclusion and alternative tax would nearly double the 1973 tax liability from $1.14 billion to $2.20 billion (row 6). Only the combination of no loss limit and the taxation of real capital gains (row 8) would leave the total tax essentially unchanged at $1.19 billion. Note that the distribution of this tax burden would be very different from the actual 1973 tax liabilities: liabilities would almost double for those with AGI over $200,000 with offsetting falls for those with incomes under $100,000.

A maximum tax rate of 50 percent would have little effect if the current definition of taxable income is maintained. This is shown in rows 5 through 8 of Table 7.5. The standard results for the current law and for price-indexed capital gains are shown for comparison in rows 1 through 4. The combination of a 50 percent maximum rate and the elimination of the capital gains exclusion and alternative rate (rows 9 and 10) significantly

12. Tax rates can still be somewhat higher than this because of the minimum tax.

Table 7.4   Tax Liabilities When Capital Gains Are Taxed like Ordinary Income

	Less than Zero	Zero to $10,000	$10,000 to $20,000	$20,000 to $50,000	$50,000 to $100,000	$100,000 to $200,000	$200,000 to $500,000	More than $500,000	All
					(millions of dollars)				
1. Tax on nominal capital gains	1	−5	23	80	159	215	291	374	1138
2. Tax on real capital gains	−0	−25	−34	−52	58	141	235	337	661
3. Tax on nominal capital gains; no loss limit	−0	−7	−6	−31	91	191	288	372	897
4. Tax on real capital gains; no loss limit	−1	−38	−94	−259	−97	72	209	325	117
5. Tax on nominal capital gains with all gains treated as short-term gains	9	30	109	406	469	562	676	804	3065
6. Tax on real capital gains with all gains treated as short-term gains	6	−8	14	174	285	421	569	736	2196
7. Tax on nominal capital gains with all gains treated as short-term gains; no loss limit	7	19	44	183	340	514	665	799	2571
8. Tax on real capital gains with all gains treated as short-term gains; no loss limit	4	−38	−112	−216	14	302	523	715	1193

NOTE: All figures relate to capital gains on corporate stock sold in 1973.

Table 7.5   Tax Liabilities on Capital Gains When the Maximum Tax Rate Is 50 Percent

		Adjusted Gross Income Class						
	Less than Zero	Zero to $10,000	$10,000 to $20,000	$20,000 to $50,000	$50,000 to $100,000	$100,000 to $200,000	$200,000 to $500,000	More than $500,000	All
					(millions of dollars)				
1. Tax on nominal capital gains	1	−5	23	80	159	215	291	374	1138
2. Tax on real capital gains	0	−25	−34	−52	58	141	235	337	661
3. Tax on nominal capital gains; no loss limit	0	−7	−6	−31	91	191	288	372	897
4. Tax on real capital gains; no loss limit	−1	−38	−94	−259	−97	72	209	325	117
−Maximum Tax Rate of 50%									
5. Tax on nominal capital gains	2	−5	23	80	164	211	255	293	1022
6. Tax on real capital gains	1	−25	−34	−52	64	142	207	265	568

7. Tax on nominal capital gains; no loss limit	0	−7	−6	−31	99	190	252	292	789
8. Tax on real capital gains; no loss limit	−1	−38	−94	−258	−85	81	187	256	49
− Maximum Tax Rate of 50%									
− All capital gains treated like short-term gains									
9. Tax on nominal capital gains	7	29	109	402	453	494	537	584	2615
10. Tax on real capital gains	5	−9	13	171	276	374	455	535	1819
11. Tax on nominal capital gains; no loss limit	6	18	44	180	329	452	529	580	2137
12. Tax on real capital gains; no loss limit	3	−38	−112	−218	15	269	419	520	857

NOTE: All figures relate to capital gains on corporate stock sold in 1973.

raises total tax liabilities. Only if this is combined with the taxation of *real* gains and a full offset of losses is the total tax kept to its current level. Again, there is a substantial redistribution within this total.

7.5 Concluding Comments

The evidence presented in this paper shows that the taxation of capital gains is grossly distorted by inflation. In 1973, the tax paid on corporate stock capital gains was $1,138 million, nearly twice the $661 million liability on real capital gains. If the limit on the deduction of real capital losses is disregarded, the net tax liability falls to only $117 million. By this standard, nearly all of the tax paid on nominal capital gains represents an excess tax caused by inflation. Moreover, our current tax rules introduce an arbitrary randomness in the taxing of capital gains; with inflation, taxpayers with equal real capital gains are often required to pay tax on very different nominal gains.

The taxation of capital gains is distorted because, when there is inflation, our current tax rules mismeasure capital gains. Other aspects of capital income and expenses, primarily interest and depreciation, are also mismeasured in the presence of inflation. The taxation of capital income is therefore more severely distorted than the taxation of wages and salaries which are correctly measured. All types of personal income, including wages and salaries as well as capital income, are subjected to artificially high tax rates because of the progressivity of the tax structure but this "bracket rate effect" is small in relation to the distortions that result from mismeasurement.

Our estimates relate to 1973 because that is the only year for which data of the type that we have analyzed is available. There is, however, no reason to think that the tax distortion for 1973 was any greater than for other recent years. Indeed, since share prices were relatively high in 1973, the ratio of real capital gains to nominal gains would also be expected to be high. More generally, it is useful to consider the effect of our current tax law on an individual who invested twenty years ago in a diversified portfolio of common stock and sold this stock at the end of 1977. According to the Standard and Poor's Index, the price of such a portfolio approximately doubled between 1957 and 1977. However, the CPI also doubled in this twenty-year period, implying that there was no real increase in the value of the stocks.[13] If the investor pays a 25 percent tax on the nominal capital gain when the stock is sold in 1977, he will actually have *lost* about 13 percent in real terms on his investment over the twenty-year period.

13. The increase in both the Standard and Poor's Index and the CPI was actually between 115 percent and 120 percent.

The problem of excess taxation of capital gains when there is inflation is not peculiar to the past twenty years but is inherent in our current tax system. Unless this aspect of the tax law is changed, the problem will continue in the future. If we abstract from fluctuations in the price-earnings ratio, the effect of retained earnings should make the real value of common stock rise at about 2 percent a year.[14] If these accruing capital gains are taxed at an effective rate of 20 percent, the net after-tax yield is 1.6 percent a year. With a 6 percent steady rate of inflation and a constant price-earnings ratio, share prices would be expected to rise at 8 percent a year. This still leaves the same real before-tax increase of 2 percent that would occur without inflation.[15] But a 20 percent capital gains tax on the 8 percent nominal capital gain leaves an after-tax nominal gain of only 6.4 percent. After subtracting the 6 percent inflation, the real after-tax gain is only 0.4 percent. The effective tax on real capital gains is thus 80 percent when the inflation rate is 6 percent. An 8 percent rate of inflation would make the effective tax rate equal to 100 percent!

The distorting effect of inflation on the taxation of capital gains could be remedied by adjusting the original cost of assets for the rise in the general price level.[16] This would reduce the effective rates of tax on real capital gains and would thereby reduce the loss in economic welfare that results from such taxation of capital income.[17] Measuring capital gains in real terms would have the further advantage of reducing the penalty for switching assets which currently distorts investor behavior.

14. If we correct the measurement of retained earnings for the artificial depreciation and inventory figures, the ratio of retained earnings to price averaged 1.9 percent for the period from 1957 through 1976. The calculation of this ratio for 1976 would proceed as follows. The uncorrected ratio of retained earnings to price is the difference between the earnings-price ratio and the dividend-price ratio, that is (8.90–3.77), or 5.13 (see the *Economic Report of the President, 1978*, table B-89). The correction factor is the ratio of retained earnings plus the capital consumption and inventory valuation adjustments to the value of unadjusted retained earnings. For 1976 this ratio is (44.5–14.1–14.5)/44.5) (all in billions of dollars), or 0.357. (See *Economic Report..., 1978*, table B-11.) Applying this adjustment factor to the 5.13 obtained above yields 1.83 as the percentage of corrected retained earnings to price for 1976.

15. Our calculations show that the effective rate on realized nominal capital gain was 24.5 percent in 1973. Since then tax legislation has raised significantly this effective tax rate through changes in the minimum tax and maximum tax. We use a 20 percent effective rate on accruing capital gains to reflect the advantages of postponement.

16. The substitution of a cash-flow or expenditure type income tax for our current system would also eliminate all such problems. See Andrews (1974) and U.S. Department of the Treasury (1977).

17. See Feldstein (1978*b*, chap. 12 below) for a discussion of the welfare loss of capital income taxation.

8 Inflation and the Taxation of Capital Income in the Corporate Sector

With Lawrence Summers

This paper presents a detailed examination of the effect of inflation on the taxation of capital used in the nonfinancial corporate sector of the U.S. economy. Our analysis shows that, with current tax laws, inflation substantially increases the effective tax rate on capital income in the corporate sector. The principal reason for this is that the historic cost method of depreciation causes a major overstatement of taxable profits, i.e., historic cost depreciation results in a large increase in the level of real taxable profits at any level of real economic profits. Current methods of inventory accounting add further to this overstatement of profits for tax purposes.

According to our most comprehensive calculation, the effect of inflation with existing tax laws was to raise the 1977 tax burden on corporate sector capital income by more than $32 billion. This extra tax burden equivalent to 69 percent of the real after-tax capital income of the nonfinancial corporate sector, including retained earnings, dividends, and real interest receipts of the corporations' creditors. Since our calculations show that the total tax burden on this corporate capital income was $92 billion, the extra tax burden raised the tax by more than 54 percent. The total effective tax rate on corporate sector capital income in 1977 was 66 percent; without the extra tax caused by inflation, the effective tax rate would have been only 41 percent.

In contrast to previous studies of the relation between inflation and corporate tax burdens, we consider not only the tax paid by the corpora-

Reprinted by permission from *National Tax Journal* 32 (December 1979): 445–70.

This paper is part of the NBER study of capital formation. The authors are grateful for comments on earlier drafts by participants in a meeting of the NBER research group on taxation and several anonymous referees. James Poterba, Stephanie Seligman, and Daniel Smith provided valuable assistance.

tions themselves but also the tax paid by the individuals and institutions that supply capital to the corporate sector.[1] This is particularly important for a correct treatment of corporate debt. Inflation implies that the nominal interest payments that corporations deduct in calculating taxable profits exceed the real cost of borrowed funds; in itself, this tends to understate real profits and to lower the effective tax rate.[2] However, the individuals and institutions that lend to the corporations are taxed on the overstated nominal interest income.[3] Our calculations show that the excess tax paid by the lenders is slightly greater than the tax saving of the corporate borrowers. Since the difference between the relevant tax rate for borrowers and lenders is quite small, the mismeasurement of interest income (or, equivalently, the real gains and losses on net corporate debt) can be ignored without seriously distorting the evaluation of the overall effect of inflation on the taxation of corporate sector capital.

In addition to our analysis of the nonfinancial corporate sector as a whole, the present study makes use of an important new source of data for individual firms on the values of both replacement cost depreciation and depreciation based on historic costs. Beginning with the year 1976, the Securities and Exchange Commission has required large corporations to provide information on replacement cost depreciation and inventory profits as part of their annual form 10-K reports. We use these data together with other information on the financial and real performance of 327 individual manufacturing firms in order to examine how inflation has raised the effective tax rates on different industries.

In the first section of this study, we ignore the mismeasurement of interest expenses and income in order to focus on the additional taxation caused by historic cost depreciation and by existing inventory accounting methods. Section 8.2 then shows that the corporate tax savings that result from overstating real interest expenses are slightly more than balanced by the greater tax burdens that the mismeasurement of interest income imposes on the individuals and institutions that directly and indirectly supply debt capital to the corporate sector. The total increase in tax liabilities on corporate source income due to inflation is then estimated in section 8.3. Section 8.4 describes inflation's impact on effective tax rates. The fifth section then uses the data on individual firms to calculate the

---

1. Studies that have focused on inflation's effect on corporate taxes include Davidson and Weil (1977), Lovell (1978), Shoven and Bulow (1976) and Tideman and Tucker (1977). The importance of looking through the corporation to examine the return to suppliers of debt and equity capital is stressed in Feldstein (1976; chap. 3 above), Feldstein, Green, and Sheshinski (1978; chap. 4 above), and Feldstein and Summers (1978; chap. 9 below).

2. Allowing the deduction of nominal interest payments that exceed real interest payments is equivalent to ignoring the real gains that accrue to corporations as inflation reduces the real value of ourstanding corporate debt. In this context, debt should of course be regarded as gross debt minus nominal assets.

3. The extent of this taxation differs substantially among the different classes of lenders.

extent of additional taxation in each of the 20 different manufacturing industries. There is a brief concluding section that discusses the implications of these higher effective tax rates for capital formation and economic performance.[4]

8.1 Depreciation Rules, Inventory Accounting and Corporate Tax Payments

A desirable taxation criterion is that real tax payments should not be affected by changes in the overall price level which do not alter real income or wealth. Our tax system violates this standard in its treatment of corporate profits. When the price level rises and firms' real profits remain constant, their real tax payments rise both because of historical cost depreciation and FIFO inventory accounting. The real cost of the depreciating of a firm's capital stock is the replacement cost of the obsolescent capital. Yet for tax purposes firms are only permitted to deduct depreciation based on the original purchase price. In inflationary periods, this may be much less than the replacement cost. Similarly, the cost of depleting inventories is the replacement cost of the goods, not their original acquisition cost. Firms which use FIFO inventory cost deduct only the acquisition cost, giving rise to phantom inventory profits.

In this section, we discuss our estimates of how much existing depreciation and inventory rules raise corporate taxes in our inflationary economy. We ignore the role of debt and limit our attention to the tax burdens at the level of the corporation; this restriction is dropped in the subsequent sections where, as we noted in the introduction, we show that explicit recognition of debt has little effect on the total additional taxation of all the capital used in the corporate sector because of the offsetting effects of inflation on the taxation of borrowers and lenders. We begin this section by examining the experience for 1977, the most recent year for which all the required information is available. We then discuss the trends in inflation's effects on the taxation of corporate source income over the period since 1954.[5]

---

4. The analysis relates only to nonfinancial corporations even when the text refers only to corporations. Throughout the study we make no attempt to assess the extent to which the initial tax burdens are shifted to other capital or to labor by changes in the allocation of capital or in the financial decisions of households and firms. We also ignore state and local taxes and, to that extent, understate total tax burdens.

5. It is important to recall that firms may use LIFO inventory accounting for tax purposes only if they also use LIFO in the "book" accounting statements that they report to shareholders and creditors. Although the extra taxes that result from FIFO accounting are in a sense voluntary, managements presumably pay these taxes because they believe that there would be greater costs of some other kind if they used LIFO and reported lower profits and assets. As long as firms do pay the higher taxes based on FIFO accounts, these taxes do affect investment and savings decisions.

8.1.1 The Experience of 1977

Before looking in detail at the data for 1977, we can summarize briefly the impact of inflation on the taxes paid by nonfinancial corporations in 1977. The cumulative effect of inflation reduced the depreciation allowed on existing plant and equipment by $39.7 billion in 1977. This raised corporate tax payments by $19 billion, or nearly one-third of the $59 billion of corporate tax liabilities for 1977. An additional $7 billion in taxes were paid on artificial inventory profits. Thus, inflation raised corporate taxes from $33 billion to $59 billion, an increase of 79 percent. Stating this in a different way, the additional corporate tax caused by inflation accounts for 57 percent of the $59 billion of corporate tax liabilities in 1977.

We can now examine the specific data used to calculate these additional tax burdens. The official national income account estimate of the 1977 real profits of nonfinancial corporations was $113.9 billion.[6] Taxable profits for those corporations were $143.5 billion in the same year. The $30 billion difference between these two profit figures is the sum of the inventory valuation adjustment and the capital consumption adjustment. The inventory valuation adjustment (IVA) of $14.8 billion implies that inflation added $14.8 billion of false inventory profits to taxable income. The capital consumption adjustment (CCA) of $14.7 billion[7] actually reflects two countervailing differences between real straight-line depreciation and the depreciation allowed for tax purposes: the accelerated depreciation rules made tax-deductible depreciation exceed straight-line depreciation by $25.0 billion while inflation reduced the value of tax deductible depreciation and raised taxable profits by $39.7 billion. We shall refer to the two components of the CCA as the "acceleration component" (CCA-A) and the "inflation component" (CCA-I). Thus historic cost depreciation plus false inventory profits together added $54.5 billion to taxable profits. With a 48 percent statutory marginal tax rate, inflation caused a $26 billion increase in corporate tax payments.

In calculating the additional corporate tax payments we have implicitly assumed that accelerated depreciation and the investment tax credit were enacted to stimulate investment and not as an offset to inflation. It is clear that these features were enacted long before adjusting taxable income for

6. *Survey of Current Business*, November 1978. For earlier years, we use the *Survey of Current Business*, March 1976, pages 53–57, and updates in the *Survey of Current Business*. Depreciation is based on straight-line depreciation at 85 percent of the Bulletin F lives with depreciation calculated at replacement cost.

7. While the CCA is the only available estimate of the appropriate adjustment of depreciation allowances, there are serious problems with its construction. It is based on estimates of "capacity disappearance" rather than as a "value reduction" standard; the two are only exactly equivalent in the case of exponential depreciation. The underlying data on asset lives are often old and may as a result be incorrect.

inflation was a serious issue. Accelerated depreciation was introduced to the tax law in 1954 (a year in which the CPI actually fell) because of a conviction that tax depreciation lives were too long. Extensions of accelerated depreciation in subsequent years appear to have been motivated by a desire to stimulate investment rather than as an offset to inflation. As Stanley Surrey noted in connection with the 1971 acceleration provisions that created the asset depreciation range (ADR) system. "The new Asset Depreciation Range system was urged by the Treasury and adopted by the Congress in 1971 not as a device needed to measure real net income . . . (but) as an incentive for the purchases of new machinery and equipment" (Surrey, 1973, p. 32). Similarly the investment tax credit was introduced as a countercyclical measure to stimulate demand in 1962, a year in which the CPI rose only 1.2 percent.

Although the tax credits and accelerated depreciation that were legislated before the recent inflation can clearly be regarded as investment incentives rather than offsets to inflation, it might be argued that the changes made in the Tax Reduction Act of 1975 (and in subsequent legislation) were intended at least partly as an offset to the inflationary distortions of the tax liabilities. It is worth emphasizing therefore that these tax changes have done relatively little to reduce corporate taxes. The accelerated depreciation component of the capital consumption adjustment rose from $20.4 billion in 1975 to $25 billion in 1977, an increase proportional to the nominal level of fixed investment in the nonfinancial corporate sector. The increase in the amount of the investment tax credit between 1975 and 1977 due to the liberalization enacted in 1975[8] cannot be measured precisely but a reasonably accurate "upper-bound" estimate can be made. If the 3 percent increase in the Investment Tax Credit rate applied to all equipment investment in 1977, the additional tax credit for nonfinancial corporations would have been only $3.4 billion. This is clearly an overestimate of the additional investment tax credit because various limitations prevent all corporations from using the full 10 percent credit and because the rate is less than 10 percent on certain types of equipment. Furthermore, the 1975 liberalization of the I.T.C. can be ascribed at least as plausibly to antirecession policy as to a desire to offset inflation's impact on taxable profits.

8.1.2 The Period Since 1954

It is useful now to see the growing impact of inflation on tax liabilities by examining the evolution of taxable income and taxes since 1954.[9] This

8. The Tax Reduction Act of 1975 raised the investment tax credit from 7 percent to 10 percent and liberalized the accelerated depreciation rules.

9. We begin with 1954 to avoid the complexities of the excess profits taxes that were levied during the Korean War. The Internal Revenue Code of 1954 represented a major overhaul of the tax law that, with amendments, continues to provide the framework for current tax legislation.

analysis shows that, although inflation has caused some increase in corporate taxes for the past two decades, the period since 1970 has seen dramatically greater tax increases induced by inflation.

Table 8.1 presents annual information on the distortion of taxable profits caused by historic cost depreciation (CCA-I) and by artificial inventory accounting profits (IVA), the additional tax due to each of these, and the proportion of actual taxes that are accounted for by these extra taxes.

Consider first the reduced depreciation for tax purposes caused by historic cost accounting. Column 2 shows that this reduction in depreciation (CCA-I) remained less than $10 billion a year until 1970 but reached $39.7 billion in 1977. The 1977 level is nearly double the 1974 level and nearly eight times the level of 1967. This is reflected in the corresponding additional taxes shown in column 5. While the additional tax due to historic cost depreciation varied between $2 billion and $3 billion a year until 1967, it has doubled every three years since then: the additional taxes rose from $2.4 billion in 1967 to $4.8 billion in 1970, $10.3 billion in 1974, and $19.1 billion in 1977. While the extra tax caused by historic cost depreciation accounted for 9 percent of actual corporate taxes in 1967 (see column 8), it accounted for 32 percent of the taxes paid in 1977.

The artificial inventory profits also remained very small until 1967, never reaching $3 billion (column 3). More recently, however, inventory profits have exceeded $10 billion a year and the resulting excess profits have accounted for more than 10 percent of actual taxes paid.

Column 10 summarizes the overall effect of both sources of increased taxation. Until 1967, the extra tax caused by inflation accounted for 10 percent to 20 percent of the corporate taxes actually paid. This implies that the excess tax raised the tax that would otherwise have been paid by up to 25 percent. During the most recent five years, however, the excess tax accounted for an average of 50 percent of the corporate taxes actually paid. This implies that corporate taxes were twice as great as they would have been if replacement cost depreciation was permitted and artificial inventory profits were not taxed.

It is important to recognize that these distortions will continue to grow even if the rate of inflation does not accelerate any further. The understatement of an asset's depreciation allowance depends on the increase in the price level since it was purchased. Hence the understatement of depreciation will rise until inflation has lasted as long as the oldest asset which is still being depreciated. The accounting conventions used in our tax system make taxes very sensitive to the rates of inflation that we have recently experienced. The substantial additional tax burden caused by inflation will continue to grow unless either the tax law or the rate of inflation changes significantly.

Table 8.1   Inflation and Corporate Tax Liabilities, 1954–77

Year	Infla-tion Rate	Overstatement of Taxable Profits			Excess Tax Due to			Percent of Actual Taxes Due to		
		Reduced Depre-ciation (CCA-I)	Inflated Inventory Profits (IVA)	Total	Reduced Depre-ciation	Inflated Inventory Profits	Total	Reduced Depre-ciation	Inflated Inventory Profits	Total
		(billions of dollars)			(billions of dollars)				percent	
	(1)	(2)	(3)	(4)	(5)	(6)	(7)	(8)	(9)	(10)
1954	−0.5	4.3	0.3	4.6	2.2	0.2	2.4	14.3	1.0	15.3
1955	0.4	4.4	1.7	6.1	2.3	0.9	3.2	11.3	4.4	15.7
1956	2.9	5.4	2.7	8.1	2.8	1.4	4.2	14.0	7.0	21.0
1957	3.0	6.0	1.5	7.5	3.1	0.8	3.9	16.4	4.2	20.6
1958	1.8	6.0	0.3	6.3	3.1	0.1	3.3	19.4	0.8	20.2
1959	1.5	5.9	0.5	6.4	3.1	0.2	3.3	14.8	1.2	16.0
1960	1.5	6.2	−0.3	5.9	3.2	−0.2	3.1	16.8	−0.9	15.9

1961	0.7	5.0	−0.1	4.9	2.6	−0.1	2.5	13.4	−0.3	13.1
1962	1.2	4.6	−0.1	4.5	2.4	−0.1	2.3	11.6	−0.4	11.2
1963	1.6	4.1	0.2	3.9	2.1	0.1	2.2	9.4	0.3	9.7
1964	1.2	3.9	0.5	3.4	2.0	0.3	2.2	8.1	1.2	9.3
1965	1.9	3.8	1.9	5.7	1.8	0.9	2.7	6.7	3.3	10.0
1966	3.4	4.2	2.1	6.3	2.0	1.0	3.0	6.8	3.5	10.3
1967	3.0	5.1	1.7	6.8	2.4	0.8	3.3	8.9	3.0	11.9
1968	4.7	6.1	3.4	9.5	3.2	1.8	5.0	9.6	5.4	15.0
1969	6.1	7.7	5.5	13.2	4.1	2.9	7.0	12.2	8.8	21.0
1970	5.5	9.7	5.1	14.8	4.8	2.5	7.3	17.5	9.1	26.6
1971	3.4	11.5	5.0	16.5	5.5	2.4	7.9	18.5	8.1	26.6
1972	3.4	12.5	6.6	19.1	6.0	3.2	9.2	17.9	9.5	27.4
1973	8.8	14.3	18.6	32.9	6.9	8.9	15.8	17.3	22.5	39.8
1974	12.2	21.4	40.4	61.8	10.3	19.4	29.7	24.1	45.4	69.5
1975	7.0	32.3	12.1	44.4	15.4	5.8	21.3	38.0	14.2	52.2
1976	4.8	36.0	14.1	50.1	17.3	6.8	24.1	32.2	12.6	44.8
1977	6.8	39.7	14.6	54.3	19.1	7.0	26.1	32.4	12.3	45.7

8.2 The Total Taxation of the Corporate Sector

We now turn to the crucial issue of corporate debt. Although inflation reduces the real value of outstanding corporate debt, this gain by corporations is not taxable income. Equivalently, corporations subtract nominal instead of real interest payments in calculating taxable profits. A number of previous writers on the relation between inflation and corporate taxes have concluded that the corporate tax saving from the exclusion of real gains on the debt is sufficient to offset the additional tax caused by the mismeasurement of depreciation and inventory profits.[10] This has been interpreted as implying that inflation has no net effect on the taxation of corporate source income.

These conclusions are misleading because they are based on consideration of only some of the taxes levied on corporate source income. The basic issue is *not* the effect of inflation on the *corporations'* tax liability but the effect of inflation on the taxation of *capital* used in the corporate sector. It is important to look through the corporation to the individuals and institutions that provide the equity and debt capital. The total tax on corporate source income includes taxes paid by the owners of corporate securities on dividends, interest payments, and capital gains. It is this total tax rather than the tax levied at the corporate level alone that affects economic incentives.

This perspective is particularly important with respect to interest payments. While corporations are permitted to deduct nominal rather than real interest payments, lenders are obliged to pay taxes on nominal interest receipts. The effect of inflation on the total taxation of interest income depends on the relative magnitude of the tax rates facing corporate borrowers on one hand and those who lend to corporations on the other. If the tax rate of corporate borrowers exceeds that of lenders, total tax payments fall. Otherwise, tax revenues rise.[11]

The effect of dividend and capital gains taxes must also be considered. The mismeasurement of income which gives rise to extra corporate tax payments reduces dividends and retained earnings. This causes a reduction in noncorporate taxes which partly offsets the increase in corporate taxes. Inflation also increases nominal capital gains but not real capital gains, leading to increases in noncorporate tax payments. A full calculation of the effects of inflation on the taxation of corporate source income requires taking account of these effects. The analysis that we present in this section shows that the relevant weighted average of the marginal tax rates paid by the individuals and institutions that lend to nonfinancial

10. For example, Shoven and Bulow (1976) and Cagan and Lipsey (1978) reached this conclusion.

11. The potential balancing between borrowers and lenders is stressed in theoretical models of the effect of inflation in Feldstein (1976; chap. 3 above), and Feldstein, Green, and Sheshinski (1978; chap. 4 above).

corporations is even greater than the marginal rate of tax that is saved by corporations and their shareholders because of the overstatement of true interest payments. More specifically, we shall show that the relevant marginal tax rate for those who lend to corporations is 0.420 while the relevant combined rate of corporations and their shareholders as borrowers is 0.404.[12] Ignoring the real gains and losses on corporate debt therefore results in an *underestimate* of the total excess tax on corporate source income that is caused by inflation. However, since the difference between the effective marginal rates of the borrowers and the lenders is quite small, the whole issue of the real gains and losses on debt (or the mismeasurement of interest payments) can be ignored without distorting the measurement of the additional tax caused by inflation.[13]

Although we believe it is important to examine the effect of inflation on the *total* tax burden on corporate source income, we shall also analyze the effect of inflation on the tax burden of the corporations and their shareholders. Our calculations, presented in section 8.3 show that the extra taxes that the corporations and their shareholders pay because of inflation substantially exceed the amount they save by ignoring their inflationary gains on their net debts. Thus whether one looks at total capital income or only at the equity investors, the data show that inflation raises the effective tax burden.

8.2.1 Noncorporate Taxation of Equity Income

Owners of corporate equity pay dividend taxes on corporate income if it is distributed or capital gains taxes if it is retained. The rates at which these taxes are levied depend on the holder. Individuals, for example, pay taxes on dividend income at regular income tax rates but pay capital gains taxes at much lower effective rates. Different financial institutions pay taxes at varying rates on capital income. As noted below, pension income is essentially untaxed while certain institutions (e.g. life insurance companies) actually face higher capital gains tax rates than dividend tax rates.

The first step in finding the effective tax rate paid on equity income is to determine the distribution of ownership of corporate equity. Table 8.2 displays the pattern of ownership of corporate equity at the end of 1976 as reported in the official flow of funds accounts prepared by the Board of Governors of the Federal Reserve System. The bulk of the equity is held by households with significant fractions held by pension funds and life insurance companies. A small portion is held by other financial institu-

---

12. The reason why the combined effective marginal tax rates for corporations and their shareholders is less than the 48 percent corporate rate is that the extra corporate tax payments lead to a reduction in taxes on dividends and retained earnings.

13. Since the lenders and borrowers are not the same individuals, inflation does cause a redistribution of net income among individuals and institutions.

Table 8.2   Effective Marginal Tax Rates on Dividends and Capital Gains

Class of Investor	Value of Holdings ($ billions)	Tax Rates on	
		Dividends	Capital Gains
Households	566.4	.39	.05
Pension funds[a]	112.9	0	0
Life insurance	34.3	.072	.15
Other insurance	17.1	.072	.15
Mutual banks	4.4	.072	.15
Commercial banks	.9	.072	.15
Other[b]	46.8	0	0
Total	782.8	.287	.047

SOURCE: Flow-of-funds data for 1976. Tax rate calculations are described in the text. Note that tax rates represent conservative assumptions rather than estimates of most likely values.

a. Includes both private pensions and the retirement funds of state and local government.
b. Comprised primarily of foreign holdings.

tions. The second and third columns of the table indicate the marginal tax rates on dividends and capital gains for each type of stockowner. We assume that retained earnings are taxed at the capital gains tax rate.[14]

We estimate that under 1976 law, the average marginal tax rate on individual dividend receipts was 39 percent.[15]

Individual capital gains are taxed at half the statutory rate on dividends. However, gains are taxed only if realized and the effective rate is reduced by the postponement of realization.[16]

Bailey (1968) has estimated that each of these factors approximately halves the effective tax rate on capital gains. Hence we assume a 5 percent

14. Assuming that retained earnings are taxed at the capital gains rate involves the implicit assumption that each dollar of retained earnings raises share prices by $1.00. Although Bradford (1979) and Auerbach (1978; appendix to chap. 4 above) have challenged this assumption by a suggesting that the existing tax rules and dividends make the equilibrium value of retained earnings less than one, the possibility of distributing the corporate net worth through mergers and stock repurchases implies that even existing tax rules do not keep the value of retained earnings below one. While the issue is still in flux, we adopt the traditional assumption that each dollar of retained earnings raises the share prices by $1.00. See also Feldstein and Green (1979).

15. The marginal tax rate was found by using the NBER's TAXSIM model to estimate the additional tax payments arising from a 1% increase in dividend payments. The TAXSIM model is described in Feldstein and Frisch (1977). We allow for an estimated 7% of equity held by institutions which are not taxed but which are included by the flow of funds statistics in the household sector; this estimate of institutional ownership is derived from the SEC Statistical Bulletin.

16. Individuals who realize capital gains are taxed on the gain which occurred while they were holding the asset. Hence capital gains which accrue on assets which are passed at death completely avoid taxation. This is because the new owner is permitted to "step up" his basis for future tax liabilities.

tax rate on capital gains. This estimate is conservative because we ignore the taxes paid under the minimum tax and preference income provisions of the tax law.

We assume that no taxes are levied on the equity income of pension funds. In fact, pension recipients do pay taxes on pension income upon receipt. The effective rate is low, however, because the tax liability is postponed and because the recipients generally have low marginal tax rates during retirement. Moreover, increased pension returns may be associated with reduced employer contributions rather than increased benefits. In order to be conservative in our estimate of the effective tax rate on capital income, we assume a zero effective tax rate on pension income.[17]

Life insurance companies and commercial banks are taxed at corporate tax rates on dividends and capital gains. They are permitted to exclude 85 percent of dividends because of the intercorporate dividend exclusion. Hence, their effective marginal tax rate on dividend income is 7.2 percent.[18] These institutions are taxed at a 30 percent statutory rate on capital gains realizations. We assume an effective rate of 15 percent on such gains because of the effect of deferral. Unlike our treatment of individuals, we assume that all gains are eventually realized.

A weighted average of the effective tax rates provides our estimates of the overall marginal effective rates on dividends and retained earnings. In order to determine the noncorporate tax rate on all equity income, it is necessary to determine how corporate profits are divided between dividends and retained earnings. We estimate this payout ratio by using the average payout ratio over the past decade.[19] The share of total profits going to dividends over this period was 46.1 percent, implying an overall tax rate on equity income of 15.7 percent.

Using this figure it is possible to find the total tax increase on equity due to a mismeasurement of corporate profits. Suppose that corporate taxable income is increased by a single dollar with no change in real income. The corporation pays 48 cents more in taxes. Shareholder income in the form of dividends and retained earnings is reduced by 48 cents, leading to a decline of 7.6 cents in shareholder tax payments. Hence, total tax payments rise by 40.4 cents. Thus, the marginal tax rate on mismeasured income is 40.4 percent. Calculations of the increase in corporate taxes

17. It can be argued that the tax treatment of pension income is equivalent to a consumption tax because income put into pensions escapes all tax until the pension is withdrawn and presumably consumed. On this view, the effective tax rate on pension dividend and interest income is zero.

18. This overstates the dividend tax rate for insurance companies because of the special rules applying to insurance companies.

19. In calculating the payout ratio, profits are adjusted for inflation effects on inventory and depreciation and on real net indebtedness. We implicitly assume that there are no "clinetele" effects, so that payout ratio is the same for the equity owned by different classes of investors.

due to historical cost depreciation or false inventory accounting overstate by about 20 percent the true additional burden on the suppliers of equity capital.

8.2.2   The Value of Corporate Interest Deductions

Corporations are permitted to deduct nominal rather than real interest payments. Increases in inflation raise the corporations' interest deductions, thereby reducing corporate tax liabilities. Although the corporate tax rate is 48 percent, the overstatement of interest expenses reduces total tax payments by less than 48 percent. This occurs because the increase in after-tax corporate income results in an increase in noncorporate tax payments on dividends and capital gains. In section 8.2.1, we showed that the effective marginal tax rate on dividends and retentions is 15.7 percent; i.e., it was demonstrated that the equity owners' tax rate on "mismeasured" corporate income was 40.4 percent. This is the correct measure of the reduction in tax liabilities due to the deduction of nominal interest. It is this 40.4 percent rate that can be compared with the marginal tax rate of corporate debt holders in order to determine the effect of inflation on the taxation of interest income and expenses. In the next part of this section we consider the extra tax paid by the holders of corporate debt.

8.2.3   The Tax on Corporate Debt Holders

We now examine the extra taxes that the holders of corporate debt pay when interest rates rise in response to a higher rate of inflation. Equivalently, we estimate the amount by which their taxes would be reduced if the taxation of interest income were indexed. We also examine the extra taxes corporations pay on their interest-bearing financial assets. In table 8.3 we display the nonfinancial corporate sectors' interest-bearing financial assets and liabilities at the end of 1976. The holders of these securities are shown in the different columns. These figures are derived directly from the official flow of funds accounts. The penultimate row provides the net corporate debt holdings of each class of investor, formed by aggregating the entries in the column. In order to calculate the effective tax rate on the holders of corporate debt, we find the weighted average of marginal tax rates for each investor class.

Before describing our estimates of the specific marginal tax rates, several features of table 8.3 deserve comment. First, most corporate debt is not in the form of bonds. Nearly half is comprised of bank borrowing and mortgages. Second, only a small proportion of corporate interest payments, less than 15 percent, goes to individuals. The largest portion goes to commercial banks. Third, it is important to recall that corporations themselves hold a large quantity of interest-bearing financial assets.

Inflation leads to the increased tax liabilities on increased income from these assets.[20]

Our estimate of the marginal tax rate facing each class of creditors is shown in the bottom row of table 8.3. These estimates are only approximate since the laws governing financial institutions are quite complex and since all of the desired information is not available. Fortunately, the estimates that are most uncertain generally apply to only small quantities of debt. When in doubt, we have selected relatively conservative assumptions. The rationale for each of our estimates now follows:

Households. According to the NBER TAXSIM model, the weighted average of the marginal tax rates on interest income is about 25 percent. However, this average includes bank deposit interest as well as interest on corporate securities. Since corporate bonds are held by more affluent taxpayers than ordinary bank account time deposits (see Projector and Weiss, 1966), the 25 percent overall figure for all interest payments is too low. We have selected a 35 percent tax rate on interest paid, thereby implying that household bondholders have lower marginal tax rates on average than household dividend recipients.

Pensions. These are conservatively treated as fully tax exempt, implying a zero marginal tax rate.

Commercial Banks. Commercial banks pay a 48 percent corporate income tax at the margin on interest receipts. Those interest receipts net of corporate tax are then subject to further taxes as dividends and retained earnings; we assume the same 15.7 percent rate for this equity income that we derived in section 8.2.1 for the equity income of nonfinancial corporations. Combining the 48 percent and the 15.7 percent implies an overall tax on this equity income of 56.1. However, when the interest rates that banks charge rise, banks also raise the interest payments that they make to their depositors. To the extent that these interest payments rise, the banks do not pay extra taxes but their depositors do. Of course, there is no increase in the interest paid on demand deposits. We assume that interest rate ceilings constrain the increase in other interest rates to 0.3 percent for each 1 percent increase in inflation.[21] When this is allowed for, the total marginal tax rate on corporations and their depositors is approximately 54 percent.[22]

Mutual Savings Banks. In some cases, these banks pay the same 48 percent tax as ordinary corporations. However, mutual savings banks with a sufficient fraction of their assets in the form of local mortgages are

20. In some cases this leads to deductions for the issuers of the assets.
21. This assumption is based on a regression for the 1954–77 period of the time deposit rate on the rate of inflation.
22. This assumes that demand deposits account for 38 percent of total bank liabilities and that the marginal tax rate on the depositors at commercial banks is 25 percent.

Table 8.3 The Distribution of the Nominal Assets and Liabilities of Nonfinancial Corporations and the Effective Marginal Tax Rate on Corporate Interest Payments

Assets	Creditors and Debtors for Interest-Bearing Corporate Assets and Liabilities								Non-Interest-Bearing Corporate Assets		Total
	House-hold	Private Pensions	Commercial Banks	Mutual S.B.	Life In-surance	Finance Companies	Other In-surance	Govern-ment	Misc.	Non-Interest-Bearing	
Time deposits	—	—	22.3	—	—	—	—	—	—	—	22.3
Consumer credit	18.3	—	—	—	—	—	—	—	—	—	18.3
Security R.P.'s	—	—	—	—	—	—	—	—	4.7	—	4.7
Government sec.	—	—	—	—	—	—	—	22.0	—	—	22.0
Commercial paper (net)	2.0	—	3.6	—	—	11.4	—	—	4.5	—	21.5
Trade credit (net)	—	—	—	—	—	—	—	—	—	71.1	71.1
Currency and demand deposits	—	—	—	—	—	—	—	—	—	47.5	47.5
TOTAL ASSETS	20.3	—	25.9	—	—	11.4	—	22.0	9.2	118.6	207.4

CORPORATE LIABILITIES										
Bonds	52.7	30.3	6.9	14.0	85.1	—	9.7	55.4	6.9	261.0
Mortgages	13.1	1.5	58.6	16.7	56.6	2.5	.3	4.6	—	153.9
Bank loans	—	—	167.0	—	—	—	—	—	—	167.0
Financial co. loans	—	—	—	—	—	30.0	—	—	—	30.0
U.S. Govt. loans	—	—	—	—	—	—	—	3.9	—	3.9
Misc. liabs.	—	—	—	—	—	—	—	—	26.7	26.7
TOTAL LIABILITIES	65.8	31.8	232.5	30.7	141.7	32.5	10.0	63.9	33.6	642.5
NET LIABILITIES	45.5	31.8	206.6	30.7	141.7	21.1	10.0	41.9	26.9	435.1
MARGINAL TAX RATES	35%	0	54%	57%	24%	57%	57%	0	0	42.0%

NOTE: Assets and liabilities refer to 1976 and are derived from the Flow of Funds accounts. Note that tax rates represent conservative assumptions rather than estimates of most likely values.

allowed to exclude a fraction of their portfolio income, a fraction that increases with the mortgage share. The overall effective rate must also reflect the extent to which mutual savings banks raise the interest rate they pay and the corresponding marginal tax rate of their depositors. We estimate a 24 percent overall rate for these institutions based on the assumption that about half of marginal income is successfully sheltered.

Life Insurance Companies. Life insurance companies are taxed according to the "Menge Formula" or "ten-to-one rule" which allows insurance companies to exclude a portion of their portfolio income before applying the 48 percent corporate tax rate (see Huebner, 1976, for a discussion of this tax rule). The procedure in the existing law is designed to separate investment income into an amount required to meet the funding requirements for existing insurance and a residual profit that is deemed taxable. To achieve this, life insurance companies pay tax on a percentage of income equal to ten times the difference between the average nominal yield on the portfolio (i) and the nominal yield that the insurance commissioners deem to be the appropriately conservative yield to use in calculating required reserves (s). Thus if the assets of the insurance company (A) are invested at a nominal yield of i, the total tax liability of the company is $T = 0.48[10(i - s)]iA$. The change in the effective tax rate caused by inflation depends on how i and s adjust. As we noted above, the nominal market yield (i) generally rises point for point for expected inflation. In contrast, the regulatory authorities have not altered s in response to inflation; historically, s has remained close to 3 percent for the past 70 years. The marginal tax rate implied by this tax formula for increases in the interest rate is an increasing function of the initial marginal tax rate. Evaluating the marginal tax rate at the relatively conservative value of i = 0.07 implies a marginal tax rate of 0.57.[23] We use this value to be conservative; at higher initial interest yields, the effective marginal tax would be even greater. Note we are also conservative in ignoring the tax paid on dividends and retained earnings of the nonmutual life insurance companies.

Finance Companies and Other Insurance. These are taxed like ordinary corporations. Combining the 48 percent corporate rate with the additional tax on dividends and retained earnings yields an overall marginal tax rate of 57.1 percent on this type of income.

Government. We assume that government neither pays taxes on interest receipts nor deducts expenses for tax purposes. While increases in

---

23. Note that at i = .07, a $1,000 portfolio earns $70. With s = .03 only 40 percent of this or $28 is taxed; the tax is $13.44 and the net income is therefore $56.56. Raising the interest rate to i = .08 implies earnings of $80 but 50 percent or $40 is taxable. The tax is thus $19.20, leaving a net income of $60.80. Note that an extra $10 of gross interest raises net interest income by only $4.24. The effective marginal tax rate is thus 57.6 percent.

interest receipts may enable governments to reduce other taxes, there is no reason to suppose that capital taxes will be reduced. Moreover, other costs of government are increased by raising interest rates.

Miscellaneous. The interest on these assets is assumed to be untaxed. Note that "miscellaneous" includes assets and liabilities of the rest of the world so our no-tax assumption implies that no taxes are paid to either the U.S. or to foreign governments by foreigners owning bonds of U.S. corporations. It is clear that our assumption that all of this income is untaxed is very conservative.

In order to calculate the marginal tax rate on interest income, we have averaged the marginal tax rates shown in the final row of Table 8.3, weighting by the share of debt owned the class of investors' share of debt. The results imply a marginal rate of 0.420 on interest income.

This implies that inflation raises the taxation of interest income, since the tax rate that lenders pay exceeds that at which corporations deduct. Allowing in the overall calculation for the impact of inflation on debt thus actually strengthens the conclusion that inflation raises the effective taxation of capital income. This effect is, however, quite small. It is equal to 1.6 percent of net interest payments (the difference between the 42 percent of lenders and the 40.4 percent of corporate borrowers or about a half billion dollars per year). This is dwarfed by the depreciation and inventory effects described in the previous section.

While several of our estimated marginal tax rates are only approximate, they pertain to relatively small amounts of debt. It is unlikely that a more exact estimate of these numbers would alter our basic conclusion that the tax on those who lend to corporations is at least as great as the rate at which corporations and their owners can deduct interest payments.

8.3   The Increased Taxation of Corporate Source Income

The first section of this paper presented calculations of the additional tax paid by corporations because of the mismeasurement of depreciation and inventories. The current section extends that calculation in three significant ways to obtain the total increased tax on corporations, on equity owners, and on all sources of capital for nonfinancial corporations.

Our calculations show that inflation raised the total tax on the income of nonfinancial corporations by $32.3 billion. This amount is substantially greater than the $26.1 billion additional tax paid by corporations themselves because of the mismeasurement of depreciation and inventory profits.

We begin by analyzing the several effects of inflation in 1977. Estimates for the years since 1954 are then presented.

8.3.1 An Analysis for 1977

We proceed in three steps to calculate the total additional taxes on corporate source income in 1977. We first calculate the excess tax paid by the corporation itself, recognizing the effect of not taxing the real gains on debt as well as the effect on depreciation and inventory profits. We then extend this to obtain the total excess tax paid by equity owners, including the effect on the tax liabilities of the corporations and the shareholders. Finally, we extend the calculation to the total excess tax including the tax paid by those who lend to the nonfinancial corporations.

The calculations in section 8.1 showed that historic cost depreciation and the existing inventory accounting practices added $26.1 billion to the 1977 tax liabilities of nonfinancial corporations. In 1977 these corporations had net interest bearing liabilities[24] of $592.2 billion and non-interest-bearing assets (primarily cash and net accounts receivable[25]) of $130.9 billion. Their net nominal liabilities were thus $461.3 billion. Since the 1977 inflation rate was 6.8 percent (the December-to-December increase in the CPI), these corporations had a real gain of $31.4 billion on their net liabilities. Excluding the gain from the corporations' taxable income saved them $15.1 billion in corporate tax. These tax savings thus offset approximately one-half of the $26.0 billion of extra tax caused by the existing tax treatment of inventories and debt. Inflation caused corporations to pay an extra tax of $11 billion in 1977.

The extra tax paid by the equity owners of the corporations differs in two ways from the extra tax paid by the corporations. First, as we discussed earlier, the extra tax paid at the corporate level leaves less income to be taxed as dividends. With a dividend payout rate of 0.46 and effective marginal tax rates of .287 on dividends and 0.047 on retained earnings, the $11 billion of extra corporate tax reduces shareholders own taxes by $1.7 billion. Second, the shareholders must eventually pay capital gains tax on the *nominal* increase in the market value of the company that results from inflation. Since this nominal increase in value is over and above the real increase due to retained earnings the extra tax paid on this nominal gain represents an extra tax caused by inflation. We shall assume that the nominal gain can be approximated by the product of the inflation rate and the real value of corporate assets.[26] The relevant marginal rate of tax on these accrued nominal gains is the effective capital gains tax rate of 0.047. The real value of the physical assets of these

24. See section 8.2 for a description of the composition of this net amount. Note that $592.2 billion is net of the interest-bearing assets of these firms.

25. These assets also include Treasury bills and other federal government securities that bear interest since the important distinguishing feature of these "non-interest-bearing assets" is that private individuals and institutions do not pay any interest on them.

26. The actual nominal gain caused by inflation is very hard to disengage from other changes in market value. Theoretical considerations imply that a change in the expected rate of inflation will cause an inverse change in the market valuation ratio which then slowly returns to its equilibrium value (see Feldstein, 1980b; chap. 10 below).

corporations (plant and equipment, inventories and land)[27] in 1977 was $1,684 billion. The inflation rate of 6.8 percent and the tax rate of 0.047 imply an additional capital gains tax of $5.3 billion. The total excess tax on the equity owners of the nonfinancial corporations is therefore the sum of three terms: the $11 billion of extra corporate income tax minus the $1.7 billion resulting reduction in personal taxes plus the capital gains tax of $5.3 billion. Inflation thus induced a net extra tax of $14.6 billion on corporations and their owners in 1977.

To obtain the total additional taxation on corporate source income that is caused by inflation, the additional taxation of corporate creditors must be added to this $14.6 billion. The net financial capital supplied by the creditors of these corporations was $595.2 billion.[28] The inflation rate of 6.8 percent imposed a real loss of $40.5 billion that should have been offset against the interest income of the creditors. The effective marginal tax rate of 0.420 on interest income implies an additional taxation of $17 billion.[29]

Combining this $17 billion with the $14.6 billion implies an extra tax on corporations and their owners of $31.6 billion. This additional tax on corporate source income was 54 percent of the corporate income tax liabilities of $59 billion and 34 percent of the combined corporate, share-holder, and lender tax liabilities of $93 billion. Stated in yet a different way, the excess tax of $31.6 billion caused by inflation is equivalent to an additional wealth tax or capital levy of 2 percent on the real corporate assets of $1,684 billion. Since these corporations earn between 10 and 12 percent on their real assets,[30] this extra tax absorbs between one-sixth and one-fifth of pretax real earnings.

8.3.2 The Period Since 1954

This same framework can be used to calculate the additional tax caused by inflation in each year since 1954.[31] Since we do not have a detailed flow-of-funds calculation of the sort presented in section 8.2 for each year, we shall use the same effective marginal tax rates for all years. The calculations therefore represent the additional tax that would have been caused for each year if the 1976 statutory tax rates and composition of creditors and debtors had prevailed; differences that result from using actual statutory rates and ownership information would be small relative to the differences over time caused by the changing history of inflation.

Table 8.4 traces the evolution of the inflation-generated additional

27. The data came from Von Furstenberg (1977).
28. We ignore the corporate assets in the form of government securities and net accounts receivable because these do not represent the supply of financial capital by private investors.
29. We neglect here the capital gains or losses accruing to firms and bondholders in existing debt when the interest rate changes.
30. See Feldstein and Summers (1977).
31. These are additional taxes due to inflation in the sense that they would not have been paid if the system were fully indexed.

Table 8.4 Changes in Tax Liabilities on Corporate Source Income Caused by Inflation, 1954–77

		Corporations			Shareholders			Creditors		
	Inflation Rate (1)	Depreciation (2)	Net Debt (3)	Total (4)	Dividends and Retained Earnings (5)	Nominal Capital Gains (6)	Equity Capital (7)	Net Corporate Interest (8)	Total Corporate Capital (9)	Extra Tax as Percent of Corporate Income Tax (10)
Year										
				(billions of dollars)						
1954	−0.5	2.4	0.1	2.5	−0.4	−0.1	2.0	−0.1	1.9	12.2
1955	0.4	3.2	−0.1	3.1	−0.4	0.1	2.8	0.1	2.9	14.4
1956	2.9	4.2	−0.5	3.7	−0.5	0.5	3.7	1.0	4.7	23.4
1957	3.0	3.9	−0.7	3.2	−0.4	0.6	3.4	1.2	4.6	24.1
1958	1.8	3.3	−0.5	2.8	−0.4	0.3	2.7	0.8	3.5	21.6
1959	1.5	3.3	−0.4·	2.9	−0.4	0.3	2.8	0.7	3.5	16.9
1960	1.5	3.1	−0.4	2.7	−0.4	0.3	2.6	0.8	3.4	17.7

1961	0.7	2.6	−0.3	2.3	−0.4	0.2	2.1	0.4	2.5	12.8
1962	1.2	2.3	−0.5	1.8	−0.3	0.2	1.7	0.7	2.4	11.6
1963	1.6	2.2	−0.7	1.5	−0.2	0.4	1.7	1.1	2.8	12.3
1964	1.2	2.2	−0.5	1.7	−0.3	0.3	1.7	0.9	2.6	10.8
1965	1.9	2.7	−1.0	1.7	−0.3	0.5	1.9	1.5	3.4	12.5
1966	3.4	3.0	−2.0	1.0	−0.2	0.9	1.7	2.9	4.6	15.6
1967	3.0	3.3	−2.1	1.2	−0.2	1.0	2.0	2.9	4.9	17.7
1968	4.7	5.0	−3.8	1.2	−0.2	1.6	2.6	4.9	7.5	22.3
1969	6.1	7.0	−5.5	1.5	−0.2	2.9	4.2	7.2	11.4	34.2
1970	5.5	7.3	−5.8	1.5	−0.2	2.3	3.6	7.3	10.9	39.9
1971	3.4	4.9	−4.1	3.8	−0.5	1.5	4.8	5.0	9.8	32.8
1972	3.4	9.2	−4.5	4.7	−0.8	1.6	4.5	5.4	9.9	29.5
1973	8.8	15.8	−12.9	2.9	−0.4	4.5	7.0	15.7	22.7	57.3
1974	12.2	29.7	−21.0	8.7	−1.3	7.2	15.6	25.0	40.6	95.1
1975	7.0	21.3	−14.5	6.8	−1.1	4.8	10.5	16.7	27.2	66.6
1976	4.8	24.1	−10.2	13.9	−2.2	3.6	15.3	11.9	27.2	56.5
1977	6.8	26.1	−15.1	11.0	−1.7	5.3	14.6	17.0	31.6	53.6

taxation of corporate source income between 1954 and 1977. Column 2 repeats the figures from table 8.1, column 7, of the excess tax at the corporate level due to the mismeasurement of depreciation and inventory profits. The corporate tax savings due to ignoring the real gains on net corporate debt are presented in column 3. It is worth noting that the additional tax paid to the mismeasurement of depreciation and inventory profits always exceeds the tax savings on the debt gains. The net excess at the corporate level, presented in column 4, remains relatively low (less than $5 billion) until 1974 when it jumped to $8.7 billion.

The reduced taxation of dividends and retained earnings due to higher corporate tax payments is shown in column 5 and the capital gains tax liability on the nominal capital gains caused by inflation is shown in column 6. Combining columns 4, 5, and 6 gives the net increase in the taxation of equity capital presented in column 7. This additional tax on equity income remained less than $5 billion until 1970 but has exceeded $10 billion annually since 1974. The additional tax on equity income since 1970 has totalled more than $80 billion.

Column 8 presents the very important additional tax on the individuals and institutions that provide debt capital to the nonfinancial corporations. This excess tax on lenders reached $5 billion in 1968 and exceeded $15 billion in 1973. The additional tax on those who lent to nonfinancial corporations has exceeded $100 billion in the brief period from 1970 to 1977.

The total additional tax on corporate source income caused by inflation is shown in column 9. Three things should be noted about these figures. First, this total extra tax caused by inflation exceeds the extra tax paid by corporations because of the mismeasurement of depreciation and inventory profits (column 2). Focusing exclusively on the extra corporate taxes paid because of the mismeasurement of depreciation and inventory profits is therefore a conservative evaluation of the total inflationary impact. Second, the total excess tax remained less than $5 billion a year until 1966, doubled by 1970 and doubled again by 1973. The excess tax has exceeded $20 billion a year since 1973. Third, the total excess tax on corporate source income has exceeded $180 billion in the period between 1970 and 1977.

Finally, column 10 states the total excess tax on corporate source income as a percentage of the corporate tax liability. Although the extra tax remained less than one-sixth of corporate income tax payments until the mid-1960s, it then quickly rose to more than one-third of the corporate income tax. For the final five years, the excess tax payments have been more than 50 percent of corporate tax liabilities.

8.4   The Effective Tax Rate on Corporate Source Income

This section presents our estimates of the total effective tax rate on the real capital income earned in the corporate sector. Our calculations show that the total tax on corporate source income in 1977, including the tax liabilities of shareholders and lenders as well as of the corporations themselves, was $91.8 billion, an effective tax rate of 67 percent on the real pretax income of the nonfinancial corporate sector. The data show that this 67 percent represents a substantial increase in the effective tax rate over the past decade and a return to the effective tax rates of the mid-1950s.

The substantial increase in the effective tax rate despite statutory reductions reflects the impact of inflation. The $32.3 billion of extra tax caused by inflation in 1977 accounts for more than one-third of the total tax on corporate source income, raising the effective total tax rate from 43 percent to 66 percent. The extra tax caused by inflation has thus offset all of the accelerated depreciation and other legislated tax reductions during the past two decades.

8.4.1   The Effective Tax Rate in 1977

The best measure of the tax burden on corporate source income is the ratio of the total tax paid on such income—including the taxes paid by shareholders and lenders as well as by the corporations—to the total real income available before tax for the shareholders and creditors. The official national income estimate of 1977 profits with the inventory valuation adjustment and capital consumption adjustment was $113.9 billion. Net nominal interest payments by nonfinancial corporations were $33.7 billion. It seems at first that the total pretax income available for shareholder and creditors could be obtained by simply adding these adjusted profits and net interest on the grounds that it is unnecessary to adjust interest payments for inflation since any correction to nominal interest expenses by the corporation would required an equal correction to nominal receipts by creditors. Although this is a generally correct principle, one further modification is required. A significant fraction of the corporations' financial assets are not liabilities of investors but of the government or of the corporations' customers. When inflation lowers the real value of these assets, the loss to the corporations is a gain to the government and to the corporations' customers and not to individual or institutional investors. The corporations' loss on these financial assets should therefore be subtracted from other corporate profits. In 1977, these assets were $130.9 billion, the inflationary loss was therefore $8.9 billion. The 1977 total pretax corporate sector income available for shareholders and creditors was therefore $138.7 billion.

Our estimated total tax of $91.8 billion on this income consists of five components. (1) The largest of these is the corporate income tax payments of $59 billion. This alone represents an effective tax rate of 42.5 percent on total corporate source income. (2) Dividends in 1977 were $39.1 billion; an effective tax rate of 0.287 on dividends implies a tax liability of $11.2 billion[32] and adds 8.1 percent to the effective tax rate. (3) The national income account estimate of $16 billion of retained earnings[33] ignores the real gain on outstanding debt. With a net debt of $461.3 billion and a 6.8 percent inflation rate, the additional real retained earnings were $31.4 billion. The total retained earnings of $47.4 billion are eventually subject to capital gains taxation with an effective tax rate of 0.047; this adds $2.2 billion to the total tax and 1.6 percent to the effective tax rate. (4) An additional capital gains tax liability results from the nominal increase in the value of corporate assets that accompanies a general rise in the price level. We abstract from the particular market fluctuations of 1977 and calculate that the real capital stock with an initial value of $1,684 billion rose by 6.8 percent. With a tax rate of 4.7 percent, this nominal increase implies an effective tax of $5.4 billion, adding 3.9 percent to the total effective tax rate. (5) Finally, the nominal interest payments of $33.7 billion were taxable income of the creditors. With a tax rate of 0.42, these interest payments involve a tax liability of $14.2 billion, adding 10.2 percent to the effective tax rate.[34] The total of these five figures of tax payments is thus $92 billion for a total effective tax rate of 66.3 percent.

Before turning to a comparison of 1977 with earlier years, it is useful to contrast the actual effective tax rate of 66.3 percent with several alternative rates that are frequently cited. Perhaps the most common measure of the corporate tax burden is the ratio of the $59 billion corporate income tax to the conventionally measured corporate profits of $143.5 billion; the resulting rate of 41.1 percent is a gross underestimate of the actual total rate. An alternative and more sophisticated rate is the ratio of the corporate income tax to the sum of corporate profits with the inventory valuation and capital consumption adjustments ($113.9 billion) plus the real gains on the net corporate debt ($31.4 billion); the resulting rate of 40.6 percent is again less than two-thirds of the total burden. These calculations underline the importance of looking beyond the corporation

---

32. This calculation uses our estimated *marginal* tax rate on dividends to measure the *average* tax rate on dividends. This causes an overstatement of the tax liability, but the error is likely to be very small.

33. This is the official figure for the undistributed profits corrected for the inventory valuation and capital consumption adjustments.

34. We are again using an estimated marginal tax rate as an average tax rate on this income. This causes some overstatement, particularly for life insurance companies. Adjusting this to use an average rather than marginal tax rate for life insurance companies might reduce the tax by up to $2 billion dollars.

to the shareholders and creditors in order to obtain a correct picture of total tax burdens on capital used in the corporate sector.

8.4.2   Variations in the Effective Total Tax Rate Since 1954

Table 8.5 traces the variations in the effective total tax rate on corporate capital since 1954. The total real income presented in column 1 is the sum of real profits as measured by the national income statistics and net nominal interest payments with an adjustment for corporate losses on government assets and net accounts receivable.

Actual corporate tax liabilities as a percentage of this total real income have declined nearly one-fifth since the mid-1950s. Moreover, there has

Table 8.5   The Effective Tax Rate on Capital Income of the Nonfinancial Corporate Sector

		Taxes as a Percentage of Total Real Income					
			Taxes on Shareholders and Creditors				
Year	Total Real Income (billions of dollars) (1)	Corporate Income Tax (2)	Dividends (3)	Real Retained Earnings (4)	Nominal Capital Appreciation (5)	Interest Income (6)	Total (7)
1954	$ 30.4	51.6	7.8	2.0	− 0.2	2.3	63.5
1955	39.8	51.1	6.8	2.1	0.2	1.8	61.9
1956	36.5	54.8	8.0	2.1	1.3	2.1	68.4
1957	35.6	53.4	8.6	2.3	1.6	2.7	68.5
1958	31.8	50.6	9.3	2.2	1.1	3.7	67.0
1959	42.0	49.2	7.4	2.2	0.7	3.3	62.8
1960	40.2	47.7	8.3	2.2	0.7	3.8	62.8
1961	41.1	47.4	8.3	2.1	0.3	4.2	62.2
1962	48.7	42.4	7.6	2.4	0.6	4.1	57.1
1963	53.8	42.4	7.6	2.5	0.7	3.9	57.1
1964	61.2	39.1	7.3	2.6	0.5	3.8	53.3
1965	70.9	38.3	7.1	2.7	0.7	3.8	52.5
1966	76.2	38.7	6.9	2.8	1.2	4.3	53.9
1967	73.8	37.5	7.4	2.8	1.3	5.2	54.2
1968	78.7	42.7	7.6	2.8	2.0	5.6	60.8
1969	74.9	44.5	8.0	2.8	3.0	7.7	66.0
1970	64.2	42.5	9.0	1.2	3.5	11.7	67.8
1971	73.7	40.5	7.9	1.1	2.1	10.7	62.3
1972	88.0	38.0	7.2	1.4	1.8	9.6	58.0
1973	90.2	43.9	7.7	2.1	5.0	11.3	70.0
1974	76.2	56.0	10.0	2.1	9.4	17.2	94.9
1975	100.2	40.8	8.4	1.7	4.8	13.6	69.3
1976	126.3	42.5	7.4	1.4	2.9	10.7	64.9
1977	138.7	42.5	8.1	1.6	3.9	10.2	66.3

been no increase at all in this ratio between 1970 and 1977. This has incorrectly led some observers to discount the argument that inflation raised real tax burdens on capital income.

The varying taxes on shareholders and creditors in columns 3 through 6 reflect variations in dividends, full retained earnings, inflationary appreciation, and interest payments. The same 1977 effective tax rates are assumed for each tax base; allowing for statutory changes would raise taxes on dividends and interest income in the earlier years and in those years but this effect would be relatively small.

The net result of these changes is shown in the total effective tax rate presented in column 7. Despite the decline in the relative corporate tax payments, the overall effective tax rate is as high now as it was in the mid-1950s. The effect of inflation has been powerful enough to offset the introduction of the investment tax credit, the cuts in the corporate tax rate, and the more rapid acceleration of depreciation.[35]

8.5   Inflation and Corporate Tax Liabilities in Two-Digit Manufacturing Industries

Although historic cost depreciation and existing accounting practices raise the tax liabilities of all corporations, their importance varies substantially among different industries. The current section presents information for each of the 20 two-digit manufacturing industries. For manufacturing as a whole, the additional taxes in 1976 caused by historic cost depreciation and existing accounting practices accounted for slightly more than half of all the federal tax liabilities of these firms. These additional taxes varied from less than 25 percent of actual taxes in a few industries to 100 percent of the taxes paid in several others. If the taxes are expressed as a percentage of the real value of capital used in these industries, the additional tax varies from less than 1 percent of capital to nearly 3 percent of capital. The very high tax rates that result in several of the industries make it particularly difficult for them to compete for capital. If these additional tax burdens persist, the allocation of capital among manufacturing industries will be substantially distorted by inflation.

Our analysis of the additional tax burdens of individual industries is based on information supplied by individual firms in their annual reports and 10-K forms. Beginning with 1976, the Securities and Exchange Commission has required the largest firms to supply information on replacement cost depreciation and on inflation-adjusted inventory gains as well as on historic cost depreciation and on their inventory profits as

---

35. We have ignored state and local taxation of corporate source income through corporate income rates, property taxes, and individual income rates. If these taxes were included, an increase in the effective tax rate would be observed and the current rate would exceed 66 percent.

they are used for tax purposes. We use the differences between the inflation-adjusted and the unadjusted figures for depreciation and inventories to measure the overstatement of taxable profits. For each industry, we then compare the total additional tax liabilities implied by these overstated profits with the actual tax liabilities paid by the firms in our sample. We also calculate the additional tax payments as a percentage of the real value of the capital used by the sample firms in the industry.[36] Finally, we use the ratio of sales by the sample firms to sales by all firms in the industry to estimate the total additional taxes caused in each industry in 1976 by historic cost depreciation and by prevailing accounting methods.[37]

Although the general approach of these calculations parallels the analysis of section 8.1, there are several differences that should be borne in mind in interpreting the results. First, the information supplied by the firms represents consolidated accounts and not just the domestic activities that were analyzed in section 8.1. Because we are forced to include the overseas depreciation and inventory gains, we overstate the extent of overtaxation. Second, the firms provide the historic cost depreciation and replacement cost depreciation as alternative measures of "book" depreciation rather than "tax" depreciation. Since the straight-line "book" depreciation is less than the accelerated "tax" depreciation, this procedure causes us to understate the extent of overtaxation. The net effect of these two countervailing biases cannot be determined from the existing data but is unlikely to be large enough to distort the conclusions of the analysis.[38]

The sample of firms for which we have information represents approximately 50 percent of the total sales of manufacturing firms. Because of the nature of the SEC requirement, the sample consists exclusively of large firms. Moreover, the coverage varies substantially among the industries with a very much smaller fraction of sales in the samples for some industries than for others. The tables in this section indicate the number of firms in each sample and the fraction of sales that the sample firms represent.[39]

36. Estimates of the replacement cost value of plant, equipment, and inventories are also required by the SEC.

37. We do not analyze the effects of inflation on real indebtedness because data on the ownership of securities by industry does not exist. The results in section 8.2 suggest that this omission is not likely to have a great impact on the conclusions.

38. These results should be viewed with caution for other reasons. There appear to be wide variations in the methods used by firms in estimating replacement cost figures. There is no necessary correspondence between the depreciation lives used by firms and those used in the construction of the aggregate statistics presented above.

39. To estimate total sales in each industry, we use the Compustat file of 2,500 firms prepared by Standard and Poor. The 1,332 manufacturing firms in this file represent 1976 sales of $1,052 billion or 87 percent of all manufacturing sales as estimated by the Federal Trade Commission. We use the Compustat file to estimate total sales by industry in order to be sure that firms are classified by industry in the same way as in our replacement cost sample.

Table 8.6 presents information on the extent of reduced depreciation and the consequent additional taxation. The first two columns show the number of firms in the sample and the percentage of the total industry sales accounted for by the sample firms. The third column shows the understatement of depreciation, i.e., the difference between replacement cost depreciation and historic cost depreciation. The additional tax liability presented in column 4 is calculated by summing (for all the sample firms in the industry) 0.48 times each firm's understated depreciation up to the limit of the tax actually paid by the firm. Note that this is a very conservative statement of the additional tax for any firm in which the limit constrains our calculated amount because it assumes that no additional profits would have been earned even at a zero tax rate and disregards the possibility of carrying losses forward. Column 5 expresses the additional tax as a percentage of the total federal tax liability of the firms in the sample while column 6 states the additional tax liability as a percentage of the replacement cost value of the firms' real capital stock.[40] The remaining two columns are estimates for all the firms in the industry and not just the sample; they are obtained by rescaling the sample values for each industry by the ratio of total industry sales to sales in the sample.

The relative importance of the additional taxes that resulted from the understatement of depreciation varied substantially among the 20 individual industries. Column 5 shows that these additional taxes represented less than one-sixth of actual 1976 tax liabilities in 6 of the 20 industries. These are primarily nondurable goods (tobacco, apparel, printing and publishing, and leather and footwear) but also include the nonelectrical machinery and instruments industries. At the other extreme, there are four industries in which the additional tax represents more than three-fourths of actual tax liabilities: primary metals, rubber, paper, and wood products.

A similar picture of very substantial variation emerges when the additional taxation is related to the replacement cost value of the firms' real capital stock (column 6). The additional tax varies from 0.4 percent of the real capital stock in the primary metals industry[41] and 0.5 percent in the nonelectrical machinery industry to 2.0 percent in the paper industry and 2.8 percent in the wood products industry.

For manufacturing as a whole, the reduction in real depreciation totalled $18 billion or half of the reduction for all nonfinancial corpora-

---

40. The real capital stock includes inventories as well as property, plant, and equipment but excludes financial assets and liabilities.

41. This tax is kept so low because the extra tax is assumed to be no greater than actual taxes paid which, in the case of primary metals, were kept low by extremely low real profits.

tions that was discussed in section 8.1. Nondurable goods industries (SIC codes 20 through 29) accounted for 58 percent of this reduced depreciation or $10.4 billion. Reduced depreciation in durable goods industries (SIC codes 30 through 39) was $7.6 billion. The additional tax caused by the understatement of depreciation was $7.6 billion, of which $4.9 billion was in nondurable goods industries and $2.7 billion was in durable goods industries.

Table 8.7 presents the combined effects of reduced depreciation and overstated inventory profits. The organization of the table parallels that of table 8.6. The results presented in column 5 show very substantial variation among industries in the importance of the extra tax as a percentage of actual taxes paid. In two of the industries (leather and nonelectrical machinery), the extra tax amounted to less than 20 percent of the actual tax paid. In contrast, four of the industries (wood and wood products; paper; rubber; and steel) would have paid no tax if depreciation had been calculated at replacement cost and if the artificial inventory profits were also eliminated. Column 6 confirms the picture of substantial variation among industries by comparing the additional tax to the replacement value of the real capital stock. The extra tax paid (as limited by the total tax paid) varied from less than 1 percent of the capital stock on the primary metals and nonelectrical machinery industries to nearly 3 percent of the capital stock in the food industry and in textiles.

For all manufacturing industries, the mismeasurement of depreciation and inventories totaled $27.1 billion or 54 percent of the aggregate reported for all nonfinancial corporations in section 8.1. Of this $27.1 billion total, 58 percent was accounted for by nondurable manufacturing. Note that this 58 percent is the same as the figure for depreciation only, implying that the mismeasurements of inventories and depreciation are distributed in the same way. The additional taxation for manufacturing firms totaled $11.3 billion, of which $7.4 billion was in the nondurable goods industries.

8.6   Conclusion

The tax laws of the United States were designed at a time when there was little or no inflation. The analysis in this paper has shown that, with the existing tax laws, inflation substantially increases the effective tax rate on capital income in the nonfinancial corporate sector. In contrast to earlier studies of the impact of inflation on corporate tax burdens, we have considered not only the tax paid by the corporations themselves but also the taxes paid by the individuals and institutions that supply capital to the corporate sector. This is particularly important for a correct treatment of corporate debt; our calculations indicate that the additional

Table 8.6   Inflation, Depreciation and Corporate Tax Liabilities in Manufacturing Industries

SIC Code	Industry	(1) N	(2) Sales Coverage (percent)	Sample Firms (3) Reduced Depreciation ($ million)	(4) Additional Taxes ($ million)	Additional Taxes as Percent of: (5) Actual Taxes Paid	(6) Replacement Value of Capital	Estimated Industry Totals (7) Reduced Depreciation ($ million)	(8) Additional Taxes ($ million)
20	Food & kindred products	28	45	574	275	24.4	1.3	1282	615
21	Cigars and cigarettes	6	70	139	37	12.1	.7	196	94
22	Textile mill products	6	25	81	39	41.6	1.5	330	158
23	Apparel & other finished products	6	22	14	7	12.2	.6	64	31
24	Lumber and products	6	83	683	252	100.0	2.5	825	304
25	Furniture & fixtures	4	69	15	7	28	.9	23	11
26	Paper & products	20	70	670	322	87	2.0	960	461
27	Publications & printing	12	50	89	43	16	1.5	178	85

28	Chemicals & products	43	62	1266	608	34	1.3	2039	979
29	Petroleum products	22	49	2241	1076	53	1.3	4543	2180
30	Rubber & misc. plastics	5	48	376	93	100.0	1.1	786	194
31	Leather & products	3	58	20	10	7.9	.9	35	17
32	Glass, clay & stone products	23	81	425	204	52.9	1.5	521	250
33	Primary metals	20	64	1451	180	100.0	.4	2265	280
34	Fabricated metal products	12	46	120	58	32.0	1.7	260	125
35	Nonelectrical machinery	45	64	414	199	10.4	.5	646	310
36	Electrical machinery	26	60	500	240	24.6	1.1	828	398
37	Transportation equipment	24	62	1243	597	22.2	1.4	1996	958
38	Instruments	12	49	94	45	12.8	.7	194	93
39	Misc. manufactures	4	41	30	15	19.9	1.0	75	36

NOTE: All figures refer to 1976. The number of firms in the sample for each industry is shown in column 1; these firms account for the percentage of industry sales in column 2.

Table 8.7 Inflation, Depreciation and Corporate Tax Liabilities in Manufacturing Industries

SIC Code	Industry	(1) N	(2) Sales Coverage (percent)	Sample Firms		Additional Taxes as Percent of:		Estimated Industry Totals	
				(3) Overstatement of profits ($ million)	(4) Additional Taxes ($ million)	(5) Actual Taxes Paid	(6) Replacement Value of Capital	(7) Overstatement of profits ($ million)	(8) Additional Taxes ($ million)
20	Food & kindred products	28	45	1339	642	57.0	3.0	2989	1435
21	Cigars and cigarettes	6	70	378	181	33.0	1.8	535	257
22	Textile mill products	6	25	153	73	78.7	2.9	623	299
23	Apparel & other finished products	6	22	46	22	40.6	2.0	211	102
24	Lumber and products	6	83	678	252	100.0	2.5	820	304
25	Furniture & fixtures	4	69	35	17	65.1	2.0	52	25
26	Paper & products	20	70	858	371	100.0	2.3	1230	532
27	Publications & printing	12	50	153	74	28.2	2.6	308	148

	Industry							
28	Chemicals & products	43	62	1796	862	48.9	1.8	2892	1388
29	Petroleum products	22	49	2970	1426	70.3	1.8	6025	2892
30	Rubber & misc. plastics	5	48	694	9.3	100.0	1.1	1448	194
31	Leather & products	3	58	59	28	22.7	2.6	101	48
32	Glass, clay & stone products	23	81	593	284	73.7	2.0	725	348
33	Primary metals	20	64	1828	180	100.0	.4	2852	280
34	Fabricated metal products	12	46	186	89	49.5	2.6	401	193
35	Nonelectrical machinery	45	64	707	339	17.8	.9	1103	529
36	Electrical machinery	26	60	949	455	46.6	2.1	1571	754
37	Transportation equipment	24	62	1644	789	29.4	1.8	2639	1267
38	Instruments	12	49	221	106	30.1	1.5	456	219
39	Misc. manufactures	4	41	51	24	33.1	1.7	124	60

NOTE: All figures refer to 1976. Overstatement of profits includes the effects of both historic cost depreciation and artificial inventory profits. The number of firms in the sample for each industrial is shown in column 1; these firms account for the percentage of industry sales in column 2.

tax paid by lenders because of inflation is actually slightly greater than the taxes that corporate borrowers save by deducting higher nominal interest payments.

The overall effect of inflation with existing tax laws was to raise the real 1977 tax burden on corporate sector capital income by more than \$32 billion. This extra tax represented 69 percent of the real after-tax capital income of the nonfinancial corporate sector, including retained earnings, dividends, and the real interest receipts of the corporations' creditors. The extra tax raised the total tax burden on nonfinancial corporate capital income by more than one-half of its noninflation value, raising the total effective tax rate from 43 percent to 66 percent.

The substantial increase in the effective tax rate on capital used in the nonfinancial corporate sector can influence the performance of the economy in a number of important ways. The most obvious of these is a reduction in the rate of capital formation in response to the reduction in the real after tax return.[42]

Moreover, since the tax rules that we have emphasized do not apply to residential real estate, the combination of inflation and existing tax rules will encourage a redistribution of investment away from the corporate sector and to residential construction and consumer durables. Within total corporate investment, existing tax rules will induce firms to invest more in inventories and less in equipment and structures.

The evidence on individual manufacturing industries presented in section 8.5 shows that there is substantial variation among industries in the extent to which inflation has caused greater tax burdens. In some industries, the additional tax induced by inflation accounts for less than 25 percent of actual taxes paid; in other industries, the additional tax induced by inflation is responsible for the entire actual tax payment. The additional tax varies from less than 0.5 percent of the real capital in two industries to nearly 3 percent in others. This substantial variation implies a further source of capital misallocations among individual industries within the overall manufacturing sector.

---

42. Although this reduction cannot be unambiguously established, in any realistic life cycle model a lower net return will reduce private saving (Summers, 1978). Some preliminary empirical evidence tends to support this view (Boskin, 1978).

III Interest Rates and Asset Yields

9 Inflation, Tax Rules, and the Long-term Interest Rate

with Lawrence Summers

Although the return to capital is a focus of research in both macroeconomics and public finance, each specialty has approached this subject with an almost total disregard for the other's contribution. Macroeconomic studies of the effect of inflation on the rate of interest have implicitly ignored the existence of taxes and the problems of tax depreciation.[1] Similarly, empirical studies of the incidence of corporate tax changes have not recognized that the effect of the tax depends on the rate of inflation and have ignored the information on the rate of return that investors receive in financial markets.[2] Our primary purpose in this paper is to begin to build a bridge between these two approaches to a common empirical problem.

The explicit recognition of corporate taxation substantially changes the relation between the rates of inflation and of interest that is implied by equilibrium theory. The Fisherian conclusion that the nominal rate of interest rises by the expected rate of inflation, leaving the real rate of interest unchanged, is no longer valid when borrowers treat interest payments as a deductible expense and pay tax on profits net of accounting depreciation.[3] A more general theory is discussed in the first section and is used there to analyze the expected impact of changes in inflation with the tax and depreciation rules in effect during the past twenty-five years. The

Reprinted by permission from *Brookings Papers on Economic Activity* 1978:1, pp. 61–99.

1. For a review of recent empirical studies, see Sargent (1976). This criticism applies also to Feldstein and Eckstein (1970), and Feldstein and Chamberlain (1973).
2. The prominent econometric studies include Krzyzaniak and Musgrave (1963), Gordon (1967), and Oakland (1972). Other major empirical studies include Harberger (1962) and Shoven and Whalley (1972). None of this research refers to either inflation or financial-market return.
3. One statement of Fisher's theory can be found in Fisher (1930).

analysis shows that changes in the rate of inflation are likely to be significantly nonneutral even in the very long run.

Since the long-term interest rate measures the yield available to individual investors, analysis of it provides an operational way of studying the incidence of changes in corporate tax rules. Oddly enough, this natural way of measuring tax incidence has not been exploited before. The first section shows how to translate the postwar changes in tax rates and depreciation rules into the changes in the interest rate that would prevail if no shifting occurred; it thus lays the foundation for econometric estimates of the actual degree of shifting set out in later sections. This approach requires separating the effects of inflation from the effects of tax changes. Since most of the postwar changes in corporate taxation have been in depreciation rules and investment credits, the effect of these changes on the long-term interest rate is of obvious importance in determining their potential stimulus to investment.

In a previous theoretical paper, Feldstein analyzed how an increase in the rate of inflation would alter the interest rate in an economy in steady-state growth. Although that model brought out the important nonneutrality of inflation and the need to revise Fisher's theories to reflect taxation, its relevance is severely limited by the assumptions that all investment is financed by debt and that capital goods do not depreciate. Both of these restrictive assumptions were relaxed in a subsequent paper in which firms were assumed to finance investment by a mixture of debt and equity and in which capital depreciates.[4] Introducing depreciation permits an analysis of the effect of allowing only historic cost depreciation for tax purposes. This more general model shows that the way inflation affects the real interest rate depends on two countervailing forces. The tax deductibility of interest payments tends to raise the real interest rate while historic cost depreciation lowers it. The net effect can be determined only by a more explicit specification of depreciation and tax rules than was appropriate in that theoretical study. Such an explicit analysis is presented in the first section below. Equally important, the empirical analysis of the subsequent sections does not assume that saving is inelastic or that all forms of investment are subject to the same tax rules.

The three main sections of our paper might also be regarded as three separate studies tied together by the common theme of inflation, taxes, and the interest rate. In the first section, we extend previous theoretical studies of the interaction of taxes and inflation by making explicit calculations based on the actual tax rules of the past two decades. These calculations show how changes in tax rules and in inflation rates have altered the maximum nominal interest rate that firms could pay on a

---

4. See Feldstein (1976; chap. 3 above) and Feldstein, Green, and Sheshinski (1978; chap. 4 above).

standard investment. An important implication of this analysis is that Fisher's famous conclusion is not valid in an economy with taxes on capital income.

The second section is an econometric analysis of the observed relation between inflation and the long-term interest rate. A novel feature of this analysis is the use of an explicit predicted inflation variable which is derived from an optimal forecasting equation based on an ARIMA (autoregressive integrated moving average) process, as described there.

The third section studies the effects of changes in tax rules and in pretax profitability. This section is the most ambitious in its attempt to link the econometric estimates to the analytic method developed in the first section. We regard its results as preliminary because all of our estimates are conditional on specific assumptions about the mix of debt and equity used to finance marginal investments and about the relative yields on debt and equity that the market imposes. We believe that it is important to explore a wider range of assumptions and that our method provides the correct framework for such an extended analysis.

A brief concluding section summarizes the major findings.

9.1 The Analytic Framework

The central analytic feature of this paper is the operational method of converting any change in tax rules and in expected inflation into the implied change in the long-term interest rate that is consistent with a fixed marginal product of capital. This method is presented in the current section and is then used (1) to analyze the effects of specific changes in tax rules, (2) to derive the relevant generalization of the Fisherian relation between inflation and the interest rate, and (3) to calculate the implied equilibrium interest rate for each year form 1954 through 1976. These estimates underpin the empirical analysis in the rest of the paper.

9.1.1 A Simple Illustrative Model

It is useful to begin by analyzing a simple illustrative case in which all marginal investment is financed by debt.[5] Moreover, the aggregate supply of loanable funds is taken as fixed.[6] We assume also that all investment is subject to the same tax and depreciation rules.[7] While these assumptions do not even approximate reality, they do permit a simple exposition of our method. Working through this simple case makes it easier to examine

---

5. That the *marginal* investments of all firms are financed by debt does not preclude their using retained earnings to finance investment; this view is developed by Stiglitz (1973, and 1976). For a contrary argument, see Feldstein, Green, and Sheshinski (1979).

6. This implies that the volume of saving is fixed and that the demand for money is interest inelastic.

7. This assumption ignores, for example, the difference between the tax treatment of investment in plant and equipment and of investment in residential real estate.

the more general framework with mixed debt-equity finance, an elastic supply of loanable funds, and differential tax rules.

We start by examining an economy with no inflation and see how tax changes alter the rate of interest. We then see how the interest rate responds to inflation under alternative tax and depreciation rules.

The diagram below illustrates the traditional determination of equilibrium interest rate (i_0), which equates the inelastic supply of loanable funds (S) to the downward-sloping investment-demand schedule (I). In the absence of taxes, each point on the investment schedule indicates the internal rate of return on the marginal project at the corresponding aggregate level of investment.[8]

The introduction of a corporate income tax with proper economic depreciation and the deductibility of interest payments does not shift this investment schedule; any investment that could pay a maximum interest rate of i before the introduction of the tax can pay exactly the same rate subsequently.[9] In contrast, an investment tax credit or acceleration of depreciation would raise the maximum potential interest rate on every project and would therefore shift the investment-demand schedule to the right to line I'. Given a completely inelastic supply of investable funds such a tax change simply raises the interest rate without any increase in investment.

Tax Changes. Analyzing quantitatively the effect of tax changes (and later of inflation) calls for an operational method of translating tax changes into changes in the interest rate—that is, a method of calculating i, in the diagram; the method must be compatible with a fixed marginal product of capital. To do this, we select a hypothetical "standard investment" and calculate the internal rate of return under different tax regimes. Consider a standard investment in equipment in which the real net output declines exponentially at δ percent a year[10] until the project is scrapped at the end of T years; the initial value of net output (a_0) is chosen so that, in the absence of any tax, the project has an internal rate of return of 12 percent.[11] Such a project has net output $a_0(1 + \delta)^{-t}$ in the tth year of its life, where a_0 is selected to satisfy

8. This is essentially Keynes's formulation of the schedule for the marginal efficiency of investment. We implicitly assume that mutually exclusive options are described by Irving Fisher's incremental method and that multiple internal rates of return can be ignored. For a cautionary note about this procedure, see Feldstein and Flemming (1964).

9. The pretax situation may be described by $f'(I) - i = 0$, where $f'(I)$ is the marginal product of investment; a tax at rate τ with the deductibility of interest does not change the implied value of i in $(1 - \tau)f'(I) - (1 - \tau)i = 0$.

10. Note that this is "output decay" and not "depreciation"; see Feldstein and Rothschild (1974) for an analysis of these concepts.

11. This is based on our earlier estimates of the pretax return on private investment in nonfinancial corporations; see Feldstein and Summers (1977). We raised the average return of 10.6 percent for 1948–76 reported there to 12 percent because we regard that sample period as overrepresenting cyclically low years, but the choice of any constant pretax rate of return does not alter our analysis.

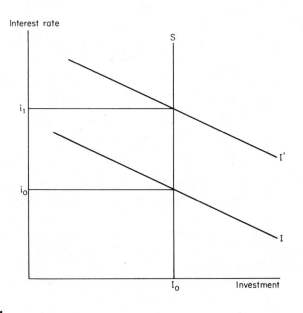

Figure 9.1

$$
(1) \qquad a_0 \sum_{t=1}^{T} \frac{(1+\delta)^{-t}}{(1.12)^t} = 1
$$

In practice, it is important to distinguish between investments in equipment and in structures because the depreciation rules and tax credits affect the two very differently; for example, the investment tax credit does not apply to structures. Our "standard investment" is therefore specified to be a mix of equipment and structures in the ratio of 1.95 to 1.[12] The specification of equation (1) is used to describe an investment in equipment with a ten-year life and an exponential decay rate of 13 percent. The net output of the investment in structures is assumed to decay at 3 percent a year and the structure is scrapped after thirty years; the output of a dollar's investment in new structures is also chosen to make the pretax rate of return equal to 12 percent. The standard investment is a thirty-year "sandwich" project, of which 66.2 percent of the investment in the first year is in a standard structure and the remainder is in equipment; the equipment is then replaced at the end of ten and twenty years.

The maximum potential interest rate corresponding to any given tax regime (that is, the value of i_1, in the diagram) is defined as the interest rate that can be paid on the outstanding balance of the loan used to

12. This figure, when used in conjunction with the procedure described below, yields an investment mix corresponding to the average composition over the past twenty years.

finance the project, where the balance is reduced to zero at the end of the life of the project. If L_t, is the loan balance at time t and x_t, is the net cash flow of the project during t (except for interest expenses), the internal rate of return is the interest rate i that satisfies

(2) $$L_t - L_{t-1} = iL_{t-1} - x_t, \; t = 1, \ldots, T$$

where $L_0 = 1$ and $L_T = 0$. In the special case of the pure equipment project and no tax, equation (2) reduces to

(3) $$L_t - L_{t-1} = iL_{t-1} - a_0(1 + \delta)^{-t}$$

The solution of this equation with $L_0 = 1$ and $L_T = 0$ is exactly equivalent to the familiar definition of the internal rate of return given by equation (1).

When a tax rate τ is levied on the net output minus the sum of the interest payment and the allowable depreciation (d_t), the loan balance changes according to

(4) $$L_t - L_{t-1} = iL_{t-1} - x_t + \tau(x_t - d_t - iL_{t-1})$$

The value of i corresponding to any tax regime is therefore available by solving for the value of i that is consistent with equation (4) for our x_t "sandwich" with $L_T = 0$ and L_0 equal to one minus the investment tax credit.

Inflation. The preceding method of analysis can also be used to analyze the effect of inflation on the investment-demand schedule and therefore on the equilibrium rate of interest if the supply of loanable funds is inelastic. More generally, the method can be extended to decompose the increase in the interest rate induced by a rise in inflation into one part due to the shift in the demand for funds and one due to a shift in the supply; we return to this decomposition below.

It is again easiest to begin by examining the case in which marginal projects are financed by debt only. Consider first the situation in the absence of taxes. In terms of equation (2) the effect of introducing a constant expected inflation at rate π is to raise the future net profit in each year by a factor $(1 + \pi)^t$ and thus to convert the fundamental equation to

(5) $$L_t - L_{t-1} = iL_{t-1} - (1 + \pi)^t x_t, \; t = 1, \ldots, T$$

For any sequence of real net profits, the internal rate of return i that satisfies the initial and terminal equations ($L_0 = 1$, $L_T = 0$) is increased by exactly the rate of inflation.[13] With a fixed supply of loanable funds, this increase in the maximum potential interest rate on all projects would raise the equilibrium interest rate by the rate of inflation.

---

13. There is actually a second-order term; the internal rate of return rises from i without inflation to $(1 + i)(1 + \pi) - 1 = i + \pi + i\pi$ with inflation.

This Fisherian conclusion is no longer valid when taxes are considered.[14] Equation (4) now becomes

(6) $$L_t - L_{t-1} = iL_{t-1} - (1 + \pi)^t x_t + \tau[(1 + \pi)^t x_t$$
$$- d(\pi)_t - iL_{t-1}]$$

where $d(\pi)_t$ is the depreciation allowed for tax purposes when there is inflation at rate π. Depending on the depreciation rule, the nominal maximum potential interest rate may rise by more or less than the rate of inflation. To see this, it is useful to consider the special case in which there is no depreciation. Equation (6) can then be written[15]

(7) $$L_t - L_{t-1} = (1 - \tau)iL_{t-1} - (1 - \tau)(1 + \pi)^t x_t$$

This is exactly the same as (5) with the real project output replaced by an after-tax value, $(1 - \tau)x_t$, and the interest rate by its after-tax value, $(1 - \tau)i$. The effect of inflation is therefore to raise the *after-tax* potential rate of interest by exactly the rate of inflation: $d[(1 - \tau)i]/d\pi = 1$, or $di/d\pi = 1/(1 - \tau)$. With the U.S. marginal corporate tax rate of $\tau = 0.48$, this implies that the maximum potential interest rate rises by almost 2 percentage points for each 1 percent of inflation. If the supply of loanable funds were perfectly inelastic, the equilibrium interest rate would also rise by nearly 2 points.

The same relationship prevails if the asset depreciates and if the historic cost basis of the depreciation is increased in proportion to the price level.[16] Although this degree of sensitivity of the interest rate may seem surprising at first, it is easily understood: each percentage point of inflation permits an increase of 2 points in the interest rate because the after-tax cost of this increase is only 1 point.[17] Moreover, this "excess adjustment" of the pretax interest rate is just sufficient to keep unchanged the after-tax return to a lender with the same marginal tax rate.[18]

The practice of allowing only historic cost depreciation reduces the real value of depreciation allowances whenever the inflation rate increases. It is equivalent to levying a tax on the accruing increases in the nominal value of the asset. This extra tax implies that the real net-of-tax yield to lenders must be reduced by inflation and therefore that an increase in

14. These remarks are developed extensively in Feldstein (1976; chap. 3 above) and Feldstein, Green, and Sheshinski (1978; chap. 4 above).

15. Note that the asset appreciates in nominal value but there is no tax due on this appreciation as such.

16. See Feldstein, Green, and Sheshinski (1978).

17. Note that with price-indexed depreciation there is no capital gains tax on the accruing increase in the nominal value of the assets or, equivalently, on the decreasing real value of the liabilities.

18. If borrowers were taxed on the *real* capital gains that resulted from the decreasing real value of their liabilities, the interest rate would rise only by the rate of inflation. To leave lenders with the same after-tax real return, the real capital losses that result from the decreasing real value of their liabilities would have to be a deductible expense.

inflation raises the nominal pretax yield by less than $1/(1 - \tau)$. Explicit calculations of this effect will now be presented.[19]

Internal Rates of Return with Pure Debt Finance. Table 9.1 presents the calculated maximum potential interest rate with pure debt finance for our standard investment under seven tax regimes. The rates are calculated first on the assumption of no inflation and then on the assumption of a constant 6 percent rate of inflation.

Consider first the results corresponding to no inflation—column 1 of table 9.1. By construction, the maximum potential interest rate (MPIR) in the absence of both taxes and inflation is 12 percent for our standard investment. Imposing the tax regime that existed until 1954 (a 52 percent corporate tax rate and straight-line depreciation) leaves the MPIR essentially unchanged at 12.4 percent.[20] Successive tax regimes liberalized depreciation and raised the MPIR. The accelerated-depreciation options introduced in 1954 were adopted only gradually, but by 1960, the mix of depreciation patterns implied an MPIR of 13.3 percent. The introduction of the investment tax credit raised it further, to 14 percent in 1963. Currently, because of a 10 percent investment tax credit and the asset-depreciation-range (ADR) method of depreciation, the MPIR has reached 14.9 percent.[21] The tax changes since 1954 have thus raised the MPIR by one-fifth of its original value.[22]

Comparing the two columns of table 9.1 reveals the ways in which taxation changes the way inflation affects the rate of interest. With no tax, a 6 percent rate of inflation raises the MPIR by 6 percentage points—from 12.0 to 18.0. In contrast, with a 52 percent tax and straight-line depreciation (regime B), the 6 percent inflation raises the MPIR by 9.2 points (from 12.4 percent to 21.6 percent). Thus $di/d\pi = 1.53$ in this regime. Note that a lender (bondholder) thus experiences an increase in the real rate of return from 12.4 to 15.6 percent. However, since the personal tax is levied on the full nominal return, the lender will receive a reduced real return after tax unless his marginal tax rate is less than 35 percent. At a personal tax rate of 50 percent, for example, the real after-tax yield on bonds falls from 6.2 percent with no inflation to 4.8 percent with 6 percent inflation.

The same pattern can be followed with all of the other tax regimes of the postwar period. The figures in column 2 show that under every

19. The theory of this relation is discussed in Feldstein, Green, and Sheshinski (1978, chap. 4); see in particular the appendix to that paper by Alan Auerbach, pp. 59–60 above.

20. The MPIR is increased in the shift from regime *A* (no tax) to regime *B* because straight-line depreciation is slightly more generous than true economic depreciation.

21. The effective rate of tax credit of 9 percent shown in the table differs from the statutory rate of 10 percent because of limitations on loss offset and carryover. Also, certain firms and types of investment are not eligible for the credit. In all our work, we use the effective rate.

22. Note that because interest is deductible, a lower tax rate actually lowers the MPIR, as illustrated by the tax cut in 1964 (switching from regime E to F).

Table 9.1   **Maximum Potential Interest Rate with 100 Percent Marginal Debt Finance, Alternative Tax Regimes, and Inflation Rates**

Percent

Tax Regime (corporate tax rate, depreciation method, and other provisions)	Inflation Rate	
	0	6 percent
(A) No tax	12.0	18.0
(B) 52 percent; straight-line depreciation	12.4	21.6
(C) 52 percent; accelerated depreciation as of 1960	13.3	22.6
(D) 52 percent; investment tax credit of 5.6 percent; depreciation as of 1963:4 with Long amendment	14.0	23.7
(E) Same as D, except Long amendment repealed	14.2	23.8
(F) Same as E, except 48 percent	14.0	23.0
(G) Current law: 48 percent; investment tax credit of 9 percent;[a] asset depreciation range	14.9	24.3

SOURCE: Derived by method described in text.

a. See text note 21.

regime, a 6 percent inflation rate would raise the nominal rate of return by between 9.0 and 9.7 percentage points.

Although the assumption that marginal investments are financed completely by debt is a useful analytic simplification, the implied interest rates shown in columns 1 and 2 are clearly inconsistent with market experience. The real long-term interest rates are not (and never have been during the postwar period) even remotely close to the high values presented in table 9.1. We turn therefore to the more relevant case of investments financed by a mix of debt and equity.

9.1.2   The Interest Rate with Mixed Debt-Equity Finance

Our view of the role of debt and equity finance starts with the observation that issuing more debt increases the riskiness of both the bonds and the stocks of the firms.[23] Issuing additional debt thus raises the interest rate that the firm must pay and lowers the price of its shares. The firm therefore does not finance all incremental investment by debt but selects a debt-equity ratio that, given tax rules and investor preferences, minimizes the cost of its capital. If the firm is in equilibrium, the mix of debt and equity used to finance an incremental investment is the same as its average debt-equity investment.[24] The interest rate than a firm can pay on

23. This view is developed explicitly in Feldstein, Green, and Sheshinski (1979). The traditional Modigliani-Miller conclusion that the cost of capital is independent of the debt-equity ratio holds generally only in a world without taxation and bankruptcy.

24. If the firm issues no new equity, it establishes its desired debt-equity ratio by its dividend policy and its debt-issue policy.

a "standard investment" depends on this debt-equity ratio and on the relation between the equity yield and the debt yield that is consistent with the preferences of portfolio investors.

In our analysis, we assume that the ratio of debt to total capital is one to three, roughly the average ratio of nonfinancial corporate debt to the replacement value of that sector's capital during the past decade. Although it would clearly be desirable to extend our analysis to make the debt-equity ratio endogenous, this generalization must be postponed until later research.

Our basic assumption about the preference of portfolio investors is that, because equity investments are riskier than debt investments, portfolio equilibrium requires a higher yield on equity than on debt. We consider two variants of the yield differential. First, we assume that the real equity yield (denoted by e) must exceed the real interest rate $(i - \pi)$ by a constant risk premium, D.[25]

$$(8) \qquad\qquad e = i - \pi + D$$

We shall examine several different values of D. Our alternative specification relates the risk premium to the differences in real *after-tax* rates of return to an investor. Computational results analogous to table 9.1 are presented for both specifications and both are examined in the econometric analysis below.

If the portfolio investor has a marginal personal tax rate θ, the real after-tax return on a bond may be written $i_n = (1 - \theta)i - \pi$. Specifying the real after-tax yield on equity (e_n) is more complex. Let p be the fraction of the real equity yield that is paid out and $(1 - p)$ the fraction that is retained. The part that is paid out is taxed at rate θ while the retained earnings are subject only to an eventual tax at the capital gains rate. We use θ_g to denote the "equivalent concurrent capital gains tax rate"—that is, the present value of the future tax equivalent to taxing the retained earnings immediately at rate θ_g. In addition to these taxes on real equity earnings, the stock investor must also pay a tax on the *nominal* capital gains that occur solely because of inflation. With inflation at rate π, the resulting nominal capital gain at rate π is subject to capital gains tax at effective rate θ_g. The real net return may therefore be written:

$$e_n = [p(1 - \theta) + (1 - p)(1 - \theta_g)]e - \theta_g\pi$$

Our after-tax alternative to equation (8) is therefore

$$(9) \qquad\qquad e_n = i_n + D$$

or

---

25. Since we assume a constant debt-equity ratio, changes in the risk premium are not induced by changes in that ratio. Note also that e includes the real gains that accrue to equity investors at the expense of bondholders.

(10) $$[p(1 - \theta) + (1 - p)(1 - \theta_g)]e - \theta_g\pi$$
$$= (1 - \theta)i - \pi + D$$

For our numerical calculations, we assume the reasonable values $p = 0.5$, $\theta = 0.4$, and $\theta_g = 0.10$.

The method of calculating the maximum potential interest rate used in the pure-debt model (discussed above) can be applied to find the values of i and e that satisfy either (8) and (9) for our "standard investment." Note that a firm's net cost of funds (N) is a weighted average of the net-of-tax interest that it pays and the yield on its equity. In nominal terms,

(11) $$N = b(1 - \tau)i + (1 - b)(e + \pi)$$

In the special case of pure-debt finance, $N = (1 - \tau)i$; the solution of the difference equation (6) provides a value for i and, since τ is known, for N as well. More generally, regardless of the mix of debt and equity finance, the solution of equation (6) can be interpreted as equal to $N/(1 - \tau)$; that is, it is equal to the cost of funds to the firm stated as if all these costs were deductible from the corporate income tax.

To calculate the value of i corresponding to any tax regime we therefore proceed in three steps. First, we solve equation (6) to obtain a value of $N/(1 - \tau)$. Second, we multiply this by $(1 - \tau)$ to obtain N. Finally with this known value of N we can solve the two equations simultaneously (11 and 8 or 10) for i and e.

Table 9.2 presents the interest rates corresponding to the pretax portfolio-balance rule of equation (8). Separate results with and without inflation are presented for three risk premiums ($D = 0.06$, 0.08, and 0.04). Note first that the implied interest rates, especially those corresponding to $D = 0.06$, are much closer to observed experience than the results based on complete debt finance in table 9.1.[26]

The numbers in column 1 (zero inflation rate) deserve comment for two reasons. First, unlike the results in the pure-debt model of table 9.1, the introduction of the corporate income tax significantly lowers the implied bond yield. This reflects the payment of a significant tax, which must reduce both the equity and debt yields. Similarly, in contrast to table 9.1, the reduced corporate tax rate in 1964 now causes an increase in the MPIR. Second, the various liberalizations of depreciation and the introduction of the investment tax credit raise the MPIR. The absolute increase is smaller than in the pure-debt case of table 9.1, but the proportional rise is substantially larger.

---

26. Note that in regimes B through G the values for $D = 0.08$ and $D = 0.04$ differ from the corresponding values for $D = 0.06$ by 0.016. This constant difference holds to the three-decimal-place accuracy of our table but is not an exact relation when the corporate tax rate τ changes.

Table 9.2   **Maximum Potential Interest Rate with One-Third Debt Finance and Selected Pretax Risk Differentials for Alternative Tax Regimes and Inflation Rates**

Percent

	Pretax Risk Differential (D)					
	6 percent		8 percent		4 percent	
	Inflation rate		Inflation rate		Inflation rate	
Tax Regime (corporate tax rate, depreciation method, and other provisions)	0 (1)	6 (2)	0 (3)	6 (4)	0 (5)	6 (6)
(A) No tax	8.0	14.0	6.7	12.7	9.3	15.3
(B) 52 percent; straight-line depreciation	2.4	7.7	0.8	6.1	4.0	9.3
(C) 52 percent; accelerated depreciation as of 1960	2.9	8.3	1.3	6.7	4.5	9.9
(D) 52 percent; investment tax credit of 5.6 percent; depreciation as of 1963:4 with Long amendment	3.3	8.9	1.7	7.3	4.9	10.5
(E) Same as D, except Long amendment repealed	3.4	9.0	1.8	7.4	5.0	10.6
(F) Same as E, except 48 percent	3.8	9.4	2.2	7.8	5.4	11.0
(G) Current law: 48 percent; investment tax credit of 9 percent;[a] asset depreciation range	4.4	10.2	2.8	8.6	6.0	11.8

SOURCE: Derived by method described in text.

a. See text note 21.

The effect of a 6 percent inflation rate is seen by comparing columns 1 and 2. With no tax, the MPIR rises by the full amount of the inflation; a 6 percent inflation raises it from 8.0 percent to 14.0 percent. The presence of taxes again changes this relation but the effect is very different with mixed debt-equity finance than in the pure-debt case. In each of the tax regimes, a 6 percent inflation rate raises the nominal interest rate by only about 5.5 percent: $di/d\pi = 0.92$. This implies that the real rate of return on debt falls even for the lender (bondholder) who is not subject to any personal tax. For a lender who pays a significant marginal tax rate, the equilibrium real net internal rate of return can easily be negative. Under regime C, the real net yield to a 50 percent taxpayer falls from 1.45 percent to -1.85 percent. With the most recent regime (G), the 6 percent inflation rate reduces the real net yield from 2.2 percent to -0.90 percent.

Table 9.3 presents the corresponding maximum potential interest rates for the net-of-tax portfolio-balance rule of equation (10). Again, the corporate income tax causes a substantial reduction in the real interest rate. The liberalized depreciation rules raise this interest rate substantially but, even in the absence of inflation, it remains significantly below the value without taxes. The most important difference between the results of tables 9.2 and 9.3 is the greater sensitivity of MPIR to inflation with the net-of-tax portfolio-balance rule of table 9.3. Comparing columns 1 and 2 shows that a 6 percent inflation rate would raise the nominal

Table 9.3   **Maximum Potential Interest Rate with One-Third Debt Finance and Selected Net-of-Tax Risk Differentials for Alternative Tax Regimes and Inflation Rates**

Percent

	Net-of-Tax Risk Differential (D)					
	6 percent		4 percent		5 percent	
	Inflation rate		Inflation rate		Inflation rate	
Tax Regime (corporate tax rate, depreciation method, and other provisions)	0 (1)	6 (2)	0 (3)	6 (4)	0 (5)	6 (6)
(A) No tax	8.0	14.0	9.3	15.3	8.6	14.3
(B) 52 percent; straight-line depreciation	0.9	8.4	3.4	10.9	2.2	9.6
(C) 52 percent; accelerated depreciation as of 1960	1.5	9.1	4.0	11.6	2.8	10.4
(D) 52 percent; investment tax credit of 5.6 percent; depreciation as of 1963:4 with Long amendment	2.0	9.9	4.5	12.4	3.2	11.2
(E) Same as D, except Long amendment repealed	2.1	9.9	4.6	12.4	3.4	11.2
(F) Same as E, except 48 percent	2.6	10.3	5.1	12.8	3.9	11.6
(G) Current law: 48 percent; investment tax credit of 9 percent;[a] asset depreciation range	3.3	11.3	5.8	13.8	4.6	12.6

SOURCE: Derived by method described in text.

a. See text note 21.

MPIR by 7.5 percent under regime B, implying $di/d\pi = 1.25$; this result is essentially independent of the differential (D) that is assumed. The faster writeoffs that are incorporated in the succeeding tax regimes reduce the extent to which inflation lowers the value of the tax depreciation. The smaller adverse effect on the value of depreciation raises $di/d\pi$; the value of 1.25 under regime B comes 1.32 with regime D and 1.33 with the current regime (G).

The maximum potential interest rates shown in tables 9.2 and 9.3 have two very important implications. First, inflation severely depresses the real net rate of return (i_n) that can be paid to a bondholder on the basis of our standard investment project. Consider an investor whose marginal tax rate is 40 percent. Table 9.2 implies that with current law and a risk differential of $D = 0.06$, a 6 percent inflation raises the nominal before-tax return from 4.4 to 10.2 percent, but reduces the real net return from 2.6 percent to 0.1 percent. With the more favorable assumptions of table 9.3, a 6 percent inflation reduces the real return from 2.0 percent to 0.8 percent. This has obvious effects on the incentive to save and to make risky portfolio investments.

The second implication relates to the firm's incentive to invest. It is frequently argued that, because their real net borrowing rate has fallen, firms now have a greater incentive to invest than they did a few years ago. The calculations of tables 9.2 and 9.3 show that the inference is wrong because inflation also reduces the maximum real net borrowing rate that firms can afford to pay on any investment. Table 9.2 with $D = 0.06$ implies that in the absence of inflation a firm could afford to pay an after-tax interest cost of 2.3 percent on the standard investment project.[27] Inflation at 6 percent reduces the maximum real after-tax interest rate for this project below zero to −0.7 percent![28] The real net cost of debt finance must thus fall by 3.0 percentage points to avoid reducing the incentive to invest. Similarly, with table 9.3, the firm could afford a net interest cost of 1.7 percent in the absence of inflation but only a negative cost, −0.1 percent, with 6 percent inflation. It is clear that the usual way of evaluating investment incentives in terms of the real net cost of finance is very misleading with the U.S. tax system when inflation is significant.[29]

9.1.3   The Effect of a Variable Supply of Investable Funds

Until now, all of our calculations have referred to the same standard investment project and therefore implicitly to a fixed supply of investable funds. Moreover, we have assumed that inflation has no effect on the

27. $(1 - \tau)i = 0.52 (0.044) = 0.0229.$
28. $(1 - \tau)i - \pi = 0.52 (0 102) - 0.06 = - 0.0070.$
29. The empirical results of the next two sections suggest that the actual real net interest rate falls by about enough to keep incentives to invest unchanged despite the low maximum potential interest rate.

supply of loanable funds to the nonfinancial corporate sector. The econometric estimation of the actual effect of changes in the corporation tax requires attention to both of these issues.

Once again we begin by considering an economy in which there is no inflation and all marginal investment is financed by debt. The notion of a fixed supply of loanable funds (the vertical S of line figure 9.1) rested on the assumption that our analysis relates to the entire economy and that the supply of saving is interest inelastic. It is important for subsequent empirical analysis to drop these two assumptions. Our econometric analysis will deal with the long-term corporate bond rate; but the demand for long-term credit comes not only from business firms, but also from investors in residential real estate, from state, local, and federal governments, and from abroad. These investment demands are not directly affected by the investment tax credit, accelerated depreciation, or changes in the corporate tax rate. This implies that the supply of loanable funds to the nonfinancial corporate sector is an increasing function of the long-term bond yield and that this supply function is not shifted by the changes in corporate tax rules. This supply elasticity would be increased by a positive response of domestic saving and international capital flows to the net interest rate.

Figure 9.2 is therefore a more appropriate representation than figure 9.1. A more liberal depreciation policy (a shift from I to I') has a more limited effect on the long-term interest rate. The magnitude depends on

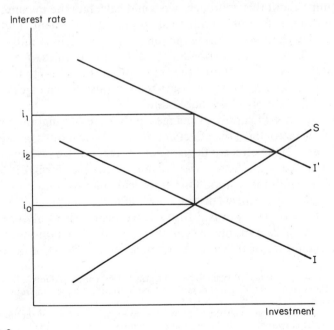

Figure 9.2

the elasticity of the supply of loanable funds to the nonfinancial business sector and therefore on both the relative size of the rest of the debt market and the degree of substitutability in investors' portfolios.

The ratio of the actual change in the long-term interest rate $(i_2 - i_0)$ to the change that would have occurred $(i_1 - i_0)$ if investment and therefore the marginal product of capital had remained the same thus measures the extent to which the tax change is shifted from corporate capital to capital elsewhere and to labor.

Our empirical analysis below focuses on the extent of tax shifting in this general sense. We look at the tax changes as summarized by the change in the corporate maximum potential interest rate and ask what impact this potential change actually had on the yields available to portfolio investors with uncommitted funds. The ratio of $(i_2 - i_0)$ to $(i_1 - i_0)$ is analogous to the definition of the incidence of corporate tax changes used in previous empirical studies.[30] This measure of incidence should be distinguished from the more general concept of the fracion of the tax change borne by capital in *all* sectors. A change in the corporate tax might be borne solely by capital even though the corporate sector bore only a modest fraction.[31] Our estimate of the ratio of $(i_2 - i_0)$ to $(i_1 - i_0)$ therefore does not measure the shift of the tax change from capital to labor. We return later to consider how well our empirical analysis of the tax-included change in the long-term bond rate measures the impact of the tax on the yield to capital in general and not just on the capital invested in the corporate sector.

To implement this approach, we could calculate the maximum potential interest rate for our hypothetical "standard investment" under the tax regime of each quarter during the sample period. This would yield the i_1 values of figure 9.2 corresponding to different tax rules. We could then estimate an equation relating the actual interest rate (i_2) to these values. In practice, however, it is necessary to allow also for changes in inflation that shift the supply of available funds.

The response of supply to changes in the rate of inflation depends on three basic factors: (1) the effect of nominal interest rates on the demand for money; (2) the effect of the real net interest rate on saving; and (3) the effect of inflation on the real yields available in other forms of investment open to portfolio investors. Our empirical analysis does not attempt to disentangle these aspects or to model explicitly the effect of inflation on yields of alternative assets.[32] Instead, we distinguish only between the changes in the rate of interest caused (1) by the inflation-induced rise in the nominal rate of return and (2) by all other effects of inflation.

30. See, for example, Krzyzaniak and Musgrave (1963) and Oakland (1972). However, these authors analyzed the effect, not on uncommitted funds, but on the return of existing investments.

31. See, for example, Harberger (1962) for an explicit analysis of the incidence of a change in the corporate tax in an economy with more than one sector.

32. Benjamin Friedman's explicit modeling of the supply of and demand for corporate debt might usefully be extended in this direction. See, for example, Friedman (1977).

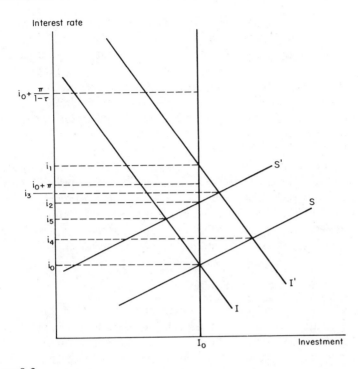

Figure 9.3

This distinction is illustrated in figure 9.3. In the absence of inflation, the equilibrium interest rate is i_0 and investment is I_0. The effect of inflation at rate π is to raise the investment-demand schedule to I'. In a pure Fisherian economy, the vertical displacement of this schedule would equal the rate of inflation: $i_1 - i_0 = \pi$. But with taxes and historic cost depreciation, this vertical shift is likely to be somewhere between π and $\pi/(1 - \tau)$, as it is in figure 9.3. Inflation will also shift the supply schedule of loanable funds from S to S'. In the pure Fisherian world, this vertical displacement would also equal the rate of inflation: $i_2 - i_0 = \pi$, implying $i_2 = i_1$. [33] More realistically, the supply shift will depend on the three factors identified in the previous paragraph. The change in the equilibrium interest rate will depend on the shifts and the slopes of both the demand and supply schedules.

As this analysis indicates, an empirical study of the relation between inflation and the interest rate should *not* be construed as a test of Irving Fisher's theory. Wih a complex structure of taxes, Fisher's conclusion would not be expected to hold. The purpose of an empirical study should instead be to assess the response of nominal long-term interest rates to inflation and therefore the effect on real after-tax yields. The statistical

---

33. Note that if the supply is perfectly inelastic (that is, if the schedule is vertical), the Fisherian result can occur with no shift in supply.

analysis presented below therefore begins by trying to measure this response of the interest rate to expected inflation;[34] in terms of figure 9.3, this coefficient equals $(i_3 - i_0)/\pi$. Our analysis can also go further and estimate how much of the increase in the interest rate would be due to a shift in the demand for funds with the supply schedule fixed $(i_4 - i_0)$ and how much to the shift in supply with a fixed demand schedule $(i_5 - i_0)$. With linear demand and supply schedules, this procedure provides an exact decomposition of the observed changes: $i_3 - i_0 = (i_4 - i_0) + (i_5 - i_0)$.

The current discussion of the effect of inflation when all marginal investments are financed by debt is extended and applied below to investments in which debt finance provides one-third of marginal capital and equity finance, two-thirds. Our analysis assumes that the debt-equity ratio is unaffected by the rate of inflation and that the *real* rates of return to debt and equity have a constant net or gross differential.

9.2   Estimating the Effect of Inflation

In this section we begin the empirical investigation of the impact of expected inflation on the long-term rate of interest. As we emphasized above, we do not regard this as a test of Fisher's conclusion since there is no reason to expect such a one-for-one impact of inflation on the interest rate in an economy in which taxes play such an important role. Instead, our aim is to estimate the net impact of expected inflation on the nominal rate of interest in order to assess the effect of inflation on the real cost of capital and the real return to investors. If the supply of loanable funds for the purchase of bonds were fixed, we would expect the equilibrium interest rate to rise in the same way as the maximum potential interest rate. In fact, however, the supply schedule is likely to be neither completely inelastic nor independent of the inflation rate. Without a much more detailed analysis, we must regard a wide range of inflation impacts as plausible a priori.

At this stage we focus on the relation between the interest rate and expected inflation. The next section introduces the effects of changes in tax and depreciation rules. Since adding the tax variable does not alter the conclusion about the effect of inflation, we prefer to start with the simple specification in which we can concentrate on making expected inflation an operational concept.

In all of our analyses, we measure the long-term interest rate by an average of yields on new issues of high-grade corporate bonds, adjusted to be comparable to the Aaa rate.[35] The use of new-issue yields is important because seasoned issues with lower coupon rates will also have

---

34. The operational specification of expected inflation is discussed below.
35. Data Resources, Inc., made this series available to us.

lower market yields owing to the more favorable tax treatment of capital gains. The new-issue yield, however, is influenced by the call-protection feature, which may make it respond more to inflation rates than it would otherwise.

The expected rate of inflation is defined in terms of the price of consumer goods and services as measured by the deflator of personal consumption expenditures in GNP. In principle, our analysis should recognize that wage rates and the prices of consumption goods, of investment goods, and of the output of nonfinancial corporations do not move proportionately and would be expected to have different effects on the supply and demand for investment funds. In practice, it is not possible to include more than one inflation variable and the choice does not alter the results in an essential way. We use expectations of the consumption price for three reasons: (1) This is the price that should affect household decisions. (2) Although firms produce investment and intermediary goods, they also purchase these goods; the consumption price may therefore be a good approximation of the price of sales by the nonfinancial corporate sector to the rest of the economy. (3) The future movement of nominal wage rates may be approximated best by the expected movement in consumer prices.

This section develops two approaches to specifying the expected future rate of inflation. The first uses the familiar distributed lag on past inflation rates, with the identifying restriction that the weights on past inflation must sum to one. Recognizing that this restriction may be invalid, we explore an alternative approach based on a series of separate optimal forecasts of inflation. In practice, the two approaches lead to very similar results.

Consider first the distributed-lag approach that has been used ever since Irving Fisher's own pioneering work on this subject. We posit that the interest rate (i) in related to expected inflation (π^*) according to

$$(12) \qquad i_t = \beta_0 + \beta_1 \pi_t^*$$

where

$$(13) \qquad \pi_t^* = \sum_{j=0}^{T} w_j \pi_{t-j}$$

with

$$(14) \qquad \sum_{j=0}^{T} w_j = 1$$

Substituting equation (13) into equation (12) yields the estimable equation

$$(15) \qquad i_t = \beta_0 + \beta_1 \sum_{j=0}^{T} w_j \pi_{t-j}$$

The key coefficient β_1 is estimable only because of the identifying restriction of equation (14).

Equation (15) was estimated by assuming that the weights on lagged inflation (that is, $j > 0$) satisfy a second-order polynomial and that $T = 16$ quarters; the coefficient of the concurrent inflation rate ($j = 0$) was unconstrained. The basic parameter estimates are presented in equation (16). (The numbers in parentheses here and in the equations that follow are standard errors.)

$$(16) \qquad i_t = 3.05 + 0.19\ \pi_t + \beta_1 \sum_{j=1}^{16} w_j \pi_{t-j}$$
$$ (0.17)\ \ (0.05)$$

$$\beta_1 \sum_{j=1}^{16} w_j = 0.64$$
$$\phantom{\beta_1 \sum_{j=1}^{16} w_j =} (0.06)$$

Sample period: 1954:1–1976:4; $\bar{R}^2 = 0.82$; Durbin-Watson = 0.21.

The identifying restriction that $\sum_{j=0}^{16} w_j = 1$ implies that $\beta_1 = 0.83$.[36] With no inflation, the interest rate would be 3.05 percent; with a sustained (and hence expected) inflation rate of 6 percent, the nominal interest rate would rise to 8.03 percent.

Sargent has rightly emphasized that the identifying restriction of equation (14) may be unwarranted.[37] The optimal weights (the w_j) depend on the nature of the process that is being forecast. If the π_t remain constant for a long time, it is clearly appropriate that the weights sum to unity and therefore predict that the same π_t will continue. But where the historic pattern of the π_t is more varied, a different set of weights will be optimal. Dropping the restriction of equation 14 leaves β_1 in (15) underidentified. This apparently led Sargent to abandon the estimation of β_1 and to attempt to test Fisher's conclusion indirectly by examining a rational expectations model of unemployment.[38] We do not think that so circuitous a route is necessary and propose instead to develop an explicit optimal forecast measure of expected inflation for use as a regressor to estimate equation (12) directly.

To derive forecasts of inflation rates, we use the optimal ARIMA forecasting procedure of Box and Jenkins.[39] We assume that the forecasts made at any time are to be based only on the information available at that time. This requires reestimating a separate Box-Jenkins equation for each quarter based on the observations available as of that quarter. To

36. That is, $0.64 + 0.19$, the latter being the coefficient of π_t.
37. See Sargent (1973).
38. Sargent concludes that his indirect evidence was ambiguous. When taxes are recognized, even the theoretical link between Sargent's equation and the inflation-interest relation is unclear.
39. In principal, of course, the Box-Jenkins procedure is too restrictive and one should derive forecasts from a completely specified econometric model. Unfortunately, doing so requires projecting all of the exogenous variables. The more general procedure that requires estimates of monetary and fiscal policy for many years ahead would not necessarily yield better forecasts than the simpler Box-Jenkins procedure. See Box and Jenkins (1970).

relax the assumption that inflation rates are generated by the same stochastic process over the entire postwar period, we specify that the ARIMA process estimated at each date is based only on the most recent ten years of data.[40] After some preliminary analysis of the data, we selected a first-order autoregressive and first-order moving-average process. With the inflation rates measured as deviations from the ten-year sample means, denoted by π, this ARIMA process can be written as

(17) $$\pi_t = \phi\pi_{t-1} + \epsilon_t - \theta\epsilon_{t-1}$$

where ϵ_t is a purely random disturbance. Equation (17) was estimated by the Box-Jenkins procedure for changing samples ending in each quarter from 1954:1 through 1976:4. The minimum mean-square-error forecast of the inflation rate in quarter $t + 1$ as of quarter t is

(18) $$\hat{\pi}_{t+1} = \frac{\phi - \theta}{1 - \theta L}\,\pi_t$$

where L is the lag operator.

A striking result of these estimates of the predicted inflation rate, shown in table 9.4, is the implied change in the sum of the optimal forecast weights on past inflation rates.[41] Because we assume that inflation rates follow a stationary process, our specification implies that the optimal weights always sum to less than one.[42] Until 1970, the implied sum of the weights was always between 0.30 and 0.40. During the 1970s, the sum of the weights has risen markedly, from 0.45 in 1970 to 0.55 in 1973 to 0.71 in 1976. Since the mean lag has remained almost constant, the rapidly rising weights imply an increased sensitivity of the optimal inflation forecast to recent experience.[43] This has potentially important implications for the changing evidence on the "accelerationist hypothesis" and other issues that we shall not explore in this paper.[44]

The expected inflation rate that affects the long-term interest rate involves a long horizon and not merely the next quarter. We can use

40. Since our sample begins in the first quarter of 1954, it is not appropriate to use a ten-year history of inflation that stretches back into World War II. The earliest inflation observation used is the first quarter of 1947; the sample is extended until a full ten years is available.

41. It follows from equation (18) that, when the process is represented as an autoregressive process, the sum of the weights is $(\phi - \theta)(1 - \theta)$.

42. Recall that our estimates are based on deviations from the sample mean so that a constant inflation rate would eventually be predicted accurately.

43. The mean lag, $1/(1 - \theta)$, was approximately 1.4 quarters until 1970 and has since been between 1.5 and 1.6 quarters.

44. The coefficients of the distributed lag on past inflation have been regarded as a test of the accelerationist hypothesis that the long-run Phillips curve is vertical. This implicitly accepts an identifying restriction like our equation (14). The evidence of an increasing coefficient on lagged inflation might be better interpreted as a changing relation between past inflation and expected inflation. For evidence of the increasing coefficients on past inflation in this context, see Gordon (1971) and Eckstein and Brinner (1972).

Table 9.4   **The Long-term Interest Rate and the
                        Predicted Inflation Rate, 1954–76**

Percent

Year	Long-term Interest Rate (i_t)	Predicted Inflation Rate (π_t^e)	Year	Long-term Interest Rate (i_t)	Predicted Inflation Rate (π_t^e)
1954	2.9	2.9	1966	5.4	2.0
1955	3.2	2.7	1967	5.8	1.9
1956	3.7	2.6	1968	6.5	2.3
1957	4.4	2.6	1969	7.7	3.1
1958	4.0	2.2	1970	8.5	3.3
1959	4.8	2.3	1971	7.4	3.6
1960	4.7	2.4	1972	7.2	3.2
1961	4.4	1.9	1973	7.7	4.3
1962	4.2	1.7	1974	9.0	8.0
1963	4.2	1.7	1975	9.0	5.2
1964	4.4	1.7	1976	8.3	5.2
1965	4.5	1.8			

SOURCES: The long-term interest rate is an average of yields on new issues of high-grade corporate bonds adjusted to the comparable Aaa rate. The series was provided by Data Resources, Inc. The predicted inflation rate is the weighted (discounted) average of ten years of quarterly Box-Jenkins forecasts (see text).

equation (18) to calculate iteratively a sequence of inflation rates in future quarters. We define the expected inflation rate π_t^e as the weighted average of the quarterly predicted inflation rates during the subsequent ten years, where the weights reflect discounting of future inflation by the interest rate. Moderate changes in the average period would have no appreciable effect on our analysis.[45]

Equation (19) presents the estimated interest rate equation based on the optimal inflation forecast:

$$(19) \qquad i_t = 2.9 + 0.94 \ \pi_t^e$$
$$(0.09)$$

Sample period: 1954:1–1976:4; $\bar{R}^2 = 0.53$; Durbin-Watson = 0.13.

The estimate 0.94 is very close to one and certainly not significantly different. Thus, this estimate, based on an optimal Box-Jenkins forecast of future inflation, is very similar to the traditional distributed-lag estimate of equation (16).

Forecasting inflation on the basis of past inflation is clearly more appropriate at some times than at others. If the reduction in inflation rates after the Korean War was properly anticipated, the estimates of expected inflation based on past inflation rates would be too high for the

45. When we return to explicit analysis of the internal rate of return in the next section, the inflation forecasts can be incorporated directly into its calculation.

early years in table 9.4. We have therefore reestimated equations (16) and (19) for the period beginning in 1960. The results are quite similar to the estimates for the entire sample: the weights sum to 0.75 with the polynomial distributed lag, and the coefficient is 0.88 when the predicted inflation variable (π_t^e) is used.

The very low Durbin-Watson statistics of our estimated equations indicate an extremely high first-order autocorrelation of the stochastic errors. This is just what we would expect in an efficient market for long-term bonds. The *change* in the long-term interest rate from quarter to quarter (and therefore the change in the price of the asset) would be expected to depend on *changes* in such fundamental determinants as the expected inflation rate with a stochastic disturbance that is serially uncorrelated and that therefore cannot be predicted. This serial independence in first differences corresponds to the observed high autocorrelation when the *level* of the interest rate is the dependent variable. The high autocorrelation of the residuals implies that our method of estimation is inefficient and that the standard errors are underestimated. We have not, however, followed the common statistical procedure of estimating the equation in first-difference form (or, more generally, after an autoregressive transformation) because we believe that doing so would introduce a substantial errors-in-variables bias. Specifically, we recognize that a variable like π_t^e is only an imperfect measure of expected inflation. Because inflation (and presumably expected inflation) has changed substantially during our sample period, most of the variance in the π_t^e series will reflect the variance of the true (but unobserved) expected inflation. A relatively small amount of "noise" will cause a correspondingly small downward bias in the coefficient of the π_t^e variable. In contrast, taking the first differences of the π_t^e series would eliminate most of the systematic component of its variance while leaving the measurement error. The result would be a very substantial bias in the coefficient. In terms of the mean-square error of the estimated coefficient, it is better to accept the inefficiency of ordinary least-squares estimation of the untransformed equation than to subject the estimates to a much more serious bias.[46]

To explore this view, we did estimate equation (19) with a first-order autoregressive transformation. The maximum-likelihood procedure implied a serial correlation of 0.99 and parameter estimates as follows:

$$(20) \qquad i_t = 5.0 + 0.14\,\pi_t^e + 0.99u_{t-1}$$
$$\qquad\qquad (1.8)\ \ (0.08)$$

Sample period: 1954:1–1976:4; $\bar{R}^2 = 0.97$; Durbin-Watson = 1.8.

We regard the very low parameter estimate of 0.14 as an indication of the relative error variance in the quarterly changes in π_t^e rather than as

---

46. As noted in the text, the substantial autocorrelation does, however, imply that our standard errors are underestimated.

evidence that the true coefficient of π_t^e is so low. This conclusion is supported by using an instrumental-variable procedure to estimate equation (19) in first-difference form:[47]

$$(21) \qquad i_t - i_{t-1} = 0.04 + 0.66 \ (\pi_t^e - \pi_{t-1}^e)$$
$$(0.04) \ (0.22)$$

Sample period: 1954:1–1976:4; Durbin-Watson = 1.86.

The estimated inflation coefficient of 0.66 (with a standard error of 0.22) is much closer to the basic parameter values of equations (16) and (19).

Although our evidence is thus roughly consistent with Irving Fisher's conclusion that the interest rate rises by the rate of inflation, both the mechanism and the implications are quite different. The rise in the nominal rate of interest reflects the impact of the tax and depreciation rules. Although the nominal interest rate rises by approximately the increase in expected inflation, the net result is far from neutral. For the individual lender, the rise in the nominal interest rate is sufficient to keep the real return *before tax* unchanged, but implies a sharp fall in the real return *after tax*. For example, a lender with a 50 percent marginal tax rate could find a real net yield of 3 percent in the absence of inflation reduced to zero by a 6 percent inflation.

Inflation is so not neutral from the firm's point of view. With an increase in the interest rate equal to the increase in inflation, the *real* net interest cost to the firm falls substantially. But, as tables 9.2 and 9.3 showed, the potential real net interest rate that the firm can pay also falls. There is neutrality with respect to the firm and therefore with respect to investment only if the actual rate falls by an equal amount. Equivalently, there is neutrality only if the actual and potential nominal interest rates rise by an equal amount. If the first rises by more than the second, the firm must adjust by reducing investment.

9.3   Changes in Tax Rules, Inflation, and Pretax Profitability

We return now to the method of analyzing the effects of changes in tax rules and inflation rates that was developed in the first section. We extend this method here to deal with forecasts of changing inflation rates and with fluctuations in the pretax rates of return.

Our analysis begins by deriving for each quarter between the first quarter of 1954 and the final quarter of 1976 the maximum potential interest rate that is compatible with our "standard investment" project. For this calculation we assume that debt finances one-third of the investment. One series of such internal rates of return is derived on the

---

47. The first-difference specification is essentially equivalent to the maximum-likelihood transformation of equation (20).

assumption of a constant 6 percent risk differential between the pretax yields on debt and equity. We refer to this variable as MPIR33G to denote a maximum potential interest rate based on 33 percent debt finance and a gross-of-tax risk differential. As table 9.2 showed, changing the risk differential from 6 percent to any other constant would change all of the internal rates of return only by a constant and would therefore not alter the regression results; in more formal language, the risk-differential parameter is not indentifiable on the basis of available experience. A second series is derived on the assumption of a constant 6 percent risk differential between the net-of-tax yields on debt and equity; we denote this MPIR33N. The risk-differential parameter is again not identifiable.

Three factors determine the changes in the MPIR variable from quarter to quarter: tax rules, inflation, and pretax profitability. For each quarter we use the tax rules that were appropriate for that quarter and assume that they would not be changed during the life of the project. We also use an optimal Box-Jenkins forecast equation to obtain quarterly forecasts of inflation rates on the basis of the information then available. The tax rules and inflation forecasts are combined using the method outlined in section 9.1 to obtain an estimated internal rate of return.

In performing that operation, it is also appropriate to relax the assumption that the "standard investment" project has the same pretax profitability in every period. In practice, the actual pretax rates of profit have experienced substantial gyrations during the twenty-five years.[48] A permanent rise or fall in the pretax profitability of investment would cause an equivalent shift in the demand for funds; even a temporary change could cause some shift. To allow for this possibility, we have also calculated an MPIR series based on the assumption that the pretax internal rate of return is not a constant 12 percent but varies from quarter to quarter.[49]

Our analysis of changing profitability is based on the series for the "net profit rate" developed in our previous paper (Feldstein and Summers, 1977). This rate is measured as the ratio of corporate profits before tax plus interest payments to the sum of fixed capital, inventories, and land. The data relate to nonfinancial corporations and are corrected for changes in the price level. Both profits and capital stock are net of the Commerce Department estimate of economic depreciation. We have interpolated the annual series to obtain quarterly figures.

It would be incorrect to assume that firms extrapolate short-run variations in profitability to the entire life of their investments. We posit instead that the demand for funds is based on a cyclically adjusted value of profitability. Specifically, we follow our earlier analysis of profitability and relate the profit rate to the concurrent rate of capacity utilization. We

48. See Feldstein and Summers (1977).
49. This is equivalent to changing the parameter a_0 of equation (1) each quarter to recalibrate the pretax rate of return.

then use this equation to estimate the profit rate that would be expected in each quarter if the capacity utilization were a standard 83.1 percent, the average for the sample period. This cyclically adjusted profit rate is then used to recalibrate the maximum potential interest rate for each quarter. We use the suffix AP to denote a variable expressing the internal rate of return that has been adjusted for variations in profitability; thus MPIR33NAP is the MPIR variable that is based on a risk differential net of tax and that has a varying profitability.

Table 9.5 shows the four MPIR variables corresponding to differentials gross of tax and net of tax and to fixed and varying profitability. Note that differences in the average level reflect the risk differential. Variations over time within each series are therefore more important than differences among the series.

Table 9.5   Values of Maximum Potential Interest Rate for
             Standard Investment Project, 1954–76[a]

Percent

Year	Constant Pretax Profitability		Varying Pretax Profitability	
	MPIR33G	MPIR33N	MPIR33GAP	MPIR33NAP
1954	5.7	5.4	4.6	4.1
1955	5.9	5.6	5.3	4.9
1956	6.0	5.7	4.1	3.5
1957	5.5	5.9	4.0	3.3
1958	6.0	5.7	4.2	3.5
1959	6.1	5.8	5.0	4.5
1960	6.1	5.8	4.6	4.0
1961	6.0	5.6	4.9	4.3
1962	6.4	6.0	5.8	5.3
1963	6.5	6.2	6.1	5.7
1964	7.1	6.8	7.0	6.7
1965	7.3	7.2	7.4	7.2
1966	7.3	7.1	6.8	6.6
1967	7.2	7.1	6.2	5.9
1968	6.9	6.7	5.7	5.3
1969	6.5	6.4	4.2	3.7
1970	6.8	6.9	3.9	3.4
1971	7.4	7.6	4.9	4.6
1972	7.7	7.9	5.0	4.6
1973	7.9	8.3	3.8	3.5
1974	8.4	9.6	2.7	2.8
1975	8.3	9.0	5.2	5.2
1976	8.2	8.8	4.8	4.8

Source: Derived by method explained in the text.

a. All MPIR variables are based on debt financing for one-third of the investment and risk differentials of 6 percent. See text for definitions of the symbols.

These MPIR values can now be used to estimate how tax changes affect the actual long-term rate of interest. If the supply of funds to the non-financial corporate sector were completely inelastic, the actual interest rate would be expected to rise by the same amount as the MPIR. In the traditional language of public finance, the full effect of changes in the tax rules would then be borne by capital in the corporate sector. More generally, however, the supply of capital to the nonfinancial corporate sector is not fixed but is an increasing function of the nominal rate of interest. The elasticity of the supply of funds to nonfinancial corporate business and the elasticity of the demand for funds by those firms together determine how much a tax-induced shift in the demand for funds raises the return to capital. For a given demand elasticity, the effect on the equilibrium interest rate of a shift in demand versus inversely with the elasticity of supply. The greater the supply elasticity, the greater will be the increase in corporate investment relative to that in the rate of interest.

Although an estimate of the elasticity of supply of funds to the non-financial corporate sector is not available, the relative magnitude of the funds raised by this sector is informative. Between 1970 and 1975, the funds raised in credit markets by all nonfinancial sectors totaled $1,029 billion.[50] Of this, corporate bonds accounted for only $107 billion. The total funds raised by corporations, including bank borrowing and mortgages as well as bonds, totaled $334 billion, or only about one-third of total funds raised. The obligations of state and local governments alone accounted for $89 billion; net borrowing for residential mortgages was $253 billion. It is clear that fluctuations in the demand for borrowed funds by corporations due to changes in tax rules and productivity may be small relative to the total flow of funds in credit markets. The potential supply of long-term lending from abroad and the elasticity of financial saving with respect to the real rate of interest strengthen this conclusion. Although a more extensive analysis of this issue would be desirable, these crude figures do suggest that the elasticity of supply of funds to the corporate sector may be substantial. If so, the effect of changes in MPIR on the actual interest rate will be correspondingly small.

In using the MPIR variable to estimate the effect on the interest rate of the shifts in the demand for funds induced by tax changes, it is important to adjust for the concurrent shifts in supply caused by changes in expected inflation. To control for such changes in the interest rate, our regression equation relates the interest rate to the expected rate of inflation (π^*) as well as to the appropriate MPIR variable:[51]

---

50. The statistics in this paragraph are from the Flow of Funds Accounts of the Federal Reserve System.

51. Our analysis uses both the polynomial distributed-lag specification and the variable constructed from Box-Jenkins forecasts. Factors other than inflation also shift the supply of funds available to the nonfinancial corporate sector: (a) shifts in saving behavior; (b) shifts in liquidity preference; and (c) shifts in the demand for funds by governments, by the rest of the world, and by investors in residential real estate. Although none of these shifts is likely

(22) $$i_t = \alpha_0 + \alpha_1\, MPIR + \alpha_2 \pi^*$$

The coefficient of the MPIR variable can therefore measure the net effect of tax changes; in terms of figure 9.3, this net effect is $(i_4 - i_0)/(i_1 - i_0)$, or the ratio of the change in the interest rate that would occur with a fixed supply curve of funds $(i_4 - i_0)$ to the change that would occur if that supply were perfectly inelastic $(i_1 - i_0)$.[52] The total impact of an increase of 1 percentage point in the expected rate of inflation can be calculated as the sum of (1) the coefficient of the expected inflation variable, α_2, and (2) the product of the coefficient of the MPIR variable and the value of $dMPIR/d\pi$ implied by calculations leading to table 9.2.

Although time is required to change investment and thereby to alter the equilibrium return on investment, the prices of bonds and stocks can adjust very quickly to reflect this eventual long-run equilibrium. A failure to adjust quickly would otherwise provide opportunities for profitable speculation. We therefore specify that the interest rate adjusts to changes in MPIR within the quarter.

The estimated coefficients of equation (22) for each of the concepts of MPIR are presented in table 9.6. Note first that the evidence favors the less restricted polynomial distributed-lag specification of shifting inflation expectations (equations 6-1 to 6-4) over the Box-Jenkins forecast (equations 6-5 to 6-8).[53] We will therefore concentrate our comments on the results based on the former specification and return to the remaining equations afterward. It is not possible to choose between the gross-risk differential concept of MPIR (equations 6-1 and 6-2) and the net-risk differential concept (6-3 and 6-4) on the basis of the goodness of fit of the equations.[54] Similarly, the evidence does not favor either the MPIR variable based on constant pretax profitability (6-1 and 6-3) or that based on changing profitability. Fortunately, the same basic conclusions are implied by all four specifications.

First, a shift in the demand for funds appears to raise the long-term interest rate by approximately one-fourth of the increase in the MPIR; a rise of 100 basis points in MPIR would thus raise the long-term interest rate by approximately 25 basis points.[55] This indicates that the supply of

---

to be caused by the changes in the tax rates that shift the demand by nonfinancial corporate business, we cannot be certain that the shifts in supply that are not caused by inflation are uncorrelated with our explanatory variables.

52. This method assumes that the response of the interest rate to a change in the demand function is the same regardless of the cause of the shift—tax rules, inflation, and pretax profitability.

53. This may reflect the fact that the MPIR variable already contains the Box-Jenkins inflation forecast.

54. The $\bar{R}^2$ values are extremely close; although this is not itself an accurate guide in the presence of high serial correlation, the Durbin-Watson statistic and the $\bar{R}^2$ together imply that the evidence offers little basis for choice between the models.

55. The point estimates vary between 0.12 with MPIR33NAP and 0.43 with MPIR33G.

Table 9.6 Effects of Changes in Taxation and Inflation on the Long-term Interest Rate[a]

Equation and Concept of MPIR[b]	Independent Variable					Summary Statistic		
	Constant	MPIR	Inflation Rate π_t	$\sum_1^{16} \pi_{t-1}$	Predicted Inflation Rate π^e	$\bar{R}^2$	Durbin-Watson	Implied Inflation Effect[c]
6-1 MPIR33G	0.53 (0.84)	0.43 (0.14)	0.15 (0.05)	0.54 (0.07)	...	0.83	0.24	1.11
6-2 MPIR33GAP	1.99 (0.56)	0.18 (0.09)	0.23 (0.05)	0.65 (0.06)	...	0.82	0.25	1.05
6-3 MPIR33N	1.38 (0.79)	0.32 (0.14)	0.14 (0.06)	0.53 (0.08)	...	0.82	0.19	1.10
6-4 MPIR33NAP	2.39 (0.45)	0.12 (0.07)	0.21 (0.05)	0.64 (0.06)	...	0.82	0.24	1.01
6-5 MPIR33G	-3.53 (-0.96)	1.13 (0.16)	...	...	0.52 (0.10)	0.69	0.28	1.61
6-6 MPIR33GAP	0.97 (1.07)	0.30 (0.16)	...	...	1.09 (0.11)	0.54	0.15	1.38
6-7 MPIR33N	-2.54 (-0.76)	1.10 (0.14)	...	...	0.25 (0.12)	0.71	0.16	1.72
6-8 MPIR33NAP	1.44 (0.83)	0.25 (0.13)	...	...	1.04 (0.10)	0.54	0.14	1.37

SOURCE: Text equation (22).

a. The dependent variable in all equations is the long-term interest rate. All equations are estimated for 1954:1 to 1976:4. The numbers in parentheses are standard errors.

b. Defined in the text.

c. The implied inflation effect is the sum of (1) the inflation coefficients and (2) the product of MPIR coefficient and $dMPIR/d\pi$ for regime G in tables 9.2 and 9.3.

funds to the corporate sector is quite elastic. Apparently, investment incentives aimed at the corporate sector do raise investment rather than dissipating because of offsetting increases in the return to debt and equity capital. In terms of figure 9.3, the estimate implies that $i_4 - i_0$ is only about one-fourth of $i_1 - i_0$ because the expansion of corporate investment reduces the pretax rate of return on investment.[56]

The extent to which the increase in corporate investment represents an increase in total national investment depends on the offsetting effect of the higher interest rate. If the total supply of investable funds were fixed, traditional investment incentives would succeed only in transferring investment to corporate business from other sectors, such as homebuilding. But the supply of investable funds is not fixed. Total investment can increase because savings rise, the net international capital flow to the United States increases, or the government reduces its deficit. Indeed, a principal rationale for investment incentives has been to maintain aggregate demand with a smaller government deficit. The effect of tax-induced changes in MPIR on total national investment requires an analysis that goes beyond the current framework.

The present study can also provide only partial information about the incidence of changes in the corporate tax rules. The estimate that α_1 is approximately 0.25 suggests that only a small part of the increase in MPIR is shifted to the corporate bondholder. The more general question of the extent to which the incidence of the tax change is shifted from capital in general to labor cannot be answered accurately on the basis of current information. The answer depends on the change in the return to capital outside the corporate sector and on the share of the corporate sector in the total capital stock. Consider, for example, a change in the corporate tax that implies an increase of 100 basis points in MPIR and that causes a rise of 25 basis points in the long-term bond rate. If the return to all other forms of capital also increased by 25 basis points and if corporate capital accounted for one-third of the total privately owned capital stock, 75 percent of the benefit of the tax change would fall on capital and 25 percent on labor.[57] Since corporate bonds and other securities are not perfect substitutes, it would probably be more reasonable to assume that the average rise in the yield on capital is less than 25 basis points. This in turn would imply that capital as a whole bears less than 75 percent of the effect of stimulative changes in corporate tax rules. The remainder would be shifted to labor through the higher productivity and

---

56. Hall and Jorgenson (1967) are not far from the truth in their assumption that the interest rate remains constant when tax incentives vary; to the extent that their assumption is wrong, they overstate the tax-induced changes in the desired capital stock.

57. More generally, the share of a corporate tax change that is borne by capital in general equals the rise in the average return to capital (relative to the change in MPIR) divided by the corporate share of the capital stock.

wages that result from increased investment. This estimate must be regarded as preliminary and subject to substantial error.

The estimated effect of changes in expected inflation support the conclusion of the second section that the long-term bond rate rises by approximately the same amount as the increase in inflation. Although the corporate MPIR variable rises by about one-fifth more than the increase in inflation, the effect of inflation on the supply of funds to the corporate sector implies that the net change is smaller than this. In terms of the last diagram, if the investment-demand schedule is shifted by inflation alone, $i_1 - i_0$ would exceed π. But $i_1 - i_0$ is found to be approximately equal to π, which implies that inflation substantially reduces the real net return to lenders.

We turn finally to the estimates of equations (6-5 to 6-8), which use the Box-Jenkins variable to indicate shifts in the supply of funds. These equations provide a less satisfactory explanation of variations in the interest rate. The results are also quite sensitive to whether MPIR is adjusted for changes in profitability. With no such adjustment, the results are quite unsatisfactory.[58] In contrast with the cyclically adjusted MPIR variable (equations 6-6 and 6-8), the results are very similar to the estimates based on the distributed lag specification of inflation. Moreover, when these equations are estimated in first-difference form (using instrumental-variable estimation) the parameter values are quite stable. The coefficient of *MPIR33GAP* is 0.53 (with a standard error of 0.44) and the coefficient of π^e is 0.96 (0.57); with *MPIR33NAP*, the corresponding coefficients are 0.31 (0.27) and 0.91 (0.46).

To examine the possibility that the long-term interest rate responds to cyclical conditions directly, we reestimated the equations of table 9.6 with capacity utilization as an additional variable. In general, its coefficient was small and statistically insignificant. In one key specification, corresponding to equation (6-2), the capacity utilization variable was significantly positive (implying that an increase of 1 percentage point in capacity utilization has the direct effect of raising the long-term interest rate by 5 basis points) and the coefficient of the MPIR variable was reduced to 0.07 with a standard error of 0.10. This suggests a further reason for caution in interpreting the point estimates of the coefficient of the MPIR variable but supports the conclusion that the actual interest rate is changed very little by tax-induced shifts in the maximum potential rate of interest.

Obviously, the estimates presented in this section must be treated as preliminary and regarded with caution. However, they offer no grounds for rejecting the conclusion of section 9.2 that an increase in the rate of

58. The coefficients of the MPIR variables in equations (6-5 and 6-7) are both unreasonably high. When these equations are estimated in first-difference form (using instrumental-variable estimation) the MPIR coefficients become very small and statistically insignificant.

inflation causes an approximately equal increase in the nominal pretax interest rate. This conclusion supports the analytic results of the first section that the tax deductibility of interest payments just about offsets the historic cost method of depreciation. Finally, the results of this section suggest that the supply of funds to the nonfinancial corporate sector is elastic enough to make a tax-induced change in the maximum potential interest rate cause a substantially smaller change in the actual interest rate.

9.4   Conclusion

The primary emphasis of this paper has been on the interaction of taxes and inflation in determining the interest rate on long-term bonds. The current U.S. tax system makes the impact of inflation much more complex than it was in Irving Fisher's time. The basic Fisherian conclusion that anticipated inflation has no effect on real variables is no longer correct.

We began our analysis by calculating the interest rate that a firm can pay on a "standard investment" project if its investment is financed one-third by debt and two-thirds by equity. The deduction of interest payments in calculating taxable income implies that this maximum potential interest rate rises by more than the rate of inflation. Offsetting this is the use of historic cost depreciation, which makes the MPIR rise less than the rate of inflation. On balance, we find that the maximum potential interest rate rises by approximately the same amount as the rate of inflation, with the sign of the difference depending on the assumption about the relation between debt and equity yields.

Our econometric estimates of the relation between inflation and the long-term interest rate confirm that the nominal rate rises by approximately the rate of inflation. This implies that the real interest rate net of tax available to investors is reduced dramatically by inflation. For example, an investor who pays a 50 percent marginal tax rate will find that a real net-of-tax return that is 2 percent in the absence of inflation vanishes when there is a 4 percent rate of inflation.

The fall in the real net rate of interest received by investors also corresponds to a fall in the real net cost of debt capital to firms. It is wrong, however, to regard this as a major stimulus to investment. The analysis of the first section shows that an inflation-induced fall in the real net-of-tax rate of interest at which firms can borrow is not a stimulus to investment because, given the tax and depreciation rules, inflation also reduces by about as much the maximum real net-of-tax interest rate that they can afford to pay on a standard investment.

Although our analysis has emphasized the interaction between taxes and inflation, we have also been interested in the effects of corporate tax changes themselves. The results of section 9.1 showed that the changes in tax rates and depreciation rules during the past twenty-five years would, in the absence of inflation, have increased the maximum interest rate that firms could afford by about 2 percentage points. Our econometric estimates in section 9.3 suggest that the elasticity of the supply of funds to purchase corporate debt is great enough that the interest rate actually rises by only about one-fourth of the potential increase induced by changes in corporate rules. The tax changes that were designed to stimulate corporate investment were therefore not offset by the resulting increases in the interest rate.

We believe that we have a useful analytic method for studying the effect of alternative tax rules. By translating the changes in tax rules and inflation into corresponding changes in the maximum rate that firms can pay for capital, we can study the changes in investment incentives and in the response of market yields. We plan to extend our analysis to include a more general model of corporate finance and to study a wider range of problems.

10   Inflation and the Stock Market

This paper discusses a crucial cause of the failure of share prices to rise during a decade of substantial inflation. Indeed, the share value per dollar of pretax earnings actually fell from 10.82 in 1967 to 6.65 in 1976![1] The analysis here indicates that this inverse relation between higher inflation and lower share prices during the past decade was not due to chance or to other unrelated economic events.[2] On the contrary, an important adverse effect of increased inflation on share prices results from basic features of the current U.S. tax laws, particularly historic cost depreciation and the taxation of nominal capital gains.[3]

This analysis shows that in order to understand the structural relation between inflation and share prices, it is crucial to distinguish between the

Reprinted by permission from *American Economic Review* 70 (December 1980): 839–47.

This study is part of the NBER program of research on Business Taxation and Finance. I am grateful to participants in the NBER Summer Institute for helpful comments, and to the NBER and the National Science Foundation for financial support. The views expressed in this paper are my own and not those of the NBER or Harvard University.

1. These price-earnings ratios are based on earnings net of real depreciation and with the inventory valuation adjustment. See my paper with Lawrence Summers (1979; chap. 8 above) for the description of the method by which these pretax price-earnings ratios are constructed. The traditional Standard and Poor's posttax price-earnings ratio, based on book profits (including inventory profits) fell from 17.45 to 9.02. An alternate measure of share-price performance, the ratio of the share price to the underlying real capital at replacement cost, fell from 1.214 in 1967 to 0.788 in 1977. For further evidence of the adverse effect of inflation on real share prices, see Charles Nelson (1976) and John Lintner (1973, 1975).

2. The analysis also shows that it is unnecessary to invoke a theory of systematic error of the type developed by Franco Modigliani and Richard Cohn (1979).

3. I emphasize that these are tax rules in the United States. Share prices in other countries that do not tax capital gains and that permit extremely rapid tax depreciation of investments may respond very differently to inflation. The relation between share prices and inflation in other countries is therefore of little relevance to the United States without a careful analysis of local tax rules.

effect of a *high* constant rate of inflation and the effect of an *increase* in the rate of inflation expected for the future. When the steady-state rate of inflation is higher, share prices increase at a faster rate. More specifically, when the inflation rate is steady, share prices rise in proportion to the price level to maintain a constant ratio of share prices to real earnings. In contrast, an *increase* in the expected future rate of inflation causes a concurrent fall in the ratio of share prices to current earnings. Although share prices then rise from this lower level at the higher rate of inflation, the ratio of share prices to real earnings is permanently lower. This permanent reduction in the price-earnings ratio occurs because, under prevailing tax rules, inflation raises the effective tax rate on corporate-source income.

This process is illustrated in figure 10.1. The top part of the figure shows the inflation rate. Until time t_0, the inflation rate is constant at π_0; it then rises to a higher steady-state level, π_1. This increase is immediately and correctly perceived. The middle part of the figure shows that until t_0 the price per share rises at a constant rate equal to the rate of growth of *nominal* earnings per share. At time t_0, the share price drops to a level consistent with the higher rate of inflation and then grows at the new

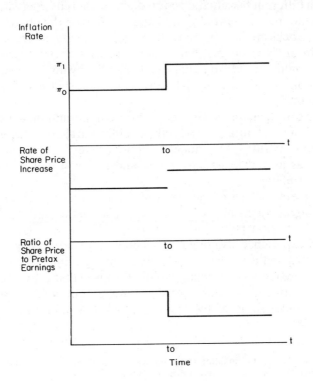

Figure 10.1

higher rate of growth of earnings per share. Finally, the lower part of the figure shows that the price-earnings ratio falls when the inflation rate increases but remains constant as long as the inflation rate is constant.

The starting point for this analysis is the way in which inflation raises the effective tax rate on corporate-source income. This is in sharp contrast to the common popular argument that share prices are depressed because inflation raises the rate of interest that can be earned by investing in bonds. It is clear that this argument should be rejected since the higher *nominal* rate of interest generally corresponds to an unchanged *real* rate of interest.[4] Indeed, since the entire nominal interest is subject to the personal income tax, the real rate of interest net of the personal income tax actually falls. The analysis of section 10.1 shows that, with existing tax rules, inflation is likely to depress the real net rate of interest by less than it lowers the real net return to equity investment. The simple valuation model that calculates the share value by discounting at the real net rate of interest leads to the conclusion that, with current tax laws, an increase in inflation reduces the price that individuals are willing to pay for shares.

Although this discounted earnings model of share valuation is a useful heuristic device, it has the serious deficiency that it implies that individuals in different tax situations would place different reservation values on the same shares. It is therefore inconsistent with the observation that the same stocks are held by individuals who face very different tax rates. The main analysis of this paper therefore uses a more general stock valuation model to derive the assets demanded by investors in different tax situations—and then calculates the share value that achieves a market equilibrium.

Numerical calculations with the market equilibrium model show how inflation can substantially depress the equilibrium share value because of our current tax rules. The model is, however, very simple. It should be regarded as an aid to understanding and not as a device for making precise calculations.

A complete analysis of the effect of inflation on share prices requires considering a wider range of alternative investments and incorporating the possibility that perceived risk varies with inflation. Explaining the historical experience also requires a model of the process by which both expectations and the capital stock adjust through time. The goal of this paper is more modest: an examination of the way that taxes and inflation interact in affecting equilibrium share prices. The final section of the paper discusses some of the ways in which this analysis could be extended.

---

4. The conclusion that inflation raises the nominal interest rate while leaving the real rate unchanged has been supported by evidence since Irving Fisher's classic study. For more recent evidence, see my paper with Otto Eckstein (1970), William Yohe and Denis Karnosky (1969) and my paper with Summers (1978; chap. 9 above).

10.1   The Effect of Inflation on the Demand Price of Shares

Consider first an economy in which there is no inflation. Each share of stock represents the ownership claim to a single unit of capital and the net earnings that it produces. There is no corporate debt and all earnings are paid out as dividends. The marginal product of capital (net of depreciation), ρ, is subject to a corporate income tax at rate τ.[5] The earnings per share that are distributed to the individual investor are therefore $(1 - \tau)\rho$. Since there are no retained earnings, the earnings per share do not grow over time and there is no change in the value per share. The individual pays personal tax at rate θ on the earnings that he receives. The individual's net earnings per share are thus $(1 - \theta)(1 - \tau)\rho$.

A simple model of share valuation implies that the price that the individual would be willing to pay per share (q) would make the net earnings per dollar of equity equal to the net interest that he would receive per dollar invested in government bonds, $(1 - \theta)r$.[6] More realistically, individuals may require a higher yield on the riskier equity investment; if this risk differential is denoted by δ, the investor's indifference condition becomes

(1)
$$\frac{(1 - \theta)(1 - \tau)\rho}{q} = (1 - \theta)r + \delta$$

The individual's demand price per share is thus

(2)
$$q = \frac{(1 - \theta)(1 - \tau)\rho}{(1 - \theta)r + \delta}$$

What happens when the rate of inflation increases from zero to a positive rate π? For simplicity, the analysis will assume an instantaneous and unanticipated increase to π which is then expected to persist forever. To evaluate the new demand price per share, it is necessary to recalculate both the net earnings per share and the real net rate of interest.

Under U.S. tax law, taxable profits are calculated by subtracting a value for depreciation from other net operating income. This value of depreciation is based on the original or "historic" cost of the asset rather than on its current value. When prices rise, this historic cost method of depreciation causes the real value of depreciation to fall and real taxable profits to be increased.[7] As a result, real profits net of the corporate

5. Since each share of stock represents one unit of capital, the marginal product of capital is also the pretax earnings per share.

6. See Mervyn King (1977). He also treats the more general case in which retained earnings cause share prices to rise.

7. When there is no inflation, the various methods of "accelerated depreciation" that are allowed for tax purposes may cause tax depreciation to exceed the economic depreciation for some assets. This is subsumed in the effective corporate tax rate τ. Accelerated depreciation does not change the conclusion that inflation reduces the real value of depreciation.

income tax vary inversely with inflation.[8] A linear approximation that each percentage point of inflation reduces net corporate profits per unit of capital by λ implies that net corporate earnings per share of capital are $(1 - \tau)\rho - \lambda\pi$.[9] After personal income tax at rate θ, the individual receives $(1 - \theta)[(1 - \tau)\rho - \lambda\pi]$.[10]

Inflation reduces these net earnings even further by imposing an additional tax on nominal capital gains. More specifically, even though the real share price remains constant at the new equilibrium value q, inflation causes nominal capital gains at the rate of πq.[11] Capital gains are taxed at a lower rate than ordinary income and only when the stock is sold; the equivalent tax rate on accrued capital gains will be denoted c.[12] The extra burden caused by taxing nominal capital gains is thus $c\pi q$. The real net earnings per share are therefore $(1 - \theta)[(1 - \tau)\rho - \lambda\pi] - c\pi q$. Note that a small increase in the rate of inflation calculated at $\pi = 0$ reduces these real net earnings by $(1 - \theta)\lambda + cq$.[13]

The effect of inflation on the real net rate of interest, $(1 - \theta)r - \pi$, depends on the response of the nominal interest rate to the rate of inflation. As noted above, the U.S. experience has been that $dr/d\pi = 1$. Thus $d[(1 - \theta)r - \pi]/d\pi = -\theta$.

For reasonable values of the tax parameters, the decrease in net earnings per dollar of equity $[((1 - \theta)\lambda + cq)/q]$ exceeds the decrease in the real net interest yield on bonds $[\theta]$. For example, with a personal tax rate of $\theta = 0.3$, a depreciation effect of $\lambda = 0.30$, an effective capital gains tax rate of $c = 0.15$, and an initial share value per unit of capital of $q = 1$, each 1 percent of inflation reduces the real net yield on equity by 0.36 percent and reduces the real net yield on debt by 0.30. If the risk premium (δ) is unchanged, this implies that the share price calculated as the discounted value of earnings per share will fall.

8. For a more complete discussion of this, see my paper with Summers (1979; chap. 8 above) and my paper with Jerry Green and Eytan Sheshinski (1978; chap. 4 above), especially the appendix by Alan Auerbach. Hai Hong (1977), Brian Motley (1969), and Richard Van Horne and William Glassmire (1972) discuss the effects of historic cost depreciation and the implication for the effect of inflation on share values; they assume a single investor whose discount rate is unchanged by inflation.

9. It can be shown that with an exponential depreciation rate of 15 percent and a growth rate of 3 percent, a 7 percent inflation rate reduces net profits per unit of capital by 0.021; this implies $\lambda = 0.30$. Recall that each share of stock represents a claim to one unit of capital.

10. This assumes that inflation does not affect the pretax profitability of capital. The calculation also ignores the transitional effect of a lower present value of the future depreciation allowable on past investments.

11. These nominal capital gains are stated in constant dollars. If the price level at time t is $e^{\pi t}$, the nominal capital gains at that time is $\pi q e^{\pi t}$.

12. That is, c is the accrual rate of capital gains taxation equivalent to the present value of the tax that will be paid in the future when the stock is sold.

13. This is also true for $\pi > 0$ if the change in q is ignored.

More specifically, the simple valuation model that calculates the individual's demand price per share by equating the real net yield per dollar of equity to the sum of the real net interest rate and the risk premium implies

(3)
$$\frac{(1 - \theta)[(1 - \tau)\rho - \lambda\pi]}{q} - c\pi$$
$$= (1 - \theta)r - \pi + \delta$$

or

(4)
$$q = \frac{(1 - \theta)[(1 - \tau)\rho - \lambda\pi]}{(1 - \theta)r - (1 - c)\pi + \delta}.$$

Differentiating q with respect to π with the condition that $dr/d\pi = 1$ implies

(5)
$$\frac{dq}{d\pi} = \frac{-(1 - \theta)\lambda + q(\theta - c)}{(1 - \theta)r - (1 - c)\pi + \delta}$$

Since the denominator is positive,[14] $dq/d\pi$ is negative if

(6)
$$q(\theta - c) < (1 - \theta)\lambda$$

Several things about this condition should be noted. First, realistic values of the tax parameters satisfy the inequality and imply $dq/d\pi < 0$. The example of $\theta = 0.3, c = 0.15$, and $\lambda = 0.30$ implies $dq/d\pi < 0$ even at $q = 1$. Second, the inequality is satisfied more easily for investors with low individual tax rates. In the important extreme case of a tax-exempt institution, $\theta = c = 0$ and the inequality is satisfied for any value of $\lambda > 0$. Finally, for some individuals with high tax rates, the inequality will not be satisfied and $dq/d\pi > 0$.[15]

This diversity of responses of q to the rate of inflation reinforces the implication of equation (4) that the demand price per share differs among investors according to their tax situation. An analysis of the effect of inflation on the market price of stock requires a portfolio model of investor equilibrium. In such a model, the risk premium (δ) is both implicit and endogenous. The risk differential changes as the investor reallocates his portfolio until a market equilibrium is achieved in which the same market value of stock is consistent with each investor's own portfolio equilibrium. The specification of such a model is the subject of section 10.2. Section 10.3 then analyzes how the equilibrium responds to a change in the rate of inflation.

---

14. This is a necessary condition for a finite value of q.
15. Recall that these calculations all assume a firm with no debt finance and no retained earnings.

10.2   A Market Equilibrium Model of Share Valuation

The market equilibrium model builds directly on the analysis of the previous section. The economy is assumed to have two assets (risky equity shares and riskless government bonds) and two types of portfolio investors (tax-exempt institutions and taxable individuals). The analysis begins by specifying the investors' portfolio equilibrium equations. When these are combined with the asset supply constraint, they implicitly define the market value per share of equity. This equilibrium model is then used in section 10.3 to calculate the effect of changing from an equilibrium with a zero rate of inflation to a new equilibrium with a positive constant rate of inflation.

The household's investment problem is to divide its initial wealth between bonds and stocks. Equation (1) showed that, in the absence of inflation, the portfolio equilibrium of the households can be written

$$(7) \qquad \frac{(1 - \theta)(1 - \tau)\rho}{q_0} = (1 - \theta)r_0 + \delta_{h0}$$

where the share price and interest rate carry a subscript zero to distinguish these initial preinflation values from the values of these variables when there is inflation. The risk premium δ_{h0} has subscripts to indicate that it refers to the household in the initial equilibrium.

The risk premium that a household requires to hold a marginal share of equity should be an increasing function of the amount of risk that the household is already bearing. More explicitly, I shall assume that δ_{h0} is proportional to the standard deviation of the return on the household's portfolio. The source of this uncertainty is the variability of the pretax equity return; the variance of ρ will be written σ_ρ^2. The after-tax variance per dollar of equity investment is thus $(1 - \theta)^2(1 - \tau)^2\sigma_\rho^2/q_0^2$. If the household has s_{h0} shares in the initial equilibrium, the dollar value of its equity investment is $s_{h0}q_0$. Since bonds are riskless, the variance of the return on the household portfolio is $s_{h0}^2(1 - \theta)^2(1 - \tau)^2\sigma_\rho^2$. If the risk premium is proportional to the standard deviation of the portfolio return,

$$(8) \qquad \delta_{h0} = \delta_h s_{h0}(1 - \theta)(1 - \tau)\sigma_\rho$$

where δ_h is a constant.[16]

Substituting (8) into (7) and rearranging terms yields the share price that is consistent with the household's chosen share ownership in the absence of inflation:

$$(9) \qquad q_0 = \frac{(1 - \theta)(1 - \tau)\rho}{(1 - \theta)r_0 + \delta_h s_{h0}(1 - \theta)(1 - \tau)\sigma_\rho}$$

16. Note that σ_ρ is a standard deviation of a rate of return and is therefore in the same units as the rate of return, i.e., percent per year. The coefficient δ_h is therefore a unit-free number.

Note that this household demand price for shares varies inversely with the quantity of shares that it holds.

For tax-exempt institutions, the relevant value of θ is zero. The portfolio equilibrium of the institution can therefore be written

(10)
$$\frac{(1 - \tau)\rho}{q_0} = r_0 + \delta_{i0}$$

where the institution's risk premium (indicated by subscript i) satisfies

(11)
$$\delta_{i0} = \delta_i s_{i0}(1 - \tau)\sigma_\rho$$

Combining these two equations yields the institution's demand price per share:[17]

(12)
$$q_0 = \frac{(1 - \tau)\rho}{r_0 + \delta_i s_{i0}(1 - \tau)\sigma_\rho}$$

The total number of shares outstanding, $\bar{s}$, constrains the combined holdings of the institution and the household investors:

(13)
$$\bar{s} = s_{i0} + s_{h0}$$

This supply constraint and the two demand equations (9) and (12) are sufficient to determine the equilibrium share price and the allocation of the shares between the two types of investors. The nature of this solution is illustrated in figure 10.2. The equilibrium relation of equation (9) is drawn as the household's demand curve for shares, $s_{h0}(q_0)$. Similarly (12) is drawn as the institution's demand curve $s_{i0}(q_0)$. These are added horizontally to get total share demand as a function of share price $s_0(q_0)$. The intersection of this market demand curve with the supply constraint line $\bar{s}$ determines the equilibrium price q_0^* and the corresponding share holdings (s_{h0}^* and s_{i0}^*).

To use this model to study the impact of inflation on share prices, it is necessary to evaluate the parameters $\delta_h\sigma_\rho$ and $\delta_i\sigma_\rho$. Although these parameters cannot be observed, their values can be inferred from the equilibrium conditions in the absence of inflation. Thus equation (9) implies

(14)
$$\delta_h\sigma_\rho = \frac{(1 - \tau)\rho - q_0 r_0}{q_0(1 - \tau)s_{h0}}$$

and (12) implies

(15)
$$\delta_i\sigma_\rho = \frac{(1 - \tau)\rho - q_0 r_0}{q_0(1 - \tau)s_{i0}}$$

17. Note that, since $(1 - \theta)$ can be eliminated from equation (9), the household and institution demand price equations differ in the absence of inflation only because of differences in δ_i.

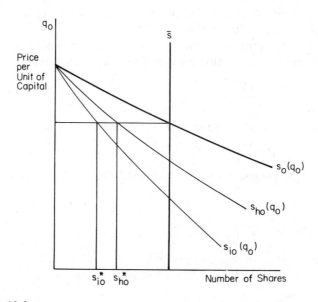

Figure 10.2

For these illustrative calculations, the pretax return to capital will be taken to be $\rho = 0.11$, the effective corporate tax rate $\tau = 0.4$, and the interest rate in the absence of inflation $r_0 = 0.03$. In 1970, households held \$700 billion of equities while institutions (including private pension plans, foundations, educational endowments, and insurance companies) held \$135 billion; I will therefore set $q_0 s_{h0} = 700$ and $q_0 s_{i0} = 135$. Together these assumptions imply

$$(16) \qquad \delta_h \sigma_\rho = (0.157 - .071 q_0)10^{-3}$$

$$(17) \qquad \delta_i \sigma_\rho = (0.815 - .370 q_0)10^{-3}$$

It is common to assume that the corporate capital stock (and therefore ρ and $\bar{s}$) will adjust until in equilibrium q equals one. An alternative view is that, with the corporate financial behavior that is optimal under existing tax laws, this arbitrage will not be fully achieved and the equilibrium value of q_0 will be less than one.[18] Section 10.3 shows how, under either assumption, the introduction of a moderate rate of inflation can cause a substantial fall in the share value.

10.3 Inflation and the Market Equilibrium Share Value

This section examines the effect of an unanticipated increase in the steady-state rate of inflation. The analysis assumes that the corporate

18. See Auerbach (1978), David Bradford (1979), and King (1977) for statements of this view.

capital stock remains constant; this implies that the total number of shares ($\bar{s}$) and the average pretax profitability (ρ) remain constant.[19]

Inflation changes the net yields on stocks and bonds in the way described in section 10.1. For households, the real net yield on equity becomes $(1 - \theta)[(1 - \tau)\rho - \lambda\pi]/q_1 - c\pi$ and the real net return on bonds becomes $(1 - \theta)r_1 - \pi$. Since the nominal interest rises by the rate of inflation,[20] $r_1 = r_0 + \pi$ and the real net return on bonds is $(1 - \theta)r_0 - \theta\pi$. The new portfolio equilibrium therefore satisfies

(18)
$$\frac{(1 - \theta)[(1 - \tau)\rho - \lambda\pi]}{q_1} - c\pi$$

$$= (1 - \theta)r_0 - \theta\pi + \delta_{1h}$$

where

(19)
$$\delta_{1h} = \delta_h s_{h1}(1 - \theta)(1 - \tau)\sigma_\rho$$

The household's demand price for shares therefore satisfies

(20)
$$q_1 = \frac{(1 - \theta)[(1 - \tau)\rho - \lambda\pi]}{(1 - \theta)r_0 - (\theta - c)\pi + \delta_h s_{h1}(1 - \theta)(1 - \tau)\sigma_\rho}$$

Similarly, the institution's demand price for shares (with $\theta = c = 0$) can be written as

(21)
$$q_1 = \frac{(1 - \tau)\rho - \lambda\pi}{r_0 + \delta_i s_{i1}(1 - \tau)\sigma_\rho}$$

Since the number of shares has not changed, it is still true that

(22)
$$\bar{s} = s_{h1} + s_{i1}$$

These three equations determine the new equilibrium share price and the corresponding allocation of shares.

Before calculating the new equilibrium explicitly, it is useful to discuss the change with the help of a diagram. Figure 10.3 combines the no-inflation demand equations originally shown in figure 10.2 with the corresponding demand equations of (20) and (21) in the presence of inflation. The dashed lines ($s_{h0}(q_0)$ and $s_{i0}(q_0)$) show the no-inflation share demands and s_0, the horizontal sum of these demand curves, gives the market demand. Comparing equations (21) and (12) shows that the institutions' demand price is lower at every value of s_{i1} but also tends to

---

19. The assumption of a fixed corporate capital stock causes the calculation to overstate the change in the share price. If q falls, capital will leave the corporate sector, raising p and thereby q. Since this would be anticipated by investors, the immediate fall would be less than that calculated here. A satisfactory solution to this problem requires a dynamic model with endogenous corporate investment decisions.

20. See note 4 for evidence that this has been the historical experience in the United States.

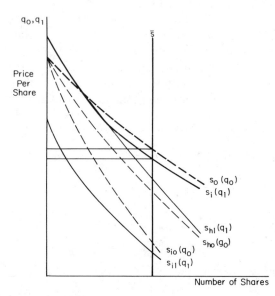

Figure 10.3

zero as s_{i1} tends to infinity; the curve $s_{i1}(q_1)$ is drawn in this way. Comparing equations (20) and (9) shows that the shift of the household demand curve is ambiguous since the numerator is reduced by $-(1-\theta)\lambda\pi$ while the denominator is reduced by $-(\theta-c)\pi$. To emphasize the possibility of a lower equilibrium price even when the household demand price rises, the household demand curve is drawn with the demand price at the initial value of $s_{h1} = 0$ greater than its previous level.

The new market demand curve $s_1(q_1)$ coincides with the household demand curve until a price is reached at which institutions are willing to hold some stock. Thereafter, the market demand curve is the sum of the two demands. The new equilibrium price occurs at a value of q_1 that is below the old equilibrium. Institutions reduce their shareholdings and individuals increase their shareholdings.

Equations (20) to (22) can be used to calculate explicitly the values of q_1 and of the separate shareholdings. Combining (20) and (21) and using $\bar{s} - s_{h1}$ for s_{i1} yields an equation for the new shareholding by households:

$$(23) \qquad s_{h1} = \frac{\delta_i \sigma_p (1-\theta)(1-\tau)\bar{s} + (\theta-c)\pi}{\sigma_p (1-\theta)(1-\tau)[\delta_i + \delta_h]}$$

Consider first the new equilibrium when q_0 was equal to 1. Using the values of $\delta_h \sigma_p$ and $\delta_i \sigma_p$ implied by equations (16) and (17), and an inflation rate of $\pi = 0.08$, equation (23) implies that $s_{h1} = 754$, i.e., inflation causes households to increase their shareholdings from 700 shares to 754 shares.[21] Substituting this value into equation (20) and setting the historic cost depreciation penalty at $\lambda = 0.30$[22] yields $q_1 = 0.812$. The share price per unit of capital falls from one dollar to 81.2 cents. Note that the value of household shares is reduced by the inflation from $700 billion to $612 billion even though they hold an increased number of shares.

A lower initial value per share does not change the conclusion that the share price falls but does reduce the relative magnitude of the fall. More specifically, if $q_0 = .8$,[23] equations (16), (17), and (23) imply that $s_{h1} = 746$. Substituting into (20) yields $q_1 = 0.729$ or 91 percent of the initial price.

10.4 Conclusion

The simple model developed in this paper conveys the idea of how a higher rate of inflation can cause a substantial reduction in the ratio of share prices to pretax earnings. The higher effective rate of tax on corporate income caused by historic cost depreciation and the tax on the artificial capital gains caused by inflation both reduce the real net yield that investors receive per unit of capital. Although the real net yield on bonds is also reduced, for many shareowners, this is outweighed by the fall in the equity yields.

The market equilibrium analysis examined the impact of inflation when both stocks and bonds are held by risk-averse investors in quite different tax situations. It also showed how the equilibrium ratio of share prices to earnings can fall even if the demand price per share for some individuals is actually increased by inflation.

Of course, the increase in the effective tax rate caused by inflation has not been the only adverse influence on the level of share prices during the last decade. The slowdown in productivity growth, the higher cost of energy, and the increased international competition have all reduced pretax profitability. Although there is no clear evidence of a permanent fall in profitability (see my paper with Summers, 1977), the transitory reduction may have caused some investors to project lower long-term pretax profitability. The higher tax rates on capital gains for high-income investors since 1969 further reduced after-tax profitability. An increase in uncertainty has also had an adverse effect on price-earnings ratios. One source of this greater uncertainty is the increasing ratio of debt to equity on corporate balance sheets. In addition, after a period of steady growth and low inflation, the events of the past decade have added uncertainty to

---

21. The other parameter values are $\tau = 0.4$, $\theta = 0.3$, $c = 0.15$, and $\bar{s} = 835$.
22. See note 9.
23. Auerbach and King show that under certain conditions the share price without inflation will be $q_0 = (1 - \theta)/(1 - c)$ if the only shareholders are individuals with these tax rates. With our current tax values, this implies 0.82.

any evaluation of the future. Finally, in considering the changes in the level of share prices over the past decade, it is important to recognize that the adverse effect of inflation has been perceived only slowly and imperfectly. Some investors have undoubtedly concluded incorrectly that even a steady rate of inflation would cause a continuing decline in the ratio of share prices to earnings. The share price level may therefore have overshot its equilibrium level.

A full understanding of the equilibrium relation between share prices and inflation requires extending the current analysis in a number of ways. The role of corporate debt and retained earnings should be included.[24] The possibility of individual investment in other assets like real estate should be recognized.[25] A more explicit portfolio model could derive asset demand equations from expected utility maximization and could recognize that some institutional holdings are really indirect ways for individuals to hold assets in a tax-favored way. Finally, the simplification that the capital stock remains constant should be replaced by a more dynamic model that recognizes the effect of inflation on capital accumulation.

24. An empirical analysis of corporate tax burdens with the existing corporate debt and retained earnings shows that inflation raises the tax burden on equity investors as well as on total corporate sector capital; see my paper with Summers (1979; chap. 8 above).

25. A model of the interaction of tax laws and inflation in determining the price of gold and land is presented in my 1980 paper (chap. 12 below).

11   Inflation, Tax Rules, and the Stock Market

11.1   Introduction

The substantial fall in the real level of share prices during the past decade has raised the cost of capital to firms and reduced their incentive to invest in new plant and equipment.[1] In a previous paper (Feldstein, 1980b; chap. 10 above) I explained how existing tax rules make the share prices of nonfinancial corporations sensitive to changes in the expected rate of inflation. An increase in the expected rate of inflation lowers the level of share prices immediately while continued inflation at any expected rate causes share prices to rise continuously to maintain their real value.

A significant feature of that paper was the explicit recognition of two classes of portfolio investors: "households" that pay an income tax on dividends and interest and a capital gains tax on nominal capital gains, and "institutions" (pension funds, nonprofit organizations, etc.) that pay no tax on portfolio income or capital gains. Both types of investors hold equity shares despite the difference between them in the relative after-tax yields on stocks and bonds because of their desire to limit risk through

Reprinted by permission from *Journal of Monetary Economics* 6 (July 1980): 309–31.

This paper is part of the NBER study of capital formation and was presented at the Rochester University Research Conference on October 25 and 26, 1979. I am grateful to James Poterba for help with these computations and to Alan Auerbach, David Bradford, Jerry Green, Mervyn King, Lawrence Summers, and other participants in the NBER summer institutes on Business Taxation and Finance for discussions. The views expressed in this paper are my own and not those of the NBER or Harvard University.

1. The cost of equity capital is an important component of the overall cost of capital if firms consider the repurchase of shares as an alternative to investment in new capacity (Tobin and Brainard, 1977) or if the firm's debt-equity ratios influence the cost of additional funds (Feldstein, Green, and Sheshinski, 1979).

portfolio diversification.[2] In the simplified framework of the earlier paper, a rise in the expected rate of inflation unambiguously depresses the price per share that institutional investors are willing to pay but may raise the demand price that household investors are willing to pay. The change in the equilibrium share price that follows an increase in expected inflation depends on the portfolio adjustment behavior of these types of investors.

Although the earlier analysis conveys the basic idea of how inflation affects share prices, it must be extended to provide a more realistic picture of the interaction of inflation and share prices. The present paper introduces three important aspects to the model of equilibrium share price behavior. First, the new analysis recognizes that firms borrow and that the existence of debt causes inflation to raise the firms' real after-tax earnings available for equity owners. Second, in contrast to the assumption in the previous paper (Feldstein, 1980a) that firms distribute all earnings as dividends, the present analysis assumes a realistic ratio of retained earnings to dividends. The effect of this is to magnify the impact on share prices of changes in inflation or other variables. Finally, the present analysis recognizes that households invest in a much wider range of assets than stocks and bonds, including real estate, consumer durables, noncorporate businesses, depletable natural resources, and such "store-of-value" assets as land, gold, and antiques; some of these investment opportunities actually become more attractive when the rate of inflation increases.[3] Households may also respond to lower prospective yields on stocks and bonds by increasing consumption. The households' broad range of alternatives to investment in equities implies in general that their opportunity cost of holding shares does not vary in the same way as that of institutions and, in particular, that it does not vary only with the real net yield on bonds. This broader set of alternatives is recognized in the current analysis by explicitly relaxing (but not completely eliminating) the previous link between the real net yield on bonds and the required yield on equities.

With these extensions, the current analysis identifies six ways in which the interaction of inflation and tax rules affects share prices: (1) Historic cost accounting for depreciation and existing methods of inventory accounting raise corporate taxes. (2) The deduction of nominal interest

2. More formally, both types of investors will generally maximize expected utility by holding mixed portfolios even though, in the absence of risk aversion, the difference in the relative after-tax expected yields on stocks and bonds would cause one type of investor to hold only one type of asset. See also Feldstein and Slemrod (1980) and Feldstein and Green (1979).

3. The interaction of inflation and tax rules affect the net yield on these assets very differently from the way they affect either stocks or bonds; see Feldstein (1980; chap. 12 below) on land and gold and Hendershott (1979) on housing.

payments lowers corporate taxes.[4] (3) The net increase in corporate tax payments reduces dividends and retained earnings, thus lowering tax payments by shareholders. (4) The nominal increase in the value of the corporation's capital stock induces a capital gains tax liability for shareholders. (5) Because households pay tax on nominal interest income, inflation lowers the real net yield on bonds as an alternative to share ownership.[5] (6) The favorable tax rules for investment in land, gold, owner-occupied housing, etc., imply that the real net opportunity cost of shareholding does not fall as much as the real net yield on bonds and may actually rise. *In considering these interactions of inflation and tax rules, it is important to distinguish households and nontaxable institutions and to recognize that share prices represent an equilibrium for these two groups.* All of these ideas are developed more fully in the present paper.

Although it is analytically useful to calculate how inflation affects share prices on the assumption that the pretax return per unit of capital is unchanged, a fall in the share price per dollar of corporate capital would in fact reduce the equilibrium size of the corporate capital stock and thereby raise the pretax return until the share price per dollar of capital returned to its initial equilibrium.[6] The current paper presents some illustrative calculations of the magnitude of the fall in the equilibrium capital stock that would result under certain simplifying assumptions.

In section 11.2 of this paper, I analyze an economy in which shares are owned only by tax exempt institutions. The more complex effects of inflation on households' demand for equity shares are examined in section 11.3. The fourth section examines the market equilibrium with both types of investors.

The limitations of the analytic structure should be stressed at the outset. The model presented here does not represent a full general equilibrium picture of the effects of inflation on share prices. Some of the values that are treated as fixed parameters should be regarded as endogenous variables in a larger system. The role and complete consequences of macroeconomic policy and debt policy remain vague. The pretax yield on capital in the noncorporate sector is not explicitly treated as an endogenous variable. The dynamic specification ignores transitional issues and focuses on steady-state values. I believe that the model is

---

4. In evaluating the impact of inflation on the *total* taxes paid on the capital income of the nonfinancial corporations, it is important to bear in mind that this reduced *corporate* tax liability is almost exactly offset by the increased tax liability of the *creditors* who must pay tax on nominal interest receipts (see Feldstein and Summers, 1979; chap. 8 above).

5. As I emphasized in Feldstein (1980*b*; chap. 10), this stands in sharp contrast to the popular notion that share prices are depressed because of high nominal interest rates.

6. Under certain conditions, the equilibrium share price per dollar of capital is unity but the presence of taxation may cause a different value; see Auerbach (1979*b*), Bradford (1979), Feldstein and Green (1979), and King (1977).

nevertheless rich enough and realistic enough to demonstrate the principal channels through which the interaction of inflation and tax rules affects share prices.

The present paper is not, however, an attempt to explain the total fall in the real value of share prices. The behavior of share prices during the past decade and a half may reflect not ony the interaction of taxes and inflation but also the cyclical downturn in economic activity and pretax profitability, the inability of investors to evaluate real corporate earnings in an inflationary environment, investors' perception of an increased risk in equity investment, etc.[7] The goal of the present paper is more modest: to examine the way in which tax rules and inflation interact in affecting the share prices of nonfinancial corporations and to show that the net effect of inflation is likely to be negative. This conclusion stands in sharp contrast to papers in which Fama (1979), Hendershott (1979), and Modigliani and Cohn (1979) have argued that the interaction of taxes and inflation has raised share prices above the even lower levels to which they would otherwise have fallen.

11.2   Institutional Investors

This section analyzes an economy in which equity shares are owned only by tax exempt institutions like pension funds and nonprofit organizations.[8] This provides a simple way of separating the effect of inflation on corporate taxes from its effects on the taxes paid by households and shows why it is important to distinguish the two classes of investors in the complete analysis. The analysis here shows that an increase in the expected rate of inflation unambiguously decreases the attractiveness of equity shares relative to bonds for this important group of investors and would therefore lower the share value per unit of capital.

Consider first an economy in which there is no inflation. Each share of stock represents the ownership claim to a single unit of capital (i.e., one dollar's worth of capital valued at its reproduction cost) and to the net earnings that it produces. The marginal product of capital (net of depreciation), f', is subject to a corporate income tax at effective rate τ_1; in the absence of inflation, this effective rate of tax is less than the statutory rate (τ) because of the combined effect of the investment tax credit and accelerated depreciation. The corporation borrows b dollars per unit of capital and pays interest at rate r. Since these interest payments are deducted in calculating corporate income that is taxed at the statutory

7. For explanations along these lines, see Fama (1979), Hendershott (1979), Malkiel (1978), Modigliani and Cohn (1979), and Summers (1980b).

8. These institutions own a significant and growing fraction of corporate stock, especially of the stock of major publicly traded corporations. Probably because of their exemption from capital gains taxes, these institutions account for a disproportionately large share of all transactions in equity shares.

rate τ, the net cost of these borrowed funds is $(1 - \tau)br$. The net return to equity investors per unit of capital is therefore $(1 - \tau_1)f' - (1 - \tau)br$. To avoid the extra notation of two different corporate tax rates, I shall define the "equivalent pretax return" ρ to satisfy $(1 - \tau)\rho = (1 - \tau_1)f'$, i.e., ρ is the pretax rate of return which, if taxed at the statutory rate, would yield the same after-tax return as occurs when the actual pretax return is taxed at the lower "no inflation" effective tax rate. The net return to equity investors per unit of capital in the absence of inflation is thus $(1 - \tau)(\rho - br)$.

What happens to this net return when the inflation rate rises? For simplicity, the analysis considers an instantaneous and unanticipated increase to π which is expected to persist forever. Under existing U.S. tax law, inflation raises taxable profits (for any fixed level of real profits) in two ways. First, the value of depreciation allowances is based on the original or 'historic' cost of the asset rather than on its current value. When prices rise, this historic cost method of depreciation causes the real value of depreciation to fall and the real value of taxable profits to rise.[9] Second, the cost of maintaining inventory levels is understated for firms that use the first-in/first-out (FIFO) method of inventory accounting.[10] A linear approximation that each percentage point of inflation increases taxable profits per unit of capital by μ implies that the existing treatment of depreciation and inventories reduces net profits by $\tau\mu$ per unit of capital per percentage point of inflation.

When there is a positive rate of inflation, the firms' net interest payments $((1 - \tau)br)$ overstate the true cost to the equity owners of the corporations' debt finance. Against this apparent interest cost it is necessary to offset the reduction in the real value of the corporations' net monetary liabilities. These net monetary liabilities per unit of capital are the difference between the interest-bearing debt (b) and the non-interest-bearing monetary assets (a).

Combining the basic net profits per unit of capital, the extra tax caused by the existing depreciation and inventory rules, and the real gain on net monetary liabilities yields the real net return per unit of capital,

$$(1) \qquad z = (1 - \tau)(\rho - br) - \tau\mu\pi + (b - a)\pi$$

If q is the share value per unit of equity (i.e., per unit of capital net of its

---

9. Specific estimates of the magnitude of this effect are discussed below. For a more general discussion, see Feldstein, Green, and Sheshinski (1978; chap. 4 above) and Feldstein (1981a), Hong (1977), Motley (1969) and Van Horne and Glassmire (1972) discuss the implications of historic cost depreciation for share values in the context of a model with a single investor whose discount rate is unchanged by inflation.

10. Although firms in principle have the option of avoiding the extra tax by using the last-in/first-out (LIFO) method of inventory accounting, a total of $7 billion in extra taxes was paid in 1977 because firms apparently regarded that as less costly in a larger sense than switching from FIFO to LIFO.

pro rata share of debt), the corporate return per dollar of equity is $e = z/q(1 - b)$.[11]

If the corporation paid all of its earnings out to shareholders in the form of dividends, e would also be the net return to the institutions that own those shares. In fact, corporations distribute a fraction d as dividends and retain the rest.[12] Since a dollar of retained earnings is worth q, each dollar of corporate earnings net of the corporate income tax is worth $d + (1 - d)q$ dollars.[13] The real net return to institutional investors per dollar of equity shares is thus

$$(2) \qquad e_{ni} = \frac{z[d + (1 - d)q]}{q(1 - b)}$$

where the subscript n indicates that this is a net return and the subscript i indicates that this is the net return for institutional investors. A simple model of share valuation implies that the price that the investor would be willing to pay per share would make the real net earnings per dollar of equity equal to the real net return on bonds, $r - \pi$. More realistically, investors require a higher yield on equity investments than they do on the apparently less risky bonds. If the risk differential required by institutional investors is denoted[14] δ_{is}, their portfolio equilibrium condition can be written

$$(3) \qquad e_{ni} = r - \pi + \delta_{is}$$

Using (2) to substitute for e_{ni} in (3) gives a portfolio equilibrium condition that can be solved explicitly for the share price,

$$(4) \qquad q = \frac{zd}{(1 - b)(r - \pi + \delta_{is}) - z(1 - d)}$$

The effect of inflation on the equilibrium share price depends on the change in the real rate of interest $(r - \pi)$ and the change in the equity

11. To see more easily that this is true, it is useful to think about the corresponding aggregates. Let K be total capital and $B = bK$ be the corresponding aggregate debt. The value of the equity shares is $q(K - B)$ and the total equity earnings are zK. The corporate equity yield is thus $zK/q(K - B) = z/q(1 - b)$.

12. I assume that d (like b) does not change with the rate of inflation. Although this is done primarily to focus attention on the more direct effects of inflation, neither ratio has changed significantly during the past 15 years.

13. If q is less than 1, institutional investors would obviously prefer to have all income distributed. Because of their different tax situation, households will generally prefer some retained earnings even if q is less than 1. The distribution fraction observed in the economy reflects the firms' balancing of these conflicting interests. For an explicit model of the determination of dividend policy, see Feldstein and Green (1979).

14. The subscript s refers to the state of the economy and can temporarily be ignored. In general, δ_{is} will be an increasing function of the number of shares that the investor holds in equilibrium. The current assumption that all shares are held by institutional investors implies that δ_{is} does not depend on the rate of inflation if we ignore any effect of changes in the constant inflation rate on the perceived riskiness of stocks.

earnings net of corporate income tax (z). Econometric studies indicate that the nominal interest rate rises point-for-point with sustained changes in the rate of inflation, $dr/d\pi = 1$.[15] It is important to emphasize that this 'Fisherian' feature of the economy is an empirical regularity and not a theoretical necessity. As Feldstein, Green, and Sheshinski (1978; chap. 4) emphasize, the response of the nominal interest rate to inflation in an economy without government bonds depends on tax rates, depreciation rules, and investor behavior.[16] The actual behavior of the interest rate depends also on government debt policy[17] and on the supply of debt by non-corporate borrowers. The remainder of the paper assumes that $dr/d\pi = 1$, i.e., that the real interest rate remains constant.

With a constant real rate of interest, (4) shows that inflation lowers the equilibrium share price if $dz/d\pi < 0$ and raises the equilibrium share price if $dz/d\pi > 0$. From (1),

$$(5) \qquad \frac{dz}{d\pi} = -(1-\tau)b - \tau\mu + b - a$$

$$= \tau(b - \mu) - a$$

Recent values of these parameters imply that $dz/d\pi$ is negative and therefore that inflation would reduce the short-run equilibrium share price in an economy in which only tax exempt institutions own shares. In 1977, nonfinancial corporations had a total capital stock of $1,684 billion and owed net interest-bearing liabilities of $509.7 billion,[18] implying that $b = 0.302$. The monetary assets of the NFCs had a value of $54.8 billion, implying that $a = 0.033$. Since the corporate tax rate in 1977 was $\tau = 0.48$, these figures imply that $dz/d\pi = 0.113 - \tau\mu$.

While it is difficult to calculate μ as precisely as τ, b and z, it is clear that $\tau\mu$ exceeds 0.113 and therefore that $dz/d\pi < 0$. Recall that $\mu\pi$ is the

15. The conclusion that inflation raises the nominal interest rate while leaving the real rate unchanged has been supported by a large number of studies. See Fisher (1930), Yohe and Karnovsky (1969), Feldstein and Eckstein (1970) and, more recently, Fama (1975) and Feldstein and Summers (1978; chap. 9 above).

16. Calculations by Feldstein and Summers (1978; chap. 9 above) show that, with existing tax rules, the interest rate would rise by slightly more than the rise in the rate of inflation if the difference in the real net yields on stocks and bonds for a typical individual investor is to be maintained. They found empirically that the interest rate movement did not maintain this real net yield difference but satisfied $dr/d\pi = 1$.

17. Feldstein (1908c; chap. 5 above) presents an explicit model of equilibrium growth that shows how different government debt policies can modify the real rate of interest in a way that is independent of the rate of inflation.

18. The capital stock, valued at replacement cost in 1977 dollars, is estimated by the Department of Commerce. The net liabilities are based on information in the flow-of-funds tables. Feldstein and Summers (1979) report the net interest-bearing liabilities of NFCs as $595 billion. For the appropriate debt measure in this work, the value of the net trade credit (72.7 billion) and government securities (12.9 billion) must be subtracted from this $595 billion. The subtraction of net trade credit reflects the assumption that the profits of NFCs include an implicit interest return on the trade credit that they extend. The new information is from the Federal Reserve Balance Sheets of the U.S. Economy.

overstatement of taxable profits per dollar of capital caused by inflation at rate π. Feldstein and Summers (1979; chap. 8) estimate that in 1977 inflation caused an overstatement of taxable profits of $54.3 billion of which $39.7 billion was due to low depreciation and $14.6 was due to artificial inventory profits. Thus in 1977 $\mu\pi = 54.3/1684 = 0.032$. The implied value of μ depends on the rate of inflation that was responsible for these additional taxable profits. For the inventory component of the overstated profits, the relevant inflation rate is the one for the concurrent year; for the depreciation component, the relevant inflation rate is a weighted average of the inflation rates since the oldest remaining capital was acquired but with greater weight given to inflation in more recent years. The consumer price index rose 6.8 percent in 1977, an average of 7.2 percent in the preceding five years, and 4.5 percent and 1.9 percent in the two previous five-year periods.[19] An inflation rate of 7.0 percent is therefore a reasonable upper bound for the relevant rate and 5.0 percent is a reasonable lower bound. A value of $\pi = 0.06$ implies that $\mu = 0.53$ and therefore that $\tau\mu = 0.256$, even at the upper bound of $\pi = 0.07$, $\mu = 0.46$ and $\tau\mu = 0.22$ Both of these values are clearly above the critical value of 0.113 required for $dz/d\pi < 0$. In the analysis that follows, I shall assume $\mu = 0.53$, a value that is also implied by an alternative calculation presented in the appendix to this paper.[20]

Two more parameter values are required to calculate explicitly the effect of inflation on the real rate of return to equity capital: the equivalent pretax rate of return (ρ) and the real interest rate ($r - \pi$). For the period from 1948 through 1976, the cyclically-adjusted rate of return on capital in the nonfinancial sector averaged 11.2 percent (Feldstein and Summers, 1977), using this value implies $f' = 0.112$. In the absence of inflation, the tax rules as of 1977 imply an effective corporate tax rate of $\tau_1 = 0.38$.[21] Since ρ is defined by $(1 - \tau)\rho = (1 - \tau_1)f'$, $\rho = 0.134$.

The real interest rate is estimated most easily for a period with low and quite stable inflation. Between 1960 and 1964, the annual rates of increase of the consumer price index varied between 1.0 percent and 1.6 percent with a mean of 1.24 percent. The interest rate on *Baa* bonds

19. The index of producer prices for finished goods rose 6.6 percent in 1977 and an average of 5.9 percent for the previous decade, essentially the same as the CPI.

20. The alternative calculation is based on selecting a hypothetical investment and seeing how inflation changes the after-tax internal rate of return with existing tax laws.

21. This figure is derived in the following way. The total 1977 tax on nonfinancial corporations (T) is equal to the tax on real capital income ($\tau_1 f' K$) plus the excess tax caused by inflation ($\tau\mu\pi K$) minus the tax reduction associated with the deduction of interest expenses ($\tau r b K$). According to the national income accounts, the 1977 tax liability of nonfinancial corporations was $59.0 billion, the net interest payments were $rbK = \$33.7$ billion, and profits (with the capital consumption and inventory valuation adjustments) were $f'K - rbK = \$113.9$ billion. Combining these with the Feldstein and Summers (1979; chap. 8 above) estimate of the excess tax due to inflation ($\tau\mu\pi K = \$19.1$ billion) and the statutory tax rate of $\tau = 0.48$ implies that the effective corporate rate in the absence of inflation would be $\tau_1 = 0.38$.

varied between an annual average of 5.19 percent in 1960 and 4.83 percent in 1964 with an overall average of 5.00 percent. These figures imply a real interest rate of 3.75 percent for *Baa* bonds.[22]

Combining these parameter estimates implies that the real rate of return to equity per dollar of capital in the absence of inflation would be (from 1)

$$(6) \qquad z = (1 - \tau)(\rho - br)$$

$$= 0.52(0.134 - 0.302(0.0375))$$

$$= 0.0638.$$

With a 6 percent rate of inflation, z falls to

$$(7) \qquad z = (1 - \tau)(\rho - br) - \tau\mu\pi + (b - a)\pi$$

$$= 0.52(0.134 - 0.302(0.0975)) - 0.48(0.53)(0.06)$$

$$+ (0.302 - 0.033)0.06$$

$$= 0.0553.$$

The rate of return at the level of the corporation thus falls by approximately one percentage point or one-sixth of its preinflation value.

The share price (4) contains two parameters that have not yet been evaluated: the dividend pay-out rate (d) and the risk differential (δ_{is}). In 1977, the corporations paid dividends equal to 45.3 percent of their real after-tax profits; this pay-out ratio has varied cyclically but averaged 45.4 percent during the preceding 15-year period. I shall assume $d = 0.45$ in all of the calculations. The risk differential (δ_{is}) can be calculated directly from the share price (4) by imposing the long-run equilibrium condition that $q = 1$. Thus (4) implies

$$(8) \qquad \delta_{is} = \frac{z}{1 - b} - (r - \pi)$$

$$= \frac{0.0638}{0.698} - 0.0375$$

$$= 0.0539.$$

Thus stocks yield 9.14 percent in this no-inflation equilibrium or 5.39 percent more than the yield on bonds.

---

22. Since the *Baa* rate fell monotonically during the early 1960s, the implied real interest rate might be as low as 3.5 percent. (The Baa rate of 8.97 percent in 1977 implies an anticipated inflation rate of approximately 5.25 percent. Since then the rise in interest rates implies an increase in anticipated inflation to between 7.50 and 7.75 percent. These calculations, of course, assume the continuous maintenance of a constant real rate of interest.)

It is now possible to calculate the effect of inflation on the short-run equilibrium share price for this economy in which all shares are owned by institutional investors. For a 6 percent inflation, (5) implies that

$$
(9) \qquad q = \frac{zd}{(1 - b)(r - \pi + \delta_{is}) - z(1 - d)}
$$

$$
= \frac{0.45(0.0553)}{(0.698)(0.0375 + 0.0539) - 0.0553(0.55)}
$$

$$
= 0.745.
$$

The short-run equilibrium share price falls to 75 percent of its no-inflation value. Note that the proportional fall in q is nearly twice as great as the proportional fall in z, a magnification that results from recognizing the effect of retained earnings.

In considering this fall in the short-run equilibrium share price, it is important to bear in mind that it treats the risk differential (δ_{is}) as fixed. Although inflation may in fact alter the perceived riskiness of investments in stocks and bonds, this is ignored here in order to focus on the interaction of inflation and tax rules.[23]

It is also important to emphasize that the new share price in (9) is calculated on the assumption that the pretax rate of return (ρ) remains unchanged and therefore that the capital stock of the corporate sector is unchanged. The lower share price would reduce investment in the corporate sector and this would cause the pretax rate of return ρ to rise. The reduced rate of investment would continue until the share price returned to its original long-run equilibrium value of $q = 1$. Ignoring this eventual return to $q = 1$ causes (9) to overstate the actual short-run fall in the share price.

To specify the capital adjustment process correctly requires at least a two-sector model of the economy in which capital and labor can both move from the nonfinancial corporate sector (and from other activities where inflation raises the effective tax rate) to activities like owner-occupied housing that are not taxed more heavily when the inflation rate rises. Consider instead a simpler calculation of the required reduction in the corporate capital stock if relative prices remain unchanged and the reduction in capital is the only way in which the pretax rate of return is increased.[24] With this simplification, it is easy to calculate the long-run reduction in the capital stock that is induced by a 6 percent inflation. It

23. The risk differential would also change with the rate of inflation because of the induced shift in share ownership. Discussion of this will be postponed until the demand for shares by household investors has been considered.

24. This would be the appropriate calculation if the only alternative to investment in corporate capital were government debt. More generally it is necessary to recognize the changes in the relative product prices and in the allocation of labor among the sectors of the economy.

follows from the share price equation (4) or (9) that returning to the original share value of $q = 1$ is equivalent to raising z to the value that prevailed in the absence of inflation or, from (6) $z = 0.0638$.

Equation (1) can be used to calculate the value ρ^* that is required to make $z = 0.0638$ *with* $\pi = 0.06$,

$$(10) \qquad 0.0638 = (1 - \tau)(\rho^* - br) - \tau\mu\pi + (b - a)\pi$$

$$= 0.52(\rho^* - 0.302(0.0975)) - 0.48(0.53)(0.06) + 0.302 - 0.033(0.06)$$

$$= 0.52\rho^* - 0.0143$$

or $\rho^* = 0.1502$. Thus the value of ρ must rise from 0.134 to 0.1502 to reestablish the long-run equilibrium. The corresponding change in the capital stock depends on the form and parameters of the production function. A Cobb-Douglas technology with a capital elasticity of 0.2 implies a 12 percent reduction in the equilibrium capital stock.

In summary, in an economy with our existing tax rules but in which all shares were owned by institutions that paid no "personal" tax on income or capital gains, a 6 percent inflation would induce a fall in the short-run equilibrium share price of nearly 35 percent and a fall in the long-run capital intensity of between 10 and 15 percent. The analysis for an economy with household as well as institutional investors is more complex and the results are more ambiguous. Before considering the behavior of this complete market equilibrium, it is useful to begin by analyzing the share valuation equation for households.

11.3 Household Investors

Household investors differ from institutional investors in three significant ways. First, households pay an income tax on dividends and a capital gains tax on the appreciation of share values. A particularly important aspect of this is the taxation of the nominal appreciation that results from capital gains. Second, because households pay tax on nominal interest income, the real net yield on bonds varies inversely with the rate of inflation. Third, households invest in a wide range of assets, a characteristic that eliminates the close link between the yields on bonds and the required yield on stocks.

This section develops the portfolio equilibrium condition for household investors and then derives the households' demand for shares as a function of their price and yield. The next section then combines the demand functions of households and institutions to study how inflation changes the market equilibrium price and capital intensity.

The real return per unit of capital after corporate income taxes but before personal taxes is the same as it was for institutional investors,

(11) $$z = (1 - \tau)(\rho - br) - \tau \mu \pi + (b - a)\pi$$

and the corporate return per dollar of equity is again $e = z/q(1 - b)$. A fraction d of this return is paid out as dividends and subject to individual income tax at rate m. The fraction that is retained adds $(1 - d)q$ to the value of the firm. This real increase in the firm's value is eventually subject to a capital gains tax when the stock is sold. The postponed tax liability can be expressed instead as an equivalent present-value tax rate c on accruing capital gains; since the actual liability is postponed and the gain taxed at less than the rate on ordinary income, $c < m$.

Inflation reduces these net earnings even further by imposing an additional tax on nominal capital gains. More specifically, even though the real share price remains constant at the new *real* equilibrium value q, inflation causes the *nominal* share price to rise at 100 π percent a year. The real value of this nominal gain at any time is thus πq per share or $\pi q(1 - b)$ per unit of capital.[25] This entails no real gain but does induce an ultimate capital gains tax liability with an equivalent accrual amount of $c \pi q(1 - b)$ per unit of capital.

The real net return to household investors per dollar of equity value is thus

(12) $$e_{nh} = \frac{z[d(1 - m) + (1 - d)(1 - c)q] - c\pi q(1 - b)}{(1 - b)q}$$

where the subscript h indicates that this is a net yield to households.

For institutional investors, portfolio equilibrium was characterized by equating this net equity yield to the sum of the real net yield on bonds and a risk differential that would in general vary with the number of shares that those investors own. For household investors, I shall adopt a similar equilibrium condition that the required net equity yield may be written as the sum of two components: a real net yield on alternative assets (n_s) and a risk differential that depends on the number of shares that households own.[26]

(13) $$e_{nh} = n_s + \delta_{hs}$$

The subscript s on n_s indicates that the real net yield on alternative assets varies with the state of the economy, i.e., with the rate of inflation.

---

25. To see why this is $\pi q(1 - b)$ note that the total real capital stock K minus the value of the debt (bK) is the capital share of the equity owners and is valued at q per unit of net capital. Thus the total equity value is $E = q(1 - b)K$. In addition to any retained earnings, the nominal value of equity rises at the rate $\pi E = \pi q(1 - b)K$. The nominal gain per unit of capital is thus $\pi q(1 - b)$.

26. The form of the dependence of δ_{hs} on the number of shares owned by households will be made explicit below. The value of δ_{hs} will also depend on the risk per share. This additive separability assumption is obviously a simplification that would only be consistent with expected utility maximization on very stringent assumptions.

For ordinary bonds, the real net yield is $(1 - m)r - \pi$; the assumption that $dr/d\pi = 1$ implies that the real net yield on such bonds falls by the fraction m of any increase in the inflation rate. Investments in other assets are treated much more favorably in an inflationary economy. Owner-occupied housing is not affected by depreciation rules, the nominal capital gains are largely untaxed, and the deductibility of nominal mortgage interest payments reduces the real net cost of mortgage finance. Investments in nondepreciable property (land, timber, depletable resources, gold, etc.) are also not affected by the historic cost depreciation rules. Although these investments entail eventual capital gains tax liabilities on their nominal appreciation, this relatively small tax is often more than offset by the tax deductibility of interest payments on the debt associated with these investments. Although investments in depreciable real estate are disadvantaged by the historic cost depreciation rule, the relatively high ratio of debt to total capital for such investments implies that even the reduction in real depreciation is often more than offset by the deductibility of nominal interest.[27] On balance, therefore, inflation may lower, raise, or leave unchanged the yield on alternative investments to which household investors compare the yield on equity.[28] The risk premium that a household requires to hold an additional share of equity should be an increasing function of the amount of risk that the household is already bearing. This relation (and the similar one for institutional investors) will be discussed explicitly in section 11.4.

Combining (12) and (13) gives an explicit equation for the price per share that household investors would be willing to pay,

$$(14) \qquad q = \frac{(1 - m)zd}{(1 - b)(n_s + \delta_{hs}) + (1 - b)c\pi - (1 - d)(1 - c)z}$$

The analysis in section 11.2 showed that the net effect of higher inflation on depreciation, inventories, and the deductibility of corporate interest expenses reduces the corporation's net of tax income, z. Equation (14) shows that this lower value of z reduces the share price. The taxation of the households' nominal capital gains, reflected in the term $(1 - b)c\pi$ in the denominator of (14), further depresses the share price. Thus if the household's required yield on equities $(n_s + \delta_{hs})$ rises or remains unchanged, the interaction of inflation and tax rules unambiguously reduces the share price that households are willing to pay. Since section 11.2 showed that the institution's demand price would unambiguously de-

27. The ratio of debt to total capital is usually much greater for commercial real estate investments than it is for nonfinancial corporations in general.

28. The change in n_s will differ among households according to their individual income tax brackets. Moreover, the new equilibrium will also involve some capitalization of yield differentials. Because of differences in tax rates among households, this capitalization cannot be complete for all households.

cline, a constant or higher value of $n_s + \delta_{hs}$ means that a higher rate of inflation would unambiguously reduce the equilibrium share price.

A significant fall in the household's required yield on equities is required to prevent a decline in their demand price for shares. Even if such a decline in $n_s + \delta_{hs}$ does prevent a decline in the household's demand price, the unambiguous reduction in institutions' demand for shares might cause a fall in the market equilibrium price of shares.

The magnitude of the decline in $n_s + \delta_{hs}$ that would maintain the household's demand for equities is easily calculated with the help of (14). It is necessary first to evaluate the two tax rates paid by household investors, m and c. For the average tax rate on dividends (m), I shall use the weighted average of shareholder marginal tax rates, weighting by the amount of dividends received; Feldstein and Summers (1979; chap. 8) report the value $m = 0.39$.[29] It is more difficult to estimate the relevant rate of capital gains tax, c. Long-term capital gains are taxed at about half of the rate on dividends[30] when the gain is realized. However, since gains are taxed only when they are realized, the effective rate is reduced by the postponement of realization. In addition, capital gains that have accrued on assets that are passed on at the death of their owner completely avoid tax on the previously accrued gain because the new owner is permitted to 'step up' his basis to the value at the time of receipt for the purpose of calculating future capital gains liabilities. A conservatively low value of $c = 0.05$ will be used.

With these values of m and c and the other parameter values that were obtained in section 11.2, it is now possible to use (14) to derive the value of $n_s + \delta_{hs}$ that is consistent with zero inflation and an initial share price of $q_0 = 1$. More specifically, with $z_0 = 0.0638$, $d = 0.45$ and $b = 0.302$, equation (14) implies that $n_s + \delta_{hs} = 0.0728$.

A rise in the inflation rate to $\pi = 0.06$ would reduce z from[31] $z_0 = 0.0638$ to $z_1 = 0.0553$ and would add $(1 - b)c\pi = 0.00209$ to the denominator to reflect the taxation of nominal capital gains. If the required rate of return on equities remains unchanged at $n_s + \delta_{hs} = 0.0728$, the demand price implied by (14) drops from $q_0 = 1$ to $q_1 = 0.632$, a more substantial reduction than the decline in the institutional investors' demand price to 0.745.

29. A 1 percent increase in the dividend receipts of each taxpayer would increase the income tax liability by 39 percent of the additional dividends. This calculation is done with the NBER TAXSIM model based on 1976 tax rates.

30. Until 1978, half of long-term gains were excludable in calculating taxable income; since then, the exclusion has increased to 60 percent. The total tax rate on capital gains also depends on the availability of the alternative tax method (until 1978), the treatment of the excluded portion of gains as a tax preference, and the reduction in the amount of earned income eligible for the maximum tax provision (until 1978).

31. See equation (7) for the calculation that $\pi = 0.06$ implies $z_1 = 0.0553$.

To prevent this decline in the household's demand price, the required rate of return would have to drop from 0.0728 to 0.0601 or less.[32] Only if such a decline in $n_s + \delta_{hs}$ occurred could the households' demand for equities increase. The possibility of such a decline and the corresponding change in the equilibrium share price when households and institutions are considered together is one of the cases considered in section 11.4.

11.4 Market Equilibrium

The separate analyses of institutional and household investors have shown how inflation affects these two components of the total demand for shares. An increase in the rate of inflation unambiguously reduces the institutional investors' demand because the real net yield on equities falls while the corresponding yield on the alternative investment on bonds does not. For household investors, the demand for equities declines unless the real net yield on the portfolio of alternative financial and real investments falls enough to offset the lower return on equities and the extra tax on nominal capital gains. If the equity demands of both households and institutions decline, the market price of shares must also decline in the short run and the capital stock of the nonfinancial corporate sector must decline in the long run.

More generally, a higher rate of inflation might reduce the real net yield on the alternative assets in which households invest by enough to increase their demand for equity shares. The change in the market equilibrium price then depends on the way in which the risk differentials of institutions and households (δ_{is} and δ_{hs}) respond to changes in the distribution of share ownership. The present section therefore begins by presenting an explicit model of the determination of δ_{is} and δ_{hs}.

The risk premium that an institution requires to hold an additional share of equity should be an increasing function of the amount of risk that the institution is already bearing. More explicitly, I shall assume that δ_{is} is proportional to the standard deviation of the return on the equity portion of the existing portfolio.[33] The source of this uncertainty is the variability of the pretax return on capital ρ;[34] the variance of ρ will be written σ_ρ^2. Equations (1) and (2) imply that the variance per dollar of equity investment is $[d + (1 - d)q]^2(1 - \tau)^2\sigma_\rho^2 / (1 - b)^2q^2$. If institutions own S_{is} shares when the economy is in state s, the dollar value of their equity

---

32. The value of 0.0601 is obtained from (14) by setting $q = 1$, $z = 0.0553$ and $(1 - b)c\pi = 0.00209$ and then solving for $n_s + \delta_{hs}$.

33. This would be the standard deviation of the entire portfolio return if bonds were completely riskless.

34. The current analysis ignores any direct effect of increased inflation on perceived risk in order to focus analytic attention on the interaction of taxes and the steady state of inflation.

investment is $S_{is}q_s$, where q_s is the price prevailing in state s. The standard deviation of the return on the equity portion of the institutions' portfolio is the product of the dollar value of the equity investment: $S_{is}[d + (1 - d)q_s](1 - \tau)\sigma_p(1 - b)^{-1}$. If the risk differential between the yields on bonds and stocks is proportional to this standard deviation, δ_{is} can be written

(15)
$$\delta_{is} = \delta_i S_{is}[d + (1 - d)q_s](1 - \tau)(1 - b)^{-1}\sigma_p$$

where δ_i is a risk-aversion constant for institutions.

Note that all of the variables that determine δ_{is} are measurable except δ_i and σ_p and that only their product matters. Recall that (8) showed that in general $\delta_{is} = z/(1 - b) - (r - \pi)$, and that with no inflation $\delta_{is} = 0.0539$. In 1967, before the inflation rate began to accelerate, institutions held approximately \$100 billion of corporate equities.[35] I shall take the share price in 1967 to be $q_0 = 1$. Measuring the total equity value in billions of dollars implies $S_{i0} = 100$. Equation (14) then indicates that $\delta_i\sigma_p = 0.724 \cdot 10^{-3}$.

The risk sensitivity parameter for households ($\delta_h\sigma_p$) can be obtained in essentially the same way. The assumption that the risk premium that a household requires to hold additional shares of equity is proportional to the standard deviation of the return on the equity portion of the existing portfolio[36] implies that

(16)
$$\delta_{hs} = \delta_h S_{hs}[d(1 - m) + (1 - d)(1 - c)q_s] \\ (1 - \tau)(1 - b)^{-1}\sigma_p$$

where δ_h is the risk aversion constant for households. The analysis in section 11.3 showed that, in the absence of inflation, an equilibrium share price of $q_0 = 1$ implies $n_0 + \delta_{h0} = 0.0728$. For any value of n_0, δ_{h0} is calculable and (16) can be used to derive $\delta_h\sigma_s$.

This specification implies that n_0 is the minimum yield on equities that is required to induce households to own any equities at all; it is equal to the real net yield to households on the portfolio of alternative assets (in the absence of inflation) plus the required risk differential when the households currently own no equities. For example, $n_0 = 0.04$ implies $\delta_{h0} = 0.0328$ and $\delta_h\sigma_p = 0.788 \cdot 10^{-4}$.[37] More generally $\delta_h\sigma_p = (0.175 - 2.406n_0)10^{-3}$; thus with $n_0 = 0.05$, $\delta_h\sigma_p = 0.547 \cdot 10^{-4}$, while

35. The flow-of-funds accounts for 1967 report that pensions and insurance companies owned \$79 billion of corporate equities at market value. Of the \$720 billion of equities owned by households, personal trusts, and nonprofit organizations, approximately \$20 billion are attributable to nonprofit organizations.

36. This would be most appropriate if the other assets in the households' portfolio could be treated as riskless but, in any case, the simple additive separability and proportionality specification of the required equity yield must be regarded as a useful approximation rather than a general result.

37. This is based on household ownership of \$700 billion of equities at market value in 1967.

with $n_0 = 0.03$, $\delta_h\sigma_p = 0.126 \cdot 10^{-3}$. The risk sensitivity parameter of households is thus approximately one-tenth of the corresponding parameter for institutions, a difference that primarily reflects the much larger total wealth of households.

The equilibrium share price and distribution of share ownership at any inflation rate must satisfy three conditions: the institutional portfolio balance condition, the household portfolio balance condition, and the requirement that the total demand for shares by households and institutions equals the existing supply. In the short run, with the stock of capital fixed, this provides three equations that simultaneously determine q_s, S_{hs} and S_{is}. In the long run, the share price must equal one and the three equations determined the equilibrium size of the corporate capital stock and its distribution between households and institutions.

Consider first the short-run equilibrium with a fixed stock of capital and a fixed number of shares $\bar{S}$. The institutional portfolio balance condition can be written, from (4),

$$(17) \qquad q = \frac{zd}{(1-b)(r - \pi + \delta_{is}) - z(1-d)}$$

where

$$(18) \qquad z = (1 - \tau)(\rho - br) - \tau\mu\pi + (b - a)\pi$$

and

$$(19) \qquad \delta_{is} = 0.724(10^{-3})S_{is}[d + (1 - d)q_s](1 - \tau)(1 - b)^{-1}$$

Note that the dependence of δ_{is} on S_{is} implies that (17) can be thought of as the institutions' inverse demand function for shares; *ceterus paribus* a higher price is associated with a smaller number of shares. The corresponding household portfolio balance condition is, from (14),

$$(20) \qquad q = \frac{(1 - m)zd}{(1-b)(n_s + \delta_{hs}) + (1-b)c\pi - z(1-d)(1-c)}$$

where

$$(21) \qquad \delta_{hs} = (0.175 - 2.406n_0)(10^{-3})S_{hs}[d(1 - m) \\ + (1 - d)(1 - c)q_s](1 - \tau)(1 - b)^{-1}$$

Finally, the demand for shares must equal the fixed supply

$$(22) \qquad S_{is} + S_{hs} = \bar{S}$$

These six equations determine the equilibrium share price q, the share ownership of households and institutions (S_{is} and S_{hs}) and the incidental parameters z, δ_{is}, and δ_{hs}.

The numerical parameter values in (19) and (21) were selected to make the equations consistent with the initial equilibrium of $\pi = 0$ and $q = 1$

with share ownership $S_{i0} = 100$ and $S_{h0} = 700$. The response of q to changes in π depends on the initial level of n_0 and on the way in which it is changed by inflation as well as on the other parameter values that have been discussed at earlier points in the paper. This is seen more clearly when (17–22) are reduced to set of three equations evaluated at $\pi = 0.06$. A subscript 1 will be used to distinguish the equilibrium values at $\pi = 0.06$ from the equilibrium value with no inflation that are subscripted with a zero. For convenience, I will define $\hat{S}_{i1} = 10^{-3}S_{i1}$ and $\hat{S}_{hi} = 10^{-3}S_{h1}$. Equations (17–19) can then be reduced to[38]

(23)
$$0.1694\,\hat{S}_{i1}q_1 + 0.2071\hat{S}_{i1}q_1^2 - 0.00423q_1 - 0.02489 = 0$$

Similarly, (20) and (21) can be reduced to

(24)
$$(0.0249 - 0.3434n_0)\hat{S}_{h1}q_1 + (0.04753 - 0.6538n_0)\hat{S}_{h1}q_1^2$$
$$- (0.2680 - 0.698n_1)q_1 - 0.01518 = 0$$

Finally,

(25)
$$\hat{S}_{h1} + \hat{S}_{i1} = 0.8$$

Consider first the implications of an initial alternative yield of $n_0 = 0.04$ that does not change at all when the inflation rate rises to 6 percent ($n_1 = 0.04$). Solving (23–25) indicates that the price falls from $q_0 = 1$ to $q_1 = 0.76$. Institutions increase their share ownership from $S_{is} = 100$ billion shares (at $q_0 = 1$) to $S_{i1} = 110$ billion shares (at $q_1 = 0.76$); the fall in the price per share implies that the total value of their equity holdings falls from \$100 billion to \$84 billion. Households reduce their share ownership from $S_{h0} = 700$ billion shares to $S_{h1} = 690$ billion shares and thus reduce the value of the equity holdings from \$700 billion to \$524 billion. The institutional ownership increases from 12.5 percent of total equities to 13.8 percent.[39]

These results are not sensitive to changes in the initial level of the alternative yield. The assumption that $n_0 = 0.03$ (instead of $n_0 = 0.04$) and that this does not change when the inflation rate rises to 6 percent implies that inflation reduces the price to $q_1 = 0.78$. Institutional holding rises to 106 billion shares and therefore to \$83 billion.

The assumed *change* in the yield on alternative assets caused by inflation does, however, have a substantial impact. If n falls from $n_0 = 0.04$ to

---

38. This uses the previous calculation that $z = 0.0553$ at $\pi = 0.06$.

39. Between 1967 and 1977, corporate equities declined from approximately 40 percent of household assets to approximately 25 percent. Equities remained at 55 percent of private pension assets and rose from 9 percent of the assets of state and local government employee retirement funds to 23 percent. Among insurance companies, equities remained at 11 percent of total assets. Thus institutions as a whole increased the fraction of their assets devoted to equities. Since the total assets of these institutions also rose somewhat faster than the total assets of households, the fraction of equities held by households declined from about 88 percent to about 78 percent.

$n_1 = 0.03$, the equilibrium price only falls from $q_0 = 1$ to $q_1 = 0.93$. This fall in n_1 implies that households would actually increase their shareholding to 715 billion shares while institutions reduced their shareholding. The fall in n_1 required to keep the equilibrium share price unchanged implies an even more implausible decrease in shareholding by institutions; if n falls from $n_0 = 0.04$ to $n_1 = 0.0264$, the equilibrium price remains unchanged at $q = 1$ but institutions reduce their shareholding from \$100 billion to \$78 billion.[40] Finally, it is interesting to note that a fall in n_1 from 0.04 to 0.0273 would be enough to increase the price that households would be willing to pay in isolation[41] but leads to a small fall in the market equilibrium price ($q_1 = 0.983$) and a substantial increase in the number of shares held by households (to 721 billion shares).

The equilibrium conditions of (17–22) can now be used to calculate the change in the pretax rate of return[42] that is required for long-run equilibrium. Instead of regarding ρ as exogenous (in equation 18) and q as endogenous, the analysis will now set $q = 1$ and solve for the value of ρ that is consistent with $\pi = 0.06$. The solution indicates that with $n_0 = n_1 = 0.04$, ρ rise from 0.134 to 0.181. The 35 percent rise in the required marginal product of capital implies a significant fall in the capital stock of nonfinancial corporations.[43] Consider again the simplifying assumptions of section 11.2 that relative prices remain unchanged and that the fall in the corporate sector capital stock is the only way to raise the pretax rate of return. A Cobb-Douglas technology with a capital elasticity of 0.2 implies that raising ρ from 0.134 to 0.181 requires a 31 percent fall in the capital stock. If inflation lowers the yield on alternative assets so that $n_1 = 0.03$, the required rate of return rises to $\rho = 0.163$ and the Cobb-Douglas technology implies a 22 percent fall in the capital stock. Although the simplifying assumptions mean that these figures are only rough approximations, they do indicate the significant effect that the interaction of inflation and existing tax rules may have on the incentive to invest.

11.5   Conclusion

The analysis in this paper has shown that, because of existing tax rules, a permanent increase in the expected rate of inflation will depress the price of equity shares and will reduce the size of the equilibrium capital stock in the affected industries. This conclusion is based on calculations

---

40. Relative to the actual increase during the period of inflation described in the previous footnote.

41. See above, at the end of section 11.3, where it is noted that any fall greater than 0.015 would raise household demand for shares.

42. And therefore, in a simplified model, in the capital stock.

43. More generally, the capital is also reduced in other activities that are more heavily taxed because of inflation.

that use likely values of the tax and financial variables and that explicitly recognize the important roles of debt finance and retained earnings.

A number of other recent studies that have reached the opposite conclusion (that the interaction of taxes and inflation does not depress share prices) are based on a faulty or incomplete description of the tax effects. For example, Fama (1979) concludes that taxes could not be responsible for the fall in real share values during the 1970s because the ratio of corporate taxes to gross corporate income (before subtracting depreciation and real interest payments) has fallen since the 1960s. I do not understand the purpose of this comparison since the denominator does not refer to equity income and the numerator does not include all of the taxes paid by equity investors. Modigliani and Cohn (1979) refer to the fact that inflation reduces the real value of depreciation but underestimate the magnitude of this effect by more than 60 percent.[44] They also ignore the extra tax on the portfolio investors and the way in which the interaction of inflation and taxes alters the real net yields available on alternative assets. Hendershott's (1979) extension and critique of Feldstein (chaps. 10, 12, and 5) avoids many of the problems of other studies; his empirical results differ from my own because of different treatment of the interest rate, inventory profits, and non-interest-bearing debt. None of the studies with which I am familiar recognizes the importance of distinguishing among investors in different tax situations, either generally or the particular distinction between households and tax-free institutions that has been emphasized here.

There are, of course, a number of ways in which this study could be extended and strengthened. Like any model of a single market, the results could be improved by imbedding the current model in a more complete general equilibrium system. In this way, the effect of reductions in the stock of nonfinancial corporate capital on the yields in other markets could be explicitly evaluated. An explicit model of the adjustment of the capital stock would permit a more accurate evaluation of the initial change in price. A better empirical specification of the yields on the

---

44. Modigliani and Cohn estimate the effect of inflation on allowable depreciation by the capital consumption adjustment (CCA) estimated by the Department of Commerce. The CCA actually reflects two countervailing differences between real straight-line depreciation and the depreciation allowed for tax purposes: acceleration makes tax-deductible depreciation exceed straight-line depreciation while inflation reduces the value of tax-deductible depreciation. In 1977, for example, the "acceleration component" *raised* tax-deductible depreciation by $25.0 billion while the "inflation component" *reduced* tax depreciation by $39.7 billion. The $14.7 billion difference between these two is the net CCA figure of the type used by Modigliani and Cohn; it is only 37 percent of the true reduction in depreciation caused by inflation. (Although the "acceleration component" grew during the 1970s, this was almost entirely due to changes in tax laws in the 1960s and to the growth of investment. The favorable tax rules and the likely future would therefore have been anticipated in the late 1960s and reflected in share prices at that time. Only the subsequent unanticipated inflation and the associated loss of real depreciation would affect subsequent share price moments.)

alternative assets in the household's portfolio would also be desirable. Finally, a more general specification of the other factors that influence the movement of share prices is a necessary prerequisite to direct empirical measurement of the extent to which the poor performance of the stock market during the 1970s is due to the interaction of inflation and existing tax rules.

11.6 Appendix: Historic Cost Depreciation and Effective Tax Rates

The text of this paper introduced the parameter μ to measure the extent to which inflation raises taxable corporate income by reducing the real value of depreciation allowances and inventory costs. Although the component of μ caused by existing inventory methods could be calculated directly, the more important depreciation component required the rather arbitrary selection of "the" inflation rate responsible for the 1977 understatement of real depreciation. The rate of $\pi = 0.06$ was selected to reflect experience during the life of the then existing capital stock. The implied value of the depreciation component of μ is 0.39. Although the results are not very sensitive to plausible variations in their inflation rate, it seems desirable to estimate this parameter by an alternative method.

The current appendix uses the "hypothetical project" technique that I employed with Lawrence Summers in an earlier study (Feldstein and Summers, 1978; see chap. 9 above). This method is completely free of the recent historic experience. It nevertheless produces a value of the depreciation parameter (say, μ_1) that is extremely close to the estimate based on the national account data. The similarity of the two results provides substantial support for this value.

Consider a "standard investment" that in the absence of taxes has an internal rate of return of 12 percent.[45] Let the "maximum potential rate of return" denote the nominal rate of return that the firm can afford to pay for funds invested in this project. In the absence of tax this would be 12 percent; with pure debt finance and economic depreciation, the firm could pay this nominal return regardless of the corporate income tax. But less than economic depreciation would reduce this maximum potential rate of return.[46]

The Feldstein-Summers study considered how a 6 percent inflation would change the maximum potential *interest* rate that a firm could pay on the standard project if the project was financed with one-third debt and two-thirds equity and if the real net equity yield to typical individual investors had to exceed their real net yield on debt by 6 percent. The

45. The "standard investment" is actually a mix of equipment and structures, each with its own exponential output decay structure. See Feldstein and Summers (1978), p. 00 above.
46. For a more complete description, see Feldstein and Summers (1978), pp. 00–00 above.

analysis showed that a maximum potential nominal interest rate of 3.3 percent with no inflation would rise to 11.3 percent with a 6 percent inflation.[47] The assumption of one-third debt finance and a 6 percent yield differential implies that a 6 percent inflation rate would lower the total maximum potential real yield on capital by 1.2 percentage points;[48] $\tau\mu_1\pi$ = 0.012 or, with the value of τ = 0.5 used in that calculation, μ_1 = 0.40. This estimate is almost identical to the value inferred from the national account data and embodied in the total value (including inventory effects as well) of μ = 0.53 that is used in the text.

---

47. These calculations assumed, in the notation of the present paper, $\tau = 0.5$, $\mu = 0.4$, $d = 0.5$, and $c = 0.1$.

48. The value of 0.012 can be derived as follows with the notation of the present paper. The assumption of a 5 percent yield differential implies $(1 - m)i - \pi + 0.06 = [d(1 - m) + (1 - d)(1 - c)](z/(1 - b)) - c\pi$. The earlier study found $i = 0.033$ when $\pi = 0$ and $i = 0.113$ when $\pi = 0.06$. These imply $z = 0.0709$ when $\pi = 0$ and $z = 0.0656$ when $\pi = 0.06$. In the present paper, $\tau\mu_1\pi$ is the change in z induced by the effect of historic cost depreciation; using this would imply $\mu_1 = 0.363$. But the Feldstein-Summers calculation assumes a rise in the real interest rate and therefore an understatement of μ_1. The total nominal return that the firm pays for funds is $N = b(1 - \tau)i + z + (1 - b)\pi$. In the absence of inflation, $N = 0.0764$ while at $\pi = 0.06$, $N = 0.1244$. The real return on capital falls from 0.0764 to 0.0694, a fall of 0.012.

12   Inflation, Tax Rules, and the Prices of Land and Gold

12.1   Introduction

Traditional theory implies that the relative price of consumer goods and of such real assets as land and gold should not be permanently affected by the rate of inflation. A change in the general rate of inflation should, in equilibrium, cause an equal change in the rate of inflation for each asset price. The experience of the past decade has been very different from the predictions of this theory: the prices of land, gold, and other such stores of value have increased by substantially more than the general price level.[1] The present paper presents a simple theoretical model that offers an explanation of the positive relation between the rate of inflation and the relative price of such real assets.

More specifically, the analysis here shows that, in an economy with an income tax, an increase in the expected rate of inflation causes an immediate increase in the relative price of such "store of value" real assets. What we have observed in the past decade can thus be understood as both (1) a series of transitions to higher relative asset prices whenever there was an increase in expected inflation, and (2) the traditional rise in these

Reprinted by permission from *Journal of Public Economics* 14 (December 1980): 309–18.

This paper is part of the NBER study of capital formation and the project on the changing role of debt and equity finance. I am grateful to the NBER and the National Science Foundation for financial support.

1. From 1968 to 1977, the consumer price level rose 74 percent. During the same period, the price of gold rose from $39 an ounce to more than $147 an ounce, an increase of 250 percent. According to the investment bankers Salomon Bros. (1978), the price of farmland rose 150 percent while the price of housing rose 110 percent.

asset prices in proportion to the general price level while the expected inflation rate remained constant.[2]

The behavior of real asset prices discussed in this paper is thus a further example of the non-Fisherian response to inflation of capital markets in an economy with income taxes.[3] In earlier papers I showed how the traditional theory of interest rates and share prices must also be changed because of the important role that income taxes now play in our economy.[4] More generally, these studies show the substantial nonneutrality of inflation in our economy.

The paper begins in section 12.2 with a simple model of the price of land and its relation to inflation. This model assumes that land and bonds are perfect substitutes in investors' portfolios. The real net yields on both types of assets must therefore be equal. Section 12.3 presents a more general portfolio equilibrium model in which assets are not assumed to be perfect substitutes. The effect of inflation on the prices of both gold and land is investigated. In order to focus on the role of taxes, the analysis ignores other important determinants of asset prices including commodity speculation, the fear of hyperinflation, and the possibility of increased supply.

12.2   The Price of Land: A First Approximation

Consider first a simple stationary economy with no inflation. There is a single produced good that can be either consumed or used in production. The population and the capital stock remain constant and there is no technical progress.[5] The lack of inflation implies that the nominal stock of money remains unchanged. The quantity of land is, of course, also fixed.

If land and real capital are perfect substitutes in investors' portfolios, the relative price of a unit of land (p_L) and of the produced good (p) must equate their relative yields.[6] If the marginal product of a unit of land in

2. The observed increase in the relative price of these assets may also reflect the increased uncertainty of future inflation rates as well as purely speculative movements that cause relative prices to depart from their long-run equilibrium. The current model ignores these issues.

3. Fisher's analyses of the effects of inflation (1930) were of course written when income taxes were much less important than they are today.

4. On interest rates, see Feldstein (1976; chap. 3 above) and Feldstein, Green, and Sheshinski (1978; chap. 4 above); see also Darby (1975). On the negative relation between expected inflation and the level of share prices, see Feldstein (1980b, d; chaps. 10 and 11 above).

5. I assume a stationary economy to avoid the extra complexity of valuing land as it becomes continually scarcer relative to the labor force and the capital stock. In a growing economy, the value of land depends on the form of technical progress. Note that the assumption of a fixed capital stock precludes the effect of land value on real capital accumulation discussed in Feldstein (1977).

6. Since we are currently examining an equilibrium at a point in time, the notation could be simplified by using the produced good as numeraire. It is, however, natural to use money as the numeraire since the analysis will soon deal with a changing price level.

terms of the produced good is pF_L, the pretax return on land is pF_L/p_L. If this return is subject to personal tax at rate θ, the net return on land is $(1 - \theta)pF_L/p_L$.[7] Similarly, the net return on real capital is $(1 - \theta)pF_k/p$, where pF_k is the marginal product of capital in terms of the produced good.[8] The equality of the net returns on land and real capital

$$(1) \qquad \frac{(1 - \theta)F_L}{p_L} = \frac{(1 - \theta)F_k}{p}$$

obviously implies that the price of land relative to the price of the produced good is just equal to the ratio of their marginal products:

$$(2) \qquad \frac{p_L}{p} = \frac{F_L}{F_k}$$

Consider what happens if the government suddenly adopts a policy of increasing the money supply at rate π. For simplicity, assume that the new rate of inflation is expected to continue indefinitely. In the new equilibrium, the prices of both the produced good and land will increase at this rate:

$$(3) \qquad \frac{\dot{p}}{p} = \frac{\dot{p}_L}{p_L} = \pi$$

But before this equation is established, the relative prices of land and of the produced good must change in order to preserve the equality of the net-of-tax real yields. Since inflation does not alter the pretax real yields, the relative prices of the two assets in the new equilibrium depends on the extent to which inflation changes real tax rates.

There are typically three important ways in which inflation changes effective tax rates. First, increases in the *nominal* value of assets are taxed as capital gains when the assets are sold; the letter c will be used to denote the equivalent accrual rate of tax on such nominal gains. Note that the assumption of a stationary economy implies that there are no *real* capital gains. The net of tax nominal rate of capital gain is thus $(1 - c)\pi$ for both assets. Second, depreciation of capital for tax purposes is based on the original cost of the asset rather than the cost of replacement. With even moderate rates of inflation, this causes a substantial reduction in the net of tax return; this will be approximated linearly by writing the real return net of income tax (but not net of capital gains tax) as $(1 - \theta)(F_k - \lambda\pi)$.[9] Third, firms are permitted to deduct nominal interest payments in calcu-

---

7. If there is a separate property tax based on the value of land, this would be reduced by a constant. Allowing for such a tax would not alter any of the conclusions of this paper.

8. Note that the price of the capital good is the same as the price of consumer goods.

9. This linear form is an approximation since λ itself depends on both the rate of inflation and the rate of depreciation. For a discussion of this approximation in the more general context of an economy with a corporate income tax as well as a personal income tax, see the appendix by Alan Auerbach in Feldstein, Green, and Sheshinski (1978; chap. 4 above).

lating taxable profits while individuals are taxed on nominal interest income; since bonds have not yet been introduced in the model, I will begin by ignoring this third aspect but will return to it later in this section.

The net nominal rate of return on land is thus $(1 - \theta)pF_L/p_L + (1 - c)\pi$ and the corresponding net real return is $(1 - \theta)pF_L/p_L - c\pi$. For real capital, the real net return is $(1 - \theta)(F_k - \lambda\pi) - c\pi$. The equality of these two real net returns thus implies:

$$(4) \qquad \frac{p_L}{p} = \frac{F_L}{F_k - \lambda\pi}$$

Because depreciation for tax purposes understates true depreciation, the real net yield on capital is reduced and the price of land rises relative to the price of reproducible capital. Only after this adjustment in relative prices has occurred will both assets increase in price at the same rate π, as indicated in (3).

It is useful to introduce bonds and to restate this analysis for an investor who equates the real net yield on land with the real net yield on bonds.[10] The key distinction between bonds and either capital or land is the absence of a nominal capital gain. Instead, the interest rate paid on these bonds rises with inflation. It is important, however, that this interest premium is subject to the ordinary rate of income tax while the nominal capital gain on land is taxed at the lower capital gains tax rate. Thus, if r is the nominal rate of interest, the net nominal yield on bonds is $(1 - \theta)r$ and the net real yield is $(1 - \theta)r - \pi$.

Equality of the net real yields on land and bonds

$$(5) \qquad \frac{(1 - \theta)pF_L}{P_L} - c\pi = (1 - \theta)r - \pi$$

implies

$$(6) \qquad \frac{p_L}{p} = \frac{(1 - \theta)F_L}{(1 - \theta)r - (1 - c)\pi}$$

Since F_L remains constant, the value of p_L/p depends on how the nominal interest rate responds to inflation. Equation (6) implies that p_L/p increases with inflation if

$$(7) \qquad \frac{dr}{d\pi} < \frac{1 - c}{1 - \theta}$$

In the United States it has long been true that the nominal interest rate rises by approximately the rate of inflation, i.e., that $dr/d\pi = 1$ provides a

10. Although the maturity of the bond is irrelevant for discussing the steady-state equilibrium, the transition is easier to consider if these bonds are assumed to have very short maturities as Treasury bills do.

close approximation of historical experience.[11] Thus, since the effective capital gains tax rate is less than the ordinary income rate ($c < \theta$), the inequality in (7) has been satisfied and inflation causes p_L to rise relative to p.

Although this simple model is able to capture the essential reason why the relative price of land varies positively with the expected inflation rate, it is easy to show that this model is not sufficient to determine the effect of inflation on the price of gold and other "pure" stores of real value. For the current purpose, the basic difference between land and gold is that gold has no *real* marginal product. The equilibrium net return on gold is simply the nominal gain caused by general inflation, $(1 - c)\pi$. The corresponding real return is thus $-c\pi$; gold has a negative real return to the extent that a capital gains tax must be paid on the nominal gain. Since the net real return on bonds is $(1 - \theta)r - \pi$, the equality of real net returns requires

$$(8) \qquad (1 - c)\pi = (1 - \theta)r$$

Even if condition (8) holds, it does not imply anything about the price of gold. Moreover, this condition would hold for different values of π only if $dr/d\pi = (1 - c)/(1 - \theta)$. Since this condition has not in fact been true, this model of investor equilibrium implies complete specialization by investors in gold or bonds.[12] What is clearly needed is a more general model of portfolio behavior. The next section presents such a model and examines its implications for the prices of gold and land.

12.3 A Portfolio Equilibrium Model of the Prices of Gold and Land

The simplest of all models of portfolio equilibrium is the condition that real net asset yields must be equal. Although this model, which implicitly assumes that the assets are perfect substitutes, may be useful for some purposes, it is clearly inadequate for analyzing the effect of inflation on the price of gold. The risks associated with holding bonds and gold are clearly different. The current section therefore presents a slightly more general model of portfolio equilibrium. After discussing the implied effect of inflation on the equilibrium relative price of gold, the model is used to extend the previous analysis of the price of land.

In place of the assumption of perfect substitutability, the current section states that the demand for gold relative to the demand for bonds is

11. This empirical result has been supported by evidence since Irving Fisher's (1930) classic study. For more recent evidence, see Yohe and Karnovsky (1969), Feldstein and Eckstein (1970), and Feldstein and Summers (1977). This behavior of the interest rate reflects both tax rules and monetary policy; see Feldstein (1980c; chap. 5 above).

12. In a more general model with more than one class of investor, differences in tax situations will cause complete specialization of asset holdings if investors disregard risk and will not hold any asset when a higher yielding alternative is available.

a linear function of the difference between the expected real net yields. If the fixed physical amount of gold is G, and its price is p_G, the nominal value of gold in investors' portfolios is $p_G G$.[13] To simplify the analysis further, I will assume a fixed real quantity of debt, B; the nominal value of the debt is thus pB. Since the real net yield on gold is $-c\pi$ and the real net yield on bonds is $(1 - \theta)r - \pi$, the portfolio equation will be written

(9)
$$\frac{p_G G}{pB} = \gamma_0 + \gamma_1 [(1 - c)\pi - (1 - \theta)r]$$

Since the demand for gold is an increasing function of the expected yield differential, $\gamma_1 > 0$; as γ_1 tends to infinity, this model tends to the earlier model of equal yields as a condition for equilibrium. With $\gamma_0 > 0$, there is a positive demand for gold even when the expected real net yield on gold is less than the corresponding yield on bonds.

Since G and B are constant, (9) implies that the relative price of gold is an increasing function of inflation if

(10)
$$\frac{dr}{d\pi} < \frac{1 - c}{1 - \theta}$$

This is the same condition as inequality (7). As I noted there, this condition has been true empirically in the United States for a long time. The simple model of portfolio equilibrium thus implies that an increase in the expected equilibrium rate of inflation raises the relative price of gold. In the new equilibrium, of course, the relative price of gold remains unchanged.

More generally, the effect of an increase in the expected rate of inflation is to reduce the real yield on gold by $c \cdot d\pi$ while it reduces the real yield on bonds by $d\pi - (1 - \theta)dr$. With the empirical approximation that $dr/d\pi = 1$, this implies that the yield on gold is reduced less than the yield on bonds if $c < \theta$, i.e., if the capital gains tax rate is less than the ordinary income tax rate. Since this is satisfied for all taxable investors, inflation shifts the yield differential in favor of gold. For quite a wide range of plausible assumptions, this change in demand can be expected to increase the relative price of gold. Note finally that in a simpler economy with no taxes on capital income ($\theta = c = 0$), inflation has no effect on the relative price of gold if $dr/d\pi = 1$.

Applying the same portfolio model to land is only slightly more complex. Since the real net yield on land is $(1 - \theta)pF_L/p_L - c\pi$, the portfolio equilibrium equation analogous to (9) becomes[14]

---

13. Treating the amount of gold as fixed implicitly assumes a closed economy. More generally, the world price of gold will depend on the demands of investors in different countries and, therefore, on their inflation rates and tax policies.

14. It would clearly be desirable to have a more general model in which the demand for each kind of asset depends on the relative yields of all assets. The current pairwise

(11) $$\frac{p_L L}{pB} = \delta_0 + \delta_1 \left[\frac{(1 - \theta)pF_L}{p_L} + (1 - c)\pi - (1 - \theta)r \right]$$

Totally differentiating this equation yields

(12) $$\frac{d(p_L/p)}{d\pi} = \frac{\delta_1 \left[(1 - c) - (1 - \theta)\frac{dr}{d\pi} \right]}{\frac{L}{B} + \delta_1(1 - \theta)F_L p^2 p_L^{-2}}$$

Since the denominator is unambiguously positive, the sign of the derivative depends on the sign of the numerator. It is easy to see that this is positive if the inequality of (10) is satisfied. Thus, if $dr/d\pi < (1 - c)/(1 - \theta)$, the simple portfolio behavior considered here implies that the relative price of land is positively related to the expected rate of inflation.

It is not possible to evaluate the magnitude of the relative price change without knowing the value of δ_1. An indication of the possible magnitude can be obtained, however, for the special case in which the real net yields on land and bonds are either equal or differ only by a constant. The portfolio equilibrium condition

(13) $$\frac{(1 - \theta)pF_L}{p_L} - c\pi = (1 - \theta)r - \pi + \beta$$

where β is an arbitrary constant yield differential, implies

(14) $$\frac{d(pF_L/p_L)}{d\pi} = \frac{dr}{d\pi} - \frac{1 - c}{1 - \theta}$$

With the approximation that $dr/d\pi = 1$, this implies that

(15) $$\frac{d(pF_L/p_L)}{d\pi} = -\left(\frac{\theta - c}{1 - \theta} \right)$$

Reasonable values of the tax parameters for individual investors may be taken as $\theta = 0.4$ and $c = 0.15$. These imply that the pretax real yield on land falls by 0.4 times the change in inflation. An inflation rate of $\pi = 0.06$ thus reduces the real pretax yield by 0.024. If the initial real pretax yield is 0.08, a 6 percent inflation reduces the yield by 30 percent. Since the physical marginal product of land (F_L) is constant, a 30 percent reduction in pF_L/p_L implies that p/p_L falls by 30 percent; thus the relative price of land rises by 43 percent. Similarly, a 10 percent rate of inflation would reduce pF_L/p_L from 0.08 to 0.04, implying a doubling of the relative price of land. While these calculations are very crude and are likely to

comparison with the yield on debt is obviously a strong simplification. It is sufficient, however, to provide an interesting generalization of the even simpler model of the previous section.

overstate the response of the land price that would be implied by a more general portfolio model, they do suggest that even a relatively small increase in the rate of inflation can have a very substantial effect on the price of land. Since gold lacks any real marginal product, its relative price is likely to be more sensitive to the expected rate of inflation.

12.4 Concluding Comments

This paper has presented a simple analysis of the relation between the expected rate of inflation and the prices of land, gold, and other nondepreciating real stores of value. In contrast to the traditional theoretical conclusion that relative prices are unaffected by the rate of inflation, the current analysis shows that, because of unindexed taxes on capital income, a higher expected rate of inflation raises the prices of land and gold relative to the general price level of produced goods. More generally, as I have noted in earlier papers, a change in the expected equilibrium rate of inflation alters the real net rate of interest, the stock market value of real capital, and the real net marginal product of investment. In an economy with capital income taxes, inflation is far from neutral.

The very rapid rise in the relative prices of land, gold, and other such assets during the recent decade of rising inflation rates is, of course, consistent with the view presented in this paper. The actual course of these prices may also have reflected such things as an increased attention to inflation, a belief that future inflation rates have become more uncertain, increased speculative demand, and changes in statutory tax rules. But even without these transitional or disequilibrium elements, the current analysis shows that changes in expected inflation can have powerful effects on the relative prices of such investment assets.

It would clearly be desirable to extend the current model by developing an explicit theory of portfolio equilibrium for investors who hold land, gold, bonds, and equity shares. The real yields on these assets would be linked because they are all dependent upon future changes in expected inflation. As a further step, the analysis should recognize that the effect of inflation on each individual's demand for each asset depends on that individual's own tax situation. The equilibrium market price can then be derived as the market clearing solution to the individuals' separate asset demand equations.[15]

---

15. Feldstein (1980b, d; chaps. 9 and 10 above) derives such a solution to the problem of valuing equity shares when there are two classes of investors in very different tax situations.

13 Inflation, Portfolio Choice, and the Prices of Land and Corporate Stock

During the rapid inflation of the past decade, the price of land has not only kept its real value but has increased far more rapidly than the general price level.[1] While elementary economic theory would predict that land and all other real assets would hold their real value when the price level rose, the increase in the relative price of land caught economists as well as others by surprise.

The reasons for the rise in the relative price of land are multiple and complex. They range from the rise in the world price of food to the political instability in the Middle East and the fears of political change in Western Europe. No single paper, let alone a short theoretical one, could hope to provide a full explanation.

There is, however, a fundamental link between general price inflation and the relative price of land that deserves particular attention. This relation is the opposite side of the same coin that causes inflation to depress the price of common stock. In essence, inflation and the tax laws interact to raise the return on land and lower the return on reproducible capital.[2] The prices of these assets must then adjust to the new inflation expectation to make investors willing to hold both types of assets in the initially existing quantities. This requires the price of land to rise (relative to the general price level) and the price of reproducible capital to fall.

Reprinted by permission from *American Journal of Agricultural Economics* 62 (December 1980): 910–16.

1. For the 1970s as a whole, the Agriculture Department's index of the price of farm land rose at an annual rate of 13 percent, nearly double the 7.4 percent annual rise in the general consumer price index.

2. In this paper, I use the term reproducible capital to refer to business capital and ignore owner-occupied housing. In many ways, owner-occupied housing behaves like land in its response to inflation.

If uncertainty could be ignored, the price changes would be such that the real after-tax rates of return were equal both before and after any change in the rate of inflation. A model of asset demand that makes this simple arbitrage assumption and ignores uncertainty can, however, be very misleading. The present paper presents an explicit model of portfolio demand and uses it to show how the rate of inflation and its variance affect the real prices of land and capital.

The present paper is thus an extension of two earlier studies in which I presented models of how the interaction of inflation and the tax rules alters the real prices of land (Feldstein, 1980; chap. 12 above) and common stock (Feldstein, 1980*b*, *d*; chaps. 10–11). Although these papers considered the role of uncertainty in a rather ad hoc way, a formal model of portfolio choice derived from utility maximization was lacking. The purpose of the present paper is to remedy that deficiency.

A basic result of the earlier papers (as well as of the present analysis) is that changes in the rate of inflation alter the relative price of assets while at any constant inflation rate the equilibrium real asset prices remain unchanged. Thus an unanticipated jump in the rate of inflation causes an immediate jump in the *level* of the land price. After this initial jump, the price of land increases at the same rate as the general rate of inflation.

This interpretation implies that the continuous increase in the price of land during the 1970s can best be thought of as a combination of (1) many small changes in the equilibrium real price of land (as the expected rate of general price inflation changed) and (2) a continuing increase in the nominal price of land at the prevailing rate of inflation. Similarly, the fall in the real value of share prices combines a series of falls in the equilibrium real price of shares with continuous increases in their nominal price.

The first section of this paper presents the model of portfolio equilibrium while the second section derives the means and variances of the asset yields. The price equations for land and reproducible capital are then developed in section 13.3. The fourth section derives the comparative static results for changes in inflation and in the uncertainty of inflation. A brief concluding section discusses some of the implications of this work and possible directions for further research.

13.1   A Model of Portfolio Equilibrium

The economy that I shall describe consists of identical individuals[3] who hold a short term nominal asset ("bills"), land, and (reproducible) capi-

---

3. The assumption of identical individuals ignores another important feature that belongs in a more complete model of portfolio choice: differences in tax rates among investors. The distinction between taxable individual investors and tax exempt institutions can be particularly important in understanding the effect of inflation on portfolio investment (Feldstein, 1980*b*, *d*; chaps. 10 and 11 above).

tal. The current price level and current inflation rate are known but the rate of inflation in the future is unknown. For simplicity, it is easiest to think of the economy switching from one expected inflation rate to another.[4]

The aggregate stocks of both land and capital are assumed fixed. While this may be a realistic approximation for land,[5] it is clearly not an appropriate model for capital. If the market price of existing capital assets[6] falls below replacement cost, the size of the capital stock will fall while a market price of existing assets above their replacement cost will cause an increase in net investment. The anticipation of the future change in the size of the capital stock will change the expected future yields per unit of capital and labor. That, in turn, will influence the initial changes in the prices of these assets. While it would clearly be desirable to incorporate this effect into the analysis, the combination of dynamic price adjustments and explicit portfolio choice under uncertainty is a more complex problem than I can currently solve.[7] I have chosen to focus on the portfolio choice aspect but I recognize the importance of extending the specification to incorporate the dynamic general equilibrium response.

Consider an individual i whose initial holdings of land, capital and money are $\bar{L}_i$ units of land, $\bar{K}_i$ units of capital, and $\bar{B}_i$ dollars of Treasury bills. These holdings reflect some previous set of expectations about asset yields and the associated covariance matrix. When the Hicksian "week" begins, there is a new set of expectations (possibly but not necessarily identical with the old ones). These expectations imply a set of equilibrium asset prices p_L and p_K relative to the numeraire; the purpose of this section is to derive equations for these equilibrium prices.

The individual's initial endowment is $W_{oi} = \bar{B}_i + p_L\bar{L}_i + p_K\bar{K}_i$ and must be redivided among new holdings (B_i, L_i, and K_i) according to the wealth constraint:

$$(1) \qquad B_i + p_L L_i + p_K K_i = \bar{B}_i + p_L \bar{L}_i + p_K \bar{K}_i$$

At the end of the "week," each unit of land is worth $P_L + R_L$, each unit of capital is worth $P_K + R_K$ and each unit of bills is worth $1 + R_B$. Thus R_L/P_L is the return per week per unit of land, R_K/P_K is the rate of return on capital, and R_B is the rate of interest. All of these are to be regarded as real after-tax rates of return. The returns to land and capital are uncer-

4. The idea of an expected time pattern of future inflation rates might be more realistic but would be more complex to analyze without adding any fundamentally new insights.

5. The effective stock of land can change through the loss of topsoil, forestations, etc.

6. This is Tobin's q value, the index of common stock prices per unit of real capital.

7. Poterba (1980) and Summers (1980c) have extended the type of analysis presented in Feldstein (1980; chaps. 10–12 above) to include an explicit capital stock adjustment process with feedback onto the path of asset prices. They assume certainty (or constant risk differentials) and therefore that the yields of all assets are always equated, at least up to a constant.

tain, while the bill return is riskless.[8] The individual's wealth at the end of the week is thus:

$$(2) \qquad W_i = (P_L + R_L)L_i + (P_K + R_K)K_i + (1 + R_B)B_i$$

If each individual has the same quadratic utility function, expected utility can be written as a linear combination of the mean and variance of W_i:

$$(3) \qquad E[u(W_i)] = E(W_i) - 0.5\,\gamma \cdot \text{var}\,(W_i)$$

where $\gamma > 0$ is a measure of risk aversion and the 0.5 is introduced to simplify subsequent calculations.

Equation (2) implies that

$$(4) \qquad E(W_i) = \bar{R}_L L_i + \bar{R}_K K_i + R_B B_i + W_{oi}$$

where the bars over the $\bar{R}_L$ and $\bar{R}_K$ denote expected yields for the one week holding period. By using equation (1), this may be rewritten

$$(5) \qquad E(W_i) = \bar{R}_L L_i + \bar{R}_K K_i + R_B[p_L(\bar{L}_i - L_i) \\ + p_K(\bar{K}_i - K_i) + \bar{B}_i] + W_{oi}$$

Equation (2) also implies that

$$(6) \qquad \text{var}\,(W_i) = \sigma_{LL}L_i^2 + \sigma_{KK}K_i^2 + \sigma_{LK}L_i K_i$$

where σ_{LL} and σ_{KK} as the variances of the one week holding period returns and σ_{KL} is the covariance.

The household's optimum portfolio is found by maximizing the value of expected utility in equation (3) subject to the constraint of equation (1). Using equations (5) and (6), this implies the first-order conditions:

$$(7a) \qquad 0 = \bar{R}_L - R_B p_L - \gamma[\sigma_{LL}L_i + \sigma_{LK}K_i]$$

and

$$(7b) \qquad 0 = \bar{R}_K - R_B p_K - \gamma[\sigma_{KK}K_i + \sigma_{KL}L_i]$$

The pair of asset demand equations may therefore be written:

$$(8) \qquad \gamma \begin{bmatrix} \sigma_{LL} & \sigma_{LK} \\ \sigma_{KL} & \sigma_{KK} \end{bmatrix} \begin{bmatrix} L_i \\ K_i \end{bmatrix} = \begin{bmatrix} \bar{R}_L - R_B p_L \\ \bar{R}_K - R_B p_K \end{bmatrix}$$

or

$$(9) \qquad \begin{bmatrix} L_i \\ K_i \end{bmatrix} = \gamma^{-1} \begin{bmatrix} \sigma_{LL} & \sigma_{LK} \\ \sigma_{KL} & \sigma_{KK} \end{bmatrix}^{-1} \begin{bmatrix} \bar{R}_L - R_B p_L \\ \bar{R}_K - R_B p_K \end{bmatrix}$$

---

8. This reflects the assumption that the inflation rate for the current week is known even though the future inflation is uncertain.

Since all of the investors are identical, each demands the same L_i and K_i.[9] Summing L_i and K_i over all individuals gives the total demand which must equal the total asset supplies: $N\bar{L}$ and $N\bar{K}$.[10] Thus

$$(10) \qquad \begin{bmatrix} \Sigma_i L_i \\ \Sigma_i K_i \end{bmatrix} = N\gamma^{-1} \begin{bmatrix} \sigma_{LL} & \sigma_{LK} \\ \sigma_{KL} & \sigma_{KK} \end{bmatrix}^{-1}$$

$$\begin{bmatrix} \bar{R}_L - R_B p_L \\ \bar{R}_K - R_B p_K \end{bmatrix} = \begin{bmatrix} N\bar{L} \\ N\bar{K} \end{bmatrix}$$

Equation (10) can thus be solved explicitly for the equilibrium asset prices as functions of the expected yields, the covariance matrix, and the initial asset quantities:

$$(11) \qquad \begin{bmatrix} p_L \\ p_K \end{bmatrix} = R_B^{-1} \left[\begin{pmatrix} \bar{R}_L \\ \bar{R}_K \end{pmatrix} - \gamma \begin{bmatrix} \sigma_{LL} & \sigma_{LK} \\ \sigma_{KL} & \sigma_{KK} \end{bmatrix} \begin{pmatrix} \bar{L} \\ \bar{K} \end{pmatrix} \right]$$

or

$$(12a) \qquad p_L = R_B^{-1}[\bar{R}_L - \gamma(\sigma_{LL}\bar{L} + \sigma_{LK}\bar{K})]$$

and

$$(12b) \qquad p_K = R_B^{-1}[\bar{R}_K - \gamma(\sigma_{KL}\bar{L} + \sigma_{KK}\bar{K})]$$

13.2   The Means and Variances of Asset Yields

I turn now to the derivation of the mean real net-of-tax returns on the three assets and the corresponding covariance matrix.

Consider first the real net rate of return on bills. If the nominal short-term rate is r, the personal tax rate is θ, and the actual current inflation rate is π, the real net-of-tax rate of return is

$$(13) \qquad R_B = (1 - \theta)r - \pi$$

Because the tax is levied on the nominal return, the real net-of-tax returns will vary with the rate of inflation. Ever since Irving Fisher's 1930 study, empirical studies have confirmed that the nominal interest rate changes approximately point for point with sustained changes in the rate of inflation;[11] in the current notation, $dr/d\pi = 1$ is a reasonable approximation. This implies that $dR_B/d\pi = -\theta < 0$; an increase in the inflation rate reduces the real net return on bills. For an inflation rate high enough, the real return can be negative. This is a particularly important feature of

9. I assume the conditions on the covariance matrix and the yield vector are such that $0 \le L_i$ and $0 \le K_i$ and $P_L L_i + p_K K_i \le p_L \bar{L}_i + p_K \bar{K}_i + \bar{B}_i$. These conditions must surely be fulfilled in an economy of identical individuals.

10. Since all individuals demand the same assets, $\bar{L}_i = \bar{L}_j$ for all i,j and the subscript can be ignored.

11. See, e.g., Yohe and Karnovsky (1969) and Feldstein and Summers (1977).

our tax system because it suggests that the usual assumption of equal yields on all assets may be wrong and a poor approximation when there is substantial inflation.

The return on a unit of land consists of an income return and a capital gain or loss. If the marginal physical product per unit of land (per week) is F_L, the net-of-tax marginal revenue product is $(1-\theta)pF_L$. Increases in the price of land are taxable capital gains. The capital gains tax rate is less than the tax rate on ordinary income and the effective tax rate is further reduced because capital gains are taxed only when the property is sold; I shall use the letter c to denote the accrual-equivalent effective tax rate, i.e., the rate which, levied on accruals, would collect the same present value of taxes as the actual rate levied on realizations. If the increase in the price of land during the week is $\dot{p}_L$, the after-tax capital gain is $(1-c)\dot{p}_L$.

The total nominal return per unit of land is thus $(1-\theta)pF_L + (1-c)\dot{p}_L$. Since a unit of land costs p_L, the nominal return per dollar invested in land is $(1-\theta)pF_L/p_L + (1-c)\dot{p}_L/p_L$. The real rate of return is the difference between this nominal rate of return and the rate of inflation: $(1-\theta)pF_L/p_L + (1-c)\dot{p}_L/p_L - \pi$. Finally, the real return per unit of land (R_L) is just the product of the real rate of return and the price per unit of land:

$$(14) \qquad R_L = (1-\theta)pF_L + (1-c)\dot{p}_L - \pi p_L$$

There are two types of uncertainty about this return, corresponding to the income and capital gain components of the price change. Since the current price level is known, the income uncertainty is caused by the uncertain marginal physical product of land. If ϕ_L is the mean marginal physical product of land and $\tilde{v}$ is the random component with the zero mean and variance σ_{vv},

$$(15) \qquad F_L = \phi_L + \tilde{v}$$

In a stationary equilibrium the price of land will rise at the same rate as the general price level: $\dot{p}_L/p_L = \pi$. Changes in the expected future rate of inflation or in the expected future value of any other factor that influences the value of land will cause the price of land to change by more or less than the current rate of inflation. The uncertain change in the price of land can be written without restriction as:

$$(16) \qquad \frac{\dot{p}_L}{p_L} = \pi + \tilde{\epsilon}$$

where $\tilde{\epsilon}$ is a random variable with zero mean, variance $\sigma_{\epsilon\epsilon}$ and covariance $\sigma_{v\epsilon}$ with the random disturbance to productivity.

Substituting (15) and (16) into (14) yields:[12]

---

12. This is the natural extension to an economy with uncertainty of the return on land derived in equation (1.5) of Feldstein (1908a).

$$(17) \quad R_L = (1 - \theta)p(\phi_L + \tilde{v}) + (1 - c)(\pi + \tilde{\epsilon})p_L - \pi p_L$$
$$= (1 - \theta)p\phi_L + (1 - \theta)p\tilde{v} - c\pi p_L + (1 - c)p_L\tilde{\epsilon}$$

The mean return per unit of land is thus

$$(18) \quad \bar{R}_L = (1 - \theta)p\phi_L - c\pi p_L$$

The variance of this return is

$$(19) \quad \sigma_{LL} = (1 - \theta)^2 p^2 \sigma_{vv} + (1 - c)^2 p_L^2 \sigma_{\epsilon\epsilon}$$
$$+ 2(1 - \theta)(1 - c)p p_L \sigma_{\epsilon v}$$

The return on reproducible capital also consists of an income return and a change in the price of the asset. Because the tax rules are based on nominal accounting definitions, a rise in the rate of inflation increases the effective tax rate on the real income from reproducible capital.[13] This is due primarily to the required use of historic cost depreciation but also reflects the method of inventory accounting.[14] If the marginal physical product per unit of capital is F_K, the net-of-tax marginal revenue product in the absence of inflation can be written $(1 - \theta)pF_K$.[15] It is convenient to approximate the extra tax burden per unit of capital as proportional to the rate of inflation; the real return per unit of capital is thus depressed by $\lambda\pi p$ at current prices. The real net of tax income per unit of capital is thus $(1 - \theta)pF_K - \lambda\pi p$. If the increase in the market price of capital[16] during the week is $\dot{p}_K$, the net-of-tax capital gain $(1 - c)\dot{p}_K$. The total nominal return per unit of capital is thus $(1 - \theta)pF_K - \lambda\pi p + (1 - c)\dot{p}_K$ and the corresponding real return per unit of capital is:

$$(20) \quad R_K = (1 - \theta)pF_K - \lambda\pi p + (1 - c)\dot{p}_K - \pi p_K$$

The income uncertainty of the return on capital reflects the uncertain marginal product of capital and can be represented by:

$$(21) \quad F_K = \phi_K + \tilde{v}$$

where $\tilde{v}$ has mean zero and variance σ_{vv}. The uncertain change in the price of existing capital assets can be written

$$(22) \quad \frac{\dot{p}_K}{p_K} = \pi + \tilde{\omega}$$

---

13. Recall that this analysis uses "reproducible capital" to refer to business capital and ignores owner-occupied real estate.

14. See Feldstein and Summers (1979; chap. 8 above) and Feldstein (1980b; chap. 10 above) for a discussion of how higher inflation increases the effective tax rate on the income of nonfinancial corporations and of their equity owners.

15. This ignores the separate corporate income tax and the differential treatment of dividends and retained earnings. Recognizing these would complicate the analysis without changing anything fundamental

16. This perhaps is best thought of as the market price of common stock, i.e., claims to the existing capital stock rather than new capital goods.

where $\tilde{\omega}$ has variance $\sigma_{\omega\omega}$ and covariance with $\tilde{\upsilon}$ of $\sigma_{\upsilon\omega}$.

Substituting (21) and (22) into (20) yields:

$$(23) \qquad R_K = (1 - \theta)p(\phi_K + \tilde{\upsilon}) - \lambda\pi p + (1 - c)(\pi + \tilde{\omega})p_K - \pi p_K$$

$$= (1 - \theta)p\phi_K + (1 - \theta)p\tilde{\upsilon} - \lambda\pi p - c\pi p_K + (1 - c)p_K\tilde{\omega}$$

The mean return per unit of capital is thus:

$$(24) \qquad \bar{R}_K = (1 - \theta)p\phi_K - \lambda\pi p - c\pi p_K$$

and the variance is

$$(25) \qquad \sigma_{KK} = (1 - \theta)^2 p^2 \sigma_{\upsilon\upsilon} + (1 - c)^2 p_K \sigma_{\omega\omega}$$

$$+ 2(1 - \theta)(1 - c)p p_K \sigma_{\upsilon\omega}$$

The covariance between the returns on capital and land depends in general on the full covariance matrix of all four random effects:

$$(26) \qquad \sigma_{KL} = E\{[(1 - \theta)p\tilde{\upsilon} + (1 - c)p_L\epsilon][(1 - \theta)p\tilde{\upsilon} + (1 - c)p_K\tilde{\omega}]\}$$

$$= (1 - \theta)^2 p^2 \sigma_{\upsilon\upsilon} + (1 - \theta)(1 - c)p p_K \sigma_{\upsilon\omega}$$

$$+ (1 - c)(1 - \theta)p p_L \sigma_{\epsilon\upsilon}$$

$$+ (1 - c)^2 p_L p_K \sigma_{\omega\epsilon}$$

13.3   The Price Equations

The means and covariance matrix of the returns on land and capital can be used with equation (12a–b) to obtain explicit price equations for land and capital. It is useful to begin by substituting the mean values R_B and $\bar{R}_L$ into (12) to obtain the price of land:

$$(27) \qquad p_L = \frac{(1 - \theta)p\phi_L - c\pi p_L - \gamma(\sigma_{LL}\bar{L} + \sigma_{LK}\bar{K})}{(1 - \theta)r - \pi}$$

Collecting and rearranging terms yields:

$$(28) \qquad \frac{p_L}{p} = \frac{(1 - \theta)\phi_L}{(1 - \theta)r - (1 - c)\pi + \gamma p_L^{-1}(\sigma_{LL}\bar{L} + \sigma_{LK}\bar{K})}$$

There are several significant things to notice about this expression for the real price of land (p_L/p). In the absence of risk aversion ($\gamma = 0$) and inflation ($\pi = 0$), the real price of land is just the discounted value of the expected return per unit of land, i.e., $p_L/p = \phi_L/r$. If there is inflation but no risk aversion, the relationship is more complex; the perpetuity at ϕ_L is discounted by $r - [(1 - c)/(1 - \theta)]\pi$. Since $(1 - c)/(1 - \theta) < 1$, this "net discount rate" can easily become "negative." That is, as π rises, $r - [(1 - c)/(1 - \theta)\pi]$ approaches zero and the implied relative price of land becomes indefinitely large. When $(1 - \theta)r < (1 - c)\pi$, the value of p_L/p

"passes through" infinity and becomes apparently negative. More generally, for many plausible tax parameters, the relative price of land is implausibly sensitive to changes in π.

These results show the importance of explicitly recognizing the role of uncertainty and risk aversion in determining p_L/p. Equation (28) shows that risk aversion can eliminate the anomalous results. With $\gamma(\sigma_{LL}\bar{L} + \sigma_{LK}\bar{K}) > 0$ in the denominator, relative asset prices are not nearly so sensitive to differences in the mean real net rates of return.

A more complete characterization of the real price of land is obtained if σ_{LL} and σ_{LK} are rewritten in terms of the underlying variances and covariances. The essential features of the analysis are preserved but the analysis is simplified by assuming that the income disturbances ($\tilde{v}$ and $\tilde{\upsilon}$) are independent of each other and of the price disturbances ($\tilde{\epsilon}$ and $\tilde{\omega}$). Such an assumption would be reasonable if investors knew that the disturbances $\tilde{v}$ and $\tilde{\upsilon}$ are serially independent so that a disturbance in one period has no implications about future values of F_L and F_K. With this simplifying assumption, the relevant variances and covariances of section 13.2 become:

$$(29) \qquad \sigma_{LL} = (1 - \theta)^2 p^2 \sigma_{vv} + (1 - c)^2 p_L^2 \sigma_{\epsilon\epsilon}$$

$$(30) \qquad \sigma_{KK} = (1 - \theta)^2 p^2 \sigma_{\upsilon\upsilon} + (1 - c)^2 p_K^2 \sigma_{\omega\omega}$$

and

$$(31) \qquad \sigma_{LK} = (1 - c)^2 p_L p_K \sigma_{\omega\epsilon}$$

Substituting these values into (28) yields

$$(32) \qquad \frac{p_L}{p} = \frac{(1 - \theta)\phi_L}{(1 - \theta)r - (1 - c)\pi + \gamma p_L^{-1}\{[(1 - \theta)^2 p^2 \sigma_{vv}}$$

$$\frac{(1 - \theta)\phi_L}{+ (1 - c)^2 p_L^2 \sigma_{\epsilon\epsilon}]\bar{L} + (1 - c)^2 p_L p_K \sigma_{\omega\epsilon}\bar{K}\}}$$

or

$$(33) \qquad \frac{p_L}{p} = \frac{(1 - \theta)\phi_L}{(1 - \theta)r - (1 - c)\pi + \gamma\{[(1 - \theta)^2 (p/p_L)^2 \sigma_{vv}}$$

$$\frac{(1 - \theta)\phi_L}{+ (1 - c)^2 \sigma_{\epsilon\epsilon} + (1 - c)^2 \sigma_{\epsilon\epsilon}]p_L\bar{L} + (1 - c)^2 \sigma_{\omega\epsilon} p_K \bar{K}\}}$$

In this form, the real price of land is defined as a quadratic function of tax rates, rates of return, the expected inflation rate, and the total wealth in land and capital. If the income risk is ignored ($\sigma_{vv} = 0$), the real price of land assumes the simple form:

(34)
$$\frac{p_L}{p} = \frac{(1-\theta)\phi_L}{(1-\theta)r - (1-c)\pi + \gamma(1-c)^2(\sigma_{\epsilon\epsilon}p_L\bar{L} + \sigma_{\epsilon\omega}p_K\bar{K})}$$

This case is also substantively interesting because the price risk can generally be expected to be large relative to the income risk and because uncertainty about the future inflation rate contributes to the price risk but not the income risk.

The analogous equation for the real market price of capital is

(35)
$$\frac{p_K}{p} = \frac{(1-\theta)\phi_K - \lambda\pi}{(1-\theta)r - (1-c)\pi + \gamma(1-c)^2(\sigma_{\omega\omega}p_K\bar{K} + \sigma_{\epsilon\omega}p_L\bar{L})}$$

13.4 Some Comparative Static Analyses

Equations (34) and (35) can be used to examine how the real prices of land and capital respond to changes in inflation, the uncertainty of future inflation, and the like. Since the stock of capital is assumed to remain constant,[17] the results can, of course, only indicate the direction and not the magnitude of the change.

The derivative of p_L/p with respect to the expected inflation rate is easily shown to be:

(36)
$$\frac{d(p_L/p)}{d\pi} = -\frac{(p_L/p)^2}{(1-\theta)\phi_L} \left\{ (1-\theta)\frac{dr}{d\pi} - (1-c) \right.$$
$$+ \gamma(1-c)^2\sigma_{\epsilon\epsilon}\frac{dV_L}{d\pi}$$
$$+ \left. \gamma(1-c)^2\sigma_{\epsilon\omega}\frac{dV_K}{d\pi} \right\}$$

where $V_L = p_L\bar{L}$ and $V_K = p_K\bar{K}$. Note first that, in the absence of risk aversion, the effect of inflation on the real price of land is positive if $(dr/d\pi) < (1-c)/(1-\theta)$. Since $c < \theta$, this will clearly be satisfied whenever $dr/d\pi \le 1$. During the increasing inflation of the 1960s and 1970s, the nominal interest rate rose by approximately the rise in the rate of inflation, causing the real net interest rate to fall by $-\theta d\pi$. In contrast, the real return on land falls only because of the smaller rate of capital gains tax on the nominal appreciation in the value of the land. Since the extra tax on bills per dollar of capital would exceed the extra tax on land, the price of land rises in the absence of uncertainty in order to equalize the yields.

Introducing uncertainty leaves this conclusion unchanged but suggests that the magnitude of the effect may be reduced. If $d(p_L/p)/d\pi > 0$,

17. See above, p. 231.

$dV_L/d\pi > 0$ since $V_L = p_L\bar{L}$ and $\bar{L}$ is constant. This positive term offsets some of the magnitude of the pure tax and interest rate effect. The economic reason for this is that as p_L rises the investor has relatively more wealth in this form which in turn raises the risk premium that the investor requires to hold even more land or, equivalently, which reduces the demand for more land and therefore the real price of land.

If the primary reason for the covariance between the unanticipated changes in the prices of land and capital ($\sigma_{\epsilon\omega}$) are the unanticipated changes in inflation, the term $\sigma_{\epsilon\omega}dV_K/d\pi$ is also likely to be positive, further reducing $d(p_L/p)/d\pi$ but nevertheless leaving it positive. For example, $dp_L/d\pi > 0$ and $dp_K/d\pi < 0$ imply $\sigma_{\epsilon\omega} < 0$ and $dV_K/d\pi < 0$ and therefore that $\sigma_{\epsilon\omega}dV_K/d\pi > 0$. Similarly, $dp_L/d\pi > 0$ and $dp_K/d\pi > 0$ imply $\sigma_{\omega\omega} > 0$ and $dV_K/d\pi > 0$ and therefore again $\sigma_{\epsilon\omega}dV_K/d\pi > 0$. The economic reason (in the relevant case in which $dp_K/d\pi < 0$) is that inflation reduces the value of the investors' reproducible capital and, since the return on capital is negatively correlated with the return on land, reduces the demand for land and therefore its price.

The effect of uncertainty is nevertheless to dampen the effect of inflation and not to reverse it. To see this, note that the opposite implies a contradiction. If $dp_L/d\pi < 0$, $\sigma_{\epsilon\epsilon}(dV_L/d\pi) < 0$ which implies an even larger positive value of $dp_L/d\pi$.

A similar analysis shows that a higher rate of inflation reduces the real value of capital[18] and that the uncertainty and risk aversion again dampen the magnitude of the effect.

Consider now the effect of an increase in the uncertainty of the future inflation rate. This increases $\sigma_{\epsilon\epsilon}$, $\sigma_{\omega\omega}$, and $|\sigma_{\epsilon\omega}|$. The relative increase in each term depends on the extent to which uncertainty and inflation is the source of the uncertainty about asset prices. Two extremes will illustrate the possible results. If most of the variation in the real price of land reflects variation in anticipated inflation while little of the variation in the inflation uncertainty will raise $\sigma_{\epsilon\epsilon}$ while leaving $\sigma_{\omega\omega}$ essentially unchanged. Moreover, if inflation is not a major source of $\sigma_{\omega\omega}$, it is possible (although not necessary) that $\sigma_{\epsilon\omega} = 0$. Total differentiation of equation (34) with respect to p_L and $\sigma_{\epsilon\epsilon}$ with $\sigma_{\epsilon\omega} = 0$ implies that $dp_L/d\sigma_{\epsilon\epsilon} < 0$, i.e., an increase in inflation uncertainty unambiguously reduces p_L while leaving p_K unchanged.

In contrast, consider the case in which inflation uncertainty is equally important for $\sigma_{\epsilon\epsilon}$ and $\sigma_{\omega\omega}$ and $\sigma_{\epsilon\omega} < 0$. If an increase in inflation uncertainty raises $\sigma_{\epsilon\epsilon}$ and $\sigma_{\omega\omega}$ by equal amounts and leaves the correlation between ϵ and ω unchanged, (34) and (35) imply that an increase in inflation uncertainty reduces both p_L and p_K. Investors respond to the

---

18. This depends on the relative magnitudes of the historic cost depreciation effect and the real interest rate effect. For an analysis with realistic parameters, see Feldstein (1980b; chap. 10 above).

increased uncertainty by demanding less land and capital and more of the riskless nominal asset.

More generally, the response of relative asset prices to an increase in inflation uncertainty will depend on the relative extent to which $\sigma_{\epsilon\epsilon}$, $\sigma_{\omega\omega}$, and $\sigma_{\epsilon\omega}$ are changed. An increase in inflation uncertainty might cause the real price of land to rise if investors wish to substitute both land and bills for capital.

13.5   Conclusion

This paper has focused on the specific question of how changes in expected inflation and in its uncertainty affect the real prices of land and of reproducible capital. The analysis shows how an explicit portfolio choice framework can be applied to derive asset price equations and how, in this framework, the interaction of taxes and increased inflation causes a rise in the real value of land and a fall in the real value of corporate equities.

Two more general points are worth noting. First, the analysis shows the inappropriateness of the common assumption that inflation is neutral, i.e., that it does not alter real magnitudes. When there are taxes on capital income, this is false and inflation can have substantial real effects.

Second, the traditional assumption that prices adjust until net-of-tax yields are equal may be very misleading. In the examples shown here, the existence of a finite price for land depends on the uncertainty of the asset yields.

This paper has shown that an explicit utility maximization model of portfolio choice can be applied to analyzing the effects of changes in the rate of inflation. A natural next step is to embed this analysis in a more general dynamic framework in which changes in the price of capital change the supply of new capital goods and therefore the future path of the real marginal products of capital and land.

IV The Effect on Investment

14   Inflation, Tax Rules, and Investment: Some Econometric Evidence

My subject here is one to which Irving Fisher devoted considerable analytic and econometric effort: the effect of inflation on financial markets and capital formation.[1] Nowadays, every student learns of Fisher's conclusion that each percentage point increase in the steady-state inflation rate eventually raises the nominal interest rate by 1 percent, leaving the real rate of interest unchanged. Moreover, since the supply of saving depends on the *real* rate of interest and the demand for investable funds also depends on the *real* rate of interest, a change in the rate of inflation would have essentially no effect on the economy's real equilibrium. I say "essentially" no effect because another great Yale economist, James Tobin, reminded us in his 1964 Fisher Lecture that an increase in the nominal interest rate could cause households to substitute capital for money in their portfolios, thereby reducing the real interest rate.

The Fisher-Tobin analysis, like most theoretical analyses of macroeconomic equilibrium, ignores the role of the taxes levied on capital income. While this may have been a reasonable simplification at some time in the past, it is quite inappropriate today. Taxes on capital income with marginal rates that are often between one-third and two-thirds can have

Reprinted by permission from *Econometrica* 50 (July 1982): 825–62.

This paper was presented as the Fisher-Schultz Lecture at the World Congress of the Econometric Society, 29 August 1980. The research is part of the NBER program on taxation and of the Bureau's special study of capital formation. The financial support of the National Science Foundation and the NBER is gratefully acknowledged.

I am grateful to Charles Horioka for assistance with calculations and to James Poterba and Lawrence Summers for earlier collaborative work. I benefited from comments on preliminary results presented at the NBER and the Harvard Public Finance Seminar and from comments on an earlier draft by several colleagues. The views expressed here are the author's and should not be attributed to any organization.

1. See, for example, Fisher (1896, 1930).

profound effects on the real macroeconomic equilibrium and on the way in which inflation affects that real equilibrium.

A simple example will illustrate the potential for substantial departures from Irving Fisher's famous neutrality result. Consider an economy in which saving and the demand for money are both perfectly interest inelastic, in which there is no inflation, and in which the marginal product of capital is 10 percent. If we ignore risk and assume that all marginal investments are debt financed,[2] the rate of interest in the economy will also be 10 percent. A permanent increase in the expected rate of inflation from zero to 5 percent would raise the nominal internal rate of return on all investments by 5 percent, which would, in turn, raise the equilibrium rate of interest in the economy from 10 percent to 15 percent. All of this is just as Irving Fisher would have it.

But now consider the introduction of a corporate tax of 100τ percent on the profits of the business with a deduction allowed for the interest payments. It is easily shown that, if economic depreciation is allowed, the interest rate that firms can afford to pay remains 10 percent in the absence of inflation. But inflation now raises the interest rate not by any increase in the inflation rate but by that increase in inflation divided by $(1 - \tau)$.[3] If τ is 50 percent, the 5 percent increase in expected inflation raises the interest rate by 10 percent to 20 percent. This is easily understood since the 10 percent increase only costs a firm a net-of-tax 5 percent, just the amount by which inflation has raised the nominal return on capital.

In this example, the effect of a 5 percent inflation rate is to raise the *real* rate of interest received by savers from 10 percent to 15 percent. Their real *net-of-tax* rate of interest will, however, depend on the extent to which the interest income is subject to personal tax. If every lender's tax rate is exactly equal to the corporate rate, the real net rate of interest will be unaffected by the rate of inflation.[4] But more generally, individual tax rates differ substantially[5] and the real net-of-tax return rises for those individuals with tax rates below the corporate rate and falls for the others. If saving is sensitive to the real net return, these changes will alter the capital intensity of the economy which in turn will change the marginal product of capital. The effect on the final equilibrium of a change in the

2. Intramarginal investments may be financed by the equity resulting from the extrepreneurs' original investment and from subsequent retained earnings. See Stiglitz (1973) for such a model.

3. Feldstein (1976; chap. 3 above) examines this simple case as well as the more general situation in which both saving and money demand are sensitive to the rate of return. If f' is the marginal product of capital and π is the rate of inflation, the nominal interest rate satisfies $i = f' + \pi/(1 - \tau)$.

4. If lenders are taxed at 100θ percent, the net-of-tax nominal interest rate rises by $(1 - \theta)/(1 - \tau)$ times the increase in the rate of inflation. With $\theta = \tau$, this is one and the real net interest rate therefore remains unchanged.

5. Individual tax rates include not only the statutory personal tax rates but the tax rates on savings channelled through pension funds, insurance, and other financial intermediaries.

expected rate of inflation will depend on the capital-labor substitutability, on the distribution of individual and business tax rates, and on the interest sensitivity of saving and money demand (as well as on the correlation between these sensitivities and the personal tax rates). In general terms, inflation will raise capital intensity in this model if the rate at which savers are taxed is less than the tax rate on borrowers.

Introducing a more realistic description of depreciation radically alters this conclusion. In calculating taxable profits, firms are generally allowed to deduct the cost of capital investments only over several years. Because these deductions are usually based on the original or "historic" cost of the assets, the real value of these depreciation deductions can be substantially reduced during a period of inflation. This raises the real tax rate on investment income and therefore lowers the real interest rate that firms can afford to offer. The change in the nominal interest rate may be greater or less than the change in inflation and depends on the balance between the positive effect of interest rate deductibility and the adverse effect of original cost depreciation. This conclusion can be extended directly to an economy with equity as well as debt finance (Feldstein, Green, and Sheshinski, 1978; chap. 4 above) and to an economy with government debt (Feldstein, 1980; chap. 5 above).

In short, the impact of inflation and of monetary policy depends critically on the fiscal setting. It is therefore unfortunate, but all too common, that theoretical analyses of inflation and of monetary policy ignore the tax structure and assume that all taxes are lump sum levies.

Because capital tax rules differ substantially among countries, inflation can have very different effects in different countries on the rate and composition of capital accumulation. In the past several years, I have tried to explore the theoretical relationship between inflation and tax rules and to measure the impact of inflation in the United States on effective tax rates (Feldstein and Summers, 1979; chap. 8 above) and on the yields on real capital, on debt, and on equity.[6] Those studies, together with the results presented in the current paper, have led me to conclude that the interaction of inflation and the existing tax rules has contributed substantially to the decline of business investment in the United States.

The rate of business's fixed investment in the United States has fallen quite sharply since the mid-1960s. The share of national income devoted to net nonresidential fixed investment fell by more than one-third between the last half of the 1960s and the decade of the 1970s: the ratio of net fixed nonresidential investment to GNP averaged 0.040 from 1965

---

6. See Feldstein and Poterba (1980b) with respect to yields on real capital; Feldstein and Summers (1978; chap. 9 above), Feldstein and Eckstein (1970), and Feldstein and Chamberlain (1973) with respect to yields on debt; and Feldstein (1980b, d; chaps. 10 and 11 above) with respect to equity yields.

through 1969 but only 0.025 from 1970 through 1979.[7] The corresponding rate of growth of the nonresidential capital stock declined by an even greater percentage: between 1965 and 1969, the annual rate of growth of the fixed nonresidential capital stock averaged 5.5 percent; in the 1970s, this average dropped to 3.2 percent.[8]

The present paper shows how U.S. tax rules and a high rate of inflation interact to discourage investment. The nature of this interaction is complex and operates through several different channels. For example, while nominal interest rates have been unusually high in recent years, the deductibility of nominal interest costs in the calculation of taxable profits implies that the real net-of-tax interest rates that firms pay have actually become negative! In itself, this would, of course, encourage, an increased rate of investment. But, since existing tax rules limit the depreciation deduction to amounts based on the original cost of the assets, a higher rate of inflation reduces the maximum real rate of return that firms can afford to pay. The effect of inflation on the incentive to invest depends on balancing the change in the cost of funds (including equity as well as debt) against the change in the maximum potential return that firms can afford to pay. This explanation of investment behavior, which is close to Irving Fisher's own approach, is developed more precisely in section 14.4 and then related to the observed variation of investment since 1955.

The interaction of tax rules and inflation can also be seen in a simpler and more direct way. The combined effects of original cost depreciation, the taxation of nominal capital gains, and other tax rules raises the effective tax rate paid on the capital income of the corporate sector by the corporations, their owners, and their creditors. This reduces the real net rate of return that the ultimate suppliers of capital can obtain on nonresidential fixed investment. This in turn reduces the incentive to save and distorts the flow of saving away from fixed nonresidential investment. Even without specifying the mechanism by which the financial markets and managerial decisions achieve this reallocation, the variations in investment during the past three decades can be related to changes in this real net rate of return. This approach is pursued in section 14.3.

In addition to these two approaches, I have also examined the implications of inflation in a capital stock adjustment model of the type developed by Jorgenson and his collaborators.[9] Those results are presented in section 14.5.

7. Data on net fixed nonresidential investment is presented in table 5.3 of the National Income and Product Accounts. The full time series is presented in table 14.1 below. All data and estimates in this paper are from the National Income and Product Accounts before the December 1980 revision.

8. See table 14.1 below for the annual values. Data on the net stock of fixed nonresidential capital is presented in the *Survey of Current Business*, April 1976 and subsequent issues.

9. See Jorgenson (1963), Hall and Jorgenson (1967), Gordon and Jorgenson (1976), and Hall (1977) among others.

14.1   On Estimating False Models

My focus in this paper is on assessing the extent to which investment responds to changes in the incentives that are conditioned by tax rules. Separate calculations based on previous research are then used to evaluate the effect on investment of the interaction between inflation and the tax rules.

Despite the extensive amount of research that has been done on investment behavior, there are still many economists who question whether investment does respond significantly to what might generally be called "price incentives" and not just to business cycle conditions.[10] One important reason for these doubts is the failure of previous studies to reflect correctly the impact of inflation. When the price incentive variable is significantly mismeasured, it is not surprising that its impact on investment is understated. A further reason, and, I believe, a more fundamental one, is that the investment process is far too complex for any single econometric model to be convincing. Moreover, making a statistical model more complicated in an attempt to represent some particular key features of "reality" or of rational optimization often requires imposing other explicit and implausible assumptions as maintained hypotheses.

The problem posed for the applied econometrician by the complexity of reality and the incompleteness of available theory is certainly not limited to studies of investment. In my experience, there are relatively few problems in which the standard textbook procedure of specifying "the correct model" and then estimating the unknown parameters can produce convincing estimates. Much more common is the situation in which the specifications suggested by a rich economic theory overexhaust the information in the data. In time series analysis, this exhaustion occurs rapidly because of the limited degrees of freedom. But even with very large cross-section samples, collinearity problems reduce the effective degrees of freedom and make it impossible to consider all of the variables or functional forms that a rich theory would suggest. These problems are exacerbated by the inadequate character of the data themselves. Even when information is available and measurement errors are small, the accounting measures used by business firms and national income accounts rarely correspond to the concepts of economic theory.

The result of all this is that in practice all econometric specifications are necessarily "false" models. They are false models not only in the innocuous sense that the residuals reflect omitted variables but also in the more serious sense that the omissions and other misspecifications make it impossible to obtain unbiased or consistent estimates of the parameters

10. See, e.g., the article by Clark (1979) and the book by Eisner (1979) for recent examples of studies that conclude that price incentive effects are economically insignificant or, at most, are quite small.

even by sophisticated transformations of the data. The applied econometrician, like the theorist, soon discovers from experience that a useful
model is not one that is "true" or "realistic" but one that is parsimonious,
plausible, and informative.

Unfortunately, econometric research is not often described in such
humble terms. The resulting clash between the conventional textbook
interpretation of econometric estimates and the obvious limitations of
false models has led to an increasing skepticism in the profession about
the usefulness of econometric evidence. While some of this skepticism
may be a justifiable antidote to naive optimism and exaggerated claims, I
believe it is based on a misunderstanding of the potential contribution of
empirical research in economics.

I am convinced that econometric analysis helps us to learn about the
economy and that better econometric methods help us to make more
reliable inferences from the evidence. But I would reject the traditional
view of statistical inference that regards the estimation of an econometric
equation as analogous to the "critical experiment" of the natural sciences
that can, with a single experiment, provide a definitive answer to a central
scientific question. I would similarly reject an oversimplified Bayesian
view of inference that presumes that the economist can specify an explicit
prior distribution over the set of all possible true models or that the
likelihood function is so informative that it permits transforming a very
diffuse prior over all possible models into a very concentrated posterior
distribution.

Although I am very sympathetic to the general Bayesian logic, I think
that such well specified priors and such informative likelihood functions
are incompatible with the "false models" and inadequate data with which
we are forced to work. I think that the learning process is more complex.
Perhaps the phrase "expert inference" best captures what I have in mind.
The expert sees not one study but many. He examines not only the
regression coefficients but also the data themselves. He understands the
limits of the data and the nature of the institutions. He forms his judgments about the importance of omitted variables and about the plausibility of restrictions on the basis of all this knowledge and of his understanding of the theory of economics and statistics. In a general way, he behaves
like the Bayesian who combines prior information and sample evidence
to form a posterior distribution, but, because of the limitations and
diversity of the data and the models that have been estimated, he cannot
follow the formal rules of Bayesian inference.[11]

As a practical matter, we often need different studies to learn about
different aspects of any problem. The idea of estimating a single complete

11. Leamer (1978) presents very insightful comments about the problems of inference
and specification search as well as some specific techniques that can be rigorously justified in
certain simple contexts.

model that tells about all the parameters of interest and tests all implicit restrictions is generally not feasible with the available data. Instead, judgments must be formed by studying the results of several studies, each of which focuses on part of the problem and makes false assumptions about other parts.

The basic reference on this type of "expert inference" isn't Jeffreys, Zellner, or Leamer. It is the children's fable about the five blind men who examined an elephant. The important lesson in that story is not the fact that each blind man came away with a partial and "incorrect" piece of evidence. The lesson is rather that an intelligent maharajah who studied the findings of these five men could probably piece together a good judgmental picture of an elephant, especially if he had previously seen some other four-footed animal.

The danger, of course, in this procedure is that any study based on a false model may yield biased estimates of the effects of interest. Although informed judgement may help the researcher to distinguish innocuous maintained hypotheses from harmful ones, some doubt will always remain. *In general, howerer, the biases in different studies will not be the same.* If the biases are substantial, different studies will point to significantly different conclusions. In contrast, a finding that the results of several quite different studies all point to the same conclusion suggests that the specification errors in each of the studies are relatively innocuous.

When the data cannot be used to distinguish among alternative plausible models, the overall economic process is underidentified. This may matter for some purposes but not for others. Even if the process as a whole is underidentified, the implications with respect to some particular variable (i.e., the conditional predictions of the effect of changing some variable) may be the same for all models and therefore unaffected by the underidentification. This "partial identification" is achieved, because the data contain a clear message that is not sensitive to model specification.

Of course, not all issues can be resolved in this satisfying way. For many problems, different plausible specifications lead to quite different conclusions. When this happens, the aspect that is of interest (i.e., the predicted effect of changing a particular variable) is effectively underidentified. No matter how precisely the coefficients of any particular specification may appear to be estimated, the relevant likelihood function is very flat. In these cases, estimating alternative models to study the same question can be a useful reminder of the limits of our knowledge.[12]

12. For a simplified formal analogy, consider the problem of estimating the elasticity of demand for some product with respect to permanent income. Since permanent income is not observed, some proxy must be used. Each potential proxy is, however, likely to introduce a bias of its own. If the estimated elasticity is similar for several quite different proxies, there is a reasonable presumption that each bias is relatively small.

14.2   Using Alternative Models of Investment Behavior

The potential advantage of using several alterative parsimonious models is well illustrated by the analysis of investment behavior. There is a wide variety of empirical issues that are of substantial importance both for understanding the economy and for assessing the importance of different government policies. How sensitive is investment to tax incentives? To interest rates? To share prices? To the expectation of future changes in tax rules or market conditions? And what is the time pattern of the response to these stimuli? While an estimate of "the correct model" of investment behavior could in principle answer all of these questions at once, it is in practice necessary to pursue different questions with different studies. The purpose of the present study, as I indicated in the introduction, is to assess the extent to which changes in tax incentives and disincentives—and particularly those changes that are due to inflation—alter the flow of investment. Focusing on this issue means that some assumptions must explicity or implicitly be made about the other issues and that the estimated effect of the tax changes is conditional on those assumptions. I find it quite reassuring therefore that estimates based on three quite different kinds of models all point to the same conclusion about the likely magnitude of the response to inflation and to effective tax rates.

The current state of investment theory also indicates the need to examine alternative models. While there is probably considerable agreement about the essential features of a very simple theoretical model of investment behavior, there is much less consensus about the appropriate framework for applied studies of investment behavior. The disagreements about empirical specification can conveniently be grouped in four areas.[13]

14.2.1   Technology

The traditional capital stock adjustment models assume that capital is homogeneous and that the purpose of investment is to increase the size of this homogeneous stock until, roughly speaking, the return on the last unit of capital is reduced to the cost of funds. An alternative and more realistic view sees capital as quite heterogeneous. There are two aspects of such heterogeneity. First, capital consists of a large number of different kinds of equipment and structures. At any point in time there may be too much of one kind of capital and too little of another. A simple aggregate relationship loses this potentially important information. A much more fundamental kind of heterogeneity is associated with the *flow* of new investment opportunities. Each year, new investment possibilities

---

13. No attempt is made here to survey the existing empirical research on investment or to examine all of the arguments about specification. For recent surveys, see Nickell (1978) and Rowley and Trivedi (1975).

are created by innovations in technology, taste, and market conditions. This exogenous flow of new investment opportunities with high rates of return can induce investment even when the total stock of capital is too large in the sense that the marginal product of an equiproportional increase in all types of capital is less than the cost of funds or the value of Tobin's q-ratio is less than one.[14]

Even within the framework of homogeneous capital models, there has been much debate about the choice between putty-putty models in which all investment decisions are reversible and the putty-clay models in which invested capital has a permanently fixed capital-labor ratio.[15] While the truth no doubt lies somewhere between these extremes (old equipment and processes can be modified but not costlessly "melted down" and reformed), the more complex putty-clay model is undoubtedly a more realistic microeconomic description than the putty-putty model.

Closely related is the issue of replacement investment, a quite significant issue since roughly one-half of gross investment is absorbed in replacement. The simplest model of replacement is that a constant fraction of the homogeneous capital stock wears out each period. A more realistic description would recognize that output decay is not exponential but varies with the age of the equipment. More generally, the timing of replacement and the level of maintenance expenditure are economic decisions that will respond to actual and anticipated changes in the cost of capital and other inputs.[16]

14.2.2   Market Environment

The conventional Keynesian picture of investment that motivates the accelerator model of investment and most other capital stock adjustment models assumes that each firm's sales are exogenous. The firm is assumed to take the price of its product and the level of its sales as given, and then to select the capacity to produce this level of output. A more general specification would recognize that the firm sets its own level of output, taking as given either the market price of its product or the demand function for its product.

There are analogous issues about the nature of the markets in which the firms buy inputs. The simplest assumption is that these markets are perfect and that the market prices do not depend on the quantities purchased. A more realistic description would recognize that the short-run supply function of labor to the individual firm is likely to be less than infinitely elastic and that, for the economy as a whole, the short-run

14. This is quite separate from the reason for investing when q is less than one that is implied by the analysis of Auerbach (1979a), Bradford (1979), and King (1977).

15. See Nickell (1978) for an extensive discussion of putty-clay specifications.

16. See Feldstein and Rothschild (1974) for a critique of the constant proportional replacement hypothesis and an analysis of the potential effects on replacement investment of changes in tax rates and interest rates.

supply price of capital as well as labor is an increasing function of the quantity purchased.[17]

Closely related is the sensitivity of adjustment costs to the volume of investment. The simplest assumption is that there are no adjustment costs and that the total cost of any total investment is independent of the speed at which it is done. In contrast, the managerial and planning costs may be a significant part of the cost of capital acquisition and may rise exponentially with the rates of net and gross investment. Abel (1978) has shown how a capital stock adjustment model can be extended to include adjustment costs and how doing so can explain why the firm increases its rate of investment only slowly even when the marginal return on installed capital substantially exceeds its cost.

14.2.3   Financial Behavior

There remains much controversy about the role of internal and external finance and about the related issue of the factors determining the cost of funds to the firm. The simplest model assumes that the costs of debt and equity funds are independent of both the debt-equity ratio and the volume of the firm's external finance. More general analyses reject the extreme Modigliani-Miller result and recognize that, beyond a certain point, increases in the debt-equity ratio raise the cost of funds. Similarly, it is frequently argued that the availablility of retained earnings lowers the cost of funds (at least in the eyes of management) and therefore affects the timing even if not the equilibrium level of investment.[18]

Tax rules significantly affect the costs to the firm of debt and equity finance. The implications of this obvious statement have been the subject of much research and debate in the past few years.[19] At one extreme is the conclusion of Stiglitz (1973) that U.S. firms should finance marginal investments exclusively by debt, retaining earnings to avoid the dividend tax and using the retained earnings to finance intramarginal investments. Auerbach (1979a), Bradford (1979), and King (1977) have argued that retaining earnings does not avoid the dividend tax but only postpones it without lowering its present value; this implies that retained earnings are substantially less costly than new equity funds and that the capital stock should be expanded even if the market valuation of additional capital is less than one-for-one.[20] These types of conclusions reflect a world of

17. Keynes (1936) emphasized that rising cost of inputs is a principal reason for the declining marginal efficiency of investment in the short run. See Brechling (1975) on the empirical importance of this.

18. See, e.g., Coen (1968) and Feldstein and Flemming (1971) for evidence on this point.

19. See, among others, Auerbach (1979a), Bradford (1979), Feldstein, Green, and Sheshinski (1979), King (1977), Miller (1977), and Stiglitz (1973).

20. For an application of this to the empirical study of investment behavior, see Summers (1980a).

certainty and one in which all individual investors have the same personal income tax rates. Although complete models with uncertainty and diverse individual tax rates have not yet been fully worked out, it is clear from partial studies (e.g., Feldstein and Green, 1979, and Feldstein and Slemrod, 1980) that these extensions can significantly alter conventional results.

14.2.4 Expectations and the Decision Process

With a putty-putty technology and reversible investment, expectations are irrelevant. But when an investment commits the firm to a future capital stock with a fixed capital-labor ratio, expectations about the future are crucial. Although simple moving averages of past variables are the most common representation of the process by which expectations are formed, this simplification may cause serious misspecification errors in some contexts. Helliwell and Glorieux (1970) and Abel (1978) have developed forward-looking models of expectations. Lucas (1976) has emphasized the potential instability of all such fixed-coefficient average representations while Sargent (1978) and Summers (1980d) have shown both the possibility and the difficulty of developing even quite simple models of factor demand that are consistent with rational expectations.

Even when investment models acknowledge that expectations are uncertain, the assumption of risk neutrality is usually invoked to simplify the analysis. In fact, investment behavior may be substantially influenced by risk aversion, changes in risk perception, and the pursuit of strategies that reduce the risk of major capital commitments.

In each of the cases that I have been describing, the researcher must choose (implicitly or explicitly) between a more tractable but usually less realistic assumption and an assumption that is more realistic but also more difficult to apply satistically. In general, the choice has gone in favor of the more tractable but less realistic specification. Moreover, implementing any one of the more complex assumptions often makes it too difficult to implement some other more realistic assumption, thus inevitably forcing the researcher to choose among false models.

The work of Jorgenson and his collaborators[21] well illustrates this problem of choice. In each case, Jorgenson and his colleagues have selected the more tractable but less realistic assumption. Because they impose the further restriction that the technology of each firm is Cobb-Douglas, the data are required only to determine the time pattern of the response of investment to prior changes in the desired capital stock.[22]

21. See the references cited in note 9 above.
22. The Jorgenson procedure also estimates a further parameter that should equal the capital coefficient in the Cobb-Douglas production function, i.e., the share of capital income in total output. Estimates of this parameter are also invariably far too low; although this indicates that the model is "false," it does not necessarily imply that the estimated effects of tax rules and inflation are misleading.

There is no separate estimation of the effect of tax rules and no specific tests of the implied effect on investment of changes in tax rules and inflation. In section 14.5, I adopt the general Jorgenson specification but relax the constraint that the technology is Cobb-Douglas and also the constraint that the response of firms to the tax-induced changes in the user cost of capital is the same as their response to other sources of variation in the user cost of capital. The results indicate that a correct measurement of the impact of inflation in the context of this model substantially increases its explanatory power and that with the correctly measured variables the data are consistent with an elasticity of substitution of one and with the assumption that firms respond in the same way to all changes in the user cost of capital.

Of course, the support for this conclusion is conditioned on all of the other false maintained assumptions. I have, however, also examined two other quite different models that do not impose these constraints. The analysis of section 14.3, which relates investment to the real net-of-tax rate of return received by the suppliers of capital, avoids any reference to financial market variables. While it is therefore obviously completely uninformative about many potentially interesting issues, it avoids conditioning the estimated responsiveness of investment on any theory of corporate finance. The specification in terms of the flow of investment avoids the assumption of homogenous capital or a putty-putty technology. Again, this makes the model uninformative about important issues but avoids constraining the results by some obviously strong assumptions of a false model. There are, of course, potential biases in this approach since it fails to distinguish different reasons for changes in investment and omits variables that may be significant (e.g., changes in government debt, international capital flow, or other factors that would in principle be reflected in financial variables).

The third approach, presented in section 14.4, avoids some of these problems but, of course, at the cost of introducing new ones. This specification relates the flow of investment to the difference between the cost of funds to the firm and the maximum potential rate of return that the firm can afford to pay on a standard investment project. The financial cost of funds is thus explicitly included. This, however, requires specifying the "true" cost of debt and equity funds and their relative importance. The specification does, however, avoid restrictive assumptions about technology and other aspects of investment behavior. But, like the other two specifications, this return-over-cost specification is a false model whose coefficients might well be biased.

The strength of the empirical evidence therefore rests on the fact that all three quite different specifications support the same conclusion that the heavier tax burden associated with inflation has substantially depressed nonresidential investment in the United States. The magnitude of the effect implied by each of these three models indicates that the adverse changes in the tax variables since 1965 have depressed investment by more than 1 percent of GNP, a reduction which exceeds 40 percent of the rate of investment in recent years.

14.3 Investment and the Real Net Rate of Return

Individuals divide their income between saving and consuming and, to the extent that they save, those resources are distributed among housing, inventories, plant and equipment, and investments abroad. Individuals make these decisions not only directly, but also through financial intermediaries, and through the corporations of which they are direct and indirect shareholders.

The most fundamental determinant of the extent to which individuals channel resources into nonresidential fixed investment should be the real net-of-tax rate of return on that investment, a variable that I will denote RN.[23] Although the idea of the real net-of-tax return is conceptually simple, its calculation involves a number of practical as well as theoretical difficulties. Because of data limitations, the calculation is restricted to nonfinancial corporations even though total nonresidential fixed investment refers to a somewhat broader set of firms. The real net return is defined as the product of the real pretax return on capital (R) and one minus the effective tax rate (1-ETR) on that return.

The pretax return is estimated as the ratio of profits plus interest expenses to the value of the capital stock. Profits are based on economic depreciation and a currect measure of inventory costs; capital gains and losses on the corporate debt are irrelevant since the calcuation deals with the combined return to debt and equity. The value of the capital stock includes the replacement cost value of fixed capital and inventories and the market value of land. The pretax rate of return is shown in column 3 of table 14.1.[24]

The effective tax rate on this capital income includes the taxes paid by the corporations, their shareholders, and their creditors to the federal government and to the state and local governments. The shareholders and creditors consist not only of individuals but also of various financial intermediaries including banks, pension funds, and insurance companies.

23. The rate of return on other types of investments might also matter. Since the interaction of inflation and tax rules raised the potential return on owner-occupied housing (Feldstein, 1980*a*; Poterba, 1980), the effect of *RN* may be overestimated but this overstatement only reflects another way in which inflational and tax rules interact to reduce nonresidential fixed investment.

24. Feldstein and Summers (1977) discuss the conceptual problems in measuring the capital income and rate of return. Feldstein and Poterba (1980*a*) use the new capital stock data provided by the Commerce Department and Federal Reserve Bank to calculate the pretax rate of return shown in table 14.1.

Table 14.1   **Investment and the Real Net Return to Capital**

Year	Investment GNP Ratio (I''/Y) (1)	Investment Capital Ratio (I''/K'') (2)	Pretax Return (R) (3)	Effective Tax Rate (ETR) (4)	Net Return (RN) (5)	Cyclically Adjusted Return — Pretax (RA) (6)	Cyclically Adjusted Return — Effective Tax Rate $(ETRA)$ (7)	Cyclically Adjusted Return — Net Return (RNA) (8)
1953	0.027	0.040	0.114	0.745	0.029	0.105	NA	NA
1954	0.023	0.033	0.107	0.687	0.034	0.117	0.754	0.029
1955	0.028	0.041	0.132	0.665	0.044	0.130	0.712	0.037
1956	0.031	0.044	0.114	0.724	0.032	0.117	0.714	0.034
1957	0.029	0.040	0.105	0.717	0.030	0.114	0.715	0.032
1958	0.017	0.023	0.090	0.707	0.026	0.113	0.713	0.032
1959	0.020	0.028	0.112	0.673	0.036	0.125	0.694	0.038
1960	0.022	0.030	0.104	0.665	0.035	0.122	0.714	0.035

1961	0.019	0.027	0.103	0.664	0.035	0.124	0.689	0.038
1962	0.023	0.033	0.117	0.615	0.045	0.130	0.643	0.046
1963	0.023	0.033	0.124	0.606	0.049	0.136	0.629	0.050
1964	0.029	0.041	0.134	0.562	0.059	0.141	0.591	0.057
1965	0.040	0.057	0.145	0.551	0.065	0.145	0.573	0.062
1966	0.045	0.064	0.145	0.560	0.064	0.137	0.595	0.055
1967	0.038	0.052	0.130	0.564	0.057	0.126	0.603	0.050
1968	0.037	0.051	0.130	0.626	0.049	0.123	0.663	0.041
1969	0.038	0.051	0.117	0.673	0.038	0.113	0.762	0.027
1970	0.031	0.040	0.096	0.705	0.028	0.106	0.792	0.022
1971	0.025	0.032	0.100	0.677	0.032	0.112	0.782	0.025
1972	0.028	0.037	0.108	0.625	0.041	0.113	0.720	0.032
1973	0.034	0.046	0.105	0.701	0.031	0.102	0.795	0.021
1974	0.031	0.040	0.082	0.901	0.008	0.096	1.079	−0.008
1975	0.014	0.017	0.086	0.724	0.024	0.115	0.852	0.017
1976	0.015	0.019	0.095	0.681	0.030	0.114	0.850	0.017
1977	0.020	0.026	0.097	0.683	0.031	0.109	NA	NA
1978	0.025	0.033	0.097	0.722	0.027	0.104	NA	NA

In an earlier study, Lawrence Summers and I did a detailed analysis of the distribution of corporate equity and debt among the different classes of shareholders and creditors and of the relevant marginal federal tax rates for each such investor (Feldstein and Summers, 1979; chap. 8 above). More recently, James Poterba and I refined this analysis and extended it to include the taxes paid to state and local governments. The effective rate of tax is shown in column 4 of table 14.1. The resulting net-of-tax rate of return is shown in the fifth column.

The pretax rate of return varies cyclically as well as from year to year but has experienced no overall trend.[25] The average return from 1953 through 1979 was 11.0 percent. The effective tax rate was quite high in the 1950s and then declined sharply in the 1960s; at the individual level this reflected a significant reduction in personal tax rates while at the corporate level this reflected changes in depreciation rules and the statutory corporate tax rate. Since the mid-1960s, the effective tax rate has moved sharply and somewhat erratically upward, primarily reflecting the overstatement of capital income that occurs when inflation distorts the measurement of depreciation, inventory profits, interest payments, and capital gains.[26] The growth of state and local taxes and various changes in personal tax rates contributed somewhat to this overall increase. The real net rate of return shows a general pattern that reflects the changing effective tax rate as well as the cyclical and year-to-year fluctuations in the pretax rate of return. This key rate of return varied around 3.3 percent in the 1950s, rose by the mid-1960s to 6.5 percent, averaged 5.0 percent for the 1960s as a whole, and then dropped in the 1970s to an average of only 2.8 percent.

Since the net rate of return varies cyclically, its estimated impact on investment can reflect cyclical as well as more fundamental influences. To separate these effects, the equations in this section relate the investment rate to a lagged cyclical measure of aggregate demand as well as to the real net return. It is also useful to consider two more explicit ways of focusing on the more fundamental changes in the real rate of return. A cyclically adjusted measure of the real net return was calculated as follows. First, the real pretax rate of return (R) is adjusted by regressing it on the difference between GNP and capacity GNP and then calculating the rate of return for each year at a standard GNP gap of 1.7 percent; this variable, denoted RA (for adjusted) and shown in column 6 of table 14.1, eliminates cyclical but not year-to-year variations in the pretax return. Since there is no trend in the pretax return, eliminating random as well as cyclical variations in the pretax return would leave only a constant.

25. Feldstein and Summers (1977) showed that the apparent downward trend in the first half of the 1970s was not statistically significant. For more recent supporting evidence, see Feldstein and Poterba (1980b).

26. This impact of inflation is discussed in Feldstein, Green, and Sheshinski (1978; chap. 4 above) and calculated in detail in Feldstein and Summers (1979; chap. 8 above).

The cyclical and random fluctuations in the effective tax rate were eliminated in a more fundamental way by using the explicit statutory provisions. Using a method developed in an earlier study (Feldstein and Summers, 1978; chap. 9 above) and described in section 14.4, I calculated the real net rate of return that a firm could afford to pay on the debt and equity used to finance a new investment that, in the absence of all taxes, would have a real yield of 12 percent. This net rate of return varies from year to year because of changes in the tax rules and in the anticipated rate of inflation. The ratio of the net rate of return on a mix of debt and equity to the assumed 12 percent real pretax return measures the changes in the effective tax rate that are not due to fluctuations in the pretax rate of return, the rate of current investment, or other year-to-year fluctuations. More formally, this ratio equals 1-ETRA and the ETRA value is shown in column 7 of table 14.1.[27]

Combining the adjusted pretax return and the adjusted effective tax rate gives the adjusted net return ($RNA = RA$ (1-ERTA)) shown in column 8 of table 14.1.

Although this variable is purged of cyclical variation, it still reflects year-to-year variation in the pretax return. Eliminating all such variation and treating the pretax return as a constant implies that all of the variation in the net return comes from the effective tax rate variable. This possibility is tested below in the context of a more general specification in which both RNA and 1-$ETRA$ are included separately.

The basic specification relates the ratio of real net investment to real GNP (I^n/Y) to the real net rate of return (RN) and the Federal Reserve Board's measure of capacity utilization ($UCAP$).[28] I use annual data and lag both regressors one year:[29]

$$(1) \qquad \frac{I^n_t}{Y_t} \, a_0 + a_1 \, RN_{t-1} + a_2 \, UCAP_{t-1} + u_t$$

where u_t is a random disturbance about which more will be said below.

Although quarterly data could have been constructed, much of the basic information that is used to calculate the net return variable is available only annually; the within-year variations in a quarterly series

---

27. This measure of the effective tax rate differs conceptually from the unadjusted measure in a number of ways. It is an *ex ante* concept for new investment rather than an *ex post* measure on existing capital. No account is taken of the important effect of inflation on the taxation of artificial inventory profits or of the changing rates of state and local taxes. The tax rates on shareholders and creditors are also measured much more crudely.

28. This specification in terms of investment flows represents a disequilibrium process rather than an equal stock adjustment. The special problems of capital heterogeneity and putty-clay technology may make this direct disequilibrium specification more appropriate, especially for explaining and predicting changes in investment over a period of ten to twenty years.

29. Note that since the equation refers to net investment, the past capital stock is not included. I return to this issue below.

would therefore be largely interpolations of doubtful economic meaning.[30]

A lag in response has been found in all previous investment studies and reflects the delays in decision making and in the production and delivery of plant and equipment. The lag also avoids the obvious problem of simultaneity between concurrent investment and capacity utilization or other measures of business cycle activity. More general lag structures and other possible explanatory variables have been considered; those results are also described below.

All of the specifications are estimated by least squares with a first-order autocorrelation correction. The autocorrelation correction algorithm estimates the first-order autocorrelation parameter simultaneously with the other coefficients using a procedure that is equivalent to maximum likelihood if the disturbances are normally distributed. The correction adds to the efficiency of the estimates and, more importantly, avoids the potentially serious downward bias in the estimated standard errors about which Granger and Newbold (1974) have so persuasively warned. For many of the basic specifications I have also checked the constraint implied by the first-order transformation and found that it cannot be rejected; I have also estimated the specification in first difference form and found similar coefficients. The evidence on this is presented below. (I might also add that simple OLS estimates without autocorrelation correction also produce essentially the same results.)

The basic result is shown in equation (2):

(2)
$$\frac{I_t^n}{Y_t} = -0.014 + \underset{(0.095)}{0.459}\ RN_{t-1} + \underset{(0.025)}{0.028}\ UCAP_{t-1}$$
$$+ \underset{(0.25)}{0.29 u_{t-1}}$$

$$\bar{R}^2 = 0.754$$
$$DWS = 2.04$$
$$SSR = 3.438\,(10^{-4})$$
$$1954\text{--}78$$

with standard errors shown in parentheses and the coefficient of u_{t-1} indicating the first-order autocorrelation parameter. Before looking at other specifications, it is useful to consider briefly the magnitude of the estimated coefficients. Since the net return variable had a standard deviation of 0.013 for the sample period, a move of RN from one standard

---

30. Extending the analysis to quarterly observations might nevertheless provide more information about the time pattern of response and about the effect of changes in capacity utilization. Of course, the combination of measurement problems and the inherent autocorrelation of the data imply that using quarterly observation would not increase the *effective* degrees of information by anything like a factor of four.

deviation below the mean to one standard deviation above would increase the investment ratio by about 0.012, approximately 1.5 times its standard deviation and 45 percent of its 25-year average value. Since the capacity utilization variable has a standard deviation of 0.044, a two-standard deviation increase in this variable would raise the investment ratio by about 0.0025 or only one-fifth of the change induced by a similar change in RN.[31]

Reestimating equation (2) in first-difference form (for 1955 through 1978) shows that the estimated coefficient of RN is quite robust: its coefficient is 0.471 with a standard error of 0.113. The capacity utilization coefficient falls to 0.008 with a standard error of 0.021 and the Durbin-Watson statistic indicates negative serial correlation. To test the constraints imposed by the first-order autocorrelation adjustment, I estimated the ordinary least squares regression of the investment ratio on its own lagged value and on one- and two-period lags in RN and $UCAP$. The reduction in the revised sum of squares was only 6 percent and the corresponding F-statistic of 0.54 was far less than the 5 percent critical value of 3.55.

Using the cyclically adjusted measure of the net return (RNA) gives greater weight to the cyclical capacity utilization variable and slightly lowers the estimated effect of changes in the fundamental determinants of the net return:[32]

$$(3) \qquad \frac{I_t^n}{Y_t} = -0.023 + 0.386\, RNA_{t-1} + 0.045\, UCAP_{t-1}$$
$$\phantom{(3) \qquad \frac{I_t^n}{Y_t} = -0.023 +} (0.106) \phantom{RNA_{t-1} + } (0.023)$$
$$\phantom{(3) \qquad \frac{I_t^n}{Y_t} = } + 0.63 u_{t-1}$$
$$\phantom{(3) \qquad \frac{I_t^n}{Y_t} = } (0.20)$$

$$\bar{R}^2 = 0.746$$
$$DWS = 2.076$$
$$SSR = 3.442\,(10^{-4})$$
$$1955\text{--}77$$

Several different more general distributed lag specifications were also estimated. There is some weak evidence that the mean lag between RN and the investment ratio is longer than a year and that the cumulative effect of RN on the investment ratio is larger than equation (2) implies. For example, when the variable RN_{t-2} is added to the earlier specification, its coefficient is 0.20 with a standard error of 0.14; the sum of the coefficients on RN_{t-1} and RN_{t-1} becomes 0.60. Second-order polynomial distributed lags with a four- or five-year span and a final value constrained

---

31. Since the standard error of the capacity utilization coefficient is relatively large, the coefficient of 0.028 should be regarded as subject to considerable error.

32. The sample is two years shorter because the information required to calculate ETRA is not available before 1954 or after 1976.

to be zero imply that the coefficients of RN_{t-1} and RN_{t-2} are significantly different from zero but that further coefficients are not; the sum of the coefficients varies between 0.45 and 0.55, depending on the exact specification. Further lags on the capacity utilization variables are never both positive and significantly different from zero.

Redefining the investment variable as the ratio of net investment to *capacity* GNP has essentially no effect; the coefficient of RN rises to 0.50 (standard error 0.10) and the capacity utilization coefficient remains essentially unchanged at 0.026 (s.e. = 0.026).

All of the equations are estimated using the *net* rate of investment because I believe that the Commerce Department's very disaggregated procedure for calculating economic depreciation, while far from perfect, is better than the alternative of studying gross investment and assuming that depreciation is a constant fraction of the past year's capital stock. Nevertheless, as a further test of the robustness of the conclusion that RN is important, I have estimated such a gross investment equation:

$$(4) \qquad \frac{I_t^g}{Y_t} = -0.123 + \underset{(0.082)}{0.314} \ RN_{t-1} + \underset{(0.028)}{0.106} \ UCAP_{t-1}$$

$$+ \underset{(0.030)}{0.163} \ \frac{K_{t-1}^n}{Y_{t-1}} + \underset{(0.295)}{0.050u_{t-1}}$$

$$\begin{aligned} \bar{R}^2 &= 0.715 \\ DWS &= 1.98 \\ SSR &= 2.70(10^{-4}) \\ &1954\text{--}78 \end{aligned}$$

These coefficients confirm the importance of RN but suggest that the net investment specification overstates the importance of RN relative to $UCAP$. However, the very large coefficient of the lagged capital variable, implying an implausible 16 percent annual depreciation rate for plant and equipment, is a warning against giving too much weight to this specification.[33]

The results are not sensitive to the use of capacity utilization to measure the effect of aggregate demand. Using the unemployment rate for men over 19 years old leaves the coefficient of RN at 0.454 (standard error = 0.077) while using the proportional gap between GNP and capacity GNP leaves the coefficient of RN at 0.405 (s.e. = 0.070). A one percentage point decline in this unemployment rate raises the investment ratio by a relatively small 0.0016; similarly, a one percentage point decline in the GNP gap raises the investment ratio by only 0.0010. Additional accelerator variables (i.e., a distributed lag of proportional

---

33. Further evidence in favor of using the net investment series is present in section 14.4 below.

changes in GNP) were insignificant when capacity utilization was included in the equation.

Several additional variables that are sometimes associated with investment were added to equation (2). Three of these variables were each insignificant and changed the coefficient of RN by less than 0.02: the ratio of corporate cash flow to GNP lagged one year; the ratio of the federal government deficit to GNP lagged one year;[34] and a time trend. When the one-year lagged value of Tobin's q variable is included,[35] its coefficient is 0.011 (with a standard error of 0.074) and the coefficient of RN drops slightly to 0.391 (s.e. = 0.117).

The actual inflation rate (lagged one year), and the predicted long-term inflation rate[36] (also lagged one year) were completely insignificant and had very little effect on the coefficient of RN. Including both the actual and expected inflation rates did not change this conclusion. The full effect of inflation on investment is captured in the current specification by the RN variable itself.

All of the specification experiments described in the past several paragraphs have also been repeated with the cyclically adjusted RNA variable with very similar results.

The specification in terms of the net return assumes that investment responds equally to changes in the pretax return and in the effective tax rate. Two tests of this assumption indicate that it is consistent with the data. If, instead of using RN_{t-1}, equation (2) is reestimated with R_{t-1} and $1-ETR_{t-1}$ as separate variables, the sum of squared residuals actually rises; i.e., the two variables actually explain less than their product does. An explicit statistical test is possible if RN in equation (2) is replaced by its logarithm; since $ln\, RN = ln\, R + ln\,(1 - ETR)$, the equality of the two coefficients of $ln\, R$ and $ln\,(1 - ETR)$ can be tested explicitly.[37] Neither coefficient is estimated very precisely (each has a t-statistic of less than 1.5) and the equality of the two coefficients is easily accepted (the F-statistic is only 0.51).

Estimating the analogous decomposition for the cyclically adjusted variables, i.e., replacing RNA by RA and $1 - ETRA$, is interesting be-

34. When the concurrent ratio of the federal deficit to GNP is included, its coefficient is -0.26 (with a standard error of 0.06) and the coefficient of RN drops to 0.21 (s.e. = 0.10). This may be evidence of crowding out or it may merely reflect the tendency of more investment to increase concurrent national income and thereby reduce the government deficit.

35. This variable is the Holland and Meyers (1979) measure, defined as the ratio of the aggregate market value of nonfinancial corporations to the net replacement cost of plant, equipment, and inventories. Essentially the same result is obtained with their broader measure in which all other nonfinancial assets are included.

36. The predicted inflation rate is based on a rolling series of ARIMA regressions; see Feldstein and Summers (1978, pp. 170–74).

37. The switch from RN to $ln\, RN$ causes a small decrease in the explanatory power of the equation.

cause it sheds light on the question of whether the year-to-year noncyclical variations in the pretax return matter. Two things should be noted. First, this substitution reduces the explanatory power of the equation as measured by the corrected $\bar{R}^2$; this favors keeping the simple specification in terms of RNA. Second, if both variables are included separately, the coefficient of the RA variable is much less than its standard error (0.033 with a standard error of 0.172) while the coefficient of the ETRA variable is statistically significant and economically important: -0.044 with a standard error of 0.017. This suggests that year-to-year fluctuations in the pretax return have not been important but that the rise in ETRA from about 0.57 in the mid-1960s to about 0.85 in the mid-1970s was enough to reduce the investment ratio by more than one percentage point.

An important indication of the plausibility and reliability of any simple model is the stability of the coefficients in different subperiods. Equations (5) and (6) show the result of splitting the sample in half:

(5)
$$\frac{I^n_t}{Y_t} = -0.066 + 0.448\, RN_{t-1} + 0.090\, UCAP_{t-1}$$
$$\qquad\qquad (0.078) \qquad\quad (0.024)$$
$$+ 0.62 u_{t-1}$$
$$(0.25)$$

$$\bar{R}^2 = 0.784$$
$$DWS = 2.20$$
$$SSR = 1.291\,(10^{-4})$$
$$1954\text{--}66$$

(6)
$$\frac{I^n_t}{Y_t} = -0.222 + 0.443\, RN_{t-1} + 0.041\, UCAP_{t-1}$$
$$\qquad\qquad (0.108) \qquad\quad (0.025)$$
$$+ 0.58 u_{t-1}$$
$$(0.32)$$

$$\bar{R}^2 = 0.839$$
$$DWS = 1.48$$
$$SSR = 0.930\,(10^{-4})$$
$$1967\text{--}78$$

The coefficients of RN are remarkably similar and the relevant F-statistic indicates that the hypothesis of equal coefficients for the two subperiods cannot be rejected at the 5 percent level.[38]

A further test of the robustness and usefulness of an equation is its performance in out-of-sample forecasts. The basic specification was reestimated for the period 1954–70 and this equation was then used to predict the investment ratio for each year from 1971 through 1978. These

38. Even the two coefficients of the capacity utilization variable do not differ in a statistically significant way; the difference between them of 0.049 has a standard error of 0.035.

Table 14.2   **Actual and Predicted Investment Ratios**

Year	Ratio			Change in Ratio		
	Actual (1)	Predicted (RN) (2)	Predicted (MPNR-COF) (3)	Actual (4)	Predicted (RN) (5)	Predicted (MPNR-COF) (6)
1971	0.025	0.019	0.024	—	—	—
1972	0.028	0.020	0.027	0.003	0.001	0.003
1973	0.034	0.028	0.033	0.006	0.008	0.006
1974	0.031	0.027	0.026	−0.003	−0.001	−0.007
1975	0.014	0.015	0.004	−0.017	−0.012	−0.022
1976	0.015	0.012	0.012	0.001	−0.003	0.008
1977	0.020	0.020	0.016	0.005	0.008	0.004
1978	0.025	0.022	—	0.005	0.002	—

NOTE: Predictors are based on equations fitted through 1970 only. Columns 2 and 5 are based on the specification of equation (1) while columns 3 and 6 are based on the specification of equation (12).

predictions are based on the two lagged variables only (RN_{t-1} and $UCAP_{t-1}$) and do not use the lagged disturbance (u_{t-1}) or any lagged dependent variable. The results shown in table 14.2 are remarkably good. The mean absolute prediction error (0.0035) is only two-thirds of the mean year-to-year change (0.0050) in the investment ratio. The year-to-year changes are also predicted quite well, with the correct sign in 6 of the 7 years and a mean error that is only one-third of the average change.

To conclude the discussion of the net return model of investment behavior, it is useful to consider its implication for understanding the decline in the investment ratio since 1966. The first column of table 14.3 shows that the investment ratio fell from 0.045 in 1966 to less than half that value in the last four years of the sample period. The 1965 value of RN was 0.065, the highest of any year in the sample, and the 1965 value of $UCAP$ was 0.896, the second highest value and only slightly below the 1966 $UCAP$ value of 0.911. Column 2 uses the estimated effect of changes in RN (i.e., 0.459 from equation 2) to calculate the investment ratio for each of the 25 sample years conditional on $RN = 0.065$; i.e., each figure in column 2 equals the corresponding figure in column 1 plus 0.459 times $(0.065 - RN_{t-1})$. Similarly, column 3 uses the estimated effect of changes in $UCAP$ to calculate the investment ratio conditional on $UCAP = 0.896$.[39] It is clear from the figures in column 2 that the fall in RN can account for most of the decline in the investment ratio since 1966 and that the fluctuations in $UCAP$ after 1966 cannot account for much of the decline. If RN had been kept at its 1965 level, net investment from 1970 to

39. Columns 5 and 6 will be considered in section 14.4.

Table 14.3   **Actual and Conditional Ratios of Net Nonresidential
                      Investment to GNP**

					MPNR-	
		RN=	UCAP=	INF=	COF=	UCAP=
	Actual	0.065	0.896	0.0	0.043	0.896
Year	(1)	(2)	(3)	(4)	(5)	(6)
1954	0.023	0.040	0.023	—	—	—
1955	0.028	0.043	0.031	0.031	0.039	0.035
1956	0.031	0.041	0.032	0.035	0.041	0.033
1957	0.029	0.045	0.030	0.035	0.036	0.032
1958	0.017	0.033	0.019	0.023	0.024	0.021
1959	0.020	0.038	0.024	0.024	0.024	0.031
1960	0.022	0.035	0.024	0.026	0.026	0.028
1961	0.019	0.033	0.022	0.023	0.023	0.026
1962	0.023	0.037	0.027	0.026	0.024	0.032
1963	0.023	0.033	0.026	0.025	0.025	0.029
1964	0.029	0.036	0.030	0.032	0.030	0.033
1965	0.040	0.043	0.041	0.042	0.040	0.043
1966	0.045	0.045	0.045	0.048	0.045	0.045
1967	0.038	0.038	0.037	0.042	0.041	0.036
1968	0.037	0.041	0.038	0.041	0.038	0.039
1969	0.038	0.046	0.039	0.043	0.042	0.040
1970	0.031	0.043	0.032	0.038	0.038	0.033
1971	0.025	0.042	0.028	0.031	0.033	0.032
1972	0.028	0.044	0.032	0.033	0.034	0.037
1973	0.034	0.046	0.036	0.039	0.038	0.039
1974	0.031	0.047	0.032	0.041	0.041	0.033
1975	0.014	0.040	0.015	0.030	0.038	0.018
1976	0.015	0.034	0.019	0.024	0.028	0.027
1977	0.020	0.036	0.023	0.028	0.033	0.027
1978	0.025	0.041	0.027	0.034	—	—

Header note: "Conditional on[a]" spans columns (2) through (6).

a. Columns 2, 3, and 4 are based on equation (2); columns 5 and 6 are based on equation (13).

1978 would have taken an average of 4.1 percent of GNP instead of the actual average of only 2.5 percent, an increase of two-thirds. By contrast, maintaining the high 1965 level of capacity utilization would only have raised the average investment-GNP ratio by 0.5 percentage points. It is also worth noting that if the 1965 level of RN had been reached a decade earlier, investment during that decade would have averaged an additional 1.2 percent of GNP. Equation (2) can also be used to estimate an approximate but explicit effect of inflation on the investment ratio. In an earlier study, Lawrence Summers and I estimated the change in the tax liability on corporate source income that is caused by the interaction of inflation and the tax laws.[40] For example, in 1977 (the last year of our study) inflation raised the tax liability by $31.9 billion or 1.9 percent of the corresponding capital stock.[41] The estimate of RN_{t-1} in equation (2) implies that a 1.9 percentage point increase in RN for 1977 would raise the 1978 investment ratio by 0.009 to 0.034; this value is shown in column 4 of table 14.3. Similarly calculated values for earlier years indicate that the interaction between inflation and the tax rules reduced investment in the 1970s by an average of 0.8 percent of GNP or about one-third of the actual level of net investment.

14.4 Investment and the Rate of Return over Cost

In the absence of taxes, the simplest specification of a firm's investment behavior is that it invests whenever the rate of return on an available project exceeds the cost of additional funds.[42] More generally, the costs of changing the rate of investment and the uncertainty associated with investment returns make the firm's decision problem more complex.[43] It is, nevertheless, useful to describe the firm's rate of investment as responding to the difference between potential rates of return and the cost of funds.

In terms of the traditional marginal efficiency of investment schedule that Keynes borrowed from Irving Fisher, an upward shift of the marginal efficiency schedule or a downward shift in the cost of funds will increase the rate of investment. If we select a particular rate of investment, we can measure the upward shift of the marginal efficiency schedule by what happens to the internal rate of return at that rate of investment.[44] A rise in the difference between the internal rate of return and the cost of funds should induce a higher rate of investment.

This idea can be extended to an economy with a complex tax structure and with inflation. A change in the tax rules or in the expected rate of inflation alters the rate of return on all projects (in a sense that I will make more precise below). These fiscal and inflation changes therefore act in a way that is equivalent to shifting the marginal efficiency of investment schedule in a simpler economy.

When we switch from a taxless economy to one with company taxes and depreciation rules, the concept of the internal rate of return must be

40. See chap. 8 above (Feldstein and Summers, 1979), table 8.4, col. 9 for the series of inflation-induced tax increases.
41. For the capital stock figures, see Feldstein and Poterba (1980a, table A-1, col. 8).
42. I have borrowed Irving Fisher's phrase "the rate of return over cost" but not his exact meaning. The model in the current section is nevertheless very close in spirit to Fisher's analysis.
43. See Abel (1978) for an explicit derivation of the optimum rule when there are endogenous adjustment costs.
44. Unless the shift is a uniform one, the answer will depend on the initial point that is selected. This is a typical index number type problem.

extended to what I shall call the maximum potential net return (MPNR). For simplicity, I shall describe this first for the case in which the firm relies exclusively on debt finance. I shall then note how the analysis is easily extended to include equity finance as well.

In a taxless economy, the internal rate of return on a project is the maximum rate of return that a firm can afford to pay on a loan used to finance that project. If L_t is the loan balance at time t and x_t (for $t = 1, 2, \ldots, T$) is the internal rate of return is the interest rate r that satisfies the difference equation:

$$(7) \qquad L_t - L_{t-1} = rL_{t-1} - x_t$$

where L_0 is the initial cost of the project and $L_T = 0$. Solution of equation (7) is exactly equivalent to the familiar definition of r as the solution to the polynomial equation:

$$(8) \qquad L_0 = \sum_{t=1}^{T} \frac{x_t}{(1 + r)^t}$$

When a tax at rate τ is levied on the net output minus the sum of the interest payment and the allowable depreciation (d_t), the maximum potential interest rate (MPIR) is defined according to

$$(9) \qquad L_t - L_{t-1} = rL_{t-1} - x_t + \tau(x_t - d_t - rL_{t-1})$$

where $L_T = 0$ and L_0 equals the initial cost of the project minus any investment tax credit.

If x_t is the *real* cash flow of the project, inflation at a constant rate π has the effect of increasing the nominal cash flow to $(1 + \pi)^t x_t$ and the MPIR rises to the value of r that solves:

$$(10) \qquad L_t - L_{t-1} = rL_{t-1} - (1 + \pi)^t x_t$$
$$+ \tau[(1 + \pi)^t x_t - d_t - rL_{t-1}]$$

Although in a taxless world the MPIR would rise by the rate of inflation, the relative importance of historic cost depreciation and the deductibility of nominal interest payments determines whether r rises by more or less than the increase in π.

The calculation of the MPIR is made operational by specifying the real cash flow from a hypothetical project and the associated series of allowable tax depreciation. I adopt here the same specifications that I used in Feldstein and Summers (1978; chap. 9 above). The hypothetical project is a "sandwich" of which 66.2 percent of the investment in the first year is a structure that lasts 30 years and the remainder is an equipment investment that is replaced at the end of 10 years and 20 years.[45] The internal

---

45. The 66.2 percent ratio is selected to produce a steady-state investment mix corresponding to the average composition over the past twenty years. Note that this specification ignores inventories and therefore the very substantial extra tax burden caused by inflation

rate of return in the absence of taxes is set at 12 percent for both the equipment and structure components. The net output of the equipment is subject to exponential decay at 13 percent until it is scrapped while the net output of the structure is subject to 3 percent decay. The depreciation rules, tax rate, and credits are then varied from year to year as the law changes.

The expected rate of inflation in each year is calculated from the consumer expenditure deflator using the optimal ARIMA forecasting procedure of Box and Jenkins (1970).[46] The calculation assumes that forecasts made at each date are based only on the information available at that time and that the ARIMA process estimated at each date is based only on the most recent 10 years of quarterly data. The calculation of the MPIR is based on the entire sequence of forecast future inflation rates and not on any single average long-term expected inflation rate.[47]

It firms did finance marginal projects exclusively by debt, it would be sufficient to relate the net rate of investment to the difference between the MPIR and the long-term nominal interest rate (as well as to capacity utilization or some other measure of cyclical demand). More generally, however, since firms do not use only debt finance, the concept of the MPIR must be extended to the maximum potential net return (MPNR), defined as the maximum net-of-corporate-tax nominal yield that the firm can afford to pay. The net rate of investment can then be related to the difference between the MPNR and the net-of-corporate-tax nominal cost of funds.

The method of calculating the MPIR in the all-debt case can be applied directly to find the value of the MPNR. In the special all-debt case, the MPNR $= (1 - \tau)r$; the solution of a difference equation like (10) is therefore equivalent to finding MPNR$/(1 - \tau)$ in the all-debt case. More generally, however, regardless of the mix of debt and equity finance, the solution of (10) can be interpreted as equivalent to MPNR$/(1 - \tau)$. Since τ is known, this yields MPNR directly. Annual values for MPNR are presented in column 1 of table 14.4

Note that the MPNR is defined in terms of a hypothetical project with a fixed pretax yield of 12 percent. All of the year-to-year variation in the MPNR is due to changes in tax rules and expected inflation. An alternative MPNR series has also been calculated in which the pretax rate of return is allowed to vary; more specifically, MPNRVP (VP for varying

with FIFO inventory accounting. While this need not affect decisions to subsitute capital for labor, it does influence the return on capital expansion to the extent that this involves greater inventories.

46. The calculation of expected inflation series is described in chap. 9 (Feldstein and Summers, 1978), pp. 170–74.

47. To meet the need for a series of expected long-term inflation rates for other purposes, Feldstein and Summers (1978; chap. 9 above) calculate a weighted average of these future inflation rates where the weights are equivalent to discounting at a fixed interest rate.

Table 14.4   Potential and Actual Net Costs of Funds

Year	MPNR (1)	MPNRVP (2)	COF (3)	MPNR-COF (4)	MPRNVP-COF (5)
1954	0.087	0.078	0.078	0.009	0.000
1955	0.089	0.084	0.077	0.012	0.007
1956	0.089	0.074	0.067	0.023	0.008
1957	0.091	0.073	0.070	0.020	0.002
1958	0.090	0.075	0.058	0.032	0.017
1959	0.090	0.081	0.060	0.031	0.022
1960	0.090	0.078	0.059	0.031	0.018
1961	0.090	0.081	0.049	0.041	0.032
1962	0.093	0.088	0.056	0.037	0.032
1963	0.094	0.091	0.056	0.038	0.035
1964	0.099	0.098	0.055	0.044	0.043
1965	0.102	0.102	0.058	0.043	0.043
1966	0.101	0.097	0.067	0.034	0.030
1967	0.101	0.092	0.061	0.040	0.031
1968	0.097	0.087	0.066	0.030	0.021
1969	0.093	0.075	0.074	0.020	0.001
1970	0.097	0.073	0.078	0.019	−0.006
1971	0.102	0.081	0.075	0.027	0.006
1972	0.105	0.082	0.071	0.034	0.010
1973	0.106	0.072	0.095	0.011	−0.022
1974	0.111	0.062	0.144	−0.034	−0.082
1975	0.110	0.083	0.108	0.002	−0.025
1976	0.109	0.080	0.107	0.002	−0.027

profitability) replaces the 12 percent assumption with a cyclically adjusted profitability series for each year's new investment that is very similar to the *RA* variable discussed in section 14.3.[48] The MPNRVP series is presented in column 2 of table 14.4.

The MPNR is the net nominal amount that firms can potentially afford to pay for funds. The actual net nominal cost of funds depends on the marginal mix of debt and equity funds. The correct assumption about this marginal mix is not clear. In the current analysis, I have assumed that firms use debt and equity at the margin in the same ratio that they do on average, i.e., that debt accounts for only one-third of total finance. This implies that the net nominal cost of funds is:

(11) $$COF = \frac{1}{3}(1 - \tau)i + \frac{2}{3}(e + \pi)$$

where i is the long-term bond interest rate and e is the real equity earnings

48. See chap. 9 (Feldstein and Summers, 1978) for a description of the cyclically adjusted return series used in the present calculation.

per dollar of share value.[49] The cost of funds series is presented in column 3.

This section examines a model that makes the rate of net investment a function of (1) the difference between the potential and actual cost of funds and (2) the rate of capacity utilization:

$$(12) \qquad \frac{I_t^n}{Y_t} = b_0 + b_1(MPNR - COF)_{t-1} + b_2 UCAP_{t-1} + u_t$$

Columns 4 and 5 of table 14.4 present the time series of this yield difference. These figures indicate that the incentive was low in the 1950s, became quite powerful in the mid-1960s, began to fail in the early 1970s and then dropped very sharply in the mid-1970s.

The pattern of the past decade reflects the fact that, because of historic cost depreciation, inflation raised the MPNR rather little while the cost of funds rose substantially.[50] Between 1966 and 1976, the cost of funds rose by four percentage points while the MPNR rose by less than one percentage point.[51]

As in section 14.2, the current analysis uses annual data and lags both regressors one year. Equation (12) and a variety of related specifications have been estimated by least squares with a first-order autocorrelation correction. Specific tests for the basic specifications show that the implied constraints are not binding, i.e., that the first-order autocorrelation correction is not inferior to a more general first-order ARMA process. Estimates in first-difference form also produce coefficients very similar to those obtained with the autocorrelation transformation.

The basic parameter estimates

$$(13) \qquad \frac{I_t^n}{Y_t} = -0.040 + \underset{(0.066)}{0.316} \; (MPNR\text{-}COF)_{t-1}$$

$$+ \underset{(0.020)}{0.073} \; UCAP_{t-1} + \underset{(0.17)}{0.70u_{t-1}}$$

$$\begin{aligned} \bar{R}^2 &= 0.784 \\ DWS &= 1.79 \\ SSR &= 2.936(10^{-4}) \\ &\quad 1955\text{-}77 \end{aligned}$$

49. The inverse of e is the product of (1) the Standard and Poor's price-earnings ratio and (2) the ratio of "book profits" to "economics profits" with correction for inflationary affects on reported depreciation, inventory profits, and debt.

50. Inflation also raised the cost of funds because the cost of equity funds was raised more than the cost of debt funds fell.

51. This is roughly consistent with a regression equation that indicates that, for the sample as a whole, each one percentage point increase in the long-term expected inflation rate reduced the difference MPNR-COF by about 1.25 percentage points. Between 1966 and 1976, the long-term expected inflation rate (demand from the ARIMA forecasts) rose 3.2 percentage points.

indicate the yield differential has a powerful effect and the variations in capacity utilization are also important.[52]

Since the return-over-cost variable had a standard deviation of 0.017 over the sample period, a move from one standard deviation below the mean to one standard deviation above would raise the investment ratio by 0.011, approximately 1.3 times its standard deviation and 40 percent of its 25-year average value. A two-standard deviation move in capacity utilization would raise investment by 0.006, or only about half as much.

Using the varying-profitability measure of the potential net return reduces the corresponding coefficient:

$$(14) \qquad \frac{I_t^n}{Y_t} = -0.031 + \underset{(0.049)}{0.219} \ (MPNRVP - COF)_{t-1}$$

$$+ \underset{(0.020)}{0.069} \ UCAP_{t-1} + \underset{(0.17)}{0.71} \ u_{t-1}$$

$$\bar{R}^2 = 0.784$$
$$DWS = 2.02$$
$$SSR = 2.931\,(10^{-4})$$
$$1955\text{--}77$$

However, since this measure is much more variable (the standard deviation of $MPNRVP - COF$ is 0.028), a two-standard deviation move implies a slightly bigger change of 0.012 in the investment ratio.

Lagged values of the regressors were insignificant and polynomial distributed lags of different lengths for the return-over-cost variable did not alter the implications of equations (12) and (13). Redefining the investment variable as a ratio to capacity GNP had no effect on the coefficients. Similarly, substituting for capacity utilization the unemployment rate for men over age 19 or the GNP gap ratio did not significantly alter the coefficient of the return-over-cost variable. Moreover, a distributed lag of proportional changes in past output was insignificant when capacity utilization was included in the equation.

The switch from the net investment equation to a gross investment equation caused some reduction in the coefficient of the return-over-cost variable (to 0.215 with a standard error of 0.072), but the extremely small and totally insignificant coefficient of the lagged capital stock variables (0.002 with a standard error of 0.093) makes this gross investment specification implausible.

A time trend and a lagged ratio of corporate cash flow to GNP were tried as additional variables; neither was significant and the coefficient of the return-over-cost variable remained unchanged. A lagged ratio of retained earnings to GNP was "mildly significant" (a t-statistic of 1.3) but

52. Because MPNR does not reflect cyclical variations in the rate of return, these parameter values are most appropriately compared with those of equation (3) rather than equation (1).

left the coefficient of the return-over-cost variable unchanged. The lagged ratio of the federal government deficit to GNP had a surprisingly positive coefficient but its inclusion did not alter the coefficient of the return-over-cost variable. The one-year lagged value of Tobin's q ratio had a coefficient of 0.012 (with a standard error of 0.009), while the coefficient of the return-over-cost variable remained essentially unchanged at 0.289 (with a standard error of 0.068). Neither the current inflation rate nor the expected inflation rate was statistically significant.

A powerful test of the appropriateness of equation (13) is obtained by estimating separate coefficients for the rate of return ($MPNR$) and cost of funds (COF) variables:

(15)
$$\frac{I_t^n}{Y_t} = -0.055 + \underset{(0.261)}{0.469} \ MPNR_{t-1} - \underset{(0.068)}{0.319 \, COF_{t-1}}$$

$$+ \underset{(0.021)}{0.074} \ UCAP_{t-1} + \underset{(0.20)}{0.66u_{t-1}}$$

$$\bar{R}^2 = 0.775$$
$$DWS = 1.81$$
$$SSR = 2.895 \,(10^{-4})$$
$$1955\text{--}77$$

A comparison of the sum of squared residuals of equations (13) and (15) shows that the coefficients of $MPNR$ and COF do not differ significantly. The separate coefficient of COF in equation (15) is almost identical to the combined return-over-cost coefficient in equation (13); the coefficient of the return variable is larger but so too is its standard error.

The separate estimate of the $MPNR$ coefficient in equation (15) is also particularly important because the $MPNR$ variable reflects only the interaction of tax rules and inflation but not the market interest rate or equity yield. The finding that the $MPNR$ coefficient is even larger than the COF coefficient is therefore powerful evidence of the effect of the tax-inflation interaction.[53]

A test of the stability of the basic coefficients over time also provides reassuring support about the plausibility and reliability of the model. Equations (16) and (17) show the result of splitting the sample in half:

(16)
$$\frac{I_t^n}{Y_t} = -0.036 + \underset{(0.266)}{0.465} \ (MPNR - COF)_{t-1}$$

$$+ \underset{(0.040)}{0.065} \ UCAP_{t-1} + \underset{(0.21)}{0.81u_{t-1}}$$

$$\bar{R}^2 \quad = 0.599$$
$$DWS = 1.24$$
$$SSR \quad = 2.276 \,(10^{-4})$$
$$1955\text{--}66$$

53. A similar analysis with the varying profitability measure of return provides even more striking confirmation: the coefficient of MPNRVP is 0.253 (s.e. = 0.155) while the coefficient of COR is −0.202 (s.e. = 0.084).

(17)
$$\frac{I_t^n}{Y_t} = -0.044 + \underset{(0.030)}{0.300} \ (MPNR - COF)_{t-1}$$

$$+ \underset{(0.011)}{0.081} \ UCAP_{t-1} - \underset{(0.43)}{0.02u_{t-1}}$$

$$\bar{R}^2 \ = 0.963$$
$$DWS = 1.75$$
$$SSR \ = 0.201 \, (10^{-4})$$
$$1967\text{--}77$$

The coefficients are quite similar and the F-statistic of 0.695 indicates that the hypothesis of an unchanged structure cannot be rejected at any conventional level of significance. The results for the varying-profitability specification are even more striking: the coefficient of the return-over-cost variable is 0.206 (s.e. = 0.089) in the first half of the period and 0.200 (s.e. = 0.033) in the second half.

Out-of-sample forecasts based on estimating equation (12) for 1955 through 1970 are shown in table 14.2. The agreement between the actual and predicted investment ratios is quite close. The mean absolute prediction error (0.0035) is the same as with the net return equation of section 14.2 and only two-thirds of the mean year-to-year change in the investment ratio. The year-to-year changes are predicted even more closely and both turning points are correctly indentified.

The parameter estimates of equation (13) can be used to analyze the sharp decline in net investment since 1966. Column 5 of table 14.3 shows the investment ratio which in principle would have been observed if the return over cost had remained at its 1965 value of 0.043. Instead of dropping to an average of only 0.025 from 1970 through 1977, it would have averaged 40 percent higher, 0.035. By contrast, even if the capacity utilization rate could have been kept at the overheated level of 0.896, the investment ratio in the 1970–77 period would only have increased 20 percent to 0.030.

The specific contribution of inflation to the decline in the value of the return-over-cost variable is difficult to determine. One simple way of measuring this effect is by a regression of the return-over-cost variable on the predicted long-term inflation rate. The coefficient in this regression (-1.27 with a standard error of 0.11) and the rise in the long-term inflation variable by 0.034 between 1965 and 1976 together imply that inflation reduced the return over cost by 0.0432 during this period. The coefficient of the return-over-cost variable (0.316 in equation 13) implies that inflation reduced the investment ratio by 0.14 over this period. This equals almost all of the 0.015 fall in the investment ratio caused by the decline in the return over cost[54] and more than half of the observed decline in the investment ratio between 1966 and 1977.

14.5   The Flexible Capital Stock Adjustment Model

The flexible capital stock adjustment model developed by Jorgenson and his collaborators is the direct descendant of that great workhorse of investment equations, the accelerator. Instead of the accelerator's assumption of a fixed capital-output ratio, the more general model allows the capital-output ratio to respond to changes in the cost of capital ownership and therefore to changes in tax rules and inflation. Implicit in the simplest version of this model are a number of very strong and generally undesirable assumptions, including homogeneous capital, a putty-putty technology, constant proportional replacement, myopic and risk-neutral decision making, and a known, exogenous financial mix. This section accepts these assumptions in order to focus on the problem of measuring the effect of inflation in the framework of this popular and influential model. The analysis shows that the traditional implementation of the model has not given adequate attention to inflation and that any attempt to analyze the recent investment experience on the basis of that implementation would be misleading

The analysis here is limited to investment in equipment. The procedure of estimating separate investment equations for equipment and structures is traditional in this framework because the tax rules differ from the two types of equipment. The implicit assumption of two independent investment demand functions, one for equipment-capital and the other for structure-capital, is clearly a poor description of reality. To the extent that investments in structures and equipment are decided as a package, the model of section 14.4 is a preferable specification.[55]

The basic model is well known and can be summarized briefly. Each firm has a desired capital stock at each time (K_t^*) and, to the extent that its actual capital falls short of the desired capital, the firm immediately orders capital goods to eliminate the difference. The sum of installed capital and capital on order is thus equal to the desired capital stock at the end of each period. This implies that in each period the net stock of outstanding orders is increased or decreased by exactly the change in the desired capital stock, $K_t^* - K_{t-1}^*$. Since there are delivery delays, the

54. This 0.015 is the difference between the actual 1977 investment ratio of 0.020 and the predicted ratio of 0.035 conditional on maintaining the 1965 level of the return over cost.
55. This specification also ignores the adverse effect of inflation through the taxation of artificial inventory profits. This will matter to the extent that inventories, equipment, and structures are part of a combined investment-output decision.

observed net investment can be represented by a distributed lag distribution of these orders:

(18)
$$I_t^n = \sum_{j=1}^{T} w_j \, (K_{t-j}^* - K_{t-j-1}^*).$$

This specification is based on an implicit assumption about replacement investment: The existing stock decays exponentially at a constant rate d, requiring replacement investment of dK_{t-1} to be made in year t to maintain the capital stock. Since firms know the delivery lag distribution exactly, they can anticipate the replacement investment that will be required in each future year (up to the length of the longest delivery lag) and can therefore order replacement investment far enough in advance to make exactly the required replacement. Gross investment is therefore given by:

(19)
$$I_t^g = \sum_{j=1}^{T} w_j \, (K_{t-j}^* - K_{t-j-1}^*) + dK_{t-1}$$

With a constant elasticity of substitution production function, the first-order conditions of profit maximization imply that the desired capital stock is related to the level of output (Q), the price of output (p) and the annual cost of capital services (c) according to:[56]

(20)
$$K_t^* = a^\sigma \, (p/c)_t^\sigma \, Q_t$$

where σ is the elasticity of substitution between capital and labor and a is the capital coefficient in the production function. Substituting (20) into (19) yields:

(21)
$$I_t^g = a^\sigma \sum_{j=1}^{T} w_j \, [(p/c)_{t-j}^\sigma \, Q_{t-j}$$
$$- (p/c)_{t-j-1}^\sigma \, Q_{t-j-1}] + dK_{t-1}$$

The accelerator model implicity assumes $\sigma = 0$ while the Cobb-Douglas technology assumed by Jorgenson and his collaborators implies $\sigma = 1$. In this section, I shall show that the flexible model with $\sigma > 0$ is more strongly supported by the data than the simpler accelerator model. The maximum likelihood estimate of σ is less than one but the likelihood function is too flat to reject the Cobb-Douglas assumption.[57]

The annual cost of capital services reflects the price level for investment goods (p_I), the real net cost of funds (R), the exponential rate of

---

56. Output is measured by the gross domestic product of nonfinancial corporations and p is the implicit price deflator for that output. The value of c is defined below.

57. I should again stress that these interferences are all conditional on very strong and obviously "false" assumptions. For example, it seems very likely that the assumption of a "putty-putty" technology causes an understatement of the true long-run elasticity of substitution if the true technology is putty-clay.

depreciation (d), the corporate tax rate (τ), the investment tax credit[58] (X) and the present value of the depreciation allowances per dollar of investment (Z):

$$(22) \qquad c = \frac{p_I(1 - \tau Z - X)\,(R + d)}{1 - \tau}$$

Inflation affects the value of this crucial variable in two important ways, through the cost of funds (R) and through the present value of depreciation (Z). In their original study, Hall and Jorgenson (1967) assumed a fixed nominal interest rate of 20 percent for the cost of funds. In the most recent of the Jorgenson studies, this assumption was replaced by the specification that $R = (1 - \tau)i$ where i is a long-term bond interest rate (Gordon and Jorgenson, 1976). This overstates the cost of debt capital (by ignoring inflation) and ignores the role of equity capital. The expected real net cost of debt capital is $(1 - \tau)i - \pi$ (where π is expected inflation) since the debt is repaid in depreciated dollars.[59] Column 1 of table 14.5 presents this measure of the real net cost of debt. Despite the rapid rise in the Baa rate itself, the real net cost of debt funds actually declined since the mid-1960s.

The cost of equity capital (e) is the ratio of equity earnings per dollar of share price. The conventional earnings-price ratio can be misleading when there is inflation since it is based on book earnings rather than real economic earnings. Book earnings overstate real earnings by using historic cost depreciation and some FIFO inventory accounting but also understate real earnings by excluding the real reduction in the value of outstanding debt that occurs because of inflation.[60] The correct earnings price ratio is presented in column 2 of table 14.5. The cost of equity funds clearly rose substantially since the mid-1960s even when the conventional series is appropriately corrected.

Defining the real net cost of funds (R) as a fixed-weight average with one-third debt (the average ratio of debt to capital for the past two decades) implies:[61]

58. To simplify notation, I use X to refer to the investment tax credit with the Long-amendment adjustment when appropriate. Data on the investment tax credit refer to actual practice and were supplied by Data Resources, Inc.

59. The putty-putty technology allows all decisions to be myopic and therefore in principle makes the short-term interest rate and short-term inflation rate the relevant variable (Hall, 1977). A more realistic description of finance and technology makes a long-term interest rate and inflation the appropriate variables. I have in fact used the Baa corporate bond rate and the long-term inflation expectation derived from the "rolling"—ARIMA estimates presented in Feldstein and Summers (1978; chap. 9 above).

60. Equivalently, book earnings are net of nominal interest payments rather than real interest payments. In my calculation, the debt is the net financial capital supplied by the creditors of the nonfinancial corporations and inflation is measured by the change in the consumer price index.

61. Note that $R + \pi$ equals the COF variable of section 14.4.

Table 14.5　　Correct and Incorrect Measures of the Cost of Capital Services

Year	Real Net Cost of Funds			Net Nominal Cost of Funds (4)	Depreciation Allowances		Relative Cost of Capital Services			
	Debt (1)	Equity (2)	Combined (3)		Correct (5)	Incorrect (6)	Correct (7)	Incorrect (8)	No Inflation No. 1 (9)	No Inflation No. 2 (10)
1954	−0.013	0.067	0.040	0.069	0.644	0.549	0.241	0.221	0.211	0.237
1955	−0.010	0.066	0.041	0.068	0.677	0.582	0.236	0.218	0.207	0.233
1956	−0.008	0.059	0.037	0.063	0.713	0.604	0.230	0.223	0.211	0.233
1957	−0.004	0.065	0.042	0.068	0.703	0.613	0.246	0.234	0.216	0.242
1958	0.000	0.053	0.035	0.057	0.745	0.620	0.227	0.228	0.214	0.235
1959	0.001	0.051	0.034	0.057	0.749	0.625	0.226	0.234	0.215	0.235
1960	0.000	0.055	0.037	0.061	0.739	0.629	0.233	0.233	0.216	0.237

1961	0.005	0.044	0.031	0.050	0.781	0.633	0.215	0.230	0.214	0.231
1962	0.006	0.064	0.044	0.061	0.756	0.652	0.231	0.218	0.205	0.230
1963	0.006	0.062	0.043	0.060	0.776	0.671	0.224	0.214	0.203	0.225
1964	0.006	0.058	0.041	0.058	0.782	0.673	0.206	0.203	0.190	0.210
1965	0.006	0.062	0.043	0.061	0.774	0.674	0.204	0.197	0.204	0.204
1966	0.009	0.076	0.053	0.073	0.740	0.675	0.226	0.206	0.190	0.213
1967	0.012	0.067	0.049	0.068	0.757	0.676	0.217	0.208	0.189	0.210
1968	0.008	0.068	0.048	0.071	0.749	0.676	0.221	0.214	0.185	0.213
1969	0.004	0.075	0.052	0.083	0.718	0.677	0.253	0.239	0.204	0.234
1970	0.011	0.084	0.059	0.092	0.695	0.677	0.263	0.241	0.205	0.234
1971	0.006	0.061	0.042	0.078	0.762	0.714	0.214	0.216	0.190	0.207
1972	0.008	0.062	0.044	0.076	0.767	0.714	0.206	0.206	0.182	0.199
1973	-0.003	0.085	0.056	0.099	0.717	0.714	0.222	0.202	0.176	0.198
1974	-0.034	0.116	0.066	0.146	0.629	0.714	0.244	0.202	0.169	0.195
1975	-0.001	0.100	0.067	0.119	0.678	0.714	0.236	0.203	0.168	0.196
1976	-0.005	0.080	0.052	0.104	0.707	0.714	0.214	0.200	0.169	0.190
1977	-0.012	0.114	0.072	0.127	0.663	0.715	0.245	0.197	0.168	0.198

$$(23) \qquad R = \frac{1}{3}\left[(1 - \tau)i - \pi\right] + \frac{2}{3}\, e$$

This series, presented in column 3 of table 14.5, shows no trend from the mid-1950s through the mid-1960s but then a gradual but substantial rise to the mid-1970s.

The second important way in which inflation affects the cost of capital services is through the value of depreciation. Since depreciation allowances are fixed in nominal terms, the real present value of the depreciation (Z) is reduced when the rate of inflation rises. This present value should be calculated using a nominal cost of funds or, equivalently, the future depreciation allowances should be restated in real terms and then discounted at the real cost of funds. Column 4 of table 14.5 presented the nominal cost of funds; this is the real cost of funds (shown in column 3) plus the expected rate of inflation.[62] The values of Z presented in column 5 reflect changes in this discount rate as well as changes in the depreciation rules.[63] In the early years, Z rose significantly but, after 1964, Z drifted down because of the rising discount rate despite the continuing acceleration of depreciation.

The importance of specifying this discount rate correctly can be seen by comparing these Z values with the alternative "$Z10$" values presented in column 6; the $Z10$ values are calculated with a constant 10 percent discount rate, the procedure used by Jorgenson and his collaborators. With a constant discount rate, the evolution of the $Z10$ variable reflects only the increasingly favorable statutory rules and therefore has actually increased during the past decade while the true value has been declining.

The composite relative cost of capital services (i.e., the c variable defined in equation (22) deflated by the output price) is presented in column 7 of table 14.5. This measure of the relative cost of capital services falls gradually from the 1950s to a low point in the mid-1960s and then begins rising again. By the end of the sample period (1977), the relative cost of capital is back to its level of the 1950s. This reversal of the incentive to invest is not observed if the inflation induced changes in Z and R are ignored; column 8 presents a false relative cost series that incorporates $Z10$ (i.e., a constant 10 percent discount rate to value depreciation) and that measures the cost of funds by the net nominal interest rate.

The Cobb-Douglas technology assumed by Jorgenson and his collaborators is a convenient place to begin testing the significance of the relative cost of capital services. I have estimated equation (21) subject to the restriction that the elasticity of substitution is one and compared it to the

---

62. In the pure debt case, this would just be the net-of-tax nominal interest rate.
63. The calculation of Z reflects the introduction of accelerated depreciation and the several reductions in the allowable depreciation life.

simpler accelerator model in which the elasticity of substitution is zero. In both specifications, the distributed lag weights were constrained to fit a third-degree polynomial (with four years of lags and a fifth year constrained to zero).

By purely statistical criteria, the evidence clearly favors the Cobb-Douglas price sensitivity model to the accelerator model. With the Cobb-Douglas technology, the $\bar{R}^2$ is 0.980 and the sum of squared residuals is 112.3. By contrast, for the accelerator model the $\bar{R}^2$ is only 0.961 and the sum of squared residuals is 215.9. An approximate likelihood ratio test strongly rejects the restriction to a zero substitution elasticity.[64]

Misspecifying the cost-of-capital series by failing to represent correctly the effect of inflation also reduces the explanatory power of the model. Following the Jorgenson procedure of evaluating depreciation allowances with a fixed 10 percent interest rate and defining the cost of funds in terms of the net nominal rate (i.e., using the incorrect c/p series presented in column 8 of table 14.5) cause the $\bar{R}^2$ to fall to 0.970 (from 0.980) and raises the sum of squared residuals to 167.4 (from 112.3).

Although relaxing the Cobb-Douglas assumption and estimating the elasticity of substitution could in principle indicate the sensitivity of investment to the cost of capital services, the data are not informative enough to provide a precise value for this parameter. With the correctly measured value of the user cost of capital, the maximum likelihood estimate of the substitution elasticity is 0.9 but the reduction in the sum of squared residuals to 112.2 is trivial.[65]

Further tests of the cost-sensitivity assumption can in principle be achieved by allowing separate elasticities with respect to the different components of the cost of capital services. In place of equation (20), the more general specification is:

$$(24) \qquad K_t^* = Q_t \left[\frac{p}{p_I} \right]^{-\sigma_1} \left[\frac{d+R}{1-\tau} \right]^{-\sigma_2} (1 - Z - X)^{-\sigma_3}$$

Instead of trying to estimate all these elasticities, three different forms of (24) were tried. The first constrains $\sigma_1 = 1$. The resulting estimates for σ_2 and σ_3 were 1.8 and 3.2, respectively, but the reduction in the sum of squared residuals to 100.4 from 112.3 in the Cobb-Douglas case is not significant. The second specification, which constrains $\sigma_1 = \sigma_3$, implies

64. In both the Cobb-Douglas and accelerator specifications, the estimated value of the depreciation rate (i.e., the coefficient of the lagged capital stock variable) is approximately 0.18, a reasonable value for equipment capital although higher than the value of 0.138 used in the cost of capital services formula and the Department of Commerce depreciation rate.

65. The value of 0.9 is obtained by searching over a grid at intervals of 0.1. It is worth noting that a mismeasurement of the cost of capital series distorts the estimate of the elasticity of substitution. Using the incorrect c/p series of column 8 leads to an estimated elasticity of substitution of 0.6. The reduction in the sum of squared residuals to 157.4 (from 167.4 in the Cobb-Douglas case) is, however, small and not statistically significant.

estimates of $\sigma_2 = 0.6$ and $\sigma_1 = \sigma_3 = 1$ but the sum of squared residuals (106.6) is again not significantly lower than in the Cobb-Douglas specification. Finally, the constraint that $\sigma_1 = \sigma_2$ implies estimates of $\sigma_1 = \sigma_2 = 0.5$ and $\sigma_3 = 1.0$; the sum of squared residuals of 97.0 is again not sufficiently low to cause a rejection of the Cobb-Douglas assumption.

The Chow test for the stability of the coefficients easily sustains the hypothesis of no change between the first and second halves of the sample, but that is more a reflection of the small sample than of any close agreement in parameter values.

It should be clear from the remarks earlier in this paper that I believe that the assumptions involved in the present model are far too restrictive and implausible for the model to be regarded as "true" in any sense. It is, however, of some importance that, even within the highly constrained assumptions of the present model, the data provide clear support for a responsiveness of investment to changes in a correctly measured cost of capital services in general and to the changes caused by inflation in particular. Although the data are not rich enough to provide precise estimates of the responsiveness of investment to the individual components of the cost of capital, it is worth noting that the evidence shows that a correct accounting of the impact of inflation substantially improves the ability of the analysis to explain the variation in investment over the past 25 years.

On the assumption of a Cobb-Douglas technology, the fall in the relative cost of capital services between the mid-1950s and the mid-1960s was enough to raise the desired ratio of equipment capital to output by nearly 12 percent.[66] Since net equipment investment averaged only about 3 percent of the equipment capital stock at the beginning of the period, the desired increase in capital would require a rise of more than 40 percent in the ratio of equipment investment to capital to achieve the desired capital output ratio within a decade and a bigger rise to achieve the adjustment sooner. In fact, the investment-capital ratio in 1966–69 was 0.065, more than double its average in 1956–65.

The subsequent rise in the value of c/p to an average of 0.235 for the years 1974–77 reversed the previous change in the desired capital-output ratio. A Cobb-Douglas technology implies a reduction in the desired capital-output ratio of nearly 10 percent between the mid-1960s and the mid-1970s. Achieving this 10 percent change in the capital-output ratio required a much larger portional fall in investment during the transition period. In fact, the rate of growth of the net equipment capital stock fell sharply, from 0.065 in 1966–69 to 0.036 in 1976–79. This in turn implied a

---

66. The value of c/p in column 7 of table 14.5 fell from an average of 0.238 in 1954–57 to 0.213 in 1964–67. The Cobb-Douglas technology implies (see equation 20) that the optimal capital-output ratio is increased by a factor of $238/213 = 1.117$.

one-third fall in the ratio of equipment investment to GNP, from 2.0 in the mid-1960s to 1.3 percent in the mid-1970s.

The specific impact of inflation in this model operates through two channels. First, inflation increases the cost of capital services by reducing the present value of depreciation allowances (Z), a reduction that reflects the increasing *nominal* cost of funds. Second, inflation can increase the cost of capital services directly by raising the real cost of funds (R).[67] The combined effect of both of these changes can be seen by comparing the actual cost of capital services (column 7 of table 14.5) with the cost of capital services calculated with the real and nominal costs of funds held constant at their 1965 levels (column 9). Instead of rising between the mid-1960s and the mid-1970s, the cost of capital falls sharply, reflecting the favorable changes in statutory tax rules. A similar, although less dramatic, conclusion appears even if the effect of inflation in raising the real cost of funds is ignored. The figures in column 10 calculate Z by using a nominal cost of funds constructed as the actual real cost of funds plus the 1965 expected inflation rate of 1.8 percent. Although the difference between columns 7 and 10 understates the adverse effect of inflation, even this measure shows that without the increase in inflation the incentive to investment would have become stronger rather than weaker in the decade after the mid-1960s.

14.6   Concluding Remarks

I began this paper by emphasizing that theoretical models of macroeconomic equilibrium should specify explicitly the role of distortionary taxes, especially taxes on capital income. The failure to include such tax rules can have dramatic and misleading effects on the qualitative as well as the quantitative properties of macroeconomic theories. The statistical evidence presented later in the paper bears out the likely importance of these fiscal effects in studying the nonneutrality of expected inflation.

In discussing the problem of statistical inference, I noted that the complexity of economic problems, the inadequacies of economic data, and the weakness of the restrictions imposed by general economic theory together make it impossible to apply in practice the textbook injunction to estimate a "true" model within which all parameter values can be inferred and all hypotheses tested. Learning in economics is a more complex and imperfectly understood process in which we develop judgments and convictions by combining econometric estimates, theoretical insights and institutional knowledge. The use of several alternative "false" models can strengthen our understanding and confidence because the *same* biases are not likely to be present in quite different models.

67. Inflation raises R to the extent that the required equity yield rises by more than the real cost of debt capital falls.

This view of the problem of statistical inference in econometrics leads me to conclude that as practicing econometricians we should be both more humble and more optimistic than is currently fashionable. We should have the humility to recognize that each econometric study is just another piece of information about a complex subject rather than *the* definitive estimate of some true model. But we should also be more optimistic that the accumulating and sifting of this econometric information will permit specialists to make better and more informed judgments.

I illustrated these theoretical and statistical ideas by estimating alternative models of investment behavior with a focus on understanding how the interaction between inflation and existing tax rules has influenced investment behavior. The results of each of these models show that the rising rate of inflation has, because of the structure of existing U.S. tax rules, substantially discouraged investment in the past 15 years.

A more general implication of these results is that monetary policy is far from neutral with respect to economic activity, even in the long run when the induced change in inflation is fully anticipated. Because of the nonindexed fiscal structure, even a fully anticipated rate of inflation causes a misallocation of resources in general and a distortion of resources away from investment in plant and equipment in particular.[68] The traditional idea of "easy money to encourage investment" that has guided U.S. policy for the past 20 years has backfired and, by raising the rate of inflation, has actually caused a reduction in investment.[69]

It would, of course, be useful to extend the current analysis in a number of ways. I am currently examining how the interaction of inflation and tax rules affects the demand for consumption in general and for housing capital in particular. Further studies should be done on the effects of inflation and tax rules on the demand for government debt, on financial markets, and on international capital flows.[70] More information about investment behavior could be developed by applying the three models of the current paper on a more disaggregated basis.

I began this paper by commenting that Irving Fisher's analysis of inflation had ignored the effects of taxation. Even so, Fisher favored the very tax reform that would eliminate the distorting effects of inflation on

68. This conclusion stands in sharp contrast to the early view of Hayek and others that inflation encourages investment by raising profits or the appearance of profits. That view not only ignored fiscal effects but also was essentially a short-run theory since wages and other costs, as well as expectations, would naturally adjust to inflation.

69. On the role of the fiscal structure in the mismanagement of monetary policy, see Feldstein (1980a).

70. Poterba (1980) and Summers (1980a) discuss the theoretical impact of inflation on the demand for housing capital. Hartman (1979) presents an analysis of the effect on international capital flows and Feldstein (1980c; chap. 5 above) treats the demand for government debt. Empirical applications are, however, still lacking.

the taxation of capital income. In a lecture published in the January 1937 issue of *Econometrica* entitled "Income in Theory and Income Taxation in Practice," Fisher advocated a progressive expenditure or consumption tax. Although his reasons for preferring such a tax did not include its inflation neutrality, my remarks today give a further reason for thinking that Fisher was right.

References

Aaron, H. 1976. "Inflation and the Income Tax." *American Economic Review* 66, no. 2 (May): 193–99.

Abel, A. 1978. "Investment and the Value of Capital." Ph.D. thesis, M.I.T.

Andrews, W. D. 1974. "A Consumption-Type or Cash Flow Personal Income Tax." *Harvard Law Review* 87, no. 6 (April).

Auerbach, A. 1979*a*. "Wealth Maximization and the Cost of Capital." *Quarterly Journal of Economics* 93, no. 3 (August): 433–46.

―――. 1979*b*. "Share Valuation and Corporate Equity Policy." *Journal of Public Economics* 11, no. 3 (June): 291–305.

―――. 1978. Appendix. In M. Feldstein, J. Green, and E. Sheshenski "Inflation and Taxes in a Growing Economy with Debt and Equity Finance." *Journal of Political Economy* 86, no. 2, part 2 (April): S68–S70. Now in chap. 4 of this volume.

Bailey, M. J. 1975. "Inflationary Distortions and Taxes." Paper presented to the Brookings Conference on Inflation and the Income Tax System, Washington, D.C., October.

―――. 1969. "Capital Gains and Income Taxation." In A. Harberger and M. Bailey, eds., *The Taxation of Income from Capital*, pp. 11–49. Washington, D.C.: Brookings Institution.

―――. 1956. "Welfare Cost of Inflationary Finance." *Journal of Political Economy* 64 (April) 93–110.

Barro, R. J. 1977. "Unanticipated Money Growth and Unemployment in the U.S." *American Economic Review* 67 (March): 101–15.

Baumol, W. J. 1952. "The Transactions Demand for Cash: An Inventory Theoretic Approach." *Quarterly Journal of Economics* 66 (November): 545–56.

Blinder, A. S. 1979. *Economic Policy and the Great Stagflation*. New York: Academic Press.

Blume, M., J. Crockett, and I. Fried. 1974. "Stockownership in the

United States: Characteristics and Trends." *Survey of Current Business* 54, no. 11 (November): 16–40.

Boskin, M. 1978. "Taxation, Saving, and the Rate of Interest." *Journal of Political Economy* 86, no. 2, part 2 (April):S3-S27.

Box. G. E. P., and G. M. Jenkins. 1970. *Time Series Analysis: Forecasting and Control.* San Francisco: Holden-Day.

Bradford, D. 1979. "The Incidence and Allocative Effect of a Tax on Corporate Distributions." National Bureau of Economic Research Working Paper no. 349, (May).

Brechling, F. 1975. *Investment and Employment Decisions.* Manchester, England: Manchester University Press.

Brinner, R. E. 1975. "Inflation and the Definition of Taxable Personal Income. In A. Aaron, ed., *Inflation and the Income Tax.* Washington, D.C.: Brookings Institution.

————. 1973. "Inflation, Deferral, and the Neutral Taxation of Capital Gains." *National Tax Journal* 26, no. 4 (December): 565–74.

Cagan, P., and R. Lipsey, 1978. *The Financial Effects of Inflation.* Cambridge, Mass.: Ballinger Publishing Co.

Clark, P. K. 1979. "Investment in the 1970s: Theory, Performance, and Prediction." *Brookings Papers on Economic Activity* 1:1979, pp. 73–113.

Coen, R. 1968. "Effects of Tax Policy on Investment in Manufacturing." *American Economic Review Proceedings* 58, no. 2 (May):200–211.

Clower, R. W. 1971. "Is There an Optimal Money Supply?—II." In M. Intrilligator, ed., *Frontiers of Quantitative Economics*, pp. 289–99. Amsterdam: North-Holland.

Darby, M. R. 1975. "The Financial and Tax Effects of Monetary Policy on Interest Rates." *Economic Inquiry* 13, no. 2 (December):266–76.

Davidson, D., and R. Weil. 1976. "Inflation Accounting: Implications of the FASB Proposal." In H. Aaron, ed., *Inflation and the Income Tax,* pp. 80–114. Washington, D.C.: Brookings Institution.

Diamond, P. A. 1975. "Inflation and the Comprehensive Tax Base." *Journal of Public Economics* 4, no. 3 (August):227–44.

————. 1970. "Incidence of an Interest Income Tax." *Journal of Economic Theory* 2, no. 3 (September):211–24.

Eckstein, O. 1978. *The Great Recession.* Amsterdam: North-Holland.

Eckstein, O., and R. Brinner. 1972. "The Inflation Process in the United States." A Study for the Joint Economic Committee, 92d Congress, 2d session.

Eisner, R. 1978. *Factors in Business Investment.* National Bureau of Economic Research, General Series no. 102. Cambridge, Mass.: Ballinger.

Fama, E. 1979. "Stock Returns, Real Activity, Inflation and Money." University of Chicago, mimeographed.

————. 1975. "Short-term Interest Rates as Predictors of Inflation." *American Economic Review* 65, no. 3 (June):269–82.

Feldstein, M. 1982. "Inflation, Tax Rules, and the Accumulation of Residential and Nonresidential Capital." *Scandinavian Journal of Economics* 84, no. 2 (June 1980): 636–50. Now chap. 6 of this volume.

Feldstein, M. C. 1981*a*. "Adjusting Depreciation in an Inflationary Economy: Indexing versus Accelerated Depreciation." *National Tax Journal* 34, no. 1 (March):29–44.

————. 1981*b*. "Aggregate Saving and the Rate of Return" (forthcoming).

————. 1981*c*. "Inflation in the American Economy." The Joseph Schumpeter Lecture of the University of Vienna, March 1981; *Empirica* (forthcoming). (A revised version will also appear in *Public Interest*, 1982.)

————. 1981*d*. "Inflation, Portfolio Choice and the Prices of Land and Corporate Stock." *American Journal of Agricultural Economics*, 62, no. 5 (December 1980):910–16. Now chap. 13 of this volume.

————. 1980*a*. "Tax Rules and the Mismanagement of Monetary Policy." *American Economic Review* 70, no. 2, (May):182–86. Proceedings of the Ninety-second Annual Meeting of the American Economic Association, Atlanta, Georgia, December 28–30, 1979.

————. 1980*b*. "Inflation and the Stock Market." *American Economic Review* 70, no. 5, (December):839–47. Now chap. 10 of this volume.

————. 1980*c*. "Fiscal Policies, Inflation, and Capital Formation." *American Economic Review* 70, no. 4 (September):636–50. Now chap. 5 of this volume.

————. 1980*d*. "Inflation, Tax Rules, and the Stock Market." *Journal of Monetary Economics* 6, no. 3 (July): 309–31. Now chap. 11 of this volume.

————. 1980*e*. "Inflation, Tax Rules, and Investment: Some Econometric Evidence." The Fisher-Schultz Lecture at the 4th World Congress of the Econometric Society, August; forthcoming in *Econometrica*. Now chap. 14 of this volume.

————. 1980*f*. "Inflation, Capital Taxation, and Monetary Policy." National Bureau of Economic Research Conference volume (forthcoming).

————. 1978*a*. "The Welfare Cost of Capital Income Taxation." *Journal of Political Economy* 86, part 2 (April):S2–S51.

————. 1978*b*. "Inflation, Tax Rules, and the Prices of Land and Gold." *Journal of Public Economics* 14, no. 3 (December): 309–18. Now chap. 12 of this volume.

————. 1978*c*. "The Rate of Return, Taxation, and Personal Saving." *Economic Journal* 88, no. 351 (September):482–87.

———. 1977a. "The Surprising Incidence of a Tax on Pure Rent: A New Answer to an Old Question." *Journal of Political Economy* 85, no. 2 (April):349–60.

———. 1977b. "Does the U.S. Save Too Little?" *American Economic Review Proceedings* 67, no. 1 (February):116–21.

———. 1977c "National Savings in the United States." In Eli Shapiro and W. White, eds., *Investment and Saving for Productivity, Growth, and High Employment.* Englewood Cliffs, N.J.: Prentice-Hall.

———. 1976. "Inflation, Income Taxes, and the Rate of Interest: A Theoretical Analysis." *American Economic Review* 66, no. 3 (December):809–20. Now chap. 3 of this volume.

———. 1974a. "Incidence of a Capital Income Tax in a Growing Economy with Variable Savings Rates." *Review of Economic Studies* 41, no. 4 (October):505–13.

———. 1974b. "Tax Incidence in a Growing Economy with Variable Factor Supply." *Quarterly Journal of Economics* 88, no. 4 (November):551–73.

Feldstein, M. S., and G. Chamberlain. 1973. "Multimarket Expectations and the Rate of Interest." *Journal of Money, Credit, and Banking* 5, no. 4 (November):873–902.

Feldstein, M. S., and O. Eckstein. 1970. "The Fundamental Determinants of the Interest Rate." *Review of Economics and Statistics* 52, no. 4 (November):363–75.

Feldstein, M. S., and J. S. Flemming. 1971. "Tax Policy and Corporate Saving and Investment Behavior in Britain." *Review of Economic Studies* 38, no. 116 (October): 415–34.

———. 1964. "The Problem of Time-Stream Evaluation: Present Values versus Internal Rate of Return Rules." *Bulletin of the Oxford Institute of Economics and Statistics* 26 (February):79–85.

Feldstein, M. S., and D. Frisch. 1977. "Corporate Tax Integration: The Estimated Effects on Capital Accumulation and Tax Distribution of Two Integration Proposals." *National Tax Journal* 30, no. 1 (March):37–52.

Feldstein, M. S., and J. Green. 1979. "Why Do Companies Pay Dividends?" *American Economic Review* (forthcoming). National Bureau of Economic Research Working Paper no. 413, December.

Feldstein, M. S., J. Green, and E. Sheshinski. 1979. "Corporate Financial Policy and Taxation in a Growing Economy." *Quarterly Journal of Economics* 93, no. 3 (August):411–32.

———. 1978. "Inflation and Taxes in a Growing Economy with Debt and Equity Finance." *Journal of Political Economy* 86, no. 2, part 2 (April):S53–S70. Now chap. 4 of this volume.

Feldstein, M. S., and J. Poterba. 1980. "State and Local Taxes and the Rate of Return on Non-Financial Corporate Capital." National Bureau of Economic Research Working Paper no. 508R, September.

————. 1980*b*. "Inflation, the Business Cycle and Corporate Profitability" (forthcoming).

Feldstein, M. S., J. Poterba, and L. Dicks-Mireaux, 1981. "The Effective Tax Rates and the Pretax Rate of Return." *Journal of Public Economics*, forthcoming. National Bureau of Economic Research Working Paper no. 740.

Feldstein, M. S., and M. Rothschild. 1974. "Towards an Economic Theory of Replacement Investment." *Econometrica* 42, no. 3 (May):393–423.

Feldstein, M. S., and J. Slemrod. 1980. "Personal Taxation, Portfolio Choice, and the Effect of the Corporation Income Tax." *Journal of Political Economy* 88, no. 5 (October):854–66.

Feldstein, M. S., J. Slemrod, and S. Yitzhaki. 1980. "The Effects of Taxation on the Selling of Corporate Stock and the Realization of Capital Gains." *Quarterly Journal of Economics* 94, no. 4 (June): 777–91.

Feldstein, M. S., and L. Summers. 1981. "Inflation, Price-Earnings Ratios, and the Cost of Capital" (forthcoming).

————. 1979. "Inflation and the Taxation of Capital Income in the Corporate Sector." *National Tax Journal* 32, no. 4 (December):445–70. Now chap. 8 of this volume.

————. 1978. "Inflation, Tax Rules, and the Long-Term Interest Rate." *Brookings Papers on Economic Activity* 1978:1, pp. 61–99. Now chap. 9 of this volume.

————. 1977. "Is the Rate of Profit Falling?" *Brookings Papers on Economic Activity* 1977:1, pp. 211–28.

Feldstein, M. S., and S. C. Tsiang. 1968. "The Interest Rate, Taxation, and the Personal Savings Incentive." *Quarterly Journal of Economics* 82 (August):419–34.

Feldstein, M. S., and S. Yitzhaki. 1978. "The Effect of the Capital Gains Tax on the Selling and Switching of Common Stock." *Journal of Public Economics* 9, no. 1 (February):17–36.

Fellner, W., K. W. Clarkson, and J. H. Moore. 1975. *Correcting Taxes for Inflation*. Washington, D.C.: American Enterprise Institute for Public Policy Research.

Fischer, S. 1979*a*. "Anticipations and the Non-Neutrality of Money." *Journal of Political Economy* 87, no. 2 (April):225–53.

————. 1979*b*. *Rational Expectations and Economic Policy*. Chicago: University of Chicago Press.

————. 1977. "Long-term Contracts, Rational Expectations, and the Optimal Money Supply Rule." *Journal of Political Economy* 85, no. 1 (February):191–205.

————. 1972. "Keyes-Wicksell and Neoclassical Models of Money and Growth." *American Economic Review* 62, no. 5 (December):880–90.

Fisher, I. 1954. *The Theory of Interest*. New York: Kelley & Millman.

———. 1937. "Income in Theory and Income Taxation in Practice." *Econometrica* 5 (January):1–55.

———. 1930. *Theory of Interest.* New York: Macmillan.

———. 1896. *Appreciation and Interest.* Publications for the American Economic Association, vol. 2.

Foley, D., and M. Sidrauski. 1971. *Monetary and Fiscal Policy in a Growing Economy.* New York: Macmillan.

Friedman, B. M. 1978. "Crowding Out or Crowding In? Economic Consequences of Financial Government Deficits." *Brookings Papers on Economic Activity* 1978:3, pp. 593–654.

———. 1977. "Financial Flow Variables and the Short-Run Determination of Long-Term Interest Rates." *Journal of Political Economy* 85, no. 4 (August):661-89.

Friedman, M. 1974. "Monetary Correction." In *Essays on Inflation and Indexation.* Washington, D.C.: American Enterprise Institute for Public Policy Research.

———. 1969. "The Optimum Supply of Money." In *The Optimum Supply of Money and Other Essays.* Chicago: Aldine.

———. 1968. "The Role of Monetary Policy." *American Economic Review* 59 (March):1–17.

———. 1942. "Discussion of the Inflationary Gap." *American Economic Review* 32 (June):308–14; reprinted in his *Essays in Positive Economics,* Chicago: University of Chicago Press.

Gordon, R. H., and D. W. Jorgenson. 1976. "The Investment Tax Credit and Countercyclical Policy." In O. Eckstein, ed., *Parameters and Policies in the U.S. Economy,* pp. 275–314. Amsterdam: North-Holland.

Gordon, R. H., and B. G. Malkiel. 1981. "Corporation Finance." In H. Aaron and J. Pechman, eds., *How Taxes Affect Economic Behavior,* pp. 121–98. Washington, D.C.: Brookings Institution.

Gordon, R. J. 1971. "Inflation in Recession and Recovery." *Brookings Papers on Economic Activity* 1971:1, pp. 105–66.

———. 1967. "The Incidence of the Corporation Income Tax in U.S. Manufacturing." *American Economic Review* 57 (September):731–58.

Granger, C. W. J., and P. Newbold. 1974. "Spurious Regressions in Econometrics." *Journal of Econometrics* 2, no. 2 (July):111–20.

Green, J., and E. Sheshinski. 1977. "Budget Displacement Effects of Inflationary Finance." *American Economic Review* 67, no. 4 (September):671–82.

Hall, R. E. 1977. "Investment, Interest Rates, and the Effects of Stabilization Policies." *Brookings Papers on Economic Activity* 1977–1, pp. 61–103.

Hall. R. E., and D. W. Jorgenson. 1967. "Tax Policy and Investment Behavior." *American Economic Review* 57 (June):391–414.

Harberger, A. C. 1962. "The Incidence of the Corporation Income Tax." *Journal of Political Economy* 70 (June):215–40.

Harris, S. 1941. *Economics of Social Security.* New York: McGraw-Hill.

Harrod, R. F. 1948. *Toward a Dynamic Economics.* London: Macmillan.

Hartman, D. G. 1979. "Taxation and the Effects of Inflation on the Real Capital Stock in an Open Economy." *International Economic Review* 20, no. 2 (June):417–25.

Helliwell, J., and G. Glorieux. 1970. "Forward-Looking Investment Behavior." *Review of Economic Studies* 37, no. 4 (October):499–516.

Hendershott, P. 1980.

———. 1979. "The Decline in Aggregate Share Values: Inflation and Taxation of the Returns from Equities and Owner-Occupied Housing." National Bureau of Economic Research Working Paper no. 370.

Hendershott, P., and S. C. Hu. 1979. "Inflation and the Benefits from Owner-Occupied Housing." National Bureau of Economic Research Working Paper no. 383.

Hendershott, P., and J. D. Shilling. 1980. "The Economics of Tenure Choice: 1955–79." National Bureau of Economic Research Working Paper no. 543.

Henderson, D. W., and T. J. Sargent. 1973. "Monetary and Fiscal Policy in a Two-Sector Aggregate Model." *American Economic Review* 63, no. 3 (June):345–65.

Holland, D. M., and S. C. Myers. 1979. "Trends in Corporate Profitability and Capital Costs." *Committee for Economic Development*, pp. 103–88.

Hong, H. 1977. "Inflation and the Market Value of the Firm: Theory and Tests." *Journal of Finance* 32, no. 4 (September):1031–48.

Heubner, S. 1976. *Life Insurance.* Englewood Cliffs, N.J.: Prentice-Hall.

Johnson, H. G. 1971. "Is There an Optimal Money Supply—I." In M. Intrilligator, ed., *Frontiers of Quantitative Economics*, pp. 279–88. Amsterdam: North-Holland.

Jorgenson, D. W. 1963. "Capital Theory and Investment Behavior." *The American Economic Review* 53 (May):247–59.

Keynes, J. M. 1936. *The General Theory of Employment, Interest and Money.* London: Macmillan and Co.

King, M. 1977. *Public Policy and the Corporation.* London: Chapman & Hall.

Krzyzaniak, J., and R. A. Musgrave. 1963. *The Shifting of the Corporation Income Tax: An Empirical Study of Its Short-Run Effect upon the Rate of Return.* Baltimore: Johns Hopkins Press.

Leamer, E. 1978. *Specification Searches.* New York: Wiley.

Levhari, D., and D. Patinkin. 1968. "The Role of Money in a Simple Growth Model." *American Economic Review* 58 (September):713–53.

Lintner, J. 1975. "Inflation and Security Returns." *Journal of Finance* 30 (May):259–80.

———. 1973. "Inflation and Common Stock Prices in a Cyclical Context." In *The New Realities of the Business Cycle*, National Bureau of Economic Research 53d Annual Report, New York.

Lovell, M. 1978. "The Profits Picture: Trends and Cycles." *Brookings Papers on Economic Activity* 1978:3, pp. 769–88.

Lucas, R. E., Jr. 1976. "Econometric Policy Evaluation: A Critique." In K. Brunner and A. Meltzer, eds., *The Phillips Curve and Labor Markets*. The Carnegie-Rochester Conferences on Public Policy, a Supplement Series to the *Journal of Monetary Economics* I. Amsterdam: North-Holland.

———. 1972. "Expectations and the Neutrality of Money." *Journal of Economic Theory* 4, no. 2 (April):103–24.

Miller, M. 1977. "Debt and Taxes." *Journal of Finance* 32, no. 2 (May):261–77.

Modigliani, F., and R. Cohn. 1979. "Inflation, Rational Valuation, and the Market." *Financial Analysts Journal* 35 (March):3–23.

Motley, B. 1969. "Inflation and Common Stock Values: Comment." *Journal of Finance* 24, no. 3 (June):530–35.

Mundell, R. 1963. "Inflation and Real Interest." *Journal of Political Economy* 71, (June):280–83.

Musgrave, J. 1976. "Fixed Nonresidential Business and Residential Capital in the U.S., 1929–75." *Survey of Current Business* 56, no. 4 (April):46–52.

Nelson, C. 1976. "Inflation and Rates of Return on Common Stocks." *Journal of Finance* 31, (May):471–87.

Nickell, S. J. 1978. *The Investment Decision of Firms*. Cambridge Economic Handbooks. Cambridge: Cambridge University Press, James Nisbet & Co., Welwyn.

Oakland, W. 1972. "Corporate Earnings and Tax Shifting in U.S. Manufacturing. 1930–1968." *Review of Economics and Statistics* 54, no. 3 (August):235–44.

Phelps, E. S. 1973. "Inflation in the Theory of Public Finance." *Swedish Journal of Economics* 75, no. 1 (March):67–82.

———. 1972. *Inflation Policy and Unemployment Theory*. New York: Norton.

Polinsky, A. M. 1977. "The Demand for Housing: A Study in Specification and Grouping." *Econometrica* 45, no. 2 (March):447–62.

Poterba, J. 1980. "Inflation, Income Taxes, and Owner-Occupied Housing." National Bureau of Economic Research Working Paper no. 553.

Projector, D., and G. Weiss. 1966. *Survey of Financial Characteristics of Consumers*. Washington, D.C.: Federal Reserve Technical Papers.

Rowley, J. C. R., and P. K. Trivedi. 1975. *Econometrics of Investment.* London: Wiley.

Salomon Bros. 1978. "Portfolio Planning: Stocks are Still the Only Bargain Left." July 3 report.

Sargent, T. J. 1978. "Estimation of Dynamic Labor Demand Schedules under Rational Expectations." *Journal of Political Economy* 86, no. 6 (December): 1009–44.

———. 1976. "Interest Rates and Expected Inflation: A Selective Summary of Recent Research." National Bureau of Economic Research, *Explorations in Economic Research* 3, no. 3 (Summer):303–25.

———. 1973. "Rational Expectations, the Real Rate of Interest, and the Natural Rate of Unemployment." *Brookings Papers on Economic Activity* 1973:2, pp. 429–72.

Sargent, T. J., and N. Wallace. 1975. "Rational Expectations, the Optimal Monetary Instrument, and the Optimal Money Supply Rule." *Journal of Political Economy* 83, no. 2 (April):241–54.

Sato, K. 1967. "Taxation and Neoclassical Growth." *Public Finance* 22: 346–67.

Shoven, J., and J. Bulow. 1976. "Inflation Accounting and Nonfinancial Corporate Profits: Financial Assets and Liabilities." *Brookings Papers on Economic Activity* 1976:1, pp. 15–57.

Shoven, J., and J. Whalley, 1972. "A General Equilibrium Calculation of the Effects of Differential Taxation of Income from Capital in the U.S." *Journal of Public Economics* 1 (November):281–321.

Stein, J. 1970. "Monetary Growth Theory in Perspective." *American Economic Review* 60, no. 1 (March):85–106.

Stiglitz, J. 1976. "The Corporation Tax." *Journal of Public Economics* 5, nos. 3–3 (April-May):303–11.

———. 1973. "Taxation, Corporate Financial Policy, and the Cost of Capital." *Journal of Public Economics* 2, no. 1 (February):1–34.

Summers, L. 1981. "Inflation and the Tax System." *American Economic Review* 71 (September):429–34.

———. 1980a. "Inflation, Tax Rules, and the Valuation and Accumulation of Capital Assets." *American Economic Review* (forthcoming).

———. 1980b"Inflation, Taxation and Share Valuation" (forthcoming).

———. 1980c. "Capital Taxation in a General Equilibrium Perfect Foresight Growth Model." Mimeographed.

———. 1980d. "Inflation, Taxation, and Corporate Investment," forthcoming.

———. 1978. "Tax Policy in a Life Cycle Model." National Bureau of Economic Research Working Paper no. 302.

Surrey, S. S. 1973. *Pathways to Tax Reform.* Cambridge, Mass.: Harvard University Press. *Survey of Current Business*, March, 1976. pp. 53–57.

Tideman, T. N., and D. Tucker. 1976. "The Tax Treatment of Business Profits under Inflationary Conditions." In H. Aaron, ed., *Inflation and the Income Tax*, pp. 33–74. Washington, D.C.: Brookings Institution.

Tobin, J. 1965. "Money and Economic Growth." *Econometrica* 33, no. 4 (October):671–84.

———. 1955. "A Dynamic Aggregative Model." *Journal of Political Economy* 23 (April):103–15.

Tobin, J., and W. C. Brainard. 1977. "Asset Markets and the Cost of Capital." In R. Nelson and B. Belassa, eds., *Economic Progress, Private Values, and Public Policy: Essay in Honor of William Fellner*, pp. 235–62. New York: Elsevier–North-Holland.

Tobin, J., and W. Buiter. 1978. "Fiscal and Monetary Policies, Capital Formation, and Economic Activity." In G. von Furstenberg, ed., *The Government and Capital Formation*. American Enterprise Institute, Reprint no. 83.

U.S. Department of the Treasury. 1977. *Blueprints for Basic Tax Reform*. Washingon, D.C.: Government Printing Office.

Van Horne, J., and W. Glassmire, Jr. 1972. "The Impact of Unanticipated Changes in Inflation on the Value of Common Stocks." *Journal of Finance* 27, no. 5 (December):1081–92.

Von Furstenberg, G. 1977. "Corporate Investment: Does Market Valuation Matter in the Aggregate?" *Brookings Papers on Economic Activity* 1977:2, pp. 347–97.

Yohe, W. P., and D. S. Karnovsky. 1969. "Interest Rates and Price Level Changes, 1952–69." *Federal Reserve Bank of St. Louis* 51, no. 12 (December):18–38.

Index